English G | 21

D3

Grundausgabe
für differenzierende
Schulformen

Vokabeltrainer-App

*Verfügbar für: iOS, Android
und Windows Phone*

English G 21 • Band D 3 • Grundausgabe

Im Auftrag des Verlages herausgegeben von
Prof. Hellmut Schwarz, Mannheim

Erarbeitet von
Susan Abbey, Nenagh, Irland
Barbara Derkow Disselbeck, Köln
Allen J. Woppert, Berlin
sowie Laurence Harger, Wellington, Neuseeland

unter Mitarbeit von
Wolfgang Biederstädt, Köln
Joachim Blombach, Herford
Helmut Dengler, Limbach
Martina Schroeder, Stedtlingen
Jennifer Seidl, München
Udo Wagner, Voerde
Herbert Willms, Herford

in Zusammenarbeit mit der Englischredaktion
Dr. Christiane Kallenbach (Projektleitung);
Dr. Eva Grabowski (verantwortliche Redakteurin);
Susanne Bennetreu (Bildredaktion); Stefanie Bayer;
Britta Bensmann; Julie Colthorpe; Dr. Philip Devlin;
Gwendolyn Düwel; Cornelia Frisse; Bonnie S. Glänzer;
Mara Leibowitz; Anne Linder; Kathrin Spiegelberg;
Uwe Tröger; Klaus G. Unger *sowie* Nathalie Schwering

Beratende Mitwirkung
Walter Droste, Spenge; Manuela Feierabend-Vonhausen,
Rossfeld; Birgit Heinemann, Neu Wulmstorf;
Ivette Huxol, Wilkau-Haßlau; Bernd Jost, Salzbergen;
Heike Jurenz, Neukirch/Lausitz; Heike Meisner,
Bad Klosterlausnitz; Gabriele Rotter, Wiesbaden;
Karl Starkebaum, Diekholzen

Illustrationen
Graham-Cameron Illustration, UK: Fliss Cary, Grafikerin;
Roland Beier, Berlin

Layoutkonzept
Aksinia Raphael; Korinna Wilkes

Technische Umsetzung
Aksinia Raphael; Korinna Wilkes;
Stephan Hilleckenbach; Rainer Bachmaier

Umschlaggestaltung
Klein & Halm Grafikdesign, Berlin

www.cornelsen.de
www.EnglishG.de

Die Webseiten Dritter, deren Internetadressen in diesem Lehrwerk angegeben sind, wurden vor Drucklegung sorgfältig geprüft. Der Verlag übernimmt keine Gewähr für die Aktualität und den Inhalt dieser Seiten oder solcher, die mit ihnen verlinkt sind.

Dieses Werk berücksichtigt die Regeln der reformierten Rechtschreibung und Zeichensetzung.

Soweit in diesem Lehrwerk Personen fotografisch abgebildet sind und ihnen von der Redaktion fiktive Namen, Berufe, Dialoge und Ähnliches zugeordnet oder diese Personen in bestimmte Kontexte gesetzt werden, dienen diese Zuordnungen und Darstellungen ausschließlich der Veranschaulichung und dem besseren Verständnis des Inhalts.

Alle Drucke dieser Auflage sind inhaltlich unverändert und können im Unterricht nebeneinander verwendet werden.

Druck und Bindung: Livonia Print, Riga

1. Auflage, 8. Druck 2019
ISBN 978-3-06-031320-4
(Schülerbuch – broschiert)

1. Auflage, 6. Druck 2019
ISBN 978-3-06-031373-0
(Schülerbuch – gebunden)

ISBN 978-3-06-032896-3 (E-Book)

PEFC zertifiziert
Dieses Produkt stammt aus nachhaltig bewirtschafteten Wäldern und kontrollierten Quellen.
PEFC/12-31-006
www.pefc.de

Dein Englischbuch enthält folgende Teile:

Introduction	Hier lernst du die jungen Leute von Band 3 kennen.
Units	die fünf Kapitel des Buches
Getting ready for a test	Hier kannst du dich gezielt auf einen Test vorbereiten.
EXTRA: Text File	viele interessante Texte zum Lesen (passend zu den Units)
Skills File (SF)	Beschreibung wichtiger Lern- und Arbeitstechniken
Grammar File (GF)	Zusammenfassung der Grammatik jeder Unit
Vocabulary	Wörterverzeichnis zum Lernen der neuen Wörter jeder Unit
Dictionary	alphabetische Wörterverzeichnisse zum Nachschlagen

Die Units bestehen aus diesen Teilen:

Lead-in	Einstieg in das neue Thema
A-Section	neuer Lernstoff mit vielen Aktivitäten und **Background File**
Practice	Übungen
Text	eine spannende oder lustige Geschichte
How am I doing?	Hier kannst du dein Wissen und Können überprüfen.

In den Units findest du diese Überschriften und Symbole:

Looking at language	Hier sammelst du Beispiele und entdeckst Regeln.
STUDY SKILLS	Einführung in Lern- und Arbeitstechniken
Dossier	Schöne und wichtige Arbeiten kannst du in einer Mappe sammeln.
All about ...	Hier übst du Wortschatz zum Thema der Unit.
WRITING COURSE	Schreibkurs in fünf Kapiteln mit Hilfen zum Schreiben von Texten
EVERYDAY ENGLISH	Übungen zum Bewältigen wichtiger Alltagssituationen
MEDIATION	Hier vermittelst du zwischen zwei Sprachen.
LISTENING	Aufgaben zu Hörtexten auf der CD
Now you	Hier sprichst und schreibst du über dich selbst.
PRONUNCIATION	Ausspracheübungen
REVISION	Übungen zur Wiederholung
WORDS	Übungen zu Wortfamilien, Wortfeldern und Wortverbindungen
Extra	Zusätzliche Aktivitäten und Übungen
👥 👥👥	Partnerarbeit / Gruppenarbeit
🎧 🎧	nur auf CD / auf CD und im Schülerbuch
≥	Textaufgaben
○ ●	leichtere Übungen / schwierigere Übungen
// ○ // ●	parallele Übungen auf zwei Niveaus
more help	Hier findest du zusätzliche Hilfen für das Lösen einer Aufgabe.

Inhalt

 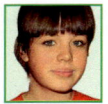

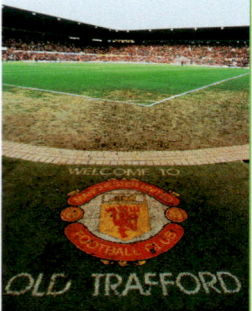

Inhalt

10,000 young people from all over the UK – Six days of brilliant music and dance – Play, sing, dance and listen to all kinds of music

National Festival of
Music for Youth

Birmingham 10–15 July

1 The festival

a) *Look at the poster. What kinds of music can you play and listen to at the festival?*

b) *What else can you do at the festival? The words in the box can help you.*

▶ *SF Learning words (p. 129)*

– listen to classical music/folk music/ jazz/reggae/pop/rock/RnB/...
– go to a concert/workshop
– learn to DJ/rap/ ...
– do hip hop/breakdance
– play the guitar/steel drum/...
– sing in a choir/rock band/...

A day at the festival 🎧

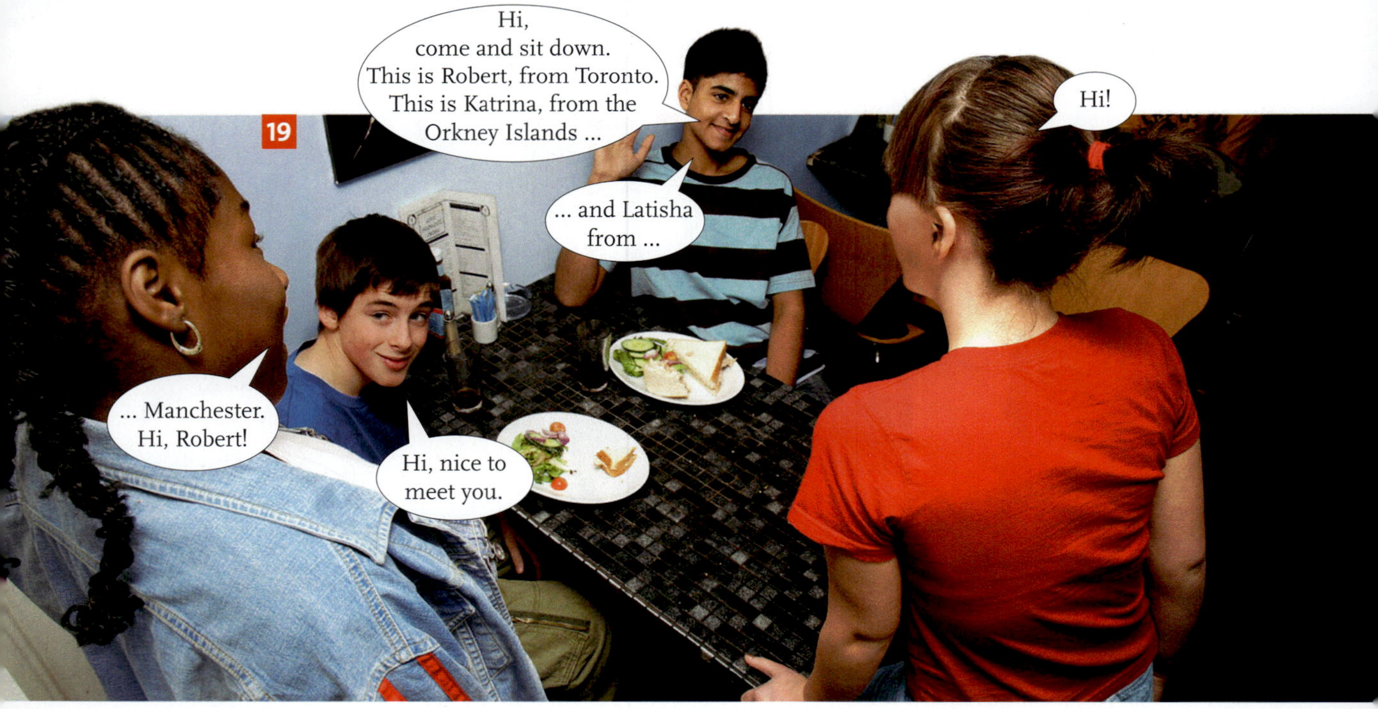

Half an hour later …

20

The islands are beautiful, but I'd really like to see London one day.

I love ice hockey …

Oh, my game's football.

I'll mail you some photos.

And that evening …

21

Your brother's band is great. We don't have anything like this in the Orkney Islands.

I've got a better idea, wait and see!

That was really great. Let's keep in touch.

Yeah! Oh and Asif, tell Hassan to come and do a gig in Manchester.

And Asif, you will send me some photos?

22

---

1   The people

a) *Look through the book. Where can you find Asif, Katrina, Latisha and Robert from the photo story?*

b) **Extra** *Start a profile for the four young people.*

> Name: …
> From: …
> Music: …
> At the festival because: …

Add more information if you can.

2   The music 🎧

Listen to four recordings from the festival. Which recording goes with which of the four young people? Why? You can use the phrases in the box.

> I think the first/second recording goes with …
> because   she plays …
>   he likes …

3   👥👥   Now you

a) *Look at these questions. Make notes.*
– What are your favourite bands or singers?
– When and where do you listen to music?
– Do you sing? When? Where?
– What instruments do you like?
– Do you play an instrument?

> drums • electric guitar • flute • guitar •
> keyboard • piano • recorder • saxophone •
> trumpet • violin

b) *Now stand (or sit) in a double circle. Ask three different partners the questions from a).*

c) **Extra** *Take notes. Report to the class on one of your partners.*

▶ *SF Learning words (p. 129) •* **Text File 1** *(p. 111) •*
WB 1–3 (pp. 1–3) • WB Revision (pp. 4–7)

My London

To:	Katrina, Latisha, Robert
Subject:	Let´s meet again

Dear All

It was great to meet you all at the festival. Let's all meet again on Messenger this Saturday at 6 pm, OK? When are you coming to London? I'd love to show you my favourite places in the capital. (See them on my website at www.asifspage.co.uk)

Asif

PS Robert, it's great that you and your parents are coming to London. CU soon!

1 The London Eye

This is the famous big wheel on the River Thames. You get great views of London from up there. But I haven't been on it yet. Visit me and we can go on it together! In this photo you can also see Big Ben and the Houses of Parliament.
Click here for my sound file.

2 Funland, London Trocadero

This is at Piccadilly Circus in the city centre. They have hundreds of video and virtual reality games here. I went there last week with my brother Hassan. Come and play with me!
Click here for my sound file.

3 Brick Lane Market

I often go there on Sunday mornings. It's near where I live. You can get great second-hand clothes there and interesting food too.
Click here for my sound file.

My favourite places in London

4 The Tower of London

The Tower is near where I live too. All the tourists go there. It's very old. Hundreds of years ago kings and queens lived here. But now the Queen lives in Buckingham Palace. Click here for my sound file.

ENTRY TO THE TRAITORS GATE

1 Asif's sound files

STUDY SKILLS Listening

a) Überlege vor dem Hören: Worum wird es in dem Hörtext gehen?
b) Keine Panik, du musst nicht alles verstehen. Konzentriere dich auf das Wesentliche.
c) Wenn du Einzelinformationen brauchst, lies die Aufgabe vorher gut durch.

a) What do you think will be in Asif's sound files?

b) Now listen to Asif's sound files. Which sound file goes with which photo?

c) Read the questions. Listen again and choose the correct answer.
1 What is the oldest part of the Tower?
   A the White Tower   B the Bloody Tower
2 Who wins the video game?
   A Asif   B Hassan
3 What time was it when Asif recorded Big Ben?
   A 6 o'clock   B 5 o'clock
4 What is the man in the market selling?
   A food   B clothes

2 Extra A day out in London
a) Think: Choose two places from Asif's website for a day out in London.

b) Pair: Compare your lists. Choose one place for both of you.

I'd like to go to …

+ It's fun/cool/fantastic/cheap/…
You can only do/see/… this in London.
I like video games/interesting food/…

– But I don't like …
It's very expensive.
You can do that in Germany too.

We've both got …   Let's do that …

c) Share: Report to the class.

▶ SF Listening (p. 133) • P 1 (p. 20) • WB 1 (p. 8)

All about ... the London Underground

1 At Queensway underground station 🎧

Robert Smith and his parents are in London.

*Robert*_____ We have to meet Asif at the London
Eye. That's near Waterloo station.

*Mr Smith*__ OK. Let's get the tickets.

*Mrs Smith*__ Hi. We are visiting London today.
Do we need single or return
tickets? Or can we buy one-day
tickets?

*Clerk*_____ One-day Travelcards are cheaper.
You can use them on the buses too.

*Mr Smith*__ What about our son? He's 14.

*Clerk*_____ There's a child Travelcard too.

*Mrs Smith*__ Great. Three Travelcards please,
two adults and one child. And how
do we get to Waterloo from here?

*Clerk*_____ Take the Central line. Change at
Bond Street. Then take the ...

▶ *What tickets do the Smiths buy?*
Tell the Smiths how they can get to Waterloo.

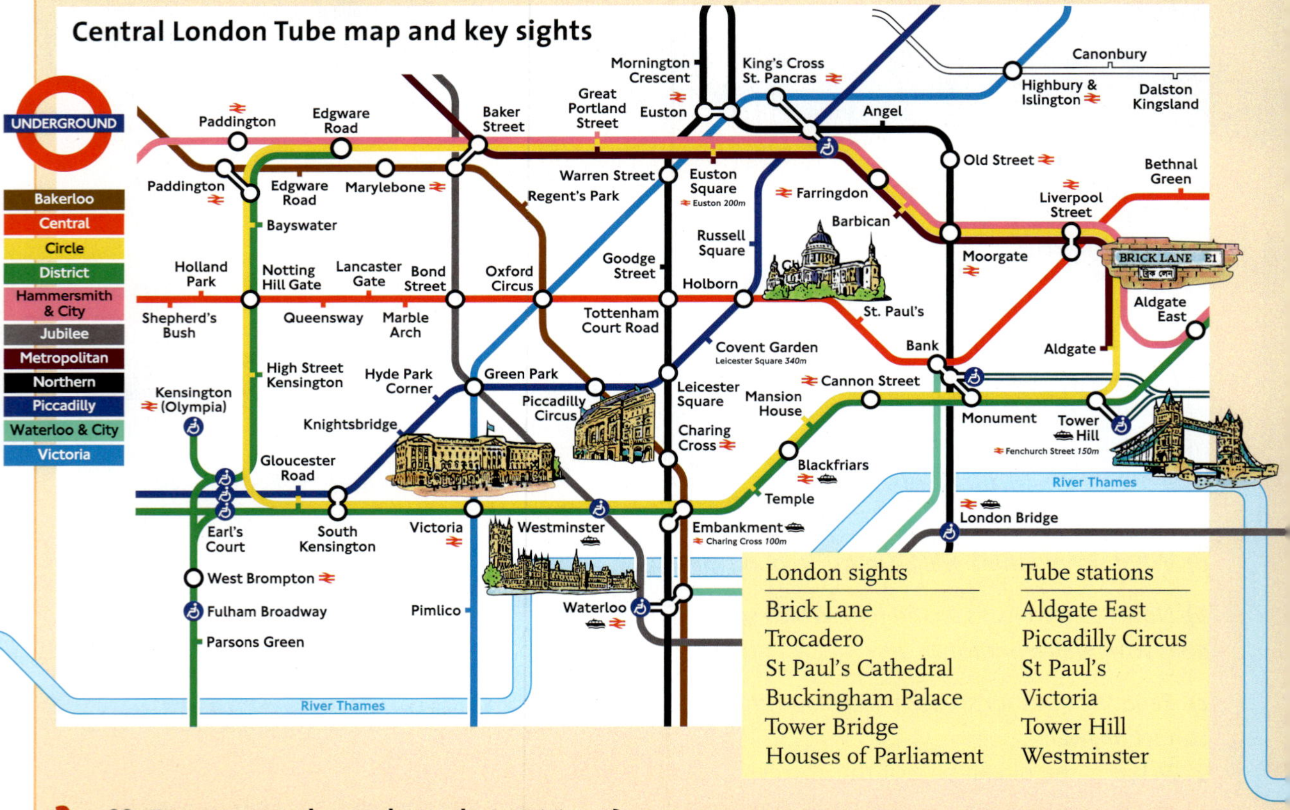

Central London Tube map and key sights

Lines: Bakerloo, Central, Circle, District, Hammersmith & City, Jubilee, Metropolitan, Northern, Piccadilly, Waterloo & City, Victoria

Stations shown include: Paddington, Edgware Road, Baker Street, Great Portland Street, Mornington Crescent, King's Cross St. Pancras, Euston, Angel, Highbury & Islington, Canonbury, Dalston Kingsland, Warren Street, Euston Square, Farringdon, Old Street, Liverpool Street, Bethnal Green, Marylebone, Regent's Park, Bayswater, Russell Square, Barbican, Moorgate, Aldgate East, Holland Park, Notting Hill Gate, Lancaster Gate, Bond Street, Oxford Circus, Goodge Street, Holborn, St. Paul's, Bank, Aldgate, Shepherd's Bush, Queensway, Marble Arch, Tottenham Court Road, Covent Garden (Leicester Square 340m), Cannon Street, Monument, Tower Hill (Fenchurch Street 150m), High Street Kensington, Hyde Park Corner, Green Park, Leicester Square, Mansion House, Kensington (Olympia), Knightsbridge, Piccadilly Circus, Charing Cross, Blackfriars, London Bridge, Gloucester Road, Temple, Earl's Court, South Kensington, Victoria, Westminster, Embankment (Charing Cross 100m), West Brompton, Fulham Broadway, Pimlico, Waterloo, Parsons Green. River Thames. BRICK LANE E1. Euston 200m.

London sights	Tube stations
Brick Lane	Aldgate East
Trocadero	Piccadilly Circus
St Paul's Cathedral	St Paul's
Buckingham Palace	Victoria
Tower Bridge	Tower Hill
Houses of Parliament	Westminster

2 👥 Excuse me please, how do I get to ...?

a) *Partner A: You want to go from* Victoria *to the
first three sights on the list. Ask your partner.*

b) *Partner B: You want to go from* King's Cross *to
the last three sights on the list. Ask your partner.*

- Excuse me please, how do I get to ...
  station?
- Take the ... line to ... / Change at ... /
  Then take the ... line to ...

▶ P 2–3 (pp. 20–21) • WB 2–4 (pp. 9–10)

3 On the London Eye

a) *Asif and Robert are on the London Eye. Look at the photos. Then listen. In what order do they take the photos?*

b) *Listen again. Find out one fact about each place.*

| … years old | … metres high |

A 'The Gherkin'

St Paul's Cathedral **C**

B Buckingham Palace

Hi, from the London Eye! **D**

4 A postcard home

London Tower Bridge

Dear Grandma

Birmingham was great. I met some nice kids at the festival. (One of them, Asif, is from London.)
We arrived in London yesterday. We visited the Tower in the afternoon and saw Tower Bridge.
This morning we went on the London Eye. It was cool! I'm going to see more of London with Asif this afternoon.

See you soon!
Love, Robert

Mrs.
2963
Vanc
Canad

> 1 Yesterday Robert arrived in …   **A** Birmingham.   **B** London.
>   2 He visited the London Eye …   **A** this morning.   **B** this afternoon.

▶ *GF 1a: Simple past (p. 143)* • *P 4–6 (pp. 21–22)* • *WB 5–8 (pp. 10–12)* • **Text File 2** *(p. 112)*

5   In Brick Lane 🎧

Asif wanted to show Robert his part of London. So he took him to Brick Lane in the East End.

'This is where my family live. They came to Britain from Bangladesh thirty years ago.'

'So are you Bangladeshi?'

'No, I'm British.'

'Have you ever been to Bangladesh?'

'No,' Asif said. 'Maybe next year.'

'Part of my family is French. Have you ever been to France?' asked Robert.

'Yeah, I've been there twice. You can go for a day trip from London.'

'Cool,' said Robert.

'I'm hungry,' said Asif. 'Do you want to eat?'

'I've had curry before. But I've never tried Bangladeshi food. Is it very spicy?'

'Well, it can be spicy or mild. My favourite dish is chicken biryani. And it's mild.'

> *Right or wrong?*   1 Asif has been to Bangladesh.
> 2 Asif has been to France.
> 3 Robert has had curry.

▶ *GF 1b: Present perfect (p. 143) • P 7–10 (pp. 23–24) • WB 9–12 (pp. 13–14)*

6   Extra Time for lunch

Scan the menu. What can Robert and Asif eat?

Robert___ I'd like something mild.
    He can have number ... or number ...

Robert___ Maybe something with chicken?
    He can have ...

Asif___ Today I want something spicy.
    He can have number ... or number ...

Asif___ I think I'll have fish.
    He can have ...

Lunch menu   (from 12 to 2.30 pm)

1 **FISH CURRY**   £3.95
with a spicy sauce and a salad

2 **CHICKEN BIRYANI**   £4.25
with Basmati rice and two mild sauces

3 **VEGETABLE DANSAK**   £3.75
in a mild sweet and sour sauce

4 **CHICKEN TIKKA**   £3.75
with spicy onions and a salad

▶ *SF Scanning (p. 134)*

7 　 Now you

a) *Have students in your group tried interesting things? Ask three people.*

| Have you ever tried | curry • bacon and eggs • English tea • carrot juice • spaghetti ice cream • Chinese/Greek/… food • … | ? |

Yes, I have.   No, I haven't.

b) *One of the group reports to the class.*

Two/Three people have tried …

Nobody has tried …

One person has tried …

c) **Extra** *Find out more details:*

Where did you try …? → At my friend's house/In Italy/In a restaurant/…

When did you try …? → Last week/Two years ago/On holiday …

▶ **Extra** *GF 1c: Present perfect/Simple past (p. 143) • P 11 (p. 24) • WB 13–14 (pp. 14–15)*

8 　 **Extra** Lost!

a) *Robert and Asif are at the bus stop. They want to go to the Trocadero. Look at the map. Complete the dialogue.*

turn left   straight on   on the left

turn right   past

b) *Now listen and check.*

Asif＿＿ Robert, I think we're lost. Let's ask that man the way.

Robert＿ Good idea.

Asif＿＿ Excuse me, please. Can you tell us the way to Piccadilly Circus?

Man＿＿ Yes, of course. Go straight on till you come to Trafalgar Square.

Asif＿＿ OK.

Man＿＿ Then … into Pall Mall. Then … into Haymarket. Go … And go … the Haymarket Theatre. Piccadilly Circus will be …

Asif＿＿ Thanks very much.

Man＿＿ You're welcome.

c) *You are at the Trocadero. Somebody asks you the way to Big Ben. What can you say?*

▶ *P 12–13 (p. 25) • WB 15–18 (pp. 15–16)*

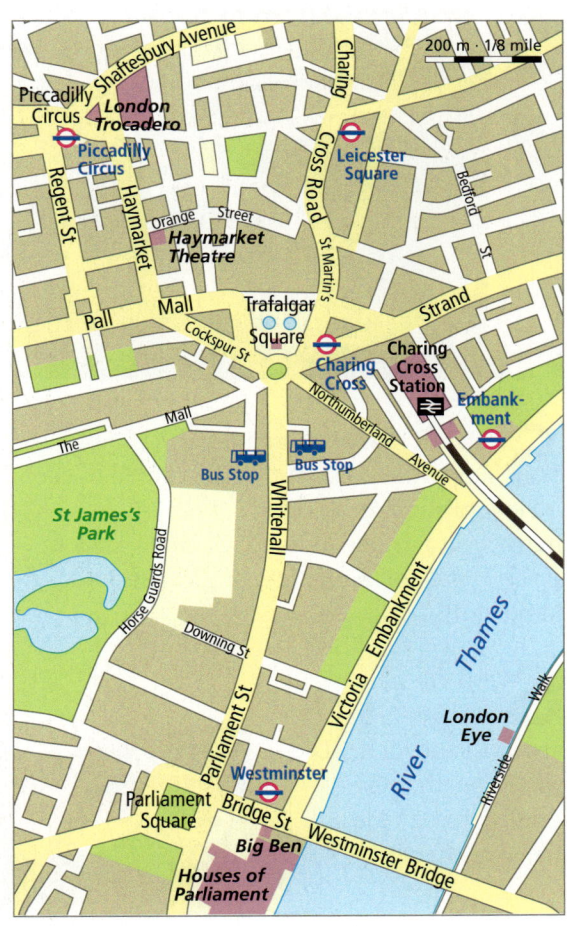

Extra **Background File** **LONDON** 🎧

Kids' day out in London ... on a budget

**London is huge. It's almost twice as big as Berlin. And it's very expensive.
So, if you've only got one day, you need to plan carefully.** ▶ *SF Understanding new words (p. 128)*

Step **1** Buy a Travelcard. You can use it on the buses or the Tube all day – after 9.30 in the morning.

Before 9.30 is the rush hour. 7.5 million people live in London (Berlin: 3.4 million) and another million come into the city to work every morning – so the rush hour is pretty busy.

Step **2** You want to go to one of London's famous musicals? No problem! Go to Leicester Square. Get cheap tickets for tonight at the half-price ticket place.

From there you can walk to Trafalgar Square and Nelson's Column, a famous London sight.

Step **3** What about some shopping? Remember, London is the capital of cool! How to shop on a budget? Well, try the markets at Portobello Road, Camden Lock or Brick Lane. You'll find lots of great second-hand stuff!

Step **4** Hungry? How about a sandwich? (Did you know that the English invented the sandwich?)

Step **5**   Now it's time for a bit of culture. Try the Natural History Museum. You can see huge dinosaurs there. Or the British Museum. You can see real mummies there. Both are FREE! And the museum shops are great for interesting souvenirs or gifts.

Step **6**   Tired now? How about a trip on the DLR (Docklands Light Railway). It goes past the new buildings in the Dockland area, east of Tower Bridge. You can use your Travelcard for this trip too.

Step **7**   On your way to the theatre, you will probably see somebody like this. She's homeless. She's selling the magazine 'The Big Issue'. Buy a magazine and help her.

1   👥👥 **A day in London**

a) *What would you like to do in London? Choose three things.*
For ideas, look at pp. 12–19. You can use guide books, the internet or tourist brochures.

> buy ... • go to ... • learn about ... • see ... •
> take ... • try ... • visit ... • walk over/along ...

b) *Plan your day in London. Report to the class.*
First we'd like to go to ...
After lunch we'd like to ...
Then ...

c) *Collect material and information. Make a poster of a day out in London.*

▶ *WB 19 (p. 17)*

1 WORDS City sights

a) 🔘 *Complete the sentences with the words in the box.*

> boat trip • map • market • museum • palace • park • views

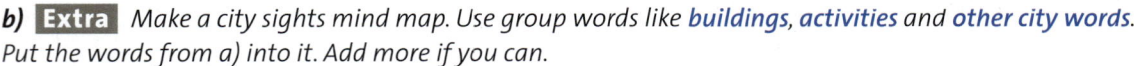

1 Take a ____ ____ on the River Thames and see lots of sights.
2 A ____ is a building with old, interesting things in it.
3 A ____ is a green place where people can walk, sit or play games.
4 From the top of the London Eye you get great ____ .
5 Every Sunday there's a great ____ in Brick Lane.
6 You can use a ____ to find your way in the city.
7 The Queen lives in a ____ .

b) **Extra** *Make a city sights mind map. Use group words like buildings, activities and other city words. Put the words from a) into it. Add more if you can.*

c) **Extra** 🔘 *Complete the text for tourists. Use your own ideas.*

> **▌Tourists!** Welcome to our city. We hope you enjoy your visit.
> If it's sunny, you can visit …
> At lunchtime, you'll probably need a snack. No problem.
> There are lots of … in the city centre.
> In the afternoon you can … For more information for your day out, go to the …
> Have a great day!

2 WORDS A transport wheel

a) 🔘 *Choose words from the box and put them in a copy of the wheel. You can use some words more than once. Some of the words are new (e.g. ⁺airport)*

> ⁺airport • bike • boat • bus •
> ⁺bus stop • car • driver • ⁺ferry •
> ⁺gate • harbour • helicopter • line •
> ⁺lorry • plane • road • river • sea •
> ship • street • station • ⁺taxi •
> ticket • train • ⁺tram • Travelcard •
> Tube • map • tunnel • …

b) *Write the verbs and prepositions from the box into your exercise book. Find words from a) to go with them. Check in the Dictionary.*

> arrive at • ask for • change to •
> get off • get on • go by • wait at

3 Extra LISTENING Travel announcements 🎧

a) Look at the pictures. Then write down the numbers 1–3. Listen to the announcements and match a picture to each number. The sounds you hear may help you.

b) Listen again and answer these questions. Remember: you don't need to understand every word.

1 Which platform do you need for the train to Bristol? Ⓐ 5 Ⓑ 9 Ⓒ 15
2 Where must you change if you want to go to Wimbledon? Ⓐ Earls Court Ⓑ Richmond Ⓒ Ealing
3 Which gate do you need if you want to fly to Berlin? Ⓐ 9 Ⓑ 2 Ⓒ 49

4 //O REVISION A visit to the London Eye (Simple past) ▶ D p. 102

a) Find the simple past forms and complete the text.

**h a d n t o o k d a r r i v e d e d i d n't s e e l c a l l e d o f o u n d t w e r e n't n d i d
n't w a i t o w e r e f w a s r d i d n't s e e o s a w w d i d n't s t a y o w e n t**

Asif and Robert *had* a really great time yesterday. In the morning Robert and his parents … the Tube to Waterloo. When they … at the London Eye, they … Asif. But then Asif … Robert on his mobile and they … him quickly. Luckily there … too many tourists there that day, so they … very long. Soon they … up on the big wheel. The view … fantastic. They … Asif's house, but they … lots of famous London sights. After the ride, Asif and Robert … with Robert's parents. They … to Asif's part of London and then to the Trocadero.

b) **Extra** *There are 13 extra letters between the simple past forms in a). Put them in the correct order. Find a place that lots of tourists visit. There's a photo of it on pp. 12–13.*

5 👥 REVISION Yesterday … (Simple past)

a) Complete the sentences for yourself.

| Yesterday: I … – I didn't … | Last weekend: I … – I didn't … | In my summer holidays: I … – I didn't … |

b) Tell your partner about yourself. Then listen to your partner and take notes about him/her.

Me
Yesterday: rode bike, didn't read
Last weekend: went shopping, didn't go to school
summer holidays: visited grandparents, didn't go to the sea

Elsa
Yesterday: went > school, didn't watch TV
Last weekend: went > cinema, didn't go shopping
summer holidays: stayed at home, didn't go > the sea

6   WRITING   A holiday postcard

a) 🔘 *Which picture goes with which postcard?*
Read the two postcards quickly and find out.

Dear Grandad

This is a great place. Yesterday we
went to the London Dungeon. That
was great but scary. This afternoon
we're going to the Tower and the
London Eye.
   Our B&B is OK - it's cheap. The
weather isn't great. Today it's rainy
and windy. But that doesn't matter.
We're having a fantastic time.

   Lots of love, Nick

5 035387 200014

Dear Jenny

   Hello from Cornwall! It's nice here. The beaches are cool.
The people here are really friendly.
   I was at a windsurfing school yesterday. The weather is
brilliant – hot and sunny. I go swimming every day. Mum and
Dad just sit in the sun! Tomorrow we're going to visit a castle.
See you soon!

Love Kate

b) *Look at the two postcards again. Find:*
1   weather words
2   activity words
3   words for sights

c) 🔘 *Write the postcard for Tom.*

Dear Sandy

I'm in 🇬🇧 We're near the 🌊

The weather is ☀️ . We go 🏊

every day. Yesterday we visited 🏰

Tomorrow we're going to go 🏄

It's really 🙂 here!

Lots of ❤️

Tom

d) more help   ▶ D p. 102
Write a postcard from an imaginary holiday in London.
You can put your postcard in your DOSSIER.
Start with a greeting:
Dear Laura / Hi Nate
Say where you are:
I'm writing to you from … / Hello from …!
Say what the weather is like:
The weather is great / terrible / …
It's hot and sunny / cold every day.
Say what the place is like:
The hotel / The city / … isn't great.
The people are friendly. / The sights are …
Say what you usually do there:
Every day we … in the afternoon because …
Say what you did yesterday:
Yesterday afternoon / … we visited a castle /
a palace / … In the evening we went to …
Say what you are going to do:
This evening / Tomorrow I'm going to go to…
Finish with a closing phrase:
Love, … / Write soon! … / See you soon, …

7 PRONUNCIATION now [aʊ] – no [əʊ] 🎧

a) Listen and repeat.

> Let's go to the disco and have a cola.

> I found a loud brown cow in my house.

b) Say these words. Which is the odd one out? Listen and check.

1	shout	snow	phone
2	nose	down	photo
3	brown	slow	clown
4	show	grow	town
5	hope	home	house
6	about	cold	cloud

8 🔘 REVISION A week in London (Present perfect)

Janina and Klara are in London. Look at their list of things to do.

a) Say what Janina and Klara have done.

1 Klara has bought clothes on a London market.
2 Janina and Klara have …
3 Janina and Klara …
4 Janina and Klara …

b) Say what they haven't done (yet).

1 Janina hasn't eaten … yet.
2 Klara …
3 Janina and Klara haven't …
4 Klara …

> **Things to do in London**
>
> | K | buy clothes on a London market ✓ |
> | J | eat Indian food in Brick Lane |
> | J + K | see the London Eye ✓ |
> | J + K | visit the Tower of London ✓ |
> | K | see a musical |
> | J + K | play video games at the Trocadero |
> | J + K | travel on the Underground ✓ |
> | K | take photos of Buckingham Palace |

9 ▥🔘 REVISION The Feely family (Present perfect) ▶ D p. 103

Match the sentence halves and make sentences about the Feely family.

1 Mrs Feely is angry …
2 Mo and Jo Feely are happy …
3 Julie Feely is proud …
4 Kitty Feely is scared …
5 Tommy Feely is ill …

because he has eaten lots of sweets.
because she has seen a big dog.
because they have had a bath.
because her kids haven't tidied their room.
because she has written a nice story.

10 WORDS Food

a) 🔘 *Match the food in the box to the shops.*
Which things can't you find in any of the shops? Where can you find them?

apples • bacon • bananas • ⁺beef • biscuits • bread • ⁺butter • cakes • carrots • cheese • cherries •
chicken • eggs • ⁺lamb • lettuce • ⁺mushrooms • ⁺onions • oranges • ⁺peas • ⁺pork • potatoes •
rolls • sausages • ⁺steaks • sweets • tomatoes • ⁺turkey • ⁺vegetable

b) `Extra` 👥 *FOOD GAME 1*
What have you got in your shopping bag?
Play a chain game.
A: I've got bacon in my shopping bag.
B: I've got bacon and bread in my shopping bag.
C: I've got bacon, bread and …

c) `Extra` 👥 *FOOD GAME 2*
Find photos or draw pictures of everything in the box in a). Glue each one onto a card. Write each word onto a different card. You can use your cards to play a food memory game.

11 `Extra` What have they done? When did they do it? (Present perfect/Simple past)

> **Remember**
>
> ***present perfect*** – *wenn keine Zeitangabe genannt wird.*
> ***simple past*** – *wenn eine Zeitangabe genannt wird, z. B.* **yesterday**, **last year**.

Write sentences. Choose the correct verb form.
1 Liz (has visited/visited) *has visited* London. She (has gone/went) *went* there <u>last summer</u>.
2 Eddie (ate/has eaten) crocodile. He (has tried/tried) it when he was in Australia.
3 Charlie (has been/was) on the London Eye. He (has been/was) on it two weeks ago.
4 Diana (has written/wrote) postcards to all her friends. She (has written/wrote) them last night.
5 Sarah and Joe (have been/were) to Brick Lane Market. They (have gone/went) there last Sunday.
6 Andy (has seen/saw) a concert in Hyde Park. It (has been/was) two months ago.

12 SPEAKING Asking for and giving information 🎧

a) *What questions might people in these pictures ask? Write them down.*

How much is	break our journey?	does the ride take?
Can we	a ticket to Richmond?	get a group ticket?
How long	it for adults?	do we have to wait for the next train?

b) *Listen to the dialogues 1 and 2. Which questions do you hear in each one?*
Mark the questions 1 or 2. Listen again and check.

c) 👥 *Prepare a dialogue with your partner like the one in the example.*
Practise the dialogue and act it out in class.

> *A:* Can I help you?   *A:* About 20 minutes.
> *B:* …   *B:* Thank you.
> *A:* Three pounds.   *A:* You're welcome.
> *B:* …

13 MEDIATION Announcements 🎧

The Meiers want to go to Richmond. Listen to the announcements. Help Tom.

Warte, da kommt eine Durchsage.

Tom, gilt die für uns?

1 Wir wollen nach Richmond, also …

Warte, da kommt noch eine Durchsage.

Gut, dass unser Zug gleich kommt.

2 Man soll … nicht unbeaufsichtigt lassen.

Das war wichtig für uns. Es ging um Reisende nach …

Oh nein, der Zug endet in … oder so. Dort sollen wir …

3

▶ *SF Mediation (p. 137)*

Only a game 🎧

> *Do you or your friends play video games? What games do you know?*

When they arrived at the Trocadero, Asif and Robert went to Funland.

'Do you want to play a virtual reality game?' asked Asif.

5 'I've never played one,' Robert said. 'What do you do?'

'You wear a helmet,' Asif said. 'Then you can see places all around you. It's like you're really there.'

10 'Cool,' Robert said.

Asif saw something in a quiet corner. 'Look at this,' he said.

There were two VR helmets and a sign in big red letters.

15 The sign said:

DANGER
Experimental game
Play at your own risk

'Let's try it,' Asif said.

'But maybe it's dangerous,' said Robert.

But he was too late. Asif was already wearing a helmet. Robert put on the other helmet.

20 'There's a menu,' Robert said. 'Can you see it?'

Tipp

Wenn du ein Wort in der Geschichte nicht kennst und wenn du es auch nicht erraten kannst, sieh in einem Wörterbuch nach.

▶ *SF English–German dictionary (p. 130)*

'Yes, I can,' Asif answered. 'We can choose a virtual world.'

'The first one is *Roman London*,' said Robert.

'Boring,' said Asif. 'What about the next one: 25 *The Great Fire of London*?' he said excitedly.

'OK,' said Robert. 'But how do we start it?'

'Push the button,' Asif told him.

'Hey, I can see my hand in the game!' Robert said. 30

'That's virtual reality,' Asif explained.

A few moments later, they were in London in the year 1666.

'Wow!' said Robert. 'This is amazing.'

The two boys were in a dark street. Robert 35 looked up. Between the houses he could see the sky. It was red.

'Look, Asif! The fire!' said Robert. 'It's so real.'

40 'Yeah,' said Asif. 'And look at all the people. They look real too. This is great.'

There were lots of people in the street. They had all kinds of things in their arms: bags, boxes, chairs, babies, musical instruments ...
45 Everybody looked scared.

'Come on,' said Robert. 'Let's find the fire.'

'Careful!' said Asif. 'It's very dirty here.'

'Too late!' said Robert. 'Look at my shoe. Yuck! It smells.'

50 'Look!' said Asif. 'What is it?'

'Rats!' Robert
55 shouted. 'Lots of rats. This is too realistic for me!'

'Who are
60 you? You talk funny,' said one woman to Robert.

'There are
65 two of them,' said a man. 'They're not from here.'

'What are you doing here?' asked the woman.

70 'Er ... We came to see the fire,' said Robert.

'They came to see the fire!' said another man.

People stopped and looked at them. They weren't friendly.

Asif said to Robert, 'Come on. I don't like   75
this. Let's go!'

They were near the Tower of London now. They had a good view of the city.

'Oh my God!' Robert was shocked. 'Look, Asif.'   80

It was terrible. There were fires everywhere.

'You know what?' Robert said. 'This isn't much fun.'

'Yeah,' Asif answered. 'Let's try a different game. Take off your helmet.'   85

Both boys took off their helmets. But nothing happened.

'We're still here! What's happening?' Asif was scared.

'I don't know! This was your idea,' Robert   90
shouted. 'Do something!'

'I know,' Asif said. 'Find the plug. Then we can stop the game.'

'But where is it?' asked Robert.

'I don't know. Try the walls of the Tower!'   95

'The walls of the Tower?' said Robert.

'Just look, Robert,' said Asif angrily. 'It's only a game!'

100 Suddenly there was a flash.

'What was that flash?' Robert asked.

'I don't know,' said Asif. 'Just look for the plug. Quickly!'

The boys felt the walls. They were hot.

105 'It's funny,' Asif said. 'I can really feel these walls.'

'So?' asked Robert.

'Well, you can see and hear things in virtual reality games. But you can't feel things.'

'And we can feel the walls,' said Robert. 'So

110 ...'

'So,' said Asif. 'I think we're really here.'

Just then somebody shouted.

'Stop those two boys. They started the fire.'

Lots of people stopped and looked.

'We didn't start the fire,' shouted Asif. 'We 115 haven't done anything!'

'They started the fire! Stop them!' another voice shouted.

'What are they going to do, Asif?' cried Robert. 'I'm scared.' 120

'Run!' said Asif.

Working with the text

1   What happens in the story?
Put the sentences in the right order.
1   They find a game in a quiet corner and want to play it.
2   The Londoners think that the boys started the fire.
3   The game gets too realistic.
4   Robert pushes the button for the Great Fire of London.
5   The boys can't stop the game because they can't find the plug.
6   Robert is scared because he thinks the people will hurt them.
7   Robert and Asif go to Funland because they want to play a virtual reality game.

2   ▐▌◯   How Robert felt   ▸ D p. 103
Finish the sentences.
1   Robert felt nervous when ...
2   He felt excited when ...
3   He felt scared when ...
4   He felt shocked when ...

> ... the people shouted at them. (ll. 112–120)
> ... he saw London in the year 1666. (ll. 32–34)
> ... he saw the fire. (ll. 79–81)
> ... Asif put on the helmet (ll. 17–19)

3   The ending   🎧
a) What do you think happens to Asif and Robert?

b) Listen. What happens at the end of the story? Choose the correct sentence.
1   Asif and Robert stopped the game and started to play another one.
2   Asif and Robert couldn't stop the game.
3   Asif and Robert stopped the game and left quickly.

4   Extra   ◉   Video games
a) What makes a video game a good game? Think of reasons.

b) What can be bad about video games? The ideas below can help you.

> If you play them all the time, ...

> If you kill people in games, ...

> ... you'll lose your friends.

> ... you'll hurt people in real life too.

> ... you don't know what's real.

> ... you won't have time for other things.

▸ WB 20 (p. 18) · **Checkpoint 1** WB (p. 19)

How am I doing? ▶ *SF Multiple choice (p. 133)*

a) *Find or choose the correct answers.*

London

1 London is on the River …
   A Trocadero. **B** Thames. **C** Tower.
2 Another word for the London
   Underground is …
   A the Tube. **B** the Eye.
   C the Travelcard.
3 The London Eye is …
   A a clock. **B** a castle. **C** a big wheel.
4 The Trocadero is near a famous square in
   the centre of London. It's called …
   A Piccadilly Circus. **B** Trafalgar Square.
5 The Queen's home in London is …
   A the Tower of London.
   B Buckingham Palace.

Words

6 What is the group word: people or tickets?
   single • return • Travelcard
7 Excuse me, how can I … to Victoria
   Station?
   A move **B** find **C** get
8 I'm hungry. I want to buy a …
   A drink. **B** postcard. **C** sandwich.
9 There are great … from the top of the
   London Eye.
   A trips **B** buildings **C** views

Writing

10 Which is a good way to start a postcard?
   A Hello from London! **B** See you soon.
   C Lots of love.

11 … we're going to visit
   London.
   A Yesterday
   B Last week
   C Tomorrow
12 Which is not the right way to end
   a postcard?
   A Love, Lisa **B** See you soon!
   C Dear Dora

Grammar

13 The boys … to the Trocadero yesterday.
   A go **B** went **C** have gone
14 Robert's parents … go to the Trocadero in
   the afternoon. They went to the Tower.
   A didn't **B** not **C** haven't
15 … you ever visited London?
   A Did **B** Has **C** Have
16 Has Asif ever tried Indian food?
   A Yes, he did. **B** No, he didn't.
   C Yes, he has.

Everyday English

17 Say it in English: Was kostet eine einfache
   Fahrkarte für einen Erwachsenen?
   A How much is a return ticket for an
   adult?
   B How much is a single ticket for a child?
   C How much is a single ticket for an
   adult?
18 … I help you?
   A When **B** Can **C** How much

b) *Check your answers on p. 214 and add up your points – one point for each correct answer.*

c) *If you had 15 or more points, well done!*
Where did you make mistakes? The chart below tells you where you can find help with your mistakes.

No.	Areas	Find out more	Exercises
1– 5	London facts	Unit 1 (pp. 12–19), P 5 (p. 21)	WB 1–2, 7, 15, 19 (pp. 8–9, 11, 15, 17)
6– 7	Word field: transport	Unit 1 (p. 14)	P 2, 4 (p. 20, 21), WB 3–4 (pp. 9–10)
8– 9	Word field: tourist words	Unit 1 (p. 17), P 11, p. 24)	WB 17 (p. 16)
10–12	Writing postcards	Unit 1, P 7 (p. 22)	WB 8 (p. 12)
13–14	Simple past (Revision)	GF 1a (p. 143)	P 4–5 (p. 21), WB 5–6 (pp. 10–11)
15–16	Present perfect (Revision)	GF 1b (p. 143)	P 8–11 (pp. 23–24), WB 10 (p. 13)
17–18	Everyday English	P 12 (p. 25)	WB 17 (p. 16)

Unit 2

Island girl

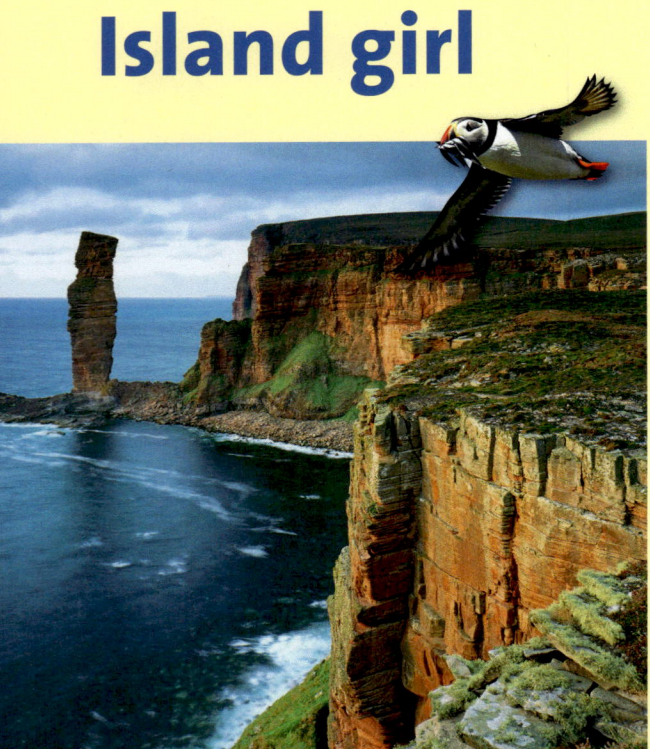

1 Island views

a) *On the map on this page, find the islands of Hoy and Mainland, and the town of Kirkwall. Find the Orkney Islands on the map on the inside cover of this book.*

b) *Which caption goes with which photo?*

A There are fish farms on the coast.

B There are lots of cows and sheep on Hoy.

C The Old Man of Hoy isn't a man. It's a huge rock.

D Some people work on the oil rigs.

E Kirkwall School has got a school hostel.

F The only way to Hoy is by ferry.

G At a ceilidh people play music and dance.

2 An interview with Katrina

There's going to be a TV documentary about Kirkwall School. A film researcher has come to interview students.

a) *Listen to the interview. Put the pictures in the correct order.*

b) *Look at the questions and choose the right answers.*

Listen to the interview again if you have to.

1 Katrina is from …
  A Hoy.   B Mainland.
2 She goes to school on …
  A Hoy.   B Mainland.
3 She goes home …
  A every day.   B on Fridays.
4 Her dad works on …
  A a fish farm   B an oil rig.
5 Katrina has got …
  A a brother.   B a sister.
6 She likes to …
  A dance.   B play the fiddle.

▶ P 1 (p. 38) • WB 1–2 (pp. 20–21)

3

4

5

6

7

All about ... electronic media

1 Keeping in touch 🎧

Katrina McFadden lives with her family on Hoy. Her grandad remembers when the first people on the island got a telephone.

Today it's different. Katrina has got a mobile and a computer. She keeps in touch with her family with text messages and phone calls when she's away at school. She sends e-mails to people too, and 'chats' with her friends on the internet.

▶ *When Katrina is at school she ...*
   A *writes letters to her family.*
   B *sends text messages to her family.*

2 Now you

a) *What media do you use? Fill in a copy of the chart for yourself.*

Mobile phone	yes	no	Computer	yes	no
– make phone calls	✓		– do homework		✓
– send text messages to family and mates	✓		– play games	✓	
– take photos		✓	– surf the internet		
– make videos			– download or mix music		
– listen to music			– chat or send instant messages		
– download logos			– talk over the internet		
– download ringtones			– send e-mails		

b) 👥 *Talk to two partners. Add their answers to your chart. Answer their questions.*
Do you make phone calls on a mobile?
Do you do homework on a computer?
Yes, I do. / No, I don't.

c) *Report to the class about your group.*

Everybody Nobody	makes calls mixes music	on a mobile. on a computer.
Only one student	downloads logos sends e-mails	on a mobile.
Two students	play games chat	on a computer.

"I MET SOMEONE WONDERFUL IN A CHAT ROOM...
AND THEN I FOUND OUT SHE'S A CAT!"

© 2000 Randy Glasbergen. www.glasbergen.com

▶ P 2–4 (pp. 38–39) • WB 3–4 (pp. 21–22) •
Text File 3 (pp. 113–114)

3 To school by ferry

On Monday morning Katrina's mum drives her from home to Lyness. It takes about half an hour. Then Katrina gets the ferry from Lyness to Houton, on the island of Mainland.

In Houton she gets a school bus to Kirkwall. That journey only takes about half an hour.

On Friday afternoon she gets the ferry back to Lyness. Her dad usually picks her up.

Hoy – Winter Timetable
Arrivals and departures, 25 Sept until 5 May

Lyness	dep	0650	1405	1640
Flotta	dep	0710	1425	—
Houton	arr	0745	1500	1715
Houton	dep	0800	1520	1730
Flotta	dep	0845	—	—
Lyness	arr	0910	1605	1810

> 1 · How long do Katrina and her mum drive from home to the ferry?
  A 30 minutes   B 15 minutes
2 What time is the ferry from Lyness on Monday morning?
  A 06.50   B 08.00
3 What time do they have to leave home?
  A after 6 am   B before 6 am

4   Now you

a) *How do you get to school? Make notes.*

b) 👥 *Tell three or more partners about your journey to school.*

c) `Extra` *Which of your partners has the longest journey to school?*

1 I usually leave the house at …
2 I walk to school. / I ride my bike.
   I go by bus/tram/train/…
   I walk to the station, and then I get a …
   My dad/… sometimes/usually drives me.
3 It takes about … minutes.
4 I arrive at school at …

5   Messages from home

Anna McFadden
Hi kat, hope u r ok. U looked a bit unhappy this morning in the car. CU on fri. Mum x

Anna McFadden
Hi k, r u ok 2 day? CU 2moro! Mum x

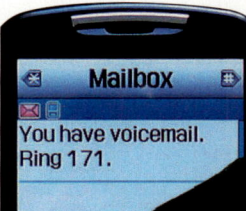

Mailbox
You have voicemail. Ring 171.

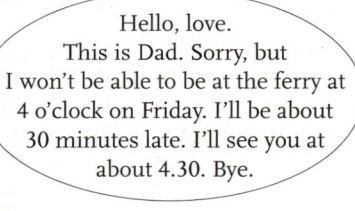

Hello, love. This is Dad. Sorry, but I won't be able to be at the ferry at 4 o'clock on Friday. I'll be about 30 minutes late. I'll see you at about 4.30. Bye.

> 1 How does Katrina's mum write these sentences in her text messages?

  I hope you are all right. • I'll see you tomorrow. • Are you OK today?

2 `Extra` Write a text message from Katrina to her dad.

▶ GF 2: will-future (p. 144) • P 5–8 (pp. 40–41) • WB 5–9 (pp. 23–24)

6   Trendy types 🎧

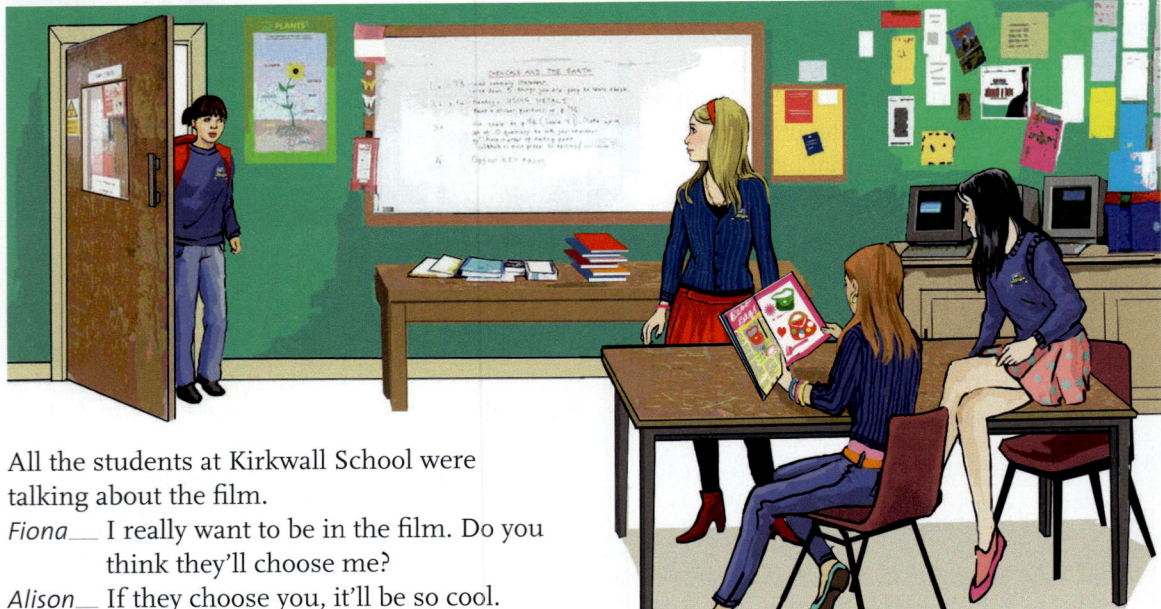

All the students at Kirkwall School were talking about the film.

*Fiona*___ I really want to be in the film. Do you think they'll choose me?

*Alison*___ If they choose you, it'll be so cool.

*Linda*___ If they choose you, you'll need some new clothes.

*Fiona*___ You're right!

*Alison*___ If you go shopping, we'll come with you.

*Linda*___ And we can go to the wee shop in Albert Street.

*Alison*___ Yes, they have those new bags.

*Fiona*___ Which new bags?

*Linda*___ You know, the bags in that magazine. I'll show you ... here.

*Fiona*___ Nice. They're really trendy. Not like Fishface's awful old rucksack. It's so uncool.

*Linda*___ Well, what do you expect? She comes from Hoy! They don't know the word 'trendy' on Hoy.

*Fiona*___ Oh oh. Here she comes!

> *Fiona or Katrina?*
1 Who wants to be in the film?
2 Who is Fishface?
3 Who comes from Hoy?
4 Who calls people names?

▶ *GF 3a: Conditional sentences (1) (p. 144) • P 9 (p. 42) •*
WB 10–11 (p. 25)

7   Extra   POEM   Billy doesn't like school really 🎧

a) *Read the poem.*
Which is wrong?

The other kids ...
Ⓐ laugh at Billy.
Ⓑ are nice to Billy.
Ⓒ make jokes about Billy's mum.
Ⓓ call Billy names.

b) *Do you think Fiona and her friends are like 'the other kids' in the poem? How?*

Billy doesn't like school really.
It's not because he can't do the work
but because some of the other kids
don't seem to like him that much.

They call him names
and make jokes about his mum.

Everyone laughs ... except Billy.
Everyone laughs ... except Billy.

by Paul Cookson

8 A Friday night chat 🎧

Katrina was tired and upset when she got back home on Friday. She went to her room and turned on the computer. Latisha was online.

*Katrina*___ I'm so glad you're online, Tish. I had a terrible week.

*Latisha*___ Why, what's the matter?

*Katrina*___ The 'Beauties' were horrible. They called me Fishface again.

*Latisha*___ If I was you, I'd forget them, Katrina.

*Katrina*___ It's hard. If people called you names, you would be upset.

*Latisha*___ They're just stupid bullies. If they called me names, I wouldn't listen.

*Katrina*___ But you're cool. If you were in my class, the 'Beauties' would be nice to you.

*Latisha*___ You're cool, Katrina. You can play the fiddle brilliantly. What can they do?

*Katrina*___ Go shopping!

*Latisha*___ Exactly! If I was you, I'd forget them.

▸ *GF 3b: Conditional sentences (2) (p. 144) • P 10–11 (p. 42) • WB 12–15 (pp. 26–27)*

> 1 Who are 'the Beauties'?
> 2 What is Katrina's problem?
> 3 What is Latisha's advice?
>   Ⓐ Forget the girls.
>   Ⓑ Listen to them.
>   Ⓒ Talk to them.
>   Ⓓ Go shopping with them.

9 Advice for Katrina

a) *Complete the e-mail to Katrina. If you don't know the words in English, look at the entries from a German–English dictionary on the right.*

Hi Katrina
I hope you are feeling better today.
I was thinking about those girls. They are (gemein) …
You must do something. It's not OK for them to (schikanieren) … you.
I think you need (Rat) … Tell your parents. Talk to a teacher.
And remember. They are stupid. You are cool!

STUDY SKILLS German-English dictionary

Das Wörterbuch gibt oft mehrere Übersetzungen für ein englisches Wort. Lies immer zuerst den gesamten Wörterbucheintrag. Wähle dann die richtige deutsche Bedeutung. Dahinter findest du das passende englische Wort.

gemein   *boshaft* mean; *gewöhnlich* common

schikanieren   to harass; *Mitschüler* to bully

Rat   advice; *Versammlung* council

b) **Extra** *Can you think of more advice for Katrina?*

▸ *SF German-English dictionary (p. 131) • P 12 (p. 43) • WB 16 (p. 28)*

Extra | Background File | SCOTLAND, a special place 🎧

Beautiful Scotland

Scotland is half the size of England and only 5 million people live there. (50 million people live in England.) It is very beautiful with lots of mountains and lakes. The tallest mountain in Britain is in Scotland. Its name is Ben Nevis.

```
A 87
Caol Loch Aillse   ¼
Kyle of Lochalsh
Am Ploc            6
Plockton
Baile Mac Ara      4
Balmacara
   (A 82)
An Gearasdan       76
Fort William
   (A 887)
Inbhir Nis         82
Inverness
```

A proud country

Scottish people are very proud of their country. Scotland is part of Great Britain, but it has its own parliament. It's in Edinburgh, the capital. It looks after important things for Scotland.

Language – not just English

People in Scotland speak English. But some people speak Gaelic too. It is a very different language to English.

The kilt

For a special day the men get out their kilts.

All the people in the photos below are wearing tartan kilts. Lots of Scottish families have their own tartan.

Highland Games

In the summer, towns and villages have 'Highland Games'. There are competitions for music and dancing and Scottish sports like 'tossing the caber'.

A bagpiper

Scottish dancing

Scottish music

Traditional Scottish music is very well-known.

There are lots of modern Scottish musicians too, like KT Tunstall and Franz Ferdinand.

Famous Scottish people

Sir Arthur Conan Doyle wrote the Sherlock Holmes stories. He was Scottish.

Do you know Robbie Coltrane? He's the actor who plays Hagrid in the Harry Potter films. He's Scottish too.

Scottish ideas

Scottish people have always had great ideas. The telephone and the television were Scottish inventions.

Did you know that scientists in Scotland were the first in the world to clone a sheep?

Scottish food

Special Scottish foods include haggis (a sort of large sausage), shortbread (not bread, but a biscuit) and Scotch pancakes.

A Scot called Macintosh invented the macintosh or 'mac'.

---

1 👥 **A Scotland quiz**

Find the answers to these questions about Scotland on pages 36–37.

1 What is the highest mountain in Britain?
2 What is the capital of Scotland?
3 Scottish men sometimes wear a tartan 'skirt'. What is it called?
4 What languages do some Scottish people speak?
5 Name some Scottish inventions.
6 What colours are the Scottish flag?

2 Extra **More about Scotland**

Find out more about Scotland. Choose one of the topics below:

– *Copy a map of Scotland. Mark on it the main towns, mountains and lakes.*
– *Learn a Scottish song.*
– *Try a Scottish recipe.*
– *Find out about some more Scottish inventions.*

▶ P 13 (p. 43) • WB 17 (p. 29) • **Text File 4** (p. 115)

1 WORDS Town and country

In the country	In the country and in the town	In a town
farmhouse, forest, ...	canal, church, ...	busy, ...

beautiful • ⁺busy • ⁺canal • ⁺car park • cathedral • church • coast • cows • department store • dirty • farm • field • forest • hill • ⁺hilly • hotel • island • lake • mountain • noisy • park • post office • pub • quiet • restaurant • river • school • sheep • station • theatre • town centre • valley • village

a) *Which words go with which photo? Which go with both photos? (The words marked ⁺ may be new to you. Guess their meaning or look them up in the Dictionary on pp. 167–188.)*

b) *Finish these sentences.*

1 In most towns and cities you can find ...
2 In the country there are ...
3 Towns are often ...
4 People like to walk by/in ...

2 [//O] WORDS Electronic media ▶ D p. 104

a) *Complete the texts with the words in the boxes.*

chat • computer • send • surf • text messages

Katrina has got her own ... in her room at home. She uses it to ... with friends and to ... the internet. It's cheaper for her to ... instant messages to her friends than to send ... on her mobile.

logo • plays • ringtone • download

Katrina loves music, so she often spends her pocket money to ... her favourite songs. She hasn't got an MP3 player, but her mobile ... MP3s. Her ... on her mobile is a picture of a fiddle, and of course her ... is fiddle music.

b) **Extra** *Choose one word from each box and make your own sentences.*

3 **Extra** PRONUNCIATION Try to sound English 🎧

a) *In English sentences important words are <u>stressed</u>. This gives English a special sound. Listen.*

b) *Listen again and repeat.*

c) 👥 *Read the dialogue. Try to sound English.*

o o o o O o Have you got a <u>mobile</u>?	O o O Yes, I <u>have</u>.
o o o O Do you send <u>mails</u>?	O o O Yes, I <u>do</u>.
o o o O o Do you make <u>phone</u> calls?	O o O <u>No</u>, I <u>don't</u>.

4   WRITING An e-mail to a friend   (Using paragraphs)

a) *This e-mail is about a special day at school. Put the parts in the correct order.*

A What did you do at the weekend? Mail back soon. Love, Lara

B We had different information points in our classroom. Our parents could listen to traditional Scottish music. ☹

C Hi Michael! Guess what I did last Saturday – I went to school! And I had a great time!

D There was an open day at our school. My class wanted to show our parents something about Scotland.

E I've sent you a photo of my dad. He's wearing Scottish clothes!

b) *Match the sentences 1–3 to the parts of the e-mail.*

This happens in A/B …

1 At the beginning say what your text is about.

2 Start a new paragraph for each new idea.

3 Finish with a general or personal statement.

c) *Write the e-mail correctly. The sentences in paragraphs A, B and C are in the wrong order.*

Dear Lara
Thanks for your mail. The photo was very funny. I went out with my dad on Saturday.

A We bought a present for my mum. First we went to a department store. It's her birthday tomorrow.

B He bought a very fast one with a cool monitor. After that we went into a computer shop. My dad wanted to buy a new computer.

C It's great. Now I can send e-mails from my desk. When we came home, we put Dad's old computer in my room.

I've sent you a photo of me and my new computer. ;-)
Write soon. Bye for now! Michael

d) more help   ▸ D p. 104
Now write an e-mail to one of your friends about a special day. You can put it in your DOSSIER.

Start with an interesting opening sentence.	– Guess what I did today! – I had a great day with … on Saturday.
Start a new paragraph for each new idea.	– We had a fantastic time. – The best part of the day was … First … After that … At lunch time … The weather was …
Finish with a general or personal statement.	– Must stop now. Please write back soon.

5   REVISION I think Katrina will ... (will-future)

a) *Look at the pairs of pictures. Write down what you think Katrina will and won't do this weekend.*

1 On Saturday morning Katrina ...

sleep till 10.30 | get up early

2 On Saturday afternoon she ...

play fiddle | listen to music

3 On Saturday evening she ...

watch TV | go to the disco

4 On Sunday afternoon she ...

help Dad | read a book

5 On Sunday evening she ...

play with her brother | pack her bag

6 On Sunday night she ...

go to bed early | chat till 12

On Saturday morning Katrina will sleep till 10.30. She won't get up early.

b) 👥 *What about you? Say two things that you will do this evening. And two things you won't do.*

6   🔘 WORDS friendly/unfriendly (Word building)

a) *Copy the chart and complete it.*

friendly	unfriendly
happy	unhappy
healthy	...
fair	
safe	
tidy	

Uncool!

b) *Complete the sentences.*
1 You aren't smiling. Are you unhappy/unfair?
2 Don't eat so much fast food. It's really unhappy/unhealthy.
3 Ben can never find anything. He's such an unsafe/untidy boy.
4 Jill never says 'hello' when you meet her. She's a really unfriendly/unhealthy person.
5 My sister can go out, but I have to stay at home. It's so unfair/untidy.
6 Don't go over that bridge. A boat hit it and now it's unfriendly/unsafe.

7 MEDIATION Using a mobile

Lucy Parker is staying with Pia Wolf. Read the dialogue. Find the English words for the German words in the box. Then complete the dialogue.

ver-/entriegeln • Knopf drücken • Geheimzahl

If I press this button, I can lock or unlock the keys, right?

Frau Wolf	Lucy kann mein altes Handy nehmen. Aber erklär's ihr bitte.
Pia	Lucy, you can use Mum's old mobile.
Lucy	Great, thanks. Oh, this looks like my mobile. If I press this button, I can lock or unlock the keys, right?
Frau Wolf	Was sagt sie?
Pia	...
Frau Wolf	Ja, das stimmt. Weiß sie, wie sie ein Gespräch annimmt?
Pia	Do you know what to do if the phone rings?
Lucy	If it rings, I have to press the green button with the telephone on it.
Pia	...
Lucy	And I finish with the red one, right?
Pia	...
Frau Wolf	Na, dann ist ja alles klar.
Pia	Yes, that's right. Is there anything else you need to know?
Lucy	Wait. Do I need the PIN code?
Pia	Ach ja, ...
Frau Wolf	Natürlich. Das ist 9 6 6 7.

8 SPEAKING Telephone messages 🎧

Pia is staying with Lucy Parker's family in Britain.

a) *Listen to the phone call and look at the message below. Write the correct message.*

Phone Message	
From:	Mr McNamara / McDonald
For:	Mr Parker / Mrs Parker
Message:	Please ring him back. / He'll ring back later.

b) *Now copy the phrases from the phone call and fill in the gaps. Then listen again and check.*

- Hello, John McNamara ___ .
- Can I __ __ Mr Parker, please?
- I'm sorry Mr Parker __ __ __ .
- __ is Pia Wolf _____ .
- Can __ ____ a message?
- Can you ask Mr Parker to ___ ___ ___ .

c) ⏺ 👥 *Look at this message. Prepare the dialogue. Listen and check. Then practise it.*

From:	Hannah
For:	Lucy
Message:	Please ring her back.

A: Melde dich.
B: Begrüße A und sag wer du bist. Frag, ob du ... sprechen kannst.
A: Bedaure, dass er/sie nicht zu Hause ist. Und sag wer du bist.
B: Frag, ob du eine Nachricht hinterlassen kannst.
A: Sag „ja".
B: Diktiere, was A wiedergeben soll.
A: Mach Notizen und sag, wenn du fertig bist.
B: Bedanke und verabschiede dich.
A: Verabschiede dich.

9   REVISION   If it's sunny, … (Conditional sentences type 1)

a) *Write a positive and a negative statement. You can use the ideas in the box.*

1   If a friend visits me next Sunday, *I'll go on a bike trip with him.*
    If a friend visits me next Sunday, *I won't practise the piano.*
2   If I've got lots of time next weekend, …
3   If I'm at home alone on Saturday, …
4   If it's sunny next Saturday, …

> **Tipp**   Hier sagst du 'Was ist wenn …'.
> Im *if*-Satz steht das **simple present**.
> Im **Haupt**satz steht meist **will-future**.

> download music • send text messages •
> surf the internet • watch DVDs • play cards •
> chat with friends • sleep late • tidy my room •
> have a party with … • go cycling/swimming •
> go for a walk • go to town • meet my friends

b) **Extra** 👥👥 *Make appointments with three students for 10, 11 and 12 o'clock. When your teacher says a time, go to your appointment. Tell your partner about your plans and listen to his/her plans.*

10   //O   Fiona's dreams (Conditional sentences type 2)   ▶ D p. 105

> **Tipp**   Fiona überlegt: Was wäre, wenn …?
> Im *if*-Satz steht das **simple past**.
> Im **Haupt**satz steht **would** oder **'d**.

Fiona often dreams about what it would be like if she lived in London. Finish her sentences.

1   If I lived in London, …

2   If my parents visited me, …

3   If I waited outside Buckingham Palace, …

4   If I was a film star, …

5   If I missed my friends, …

6   If I wanted to see my family at home, …

| … I would be very happy. | … maybe I'd see the Queen. | … I'd wear beautiful clothes. |
| … we'd go on the London Eye. | … I'd go by plane. | … I'd chat with them on the internet. |

11   Extra   O   What if …? (Conditional sentences type 2)

a) *Complete the sentences with ideas from the box.*

1   If I lived on an island, I'd …
2   If my parents had a million euros, we'd …

b) 👥 *Compare your sentences with your partner's. Are they the same or different?*

> have more time/buy a boat •
> buy a house in …/a castle in …/… •
> travel around the world/
> give lots of money to …

12 STUDY SKILLS Using a German-English dictionary

Find the correct English words for the underlined German words in the following sentences.

1 Katrina hat Latisha <u>um Rat</u> gebeten.
Katrina asked Latisha ____ _____ .

2 Latisha <u>hatte Mitleid mit</u> Katrina.
Latisha felt _____ ____ Katrina.

3 Katrina war sehr <u>dankbar für</u> Latishas Hilfe.
Katrina was very _____ ___ Latisha's help.

4 Die anderen Mädchen <u>machen sich lustig über</u> Katrina.
The other girls _____ _____ of Katrina.

5 Der Witz war nicht sehr <u>lustig</u>.
The joke wasn't very _____ .

> **Tipp**
>
> *Was bedeuten die Kurzformen **jn**. oder **jm**.?*
> *Schau auf S. 150, wenn du nicht sicher bist.*

Rat advice; *Ratschlag* piece of advice; *Versammlung* council; **jn. um Rat fragen** ask sb. for advice

Mitleid pity (*mit* for); **...haben mit** feel sorry for

dankbar grateful (*jm* to sb.; *für* for); *lohnend* rewarding

lustig funny; *fröhlich* cheerful; **es war sehr...** it was great fun; **sich ... machen über** make fun of

---

13 Extra 🔘 👥 Loch Ness and Edinburgh

Partner B: Look at p. 99.

a) *Partner A:*

A student has written this text about Loch Ness. There are five mistakes in it. Read the text through quietly. Then read it out to your partner. He/She will correct the mistakes.

Loch Ness

Loch Ness is one of the most famous places in Wales. It is a lake in Scotland. The word 'loch' means mountain. Loch Ness is 7 kilometres long. It is the longest lake in Britain.

Some people say that there is a big fish in the lake. They have given it a name: Nessie. Every year one or two tourists come to Loch Ness to try and see her.

b) *Read the box below. Then listen to your partner's text about Edinburgh. When you hear a mistake, say **Stop!** Correct the sentence with facts from the box.*

> **Facts about Edinburgh**
>
> 1 Edinburgh is the capital of <u>Scotland</u>.
> 2 More than <u>13</u> million tourists visit Edinburgh every year.
> 3 Visitors come to see famous places like <u>Edinburgh Castle</u>.
> 4 Alexander Graham Bell had the idea for the first <u>telephone</u>.
> 5 J.K. Rowling wrote her first Harry Potter <u>book</u> in a café in Edinburgh.

Orkney Star 🎧

> *Before you read **Orkney Star**, look at the pictures. What do you think the story is about?*

It was Monday morning. Another weekend was over.

'Katrina!' her mum called. Katrina was still upstairs in her room. She took her old teddy and pushed him into her bag. She picked up her fiddle. Then she turned off the light and went downstairs.

'There you are, love. Have some breakfast. Would you like a cup of tea?'

'I'm not hungry, Mum.'

'Och, you must eat something. And the boat will be cold. Have you got your scarf?'

'Oh, Mum.'

They drove to the ferry along the dark roads. It was a horrible morning, rainy and very windy.

'I hate Mondays,' said Katrina.

Her mum smiled. 'It'll be OK. Don't worry. Have a good week. We'll see you on Friday!'

In Assembly that morning the head teacher had some exciting news.

'I have a letter here from Scottish Television. You know that they want to make a documentary at our school. Well, they've chosen a student from S3 to be the star.'

Fiona smiled at Alison. 'I'm sure it will be me!' she whispered.

'And … it's … Katrina McFadden. So, good luck to Katrina.'

At break the 'Beauties' came up to Katrina.

'Amazing, Katrina!' Fiona said. 'What a surprise for you. We can help you if you like.'

'Help me?' Katrina said.

'Yes,' said Linda. 'We can help you to buy some new clothes.

'And a new bag!' added Alison.

'Yes,' said Fiona. 'And the film crew can come with us!'

'But I don't need new clothes, or a new bag,' said Katrina.

'Well, what about your hair? We can help you with that,' said Fiona.

'It's OK, thanks,' said Katrina.

The 'Beauties' walked away.

'Now we won't be able to get into the film!' said Linda crossly.

The day of the filming was cold and windy. Katrina walked across from the hostel in her wellies and anorak. She didn't know if she was more excited or more scared.

'Film people are very trendy,' she thought. 'They'll probably all look like the 'Beauties'.'

'Ah, here she is!'
said the head teacher.
'Katrina, this is the
60 director's assistant,
Miss Burns.'

'Hello there,
Katrina. I'm
Sheena. Nice to
65 meet you.'

Sheena was about
23. She wore jeans, big
green wellies and
a green anorak. Just like
70 Katrina.

Katrina smiled. 'Hello, Sheena,' she said.

*

'This is the crew, Katrina,' said Sheena.
'Hi, Katrina. I'm Bill, the director.'
'Hi!' said Katrina nervously.

75 The electrician smiled at her. 'I'm Fred,' he
said.

'And I'm Emma. I'm the sound assistant.
Can I put this little microphone on your
sweatshirt?'

80 'And I'm Alistair,' said the cameraman. 'If
you're nice to me, you'll look good in the film.
If you aren't nice to me, well ...'

Katrina laughed.

*

'OK Katrina, we're going to start with an
85 interview,' said Bill. 'Ready?'

Katrina didn't feel ready, but Bill smiled at
her and Sheena smiled at her ...

'Katrina, where are you from?'
'I'm from Hoy. It's a small island.'
90 'Tell me more about your home.'

The interview was going well, but suddenly
there was a loud noise. It was the bell for
break.

'Let's stop for a bit,' said Bill. 'We can go out
and film the kids at break.'   95

*

Later they went to film the hostel. They saw
Fiona and her friends. Sheena whispered to
Katrina, 'Who are the girls with the trendy
clothes? Are they your friends?'

'Oh no,' smiled Katrina, 'They're not my   100
friends. They're the 'Beauties'.'

'Beauties? I don't think so!' said Sheena.
'Clones, maybe, but not beauties!'

'They call me Fishface,' said Katrina.

'That's not very nice,' said Sheena. 'They are   105
just jealous.'

'Jealous?' said Katrina. 'Of me?'

'Yes,' said Sheena. 'You're great, you're
a great fiddle player, and you're the star of our
film ... Of course they're jealous!'   110

*

The filming finished on Friday evening at
Katrina's home on Hoy. After dinner Mrs
McFadden said: 'There's a ceilidh this evening.
You must join us!'

'Don't worry,' laughed Katrina. 'It's only   115
a dance!'

So they all went to the community hall. And
they all danced!

Working with the text

1   //○   **What's the story about?**   ▶ *D p. 105*

a) *Here are headings for the different parts of the story. Put them in the right order.*

Page 44	Page 45
Katrina and the 'Beauties'	'Clones, maybe, but not beauties.'
The filming starts	The film crew
Katrina will be a star	On Friday on Hoy
At home on Monday morning	Katrina meets Sheena
The journey to school	

b) ○ *Write one sentence about each part. Match the sentence halves.*

1	Katrina picked up her things and	Katrina felt unhappy.
2	In the car	went downstairs.
3	The head teacher told the school	she said no.
4	The 'Beauties' wanted to help Katrina but	looked like Katrina.
5	Sheena, the director's assistant	the news about Katrina.,

6	The film crew were	questions about her life.
7	Bill asked Katrina	the 'Beauties' were beautiful.
8	Sheena didn't think	went to a ceilidh.
9	On Friday evening the film crew	nice to Katrina.

2   **The interview**   more help   ▶ *D p. 106*

Think of questions for an interview with Katrina. Here are some ideas.

Where are you from?   How do you get to school?

Tell me about your family/...   What is Hoy like?

What instruments do you play?

Do you like the hostel/school/...?

Then write the interview like this:
Director___ Katrina, where are you from?
Katrina___ I'm from ...
Director___ ...

▶ WB 18 (p. 30) · **Checkpoint 2** WB (p. 31) · **Selbsteinschätzung 1–2** WB (pp. 34–35)

How am I doing?   ▶ *SF Multiple choice (p. 133)*

a) Choose the correct answers.

Scotland

1 Hoy and Mainland are two of the Orkney ...
   A islands   B lakes   C hills   D towns
2 The capital of Scotland is ...
   A London   B Kirkwall
   C Edinburgh   D Glasgow
3 What do you do at a ceilidh?
   A dance   B go shopping
   C do sport   D cook
4 The Old Man of Hoy is a huge ...
   A mountain   B tower
   C rock   D river

Words

5 Where won't you find many trees?
   A in a forest   B in a city park
   C in a car park   D in the country
6 Which word doesn't fit?
   A coast   B mountain   C lake   D river
7 It's usually cheaper to send somebody a ... than to make a phone call.
   A logo   B text message
   C download   D chat
8 The film crew had a ... time on Hoy.
   A huge   B big   C large   D great

German–English dictionary

9 Which word won't you find between 'Perücke' and 'Pflaster'?
   A Pflanze   B Pfanne
   C petzen   D Person

10 You want to translate 'geht' in the sentence 'Die Spülmaschine geht nicht.' You look up 'gehen' and find these German meanings. Where will you find the translation – under:
   A laufen?   B funktionieren?
   C dauern?   D handeln?

Grammar

11 If my friend ... me a text, I'll answer it.
   A will send   B send   C sends   D sent
12 If my brother goes to the party, I ... at home.
   A will stay   B stayed
   C would stay   D stays
13 If I ... you, I'd tell my teacher.
   A was   B would be   C am   D are

Everyday English: On the phone

14 This is Emily ...
   A on the phone.   B speaking.
   C speak.   D talking.
15 Can I leave a ...
   A message?   B news?
   C note?   D newspaper?

b) Check your answers on p. 214 and add up your points – one point for each correct answer.

c) If you had 12 or more points, well done! Where did you make mistakes? The chart below will tell you what you can do to improve your English.

No.	Areas	Find out more	Exercises
1–4	Scotland facts	Unit 2 (pp. 30–37)	WB 1, 17 (pp. 20, 29)
5–6	Word field: town and country	Unit 2 (pp. 30–31), P 1 (p. 38)	WB 2 (p. 21)
7–8	Word field: electronic media	Unit 2 (p. 32)	P 2 (p. 38), WB 3, 5 (pp. 21, 23)
9	The German word 'groß'	Vocabulary (p. 156)	—
10–11	German–English dictionary	Unit 2, A 10 (p. 35), SF (p. 131)	P 12 (p. 43), WB 16 (p. 28)
12–13	Conditional sentences (1)	GF 3a (p. 144)	P 9 (p. 42), WB 10 (p. 25)
14	Conditional sentences (2)	GF 3b (p. 144)	P 10–11 (p. 42), WB 12, 14–15 (pp. 26–27)
15–16	Everyday English		P 7–8 (p. 41), WB 5, 9 (pp. 23, 24)

1 WORDS In the country

Words about the country are important in the practice test on pp. 50–51.
a) *Complete the mind map with country words and phrases.*

quiet
what it's like — IN THE COUNTRY — places and things — forest / river
horse
animals — what you can do there — ride a horse / go ...

b) 👥 *Swap with a partner and compare. Can you add anything?*

2 STUDY SKILLS Describing pictures ▶ *SF Describing pictures (p. 132)*

In the test you will have to describe a picture.

Where are these people/things in the picture?

1 farmer   3 birds   5 mountains
2 bike   4 horse   6 boy

at the top • in the middle •
in the background • in the foreground •
on the left • on the right • in front of •
behind the horse • next to • between

1) *farmer – on the left / next to the carrot field*
2) *bike – ...*

3 The birds are flying (Present progressive)

*Um zu sagen, was in einem Bild gerade passiert, benutze das **present progressive**:*

The birds **are flying**.

*Eine Form von **be** + **-ing**-Form des Verbs*

a) *Write the **-ing form** of the verbs in the box. Be careful with the spelling.*

arrive • chat • cycle • eat • fly • give • get •
hide • meet • play • take • win • write

arrive – arriving
chat   –   ...

b) *Complete the sentences. Use the **present progressive**.*
1 I can see some birds. They*'re flying* (fly) in the sky.
2 That must be the farmer next to the wall. He ... (talk) to somebody on his mobile.
3 The dog looks happy. It ... (play) with a ball.
4 The rabbits ... (eat) carrots in the field.
5 I think the girl is the farmer's daughter. She ... (give) the horse an apple.
6 Maybe that's her brother. He ... (hide) behind the horse.

4 Katrina's day (Simple past)

*When you write a short story or report, do this in the **simple past**.*
*Use the **simple past forms** of the verbs in the following sentences.*

1 Yesterday Katrina … (get up) at twenty to six.
   Yesterday Katrina got up at twenty to six.
2 Later she … (have) breakfast.
3 It … (be) windy and rainy when her mum …
   (drive) her to the ferry at Lyness.
4 Two hours later she … (arrive) at school.

5 At Assembly there … (be) announcements.
6 Katrina … (be) very surprised when she …
   (hear) her name.
7 She … (hear) the other announcements.
8 After school she … (call) her parents and …
   (tell) them the news about the TV film.

5 Spelling (Plural of nouns)

Remember that nouns have different plural forms.
Write the plural of the words from the box in
a copy of the chart.

book • bookshelf • box • class • day • family •
film • hobby • man • mouse • party • pen •
sheep • thief • watch • wife • woman

-s	-es	-ies	-ves	irregular
books			bookshelves	

6 STUDY SKILLS Writing (Linking sentences)

Time phrases and linking words can make stories and reports clearer and more interesting.
Read this story. Choose the right word or phrase for each gap.

An appointment in Victoria Road

… (Every day in August/One day in August)
Asif found a note from his brother, Hassan:

> Meet me at 73 Victoria Road
> at 11.45.
> I need your help.
> Hassan

It was 8.55. Asif had enough time to do a few
other things before he left. … (First/Tomorrow)
he checked his e-mails. … (After that/First) he
tidied his room. … (At eleven o'clock/At eight
o'clock) he left the house. It was very hot, …
(because/so) he took a bottle of water.

73 Victoria Road was a pet shop. 'What can
Hassan want here?' Asif wondered. 'And
where is he?' Asif drank some water and

waited, but Hassan didn't come. … (An hour
later/An hour earlier) Asif went home again.
   'Where were you?' Hassan asked when Asif
got home.
   'I waited at that pet shop for hours,' Asif
said.
   'But 73 is a music shop,' Hassan answered.
'I had to get a big new drum for the band. And
… (just/so) I needed help.'

… (Suddenly/Because) Asif had an idea.
'There's more than one Victoria Road in
London, isn't there?' he asked.
   'And you went to the wrong one!' Hassan
said.
   Asif smiled, … (and/but) he didn't really
think that it was very funny.
   'Listen,' he said. '… (If/Then) you want my
help again, give me the correct address.'

▶ WB (pp. 32–33)

1 Reading

Robin Hood and Little John

Everybody knows the story of Robin Hood, the 'thief' who stole from rich people so that he could give the money to poor people. And everybody knows about 'Little' John, the big tall man who was Robin's number 2 man. Do you know how they met?

One day Robin was fed up and bored. So he decided to go out into the woods to look for some fun.

That same day, the shepherd[1] John Little was fed up too. The terrible Sheriff of Nottingham took away all his land, so he had to go to the nearest town to look for work. To get there, he had to go through Sherwood Forest, where there were many thieves and robbers.

And so it happened that John and Robin found themselves in the same place at the same time: on a very narrow[2] bridge over a river. They met in the middle.

Robin spoke first. 'Please go back, sir, so that I can pass. I was on this bridge before you.'

John was sure that that wasn't true, and he didn't want to go back.

'No, sir,' John answered, 'I believe I was here first. You go back.'

Robin said. 'You have a staff[3], I see. If you wait here, I will quickly make a staff. Then we will have a fair fight[4].'

John waited on the bridge while Robin cut a tree and made a staff for himself. Robin went back on the bridge, and the two men fought.

It didn't take long till Robin was in the water. John ran down to pull him out of the river.

'You saved me!' said Robin, surprised. 'You are a good man. What is your name, sir?'

'John Little,' answered the big man.

Robin thought that was a very funny name for such a big man, and he laughed. 'From now on, I will call you Little John. If you like, Little John, you can join me and my men and wear the green clothes of my band of thieves.'

And so it happened that Robin Hood and Little John became best friends and had many adventures as they fought against the Sheriff of Nottingham.

---

[1] shepherd ['ʃepəd] *Schafhirte*   [2] narrow ['nærəu] *schmal*
[3] staff [stɑːf] *Stock*   [4] fight [faɪt] *Kampf*

a) *Choose the right answers:*

1 Robin Hood was …
   A a sheep farmer.
   B a friend of the poor.
   C Little John's number 2 man.

2 Robin met John Little …
   A in a river.
   B on a bridge over a river.
   C under a big tree.

3 When Robin met John, he first wanted to …
   A push him into the water.
   B kill him.
   C cross the bridge and move on.

4 John …
   A gave Robin his staff.
   B killed Robin.
   C pulled Robin out of the water.

b) *Find a correct sentence half for the three sentence parts below:*

1 Robin Hood went out into the woods …
2 Sherwood Forest was a dangereous place …
3 Robin and John became friends …

… because he wanted to find work.
… because there were lots of thieves and robbers.
… because John saved Robin.
… because both of them liked to fight.
… because he wanted to do something exciting.

2 Speaking

Talk about the picture.
– Where are the things/people/animals in the picture?

> the sea • the girls • the woman •
> the farmer • the dog • the children •
> the two men

– What are the people doing?

> It's a picture of the country. In the background you see the sea. In the foreground there's ... On the right ...

> Two girls are cycling. A farmer is standing on the road. ...

3 Writing

Look at the woman and the farmer in the foreground of the picture. Answer the questions about them.

A meeting on a country road
– Who meets on a country road?
– How old is the woman?
– What is she wearing?
– What's her job?
– Why is she looking at her watch?
– What else is she doing?
– Do you think she is happy or angry? Why?
– Write two sentences about the farmer.
– What do you think she said to him?
– What do you think he said to her?

> A meeting on a country road
> One day a young ...
> I think ...
> She's ...
> Maybe she ...
> ...

Remember

Alles, was du aufschreibst, solltest du auf sprachliche Richtigkeit überprüfen:
• *in Bezug auf die Rechtschreibung*
• *in Bezug auf die Grammatik.*

Sport and more

1 A teenager's room

a) 👥 *What can you see in the room?*

- There's a/There are … on the floor/desk/wall.
- In the corner there is …
- On the left/right I can see …
- In the foreground/background …
- I like/don't like the colours/…

b) `Extra` *Describe your room.*

- I've got my own room. / I share a room with …
- My room is big/small/tidy/…
- I've got a … in my room.
- I'd like a TV/a computer/… in my room.

2 A profile

a) *Look at the room. Write a profile for this person.*

Age: 13/14

Sex: female/male

Location: Manchester, UK/Chemnitz, Germany

About me: I love/hate/quite like sport! I play hockey/football/tennis/handball/…

I also like: music/swimming/judo/reading/shopping/animals

My favourite team: Manchester United/Liverpool/Barcelona

My favourite things: my steel drum/my old teddy/ my mobile/my TV/my clothes/my computer

My favourite place: France/the Caribbean/Germany

My favourite colour: black/blue/red/orange/…

b) *Write your own profile. Use the ideas in a). You can put it in your DOSSIER.*

▶ P 1 (p. 60) • WB 1–2 (pp. 36–37)

1   A Friday evening chat with friends

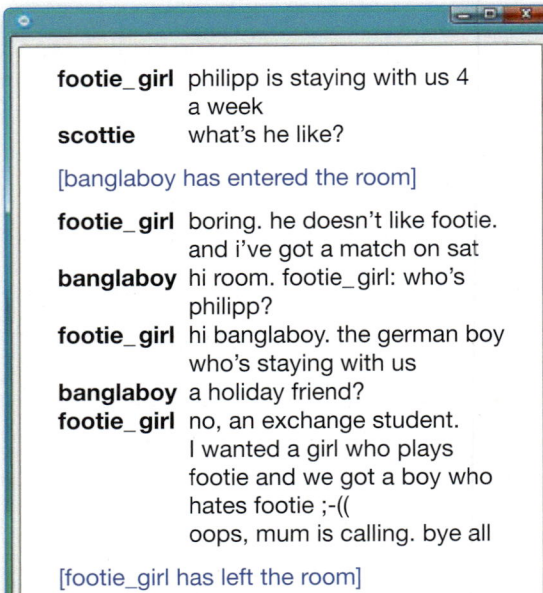

footie_girl   philipp is staying with us 4
            a week
scottie   what's he like?

[banglaboy has entered the room]

footie_girl   boring. he doesn't like footie.
            and i've got a match on sat
banglaboy   hi room. footie_girl: who's
            philipp?
footie_girl   hi banglaboy. the german boy
            who's staying with us
banglaboy   a holiday friend?
footie_girl   no, an exchange student.
            I wanted a girl who plays
            footie and we got a boy who
            hates footie ;-((
            oops, mum is calling. bye all

[footie_girl has left the room]

> *What does it mean?*

1 *4 a week*
Ⓐ for four weeks
Ⓑ for one week

2 *footie*
Ⓐ foot
Ⓑ football

3 *a match on sat*
Ⓐ a match on
  Saturday
Ⓑ a match on
  satellite TV

2   The exchange student 🎧

Mrs Byrd_ I hope you like this, Philipp. It's a
            chicken dish that my grandma
            made. She was from Trinidad.
Philipp___ Er, OK. Thank you. Do you say
            'Good appetite' in English?
Mrs Byrd_ No, we don't. Is that what you say in
            German? Some people say 'Enjoy'.
Latisha___ But usually we just start. Come on!
            I'm hungry.
Philipp___ This is delicious. I like chicken.
Mrs Byrd_ Good. And are there things that you
            don't like?
Philipp___ I eat most things. Well, I don't like
            ... er ... *Nieren*. How do you say that?
Mrs Byrd_ Try and explain.
Philipp___ It's a kind of meat that some people
            don't like. It isn't like steak.
Latisha___ I bet it's liver. I hate liver.

> 1 *Who's footie_girl? Mrs Byrd or Latisha?*
   2 *How do you say 'Guten Appetit' in English?*
   3 *Latisha wasn't right about the English word
      for 'Nieren'. Check in a dictionary.*

▶ *GF 4: Relative clauses (p. 145) • P 2–4 (pp. 60–61) •*
WB 3–5 (pp. 37–38)

Looking at language

*In **1** und **2** beschreiben Latisha und
Mrs Byrd Menschen und Dinge näher.*
***a)** Vervollständige die Sätze aus Text **1**:*
– the German boy who is staying with us

– I wanted a girl ... plays footie.
– We got a boy ... hates footie.

***b)** Vervollständige die Sätze aus Text **2**:*
– It's a chicken dish ... my grandma
  made.
– Are there things ... you don't like?
– It's a kind of meat ... some people
  don't like.

***c)** Wie lautet die Regel?*

*Wenn du über Menschen
redest, benutze ...*   **that** or **who** ?

*Wenn du über Dinge
redest, benutze ...*   **who** or **that** ?

3 Saturday morning in town 🎧

1

2

'Well, here we are,' Latisha said as she and Philipp got off the bus. 'This is the Quays.'

'Keys? Like for the door?' Philipp asked.

Latisha smiled. 'No,' she said, 'a quay is also a place that is next to a river. Ships stop there.'

'Oh, OK. Well, it's nice,' said Philipp.

'Do you want to go to Old Trafford now?' said Latisha. 'It's near here.'

'Old Trafford?'

'It's a stadium. You know, the place where Manchester United play. It's great. You can walk up the tunnel onto the pitch.'

'Oh no,' Philipp said. 'I'm not interested in football! Let's walk around here. It's nice.'

'OK, if we do that, will you come to my football match this afternoon?'

'I think that's fair. OK.'

> ▶ Which picture shows the Quays? Which one shows Old Trafford?

4 Extra 👥👥 GAME What is it?

a) *One person in the group chooses one sentence from the yellow box and reads it out.*

> It's a person who looks after a school.
> It's an animal that likes water.
> It's a thing that you put cornflakes in.
> It's an instrument that makes a lot of noise.
> It's something that you wear when it's cold.
> It's a place where you can watch a film.

The others in the group work alone. They choose an answer from the orange box and write it down. Who is right?

> anorak • bowl • camera • caretaker • cat • cinema • drum • frog • glass • radio • teacher • T-shirt

That's the right answer. One point for you.

That's wrong.

b) *Go on. The next person reads a sentence from the yellow box in a). The others choose an answer.*

STUDY SKILLS | **Paraphrasing**

Wie erklärt Latisha das Wort **quay** *in 3?*

Um ein Wort zu umschreiben, kann man ein allgemeines Wort (z. B. **a person**, **something**) *nehmen, das mit einem durch* **who**, **that** *oder* **where** *eingeleiteten Satz näher erklärt wird, z. B.:*

… **a person who** cooks in a restaurant.

… **an animal that** you can only find in Australia.

… **something that** you put on a letter.

… **a place where** buses stop.

▶ SF Paraphrasing (p. 138) • P 5–6 (p. 62) • WB 6–7 (pp. 38–39)

All about ... activities

5 **Sporty or not?** 🎧

I love sport because I like to be fit. I'm a Manchester United fan and I play for a girls' team, Manchester United U14s. We wear red shirts. We won our last match 2 nil against Stoke. I scored a goal!

We usually train once a week. Our coach shouts a lot, but he's OK.

Latisha is sporty, but I'm not. I like swimming. And I play table tennis and billiards with my friends at the youth club. But I play for fun. I don't like matches and competitions.

I do sport for fun too. I like Boxercise. I do it in the lunch hour at school. It's great when you feel angry!

> *Are you more like Latisha or Philipp? Which of these activities look interesting?*

6 **Now you**

a) *What sports or activities do you do? Choose one. Draw a picture or find a photo of it.*

when?

why I like it

where?

MY ACTIVITY:
...

with who?

what I wear

b) *Make notes about your activity. If you don't know a word, use a German-English dictionary.*

c) Extra 👥 *Talk to a partner. Tell him/her about your activity. Your picture can help to explain new words*

d) *Write a short text that goes with your picture for your DOSSIER.*

I love basketball. I play after school on Thursdays. It's fun to play with my team. The other girls are very nice. We wear ...

I'm not sporty. But I do other activities. I like ...

I like football. I don't play in a team. I play with friends in the local park. I'm also a Werder Bremen fan. I watch ...

e) Extra *Hang up the texts in your classroom. Read them. Can you guess who wrote them?*

▶ P 7–9 (p. 62–63) • WB 8–9 (pp. 39–40) • **Text File 5** (p. 116)

7 Latisha's match

a) *Listen. Did Philipp enjoy Latisha's match?*

b) *Answer the questions below. Listen again if you have to.*
1 What's the name of Latisha's team?
2 What colour is her team wearing?
3 What's the score two minutes before the end of the match?
4 Who scores the final goal for Manchester?
5 Who's shouting at the end?

▶ P 10 (p. 64) • WB 10–11 (pp. 40–41)

8 A match report

Manchester
JUNIOR FOOTBALL NEWS

Manchester United U14s beat Rochdale

Manchester United U14 girls beat Rochdale in a very exciting match in Manchester on Saturday. Both teams played well, but Manchester was the stronger team in the end.

In the 59th minute Manchester's Latisha Byrd scored the final goal of the match. The final score was 3–2. That means that Manchester are now in the cup final. Good luck, girls!

The Rochdale goalkeeper couldn't stop this goal

> *Copy and complete the chart.*
> *Answer the 5 Ws.*

When was the match?	Saturday
Who played?	
Where was the match?	
What was the final score?	
Who scored the last goal?	

9 [Extra] Now you

Think of a good match that you played in, went to or watched on TV. It can be football, handball, volleyball, basketball, …
*Make a chart about the match like the one in **8**.*
Tell a partner about it.

I saw a great match on TV at the weekend …

I went to a great match at my local stadium last summer …

▶ P 11–12 (p. 65) • WB 12–14 (pp. 42–43) • **Text File 6** (p. 117)

Extra   **Background File**   **Greater Manchester Youth Games**

Every year there is a big sports competition for young people from the Manchester area. It's called the Greater Manchester Youth Games. At the games young people do all kinds of sports. The kids aren't brilliant athletes. They just love sport! They all train for months to prepare for the games.

Athletics is for people who love to jump, run and throw.

Some people say that cricket is a very English sport. But it is also popular in Australia, New Zealand, India, Pakistan and the Caribbean.

This is tag rugby. You play with a rugby ball, but it's safer than real rugby.

This is netball. It's a bit like basketball. But it's only for girls and they play outside, not inside.

1   Different kinds of sport

a) *Look at the photos. Name all the sports.*

b) *Choose one of the sports and find out more about it.*
– Where do you do it?
– Which things do you need for this sport?
– How many people are there in a team?
– Can you do it in Germany?

c) *Tell the class about your sport.*   ▶ WB 15 (p. 43)

1 👥 WORDS Rooms

a) *Make one copy of this picture on a big piece of paper for you and your partner.*

b) *Take it in turns to read out the sentences in the blue and green boxes. Draw the things in the right place in your room. Partner A starts.*

Partner A	Partner B
1 The clock is on the wall on the left.	1 The desk is on the left under the clock.
2 The chair is on the left in the foreground.	2 The bed is under the window.
3 The lamp is on the desk.	3 The birdcage is in the middle in the foreground.
4 The guitar is on the floor between the birdcage and the chair.	4 The shelves are next to the window on the right.

c) *Look at p. 99 and check your picture.*

d) **Extra** ⬤ *Make a new copy of the empty room in a). Draw the things below in the room. Then write sentences like the ones in b) about your room.*

Read out your sentences to another pair. They have to draw the things in the right place in the empty room. Check their picture.

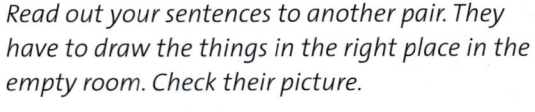
clock · fridge · cupboard · washing machine

table · sink · chair · dog basket

▶ SF Describing pictures (p. 132)

2 PRONUNCIATION (Different stress in English and German words) 🎧

a) *The stress is sometimes different in English and German words. Listen carefully.*
Appet<u>i</u>t · <u>A</u>pril · brill<u>ant</u> · Instrum<u>ent</u>
app<u>e</u>tite · <u>A</u>pril · <u>brill</u>iant · <u>in</u>strument

b) *Listen again and repeat the English words.*

c) *Copy these German and English words into your exercise book. Say the words. Mark the stress.*
Problem · Programm · Pullover · Thermometer
problem · programme · pullover · thermometer

d) *Listen and check. Repeat the English words.*

3   [//○]   What would you like? (Relative clauses)   ▶ D p. 106

a) Write sentences.

I'd like	a teacher a friend an aunt	who	listens to my problems. gives me lots of nice presents. explains things well and is funny.
I'd like	a car a computer a camera	that	takes good pictures. is fun to drive. is really fast and easy to use.

b) **Extra** *What would you like? Make your own sentences*

4   A quiz (Relative clauses)

a) Make questions. Use **who** *for people and* **that** *for things.*

b) 👥 *Then do the quiz with a partner. You can check the answers on p. 101.*

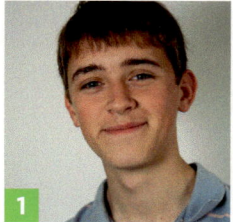

What's the name of the boy ... is visiting Latisha?
What's the name of the boy who ...?
Ⓐ Patrick
Ⓑ Philipp

1

What's the name of the big wheel ... you can see on the River Thames in London?
What's the name of the big wheel that ...?
Ⓐ Big Ben
Ⓑ The London Eye

2

What's the name of the instrument ... Latisha plays?

Ⓐ the steel drum
Ⓑ the fiddle

3

What's the name of the books ... J. K. Rowling wrote?

Ⓐ Famous Five
Ⓑ Harry Potter

4

What's the name of the actor ... you can see in the 'Pirates of the Caribbean'?

Ⓐ Keira Knightley
Ⓑ Beyonce Knowles

5

Who's this England football player ... first played for Manchester United in 2004?

Ⓐ Wayne Rooney
Ⓑ Michael Owen

6

What's the name of the country ... Robbie Williams comes from?

Ⓐ USA
Ⓑ Great Britain

7

What's the name of the writer ... wrote the Sherlock Holmes books?

Ⓐ Sir Arthur Conan Doyle
Ⓑ Sir Paul McCartney

8

5 👥 STUDY SKILLS Paraphrasing

Partner B: Go to p. 101.

a) *Partner A: Explain the words in the green box to your partner. Match the sentence halves.*

1 It's a person who …
2 It's something that you use to …
3 It's an animal that …
4 It's a fruit that …
5 It's a place where …

b) *Listen to your partner and guess his/her words.*

waiter • cooker • lion • cherry • palace •

… cook your food.
… is small and red.
… brings your food in a restaurant.
… kings and queens live.
… lives in Africa and looks like a big cat.

Oh, do you mean a …?

6 REVISION If Latisha … (Conditional sentences)

> **Remember**
>
> *Kein* **will** *im Nebensatz mit* **if**!

a) *Complete these sentences.*

1 If Latisha goes/will go *goes* to the Quays with Philipp, he is/will be *will be* happy.
2 Latisha is/will be sad if Philipp won't go/doesn't go to the football match with her.
3 Latisha doesn't play/won't play well in her match if she goes/will go to bed late.
4 If Latisha's team will win/wins the match, they are/will be in the final.
5 If Latisha's mum cooks/will cook kidneys, Philipp eats/won't eat them!

b) *Complete these sentences about yourself.*

1 If I went to Manchester, I would go/wouldn't go to Old Trafford.
2 If I had a ticket, I would go/wouldn't go to a Manchester United match.

7 Extra LISTENING Keep fit in your English lesson 🎧

a) *Match the instructions and the pictures.*

… and let your arms hang down.

… and stretch your fingers out.

… and turn your head.

… and bring your knees up, keep your back straight!

 **1**

 **2**

 **3**

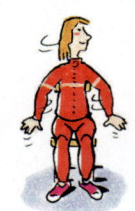 **4**

b) *Listen and do the exercises.*

8 WORDS Sports

a) [O] *Look at the pictures. Name the sports.*

American football · badminton · inline skating ·
riding · running · skiing · swimming · table tennis

b) *Name the missing equipment.*
In picture 1 the … is/are missing.

⁺skis

badminton ⁺racket

skates and ⁺pads

⁺saddle

table tennis ⁺bat

running shoes

helmet   ⁺swimming trunks/⁺swimsuit

c) **Extra** *Where can you do these sports?*
You go skiing on a ski slope.
You play badminton in a …

pool · ⁺riding stable · ⁺running track · ⁺skate park ·
⁺ski slope · ⁺sports hall · stadium

9   [//O] REVISION Hobbies (Word order in subordinate clauses)   ▸ D p. 106

Remember						
	S	V	O	S	V	O
English:	Latisha wears a red shirt when she plays football.					
German:	Latisha trägt ein rotes Hemd, wenn sie Fußball spielt.					
	S	V	O	S	O	V

a) *Complete these sentences.*
1 Latisha likes football because it (an exciting game/is).
2 Latisha is unhappy when her team (a match/loses).
3 Philipp doesn't usually go to football matches because he (football/doesn't like).
4 Philipp had a good time when he (to Latisha's match/went).
5 Latisha was happy because Philipp (to her match/came).
6 Latisha was very happy when she (a goal/scored).

b) *Write two sentences about your hobbies and free time activities.*

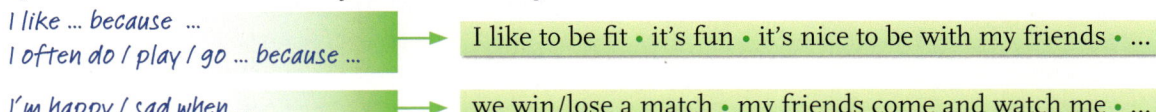

I like … because …
I often do / play / go … because …   ⟶   I like to be fit · it's fun · it's nice to be with my friends · …

I'm happy / sad when …   ⟶   we win/lose a match · my friends come and watch me · …

10 WRITING A report (Collecting and organizing ideas)

a) *In a report on a match or another event,*

you want:	you don't want:
– quick information on what happened – the answers to questions like: **Who? What? Where? When? Why? How?**	– details that are not important – personal thoughts of the writer

Which of these sentences would you not put in a report?

'A great day for football,' I thought. 'Not too warm and not too cold.'

Manchester United U14s beat Rochdale 3–2 in an exciting match in Manchester last Sunday.

Both teams played well. It was 2–2 at half-time.

Last Saturday I went to bed early because I had a match on Sunday.

Our coach was angry because the other team arrived late.

b) *Here are some ideas for a report. Organize the ideas in a chart like this:*

Who?	What?	Where?	When?	How?
	first match of the year			

Bristol South against Redcliffe

the first match of the year

boys' U14 football

half-time 0–0

slow start

final score: Redcliffe 0, South 1

in Redcliffe

last Sunday

second half better

South's Tim Hooley best player

lots of mistakes by Redcliffe

c) *There are 10 mistakes in this report. Use your chart from b) to find the mistakes. Then rewrite the report.*

★ **Bristol South U14 girls' rugby team played against Redcliffe last Saturday in Manchester.**

It was the second match of the year, so both teams made a fast start. At half-time the score was 1–1.

After the break both teams played better. But in the end Redcliffe won because Bristol South made lots of mistakes. The final score was Redcliffe 0 Bristol South 1. The best player on the pitch was South's John Hooley. He scored the only goal of the match.

d) [more help] ▶ D p. 107 *Use the information in this chart to write a similar report.*

Who?	What?	Where?	When?	How?
• Manchester U14s against Stoke U14s • best player: Latisha Byrd	• girls' football • cup final • final score 2–1	• in Manchester	• on Sunday afternoon	• fast start half-time 0–1 for Stoke • Stoke: 1st half – played well • 2nd half – mistakes • after break – Manchester stronger • Byrd scored two goals

11   SPEAKING Talking to people at meals 🎧

a) ⊙ *Philipp is the guest. The Byrds are his host family. Who says these things – the host or the guest? Collect the phrases in a list.*

| The meal was really delicious. |
| I'm really full. |

| Would you like chips or mashed potatoes with your meal? |

| I'd like peas, please. |
| How about a nice cup of tea? |

| Help yourself to some salad. |
| Have some more chips. |

host	guest

b) ⊙ 👥 *Compare your lists. Then listen and check.*

c) 👥👥 *Try these dialogues in groups of three.*

Dialogue 1
A: Frag, ob B Spaghetti oder Kartoffeln möchte.
B: Sag, du möchtest Spaghetti.
C: Fordere B auf sich etwas Salat zu nehmen.
B: Bedanke dich.
A: Biete noch ein bisschen Fleisch an.
B: Bedanke dich, lehne aber höflich ab, weil du satt bist. Dann bedanke dich für das leckere Essen.

⊙ Dialogue 2
A: Schlag vor, ein Glas Milch zu trinken.
B: Sag, du möchtest Tee.
C: Frag, ob B Milch und Zucker möchte.
B: Sag, du magst ganz viel Zucker, aber keine Milch.
A: Fordere B auf, sich etwas Kuchen zu nehmen.
B: Sag, dass du satt bist, aber sag ja.

d) *Check your dialogues with the CD.*

12   MEDIATION Talking about Manchester

SALFORD QUAYS TRAFFORD WHARF OLD TRAFFORD
THE QUAYS
greater manchester's waterfront

What to do at The Quays

Just ten minutes from Manchester city centre

Ordsall Hall Museum
Ordsall Hall is 600 years old. Check out the webcam. If you're lucky, perhaps you'll see the ghost who walks through the Great Hall.

Old Trafford
A must for football fans. Home to Manchester United. Take a tour, walk up the tunnel onto the pitch where Manchester United stars play every week.

Philipp is showing his sister Carolin pictures of Manchester. Complete the dialogue.

Philipp__ Diese Gegend nennt man 'the Quays'. Ich war da mit Latisha.
Carolin__ Ist das im Stadtzentrum?
Philipp__ …
  Wir waren in diesem Museum.
Carolin__ Was ist besonders daran?
Philipp__ …
Carolin__ Old Trafford kenne ich vom Namen her. Was kann man da machen – außer Fußball schauen?
Philipp__ Wir waren nicht drin, aber es steht hier, dass …

▶ *SF Mediation (p. 137)*

Who needs legs? 🎧

Partner B: Go to p. 100.
Partner A: Read this text.

Nathan Stephens was born
in a village in Wales on 11th
April 1988. As a little boy
Nathan loved sport.
5 He started school in 1993.
At school he played football
and in his free time he
learned to ride. He loved
animals. 'When I grow up,' he said, 'I'm going
10 to work with animals.'
   For his ninth birthday Nathan asked his
parents for a pair of riding boots and a new
riding hat.
   He was really excited
15 when he came down to
breakfast on 11th April
1997 and there they were.
   After school that day
some cousins and friends
20 came to tea.

It was a sunny
spring day so after
tea the boys asked if
they could go down
to the old railway   25
line to play. Trains
didn't go there any
more so it was
a favourite place for
kids to play.   30
'Stay away from the new railway line where
the trains are,' called Nathan's mum as they
ran outside.
   Nathan remembers that afternoon. 'Our
parents always said to us: "Don't go near the   35
new railway line." But I saw this slow train
and I tried to jump onto it. I fell ... under the
train. It cut off both my legs.'
   'A doctor and paramedics were already there
when I arrived,' says Nathan's mum. 'All he   40
said to me as they put him in the ambulance
was, "Sorry, Mum".'

Working with the text

1   Who is Nathan Stephens?

a) 🔘 *Complete these notes:*

> Nathan was born in _____ on _____.
> As a little boy he played _____ and he
> learned to _____.
> On his ninth birthday he went to play at
> _____.
> There he tried to _____.
> The train cut off _____.

b) 👥 *Answer your partner's questions about Nathan. Then ask him/her what happened next. Take notes.*
– When did Nathan learn to walk again?
– What sport did he start when he was ten?
– When did he win his first athletics medals?
– What are his hopes?

2   👥 Timeline

a) *Copy and complete this timeline with your partner. Scan both texts again if necessary.*

> Nathan
> born
> ├──┼──┼──┼──┼──┼──┼──→
> 1988 1993 1997 1998 2002 2004 2006 After 2006

b) **Extra** *What did Nathan do after 2006? Find out with the help of the internet.*

> **DOSSIER Timeline for ...**
>
> *Find out about an interesting person (a sports star, a film star, ...). Draw a timeline for him/her.*

▶ *WB 16 (p. 44)* • **Text File 7** *(pp. 118–120)* •
Checkpoint 3 *WB (p. 45)*

How am I doing?

a) *Find or choose the correct answers.*

Scanning – Facts from the unit
If you can't remember the answers, go back into the unit and scan for them.

1 It's the instrument that Latisha plays.
   Ⓐ the steel drum   Ⓑ the guitar
   Ⓒ the fiddle

2 It's the name of the stadium where Manchester United play.
   Ⓐ the Quays   Ⓑ Old Trafford
   Ⓒ Rochdale

3 It's what some English people say when they start to eat.
   Ⓐ Come on, hurry!   Ⓑ Good appetite.
   Ⓒ Enjoy.

4 It's the country that Latisha's grandmother came from.
   Ⓐ Scotland   Ⓑ Trinidad
   Ⓒ New Zealand

Explaining words

5 It's a fruit that is green and sweet. It comes from a country that is near Australia.

 Ⓐ    Ⓑ    Ⓒ

6 Look at the picture:
   Ⓐ It's somebody who plays sport.
   Ⓑ It's somebody who trains a team.
   Ⓒ It's somebody who is a fan.

Words

7 Which word doesn't fit?
   Ⓐ pitch   Ⓑ stadium   Ⓒ hall   Ⓓ bat

8 Which word doesn't fit?
   Ⓐ shelves   Ⓑ bed   Ⓒ desk   Ⓓ pet

9 Which of these things will you probably not find in a teenager's room?
   Ⓐ shelves   Ⓑ fridge   Ⓒ lamp   Ⓓ TV

Writing

10 Which of these sentences is a good way to start a report?
    Ⓐ The match was OK but our team played badly.
    Ⓑ About 100 people were at the stadium in Manchester to watch the U14 girls football final last Saturday.

11 Look at sentence 10B. Which questions does it answer?
    Ⓐ Who?   Ⓑ Where?   Ⓒ When?
    Ⓓ What?

Grammar

12 I've just met a girl … comes from England.
    Ⓐ who   Ⓑ where   Ⓒ which   Ⓓ how

13 Put the following in the right order to finish the sentence: Manchester is a city …
    I / to visit / that / want

Everyday English

14 Which phrase means 'Das war lecker'?
    Ⓐ I'm really full.   Ⓑ That was delicious.
    Ⓒ I'm hungry.

15 Which phrase is different?
    Ⓐ Have some salad.   Ⓑ Help yourself to some salad.   Ⓒ I don't really like salad.

b) *Check your answers on p. 214 and add up your points – one point for each correct answer.*

c) *If you had 12 or more points, well done! Where did you make mistakes? The chart below will tell you where to go for help with your English.*

No.	Areas	Find out more	Exercises
1–4	Unit facts, Scanning	Unit 3 (pp. 52–57, 66) SF (p. 134)	WB 15–16, (pp. 43–44)
5–6	Explaining words	Unit 3 (p. 55), SF (p. 138)	P 5 (p. 62), WB 7 (p. 39)
7–8	Word field: sports	Unit 3 (p. 56)	P 8 (p. 63), WB 8–9, 15 (pp. 39–40, 43)
9–10	Word field: the house	Unit 3 (p. 52)	P 1 (p. 60), WB 1 (p. 36)
11–12	Writing reports		P 10 (p. 64), WB 11 (p. 41)
13–14	Relative clauses	Unit 3 (p. 54), GF 4 (p. 145)	P 3–4 (p. 62), WB 4–5 (p. 38)
15–16	Everyday English		P 11 (p. 65)

Growing up in Canada

A

B

C

D

E

F

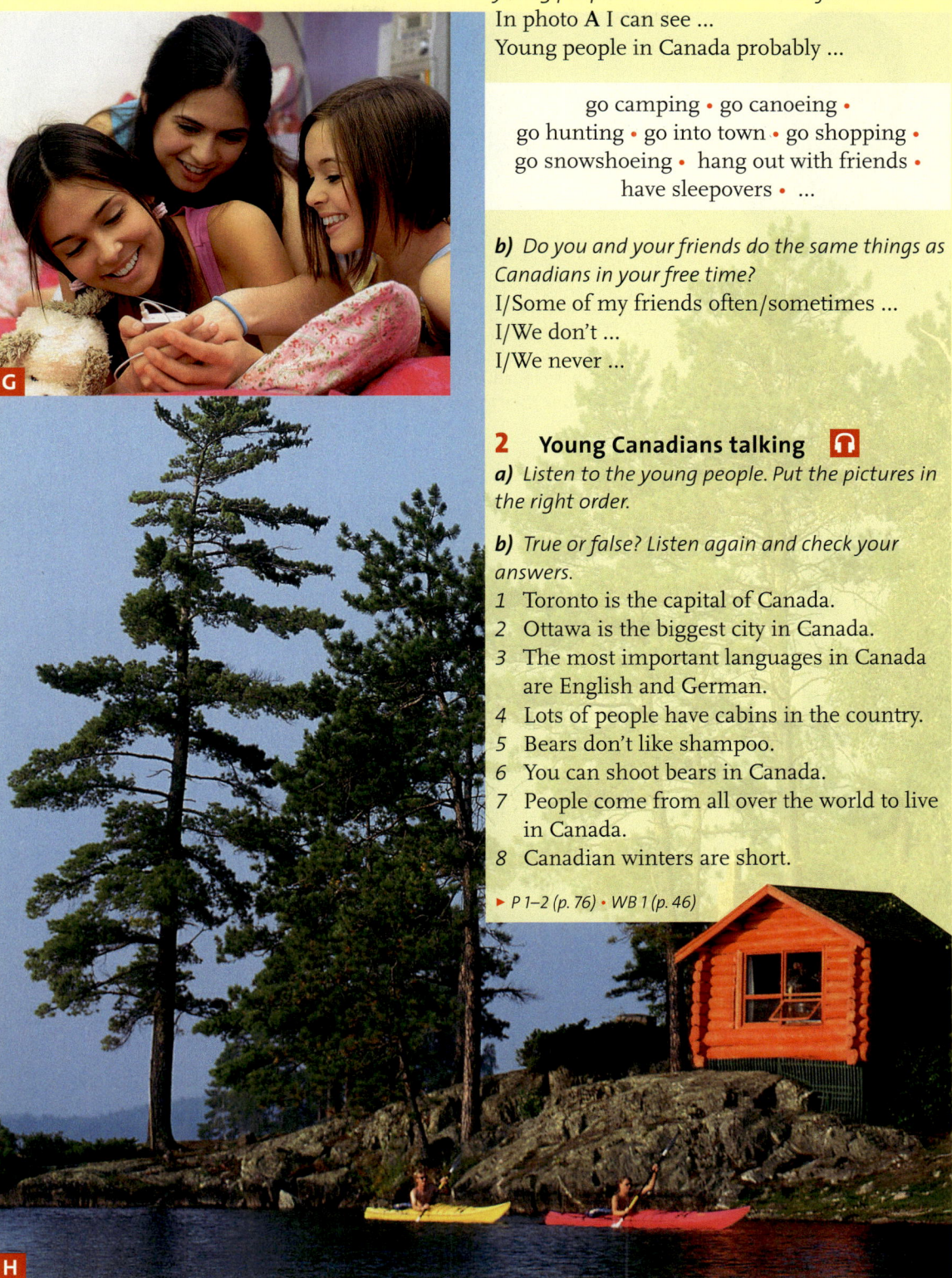

G

H

1 👥 Growing up in Canada

a) What can you see in the photos? What do young people in Canada do in their free time?
In photo **A** I can see …
Young people in Canada probably …

> go camping • go canoeing •
> go hunting • go into town • go shopping •
> go snowshoeing • hang out with friends •
> have sleepovers • …

b) Do you and your friends do the same things as Canadians in your free time?
I/Some of my friends often/sometimes …
I/We don't …
I/We never …

2 Young Canadians talking 🎧

a) Listen to the young people. Put the pictures in the right order.

b) True or false? Listen again and check your answers.
1 Toronto is the capital of Canada.
2 Ottawa is the biggest city in Canada.
3 The most important languages in Canada are English and German.
4 Lots of people have cabins in the country.
5 Bears don't like shampoo.
6 You can shoot bears in Canada.
7 People come from all over the world to live in Canada.
8 Canadian winters are short.

▶ P 1–2 (p. 76) • WB 1 (p. 46)

All about ... adults and teenagers

1   They just don't understand 🎧

> My mom doesn't like my music. She says it's too loud. And she hates rap music.

Robert

> I have to go to bed very early on school nights. My friends are allowed to watch TV till 12 o'clock. It's not fair.

Emily

> I'm not allowed to use the house phone. The last phone bill was very big. My parents say it's my fault. But I have to talk to my friends. I think they're too strict.

Ashley

> I'm not allowed to colour my hair. And I can't get a piercing. It's not fair. My parents are so old-fashioned.

Sam

> I'm grounded. I'm not allowed to go out for a week. I did badly in a test but it's not my fault. Everybody did badly.

Jordan

> My dad says I spend too much money on clothes. It's not true. I haven't got anything to wear.

Jessica

▷ *1 What things do these kids argue about with their parents?*

2 Do you think their parents are ...
Ⓐ *too strict?*   Ⓑ *quite strict?*   Ⓒ *OK?*

2   Now you: I'm allowed to ...
a) 👥 *Make two lists. Collect as many ideas as you can.*

> Teenagers often are not allowed to play loud music, ...
>
> Teenagers are usually allowed to go to youth clubs, ...

b) Write down one thing that you're not allowed to do and one thing you are allowed to do.

c) 👥 *Talk to a partner. Are your parents strict about the same things?*
A: I'm allowed to watch TV till 12 o'clock. What about you?
B: I'm not allowed to do that. I'm allowed to ...

▶ *GF 5: Modals and their substitutes (p. 146)* •
P 3–4 (pp. 76–77) • *WB 2–3 (pp. 47–48)*

3   A school discussion – Part 1 🎧

Students at Robert's school don't have to wear a uniform, but there is a dress code. This means there are rules about clothes, hair and jewellery.

> 1 Who's for the school dress code?
> 2 Who's against it?

Sam ___ I think the school dress code is too strict.

Ashley ___ I agree. My brother bought himself some new jeans. But he isn't allowed to wear them because they're too baggy.

Jessica ___ I think the teachers are too strict about piercings too. Why do we need a dress code?

Robert ___ You're right. I often ask myself the same question.

Emily ___ I don't agree. I think some people wear very stupid things. They can only blame themselves if teachers are strict. I sometimes think a uniform is a good idea. It would be easier.

Jordan ___ That's a good point. I don't have time to worry about my clothes in the morning. Lots of people are like me. We don't have time to look at ourselves in the mirror. A uniform is a good idea.

Sam ___ You must be mad! I don't want to wear a boring uniform.

4   The discussion – Part 2

a) Copy the chart below. Write down the phrases that the students use to agree and to disagree.

agree	disagree
I agree You're …	…

b) What about your school? Write four sentences.

I think / I don't think …
… our teachers are too strict.
… a school dress code is a good idea.

I think it's OK / I don't think it's OK …
… to wear lots of jewellery.
… to wear baggy/short/tight/… clothes.
… to have lots of piercings.
… to show your underwear/stomach.
… to have long/short/coloured/… hair.

▶ GF 6: Reflexive pronouns (p. 147) • P 5–6 (p. 77) • WB 4–6 (pp. 48–49)

c) 👥 Tell a partner what you think.

I don't think …

I think …

You're right. That's a good point.

I don't agree. You must be mad!

Looking at language

Schreib die Tabelle ab. Ergänze die fehlenden Pronomen mit **-self/-selves** aus Text **3**.

	-self		-selves
I	myself	we	…
you	yourself	you	yourselves
he she it	… herself itself	they	…

5 Plans for the weekend 🎧

*Ashley*__ Hey guys! You know I'm having a party on Saturday. Are you coming?

*Emily*__ I'm coming. But I have to be home by ten o'clock.

*Ashley*__ And you, Jordan? Are you coming?

*Jordan*__ I'm not allowed to go.

*Robert*__ Why not?

*Jordan*__ I'm grounded, remember!

*Robert*__ Oh yeah, I forgot. We're driving out to our cabin for the weekend.

*Jessica*__ When are you leaving?

*Robert*__ Saturday morning. I'm doing a gig at the youth centre on Friday.

*Jordan*__ Cool.

*Jessica*__ What are you doing on Sunday, Em?

*Emily*__ I'm not doing anything.

*Jessica*__ Do you want to come with me and my sisters to Wonderland on Sunday?

*Emily*__ Great! – Oh look, here comes Sam.

*Sam*__ Hi, guys. Robert, I have to talk to you.

▷ *Who's going to the party? Who isn't going? Why not? Which is Robert's diary?*

		A
Fri	buy present for Ashley after school	
Sat	go to party	

		B
Fri	do gig at youth centre	
Sat	drive to cabin	

6 Plans for Saturday

a) *Make a list of things that you often do on Saturdays. Brainstorm.*

> go to the cinema, stay in bed late, watch TV, buy a new CD, read a book, meet friends, look after my sister, visit Jenny / …, tidy room, clean …, …

b) *Plan your dream Saturday.*

	Saturday
morning	get up late, meet friends in park
afternoon	go shopping with Mum
evening	watch DVD with Jo

c) 👥 *Compare your plans.*

A: What are you doing in the morning/afternoon/…?

B: I'm getting up late, then I'm … What about you?

STUDY SKILLS **Brainstorming**

Brainstorming erfolgt in zwei Schritten:
1 Schreib alle Ideen auf. Es ist zunächst völlig egal, ob sie gut sind oder nicht. Es muss nur schnell gehen!
2 Wenn du fertig bist, wähle die besten Ideen aus und sortiere sie.

▶ SF Brainstorming (p. 139)

d) **Extra** *Write about your plans for your DOSSIER.*

> My plans for a dream Saturday
>
> On Saturday morning I'm getting up really late. Then …

▶ GF 7: Present progressive with future meaning (p. 148) • P 7–8 (pp. 78–79) • WB 7–8 (pp. 50–51)

7 Extra Dragon boats

a) *Listen. What does Sam want from Robert?*

b) *Read the questions below. Then listen again and answer them.*

1 How many people are there in a dragon boat crew?
2 How many dragon boaters are there in Toronto?
3 What does Robert's mum say about Robert?
4 What does Robert want to do in the end?

► *SF Listening (p. 133)*

8 Friday evening: Robert's gig at the youth centre 🎧

The youth leader went to the microphone.
  'Welcome to our holiday weekend disco. We've got three DJs tonight. They've all taught themselves to DJ. And they're all very different. Maybe they'll learn something from each other tonight. – Our first DJ is Robert 'DJ Bobby' Smith.'
  Robert jumped onto the little stage.
  'Hi, everybody. I'd like to start with a mix of all your favourite Canadian pop stars. First, Avril Lavigne with one of her first big hits, ...'

► *P 9 (p. 79)* • *WB 9 (p. 51)*

9 SONG Sk8er boi by Avril Lavigne 🎧

> # Sk8er boi *by Avril Lavigne*
>
> *(Chorus)*
> *He was a sk8er boi, she said see ya later boy*
> *he wasn't good enough for her,*
> *she had a pretty face but her head was up in space,*
> *she needed to come back down to earth.*

▷ *Who's the song about? Do you think it's a happy or a sad song? Do you like this kind of music?*

► *P 11–12 (p. 80)* • *WB 10–11 (p. 52)*

Extra   **Background File**   **CANADA** 🎧

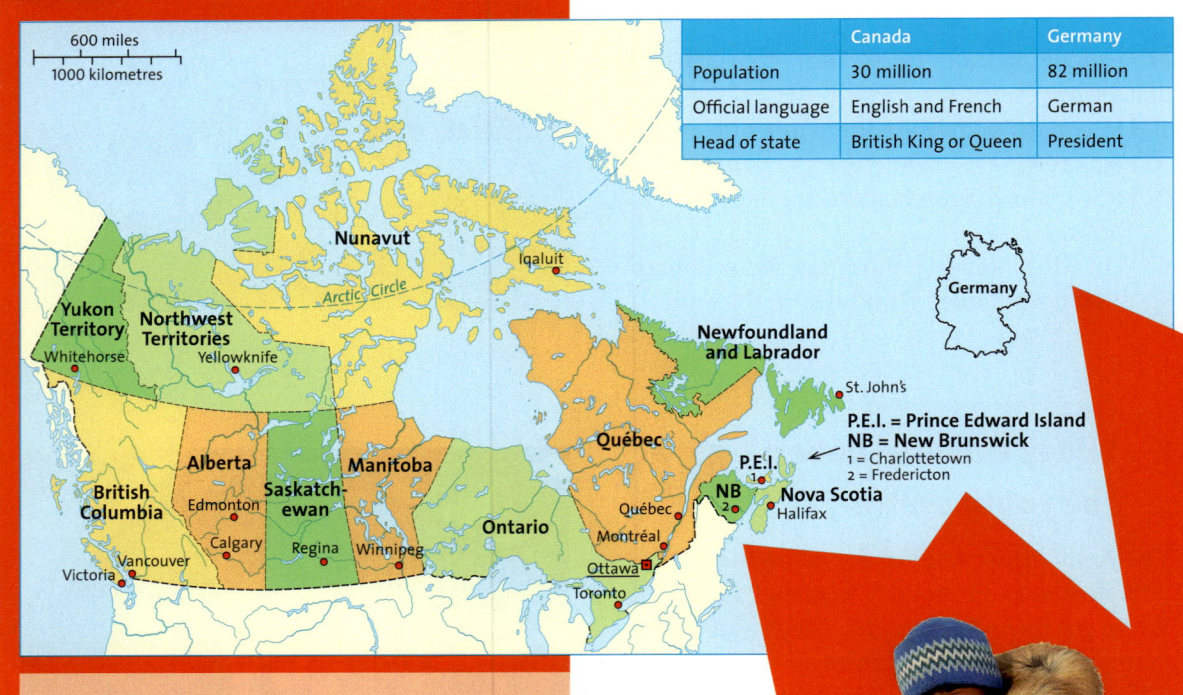

	Canada	Germany
Population	30 million	82 million
Official language	English and French	German
Head of state	British King or Queen	President

600 miles
1000 kilometres

Nunavut
Iqaluit
Arctic Circle

Yukon Territory
Whitehorse

Northwest Territories
Yellowknife

Newfoundland and Labrador
St. John's

Germany

British Columbia
Victoria
Vancouver

Alberta
Edmonton
Calgary

Saskatchewan
Regina

Manitoba
Winnipeg

Ontario

Québec
Québec
Montréal
Ottawa
Toronto

P.E.I.
NB
Nova Scotia
Halifax

P.E.I. = Prince Edward Island
NB = New Brunswick
1 = Charlottetown
2 = Fredericton

First Canadians

Aboriginals like the Inuit and the First Nations (Indians) have lived in Canada for thousands of years. But today only about 4.4% of the Canadian population is Aboriginal.

In 1999 the Inuit were allowed to found the territory of Nunavut – 'Our land' in their language. Many other Aboriginal people live on reserves all across Canada.

You can listen to an Inuit legend. Look at p. 79.

Canadian settlers

The Vikings were the first Europeans in Canada.

In the 16th century the first French people settled in Canada and Canada became New France.

In 1763 France lost Canada to the British. But today people in the province of Quebec still speak French.

People still want to go and live in Canada. Today it is a very multicultural place.

Canadian sports

Canadian Aboriginals played the game of **lacrosse** first. Today it's Canada's national summer sport. It is a very fast team sport.

Ice hockey is Canada's national winter sport – the Canadians just call it 'hockey'. Toronto's team – the Maple Leafs – is one of the best teams in the country.

1 Facts about Canada

Find the answers to these questions on pp. 74–75.

1 What is Canada's national winter sport?
2 Is Canada bigger or smaller than Germany?
3 Where do more people live – in Germany or in Canada?
4 It's on the Canadian flag and the name of a famous hockey team. What is it?
5 Which people lived in Canada first?

2 Now you

a) Look again at pp. 74–75. What did you already know about Canada? What didn't you know?
I knew that …
I didn't know that …

b) ◉ *What interesting facts could you tell a visitor about Germany? Write a short text. Add pictures. You can put it in your DOSSIER.*

▶ *WB 12 (p. 53)*

1 👥 WORDS Numbers

Fill in the gaps with words and phrases from the box.

> ten-kilometre walk • ⁺per cent (%) •
> ⁺150-kilogram bear • ⁺six point seven (6.7) •
> ⁺sixteen-year-olds •
> ⁺80 km per hour (kph) • ⁺million

1 About 30 … people live in Canada.
2 You can't go more than … on most Canadian roads.
3 … can drive in some places in Canada.
4 He was tired when he got home from his …
5 I hope I don't meet a … in the forest!
6 French is the first language for … million Canadians.
7 That's about twenty … of all Canadians.

2 🔘 REVISION About Canada (Relative clauses)

*Make sentences with **who** or **that** about Canada.*

> **Tipp**
>
> **who** für Menschen und **that** für Dinge

	who that	
1 Canada is a country		is near the USA.
2 Snowshoeing is something		lots of Canadians do in winter.
3 Avril Lavigne is a singer		was born in Canada.
4 French is the language		about seven million Canadians speak.
5 French-Canadians are people		live in Canada and speak French.
6 The black bear is one of the animals		you can find in the Canadian forests.
7 A snowmobile is something		lots of Canadians drive in winter.

snowmobile

Avril Lavigne

3 WORDS Adults and teenagers

a) 🔘 *What do adults say? What do teenagers say? Make two lists.*

> It's not fair. • It's too loud. •
> You're grounded. • They don't understand. •
> They're too strict. • It's not my fault. •
> My parents are old-fashioned. •
> You're not allowed to have a sleepover. •
> I'm not allowed to get a piercing. •
> You have to do more homework.

b) **Extra** *Write about your family.*

> • I often / never fight with my mum / dad / …
> • He / She always says …
> • I have to …
> • I'm (not) allowed to …
> • I think my parents are strict / OK / cool / …

4 //○ **School rules** *(have to and be allowed to)* ▶ D p. 107

a) *Write the rules of Robert's school.*

> – arrive on time for school
> – turn off phones in the classroom
> – clean the tables after lunch
> – be friendly to other students

> – wear caps and jackets in class
> – eat in the classroom
> – cycle or skate in the school building
> – smoke in the school yard or building

Students have to arrive in time for lessons.   *They aren't allowed to …*

b) **Extra** 👥 *What do you have to do at your school ? What aren't you allowed to do?*

5 //○ **What are they saying?** (Reflexive pronouns) ▶ D p. 108

Match the speech bubbles and the pictures.
The girl/boy in picture 1/2/… is saying '…'

> She taught herself to paint.

> Did you hurt yourself?

> We really enjoyed ourselves.

> Look at the cat. It's cleaning itself.

> I'm going to buy myself something nice.

> Please, help yourselves.

> Don't cut yourself!

> Look. He's looking at himself in the mirror.

6 //○ **Mum and Dad are on strike** (Reflexive pronouns) ▶ D p. 108

Complete the sentences with the correct reflexive pronoun.

1 Mr and Mrs Jones are on strike. They want to enjoy himself/themselves.
2 Mrs Jones usually makes Jack's lunch, but today he has to cook for herself/himself.
3 Mr Jones usually looks after Jill in the afternoon, but today she has to look after herself/himself.
4 Jill doesn't understand. 'Why do I have to look after herself/myself today?'
5 Mrs Jones usually teaches Jack the guitar in the evening, but today she says, 'Sorry, Jack, but you'll have to teach yourself/himself.
6 Jack says to Jill, 'Mum and Dad don't want to cook. We have to cook for ourselves/yourselves.'
7 'Don't blame us,' their parents say. 'You two were terrible yesterday. You two can only blame themselves/yourselves!'

7 WRITING Telling a story (The steps of writing)

| Step 1 | Before you write |

What happened when Jessica and Emily were at the fun park? Brainstorm your ideas.

1 **Wonderland** – the biggest fun park in Canada

2 Go-karts are great fun!

3 **Splash Works** –don't be afraid to get wet!

4 A ride in every weather?

| Step 2 | Writing |

a) *Now write the story. For your first paragraph you can use the following ideas:*

> So they went to Wonderland.

> It's the biggest fun park in Canada.

> Jessica and Emily wanted to do something special.

> It was Sunday.

b) *How can the story go on? Add the words in brackets to these sentences.*

> They tried the go-karts. (First)
> They were exciting. (really)
> They went on rides. (after that, lots of, other)

c) *Join these sentences with the linking words.*

> Emily wanted to go to 'Splash Works'. It looked exciting. (because)
> It was great fun. They got very wet. (but)

d) *Try and write a good end for the story. You can use the ideas in the box on the right.*

e) *Don't forget a title for the story.*

> A great day   A day at Wonderland

> On Sunday afternoon

Tipp

Deine Geschichte sollte bestehen aus: Einleitung (beginning), Mittelteil (middle) und Schluss (end).

▸ *Writing course: Using paragraphs (p. 39)*

Tipp

*Gestalte deinen Text interessanter! Verwende **Adjektive** (great, hungry) und **Zeitangaben** (**time phrases:** after that, before lunch).*

Tipp

*Versuche, die Sätze miteinander zu verbinden (**linking words:** and, because, but, so).*

> after that • start to rain • everybody •
> leave • but • the girls • stay •
> have a great time • park • empty

| Step 3 | Revising | more help | ▸ D p. 109

Check your story for mistakes. Check the spelling. Did you write in the simple past? Is the story clear?

Tipp

Bitte einen Partner/eine Partnerin deine Geschichte zu lesen.

8 👥 **Plans for the week** (Present progressive with future meaning)

Partner B: Go to p. 101.

a) *Partner A: Ask your partner about his/her plans for the week.*

A: On Monday evening I'm visiting Grandad. What about you?

B: I'm going ... On Tuesday evening I'm ... What about you?

A: ...

b) *When are you doing the same things?*
We're doing the same thing on ... and ...

	afternoon ☀	evening ○
MON		visiting Grandad
TUE		going to basketball training
WED	playing in a basketball match	
THU		watching a DVD at my friend's house
FRI		having a sleepover
SAT	taking my brother to park, going shopping in the afternoon	

9 Extra **Are they looking at themselves or each other?** (each other/ themselves)

Look at the pictures. What are they doing? Use themselves or each other.

1 They're looking at ...

2 They're looking at ...

3 They're thinking of ...

4 They're thinking of ...

5 They're taking photos of ...

6 They're taking photos of ...

7 They're teaching ...

8 They're teaching ...

10 Extra **LISTENING Kahasi and the loon – an Inuit legend** 🎧

a) *Listen to the story. Which picture shows ...*
① a leaf? ② a loon? ③ a blanket? ④ a walrus?

A B C D

b) *Choose the correct answers. Listen and check.*

1 Kahasi lived in Canada/France.
2 He slept/went hunting every day.
3 A bird told Kahasi to go running/swimming every morning.
4 Kahasi helped the people because they were lazy/hungry.
5 The people threw Kahasi up in a blanket/basket.
6 Kahasi saw bears/walruses on the ice.
7 The hunters/Kahasi killed the animals.

EVERYDAY ENGLISH

11 SPEAKING A classroom discussion

*a) Listen to these three songs by Canadian musicians.
What do you think of each one? Who would like it?
Write two sentences about each song.*

I think	the first song the second song the third song	was

brilliant :-))
nice :-)
easy to listen to :-)

boring :-((
old-fashioned :-((
nothing special :-(

People in our class My parents Young kids	like don't like	that kind of music.

*b) Complete the dialogue. Use the phrases on the right.
Then listen and check.*

A: _____ the first song was boring. What do you think?
B: You're right. My parents like that kind of music.
C: _____ I think it was old-fashioned.

B: What about the second song? I think it was nice.
C: _____ It was nothing special.
A: _____ I think it was boring.

C: What about the third song? I think that was brilliant.
A: _____ People in our class like that kind of music.
B: _____ It was really boring.

I think

You're right.

I don't agree.

You must be mad.

I agree.

That's a good point.

c) 👥 *Talk about the songs with your partner.*

12 MEDIATION Canadian neighbours

a) ⊙ *Lena and her younger brother Jannis are
staying at a holiday park. There's a Canadian
family next door.
Look at the pictures. Listen to two dialogues.
Match a picture to each dialogue.
Dialogue 1 goes with picture …*

b) Listen again. What can Lena tell Jannis?

Tipp

*Keine Panik, du musst nicht alles verstehen.
Und übersetze nicht alles wörtlich, gib nur das
Wesentliche weiter.*

▶ *SF: Mediation (p. 137)*

A

B

C

Two newspaper articles

> *Read the articles. You don't have to understand every word.*

1
Dog helps to kill bear

JULY 22, 2006

A man killed a black bear with a 15-cm hunting knife yesterday. The man says the bear attacked him and his dog while he was canoeing in northern Ontario. He thinks the bear saw him as "lunch".
Tom Tilley, a 55-year-old from Waterloo, Ontario, was in the forest north of Wawa. He says his dog Sam made lots of noise when he saw the bear. So Tilley had time to find his knife. Then the bear attacked Sam. As Sam fought the 90-kg bear, Tilley jumped on it and killed it with his knife. Doctors say Tilley and his dog will be fine.

2
Woman is victim of latest bear attack

SEPTEMBER 8, 2005

A bear killed an Ontario woman and hurt her husband badly at Missinaibi Lake on Saturday. The attack happened late on Saturday afternoon. The victims were camping at the lake, about 80 km north of Chapleau, Ontario.
Police gave their names as Sarah Bennett, 31, and Marc Bennett, 30. Mrs Bennett was a doctor.
"The man attacked the bear with a knife, but he couldn't save his wife," policewoman Karen Farand said. "The bear escaped into the forest."

Working with the text

1 ◎ **In the article or not?**

*Are these things in article **1** or in article **2**?*

1 The attack happened in Ontario.
2 A man was canoeing.
3 A man and a woman were camping.
4 The dog fought with the bear.
5 The man had a knife.
6 The man killed the bear.
7 A person died.
8 The bear escaped.

	Article 1	Article 2
1	Yes	...
2	...	...
3		
4		
5		
6		
7		
8		

2   **The 5 Ws**

*Make a chart with the 5 Ws (**who**, **where**, **when**, **what**, **why**) for each of the articles.*
Do they answer all the questions?

	Who?	Where?	When?	What?	Why?
Article 1	Tom		yesterday	a bear attacked	
Article 2				a bear attacked doctor	

▶ WB 13 (p. 54) • **Checkpoint 4** WB (p. 55) • **Text File 8** (p. 121) • **Selbsteinschätzung 3–4** WB (pp. 58–59) • **Text File 9** (pp. 122–123)

Extra **A fishing trip** 🎧

> *Look at the pictures. Who are the people?*
Try and guess the right order of the pictures. Then listen and check.

A

B

C

D

E

F

Working with the text

1 Tell the story

Match the sentence halves and tell the story.

1 Robert and his father went on …	trouble.
2 The trip started well when Robert caught …	a big fish.
3 Then Mr Smith saw …	a plan.
4 When Mr Smith lost his canoe, they were in …	a fishing trip.
5 Robert had …	escaped.
6 Mr Smith threw Robert's fish to the bear and then he and Robert …	followed them.
7 They thought they were OK, but the bear …	a bear.
8 Luckily the bear ran away when Mrs Smith arrived in …	the car.

How am I doing?

a) *Find or choose the correct answers.*

Canada

1 The capital of Canada is ...
   A Ottawa.   B Toronto.   C Montreal.
2 The biggest city in Canada is ...
   A Ottawa.   B Toronto.   C Montreal.
3 Canada is ... than Germany.
   A bigger   B smaller
4 The number of people who live in Canada is ... than the number in Germany.
   A bigger   B smaller
5 The two most important languages in Canada are English and ...
   A Spanish.   B Italian.   C French.

Words

6 You don't need snow or ice for it:
   A ice hockey   B snow shoeing
   C football   D ice fishing
7 Which of these do you do or have in a house or flat?
   A hunting   B a sleepover
   C camping   D fishing
8 What do parents say to kids?
   A It's not my fault.   B It's not fair.
   C You're grounded.   D You're too strict.
9 What do kids say to parents?
   A You're so old-fashioned.
   B You always argue with your brother.
   C You never help around the house.
   D You're grounded.

Discussions

10 Which phrase is different?
   A You're right.   B I agree.
   C That's a good point.   D You're mad.

Writing

11 Every story needs three parts, put them in the correct order:
   ..., ... and ...
   A an end   B a middle   C a beginning
12 It was really cold ... we stayed inside.
   A so   B because   C then
13 I worked harder ... I did badly in the test.
   A while   B after   C then

Grammar

14 I ... go to the disco because my parents think I'm too young.
   A have to   B don't have to
   C am allowed to   D am not allowed to
15 If you want more pocket money, you'll ... do more jobs at home.
   A must   B have to   C had to   D can
16 Robert enjoyed ... at the disco.
   A herself   B itself   C himself
17 What are you ... at the weekend?
   A do   B will do   C doing

b) *Check your answers on p. 214 and add up your points – one point for each correct answer.*

c) *If you had 14 or more points, well done! Where did you make mistakes? The chart below will tell you what you can do to improve your English.*

No.	Areas	Find out more	Exercises
1– 5	Canada facts	Unit 4 (pp. 68–75)	P 2 (p. 76), WB 1, 10, 12 (pp. 46, 52, 53)
5– 9	Words	Vocabulary Unit 4 (pp. 161–163)	WB 1b, 2a, 11 (pp. 46, 47, 52)
10	Discussion	Unit 4 (p. 72)	P 11 (p. 80)
11–13	Writing	Unit 4, P 7 (p. 78)	WB 7 (p. 50)
14–15	Modal substitutes	GF 5 (p. 146)	P 4 (p. 77), WB 3 (p. 48)
16	Reflexive pronouns	GF 6 (p. 147)	P 5–6 (p. 77), WB 4–5 (pp. 48–49)
17	Present progressive with future meaning	GF 7 (p. 148)	P 8 (p. 79), WB 8 (p. 51)

1 👥 STUDY SKILLS Understanding new words ▶ *SF Understanding new words (p. 128)*

▶ *SF Understanding new words (p. 128)*

> **Tipp**
>
> *In einem Test liest oder hörst du manchmal ein unbekanntes Wort, aber oft kannst du die Bedeutung erraten.*

Guess what the green words mean in German.

1 North Rhine-Westphalia and Saxony are two of Germany's 16 states.
2 Beer is a traditional German product. Every part of Germany produces beer.
3 It's important to pack glasses and other breakable goods carefully.
4 Greenpeace is an organization that tries to save whales and other animals.
5 Recycling is easy: just take your old glass to the bottle bank.
6 It was a terrible storm. Almost everybody on the ship was seasick.
7 In this factory robots do all the work.

2 SPELLING Same sound, different words

> **Tipp**
>
> *Manche Wörter werden gleich ausgesprochen, aber anders geschrieben. Vorsicht beim Schreiben!*

Find the missing words.

1 **hour, our** ['aʊə]
The train was late. I waited for over an ...
Is that ... train over there?
2 **son, sun** [sʌn]
The Browns have a ... and a daughter.
They both wear hats when the ... shines.
3 **their, there** [ðeə]
Who's ... ? – Oh, it's Malte and Hauke.
They've got ... new bikes with them.
4 **know, no** [nəʊ]
Do you ... our new teacher, Mrs Sprengel?
... , I haven't met her yet.
5 **hear, here** [hɪə]
There are lots of birds ... in the forest.
Can you ... the woodpecker?
6 **sea, see** [siː]
We stayed in a caravan near the ...
You can ... the beach from there.
7 **wear, where** [weə]
... is my new dress?
I'd like to ... it to Matt's party.
8 **weak, week** [wiːk]
Last ... the doctor told my grandma she had a ... heart.

3 WRITING The 5 Ws and how ▶ *Writing course 3: A report (p. 64)*

▶ *Writing course 3: A report (p. 64)*

> **Tipp**
>
> *In einem Test musst du manchmal einen Bericht schreiben.*
> *Denk daran, folgende Fragen zu beantworten: **who**, **what**, **when**, **where**, **why** und **how**.*

Write the text. Put the phrases from the chart into the text.

who	what	when	where	why	how
the whole family	our visit to the zoo	on Sunday	50 miles away	it was my little sister's birthday	we went by bus

A great day in the school holidays
The best thing about my school holidays was ... (1). We don't often go there, because it's so expensive. But we went last weekend because ... (2). Mum and Dad said that ... (3) could go.

Mum had to work on Saturday so we went ... (4). The zoo isn't near here. It's ... (5). Mum and Dad didn't want to drive, so ... (6).

It was great to see all the animals. We stayed all day and we enjoyed every minute.

4 Ashley's visit to Niagara Falls (Word order)

> **Tipp**
>
> *Denk daran, dass die Wortstellung im Englischen und im Deutschen oft unterschiedlich ist!*

> **Denk daran**
>
> *ORT vor ZEIT!*
> *In Satz 1 ist Niagara Falls der ORT, also steht er vor last June. Die Regel gilt auch für Satz 2 und andere Sätze. Für welche?*

> *S-V-O lautet die Regel im Englischen.*
> *Satz 3:   S = Ashley   V = forgot*
> *Satz 4:   S = they   V = arrived*
> *Und in Satz 7?*

Choose the right place in the sentences for the words in brackets.

1 Ashley and her dad went ? to Niagara Falls ? . (last June)
   Ashley and her dad went to Niagara Falls last June.
2 Their bus left ? at six am ? . (Toronto)
3 They almost didn't get the bus because Ashley ? her rucksack ? . (forgot)
4 At one minute to six ? they ? at the bus stop. (arrived)
5 When they ? to Niagara ? , they saw the amazing waterfalls. (got)
6 They went ? after lunch ? . (to Victoria Park)
7 Everything was so interesting that Ashley ? to stay another day ? . (wanted)

5 We went on a great trip (Prepositions)

Complete the sentences with the correct prepositions.

1 We went ... a great trip. (in/on)
2 We listened to the weather report ... the radio. (in/on)
3 We left early ... the morning and arrived late ... night. (in/on, at/in)
4 There wasn't a cloud ... the sky. (in/on)
5 I was really interested ... the railway museum. (in/on)
6 All the information was ... English. (in/of)
7 I had to translate it ... German. (in/into)
8 There were lots of cars ... the city centre. (in/on)
9 It was quicker to walk than to go ... car or bus. (by/with)
10 I was tired, so I slept ... the train. (at/on)

6 If we go to Toronto ... (Conditional sentences type 1)

You're on holiday in Canada. You're planning a day trip to Toronto with a friend.
Match the sentence halves.

1 If we go to Toronto, ...	if it rains.
2 If we leave early, ...	we can go on a walking tour.
3 If we take sandwiches with us, ...	we'll have more time in Toronto.
4 If we check on the internet, ...	we'll have a great time.
5 If you like walking, ...	we can eat them in a park.
6 We'll see more of the city ...	we'll know when the museums open.
7 We'll have to do something inside ...	if we don't have a good map.
8 We won't be able to find places ...	if we go on a bike tour.

▶ WB (pp. 56–57)

1 Listening 🎧

Part 1 On the way to Green Gables

Listen to the Brown familiy. Choose the correct answer for each question.

1 Who left a voicemail for the kids?
  A their mother
  B their father
  C their friend

2 What kind of sandwiches does the boy like?
  A cheese and tomato
  B cheese
  C chicken

3 What is Green Gables?
  A a book
  B a school
  C a farmhouse

4 How are they going to Green Gables?
  A They're walking.
  B They're going by bus.
  C They're going by car.

Part 2 A visit to Green Gables

Michael is a student in Canada and he's working as a tour guide[1] on Prince Edward Island this summer. Today he's taking the Brown family and other visitors to the farmhouse Green Gables.

Listen. Choose the correct answer for each question.

1 Linda …
  A is a girl who has lost her parents.
  B works as a bus tour guide.
  C knows a lot about Anne of Green Gables.

2 There are …
  A two books about Anne of Green Gables.
  B six books about Anne of Green Gables.
  C eight books about Anne of Green Gables.

3 Lucy Maud Montgomery …
  A was a farmer.
  B wrote books for children.
  C helped a young girl without parents.

4 Lucy Maud Montgomery was born in …
  A 1847.
  B 1874.
  C 1908.

[1] tour guide [gaɪd] *Reiseleiter/in*

2 Reading

Read about St. Jacobs, a village near Toronto, Canada, where Mennonites[1] live. Then answer the questions on the right.

✍ Visit St. Jacobs
Explore St. Jacobs on foot with our new walking-tour brochure. On sale at the Visitor Centre: $2

✍ St. Jacobs Farmers' Market
Thurs. and Sat. 7 am to 3.30 pm. Fresh, healthy food. Great atmosphere. Mennonite farmers travel to market by horse and buggy to sell their vegetables, sausages and maple syrup.

✍ The Mennonite Farm Tour
On market days only. The 1-hour tour starts and ends at the Farmers' Market. Travel in a horse-drawn trolley, see the farms at work and enjoy the country. ➜ Adults $15. Children $7.50

[1] Mennonites ['menənaɪts] *Mennoniten*
[2] maple syrup ['meɪpl ˌsɪrəp] *Ahornsirup*

1 You can buy a $2 brochure about …
  A how to see St. Jacobs on foot.
  B Mennonite history.
  C railway history in Ontario.

2 The Mennonite Farm Tour …
  A is seven days a week.
  B is on Thursdays and Saturdays.
  C starts at the Maple Syrup[2] Museum.

3 You do the Farm Tour at 12.30. How much time do you have at the market after the tour?
  A under 1 hour
  B 2 hours
  C over 2 hours

3 👥 Speaking

Partner A and **Partner B** You're planning a day trip to St. Jacobs. Read the instructions below. You can make notes for your dialogue. Then act out the dialogue.

A You want to go to the Visitor Centre first. I'd like to …	B Ask why.
Say you can buy a walking-tour brochure. If we go there, we can …	*Ask how much the brochure is.*
Say how much the brochure is.	*Say OK. But you want to go on the farm tour.* I'd like to …
Ask why.	*Answer.* If we go on the tour, we can see …
Ask how much the farm tour is.	*Say how much the farm tour is.*
Say the tour is too much. Have you got another idea? That's too much. Let's …	*Agree or disagree with your partner's idea.* That's a good idea. / No, I'd like to …

4 Writing

Yesterday you visited St. Jacobs. Write a short e-mail about your visit (40–50 words).
Where did you go yesterday? **Who** did you go with? **When** did you get there? **What** did you see? **How** was the day? **Why**?

Where	Who	When	What	How	Why
St Jacobs					

A teen magazine

⊙ Harbourfront centre

Harbourfront Community Centre · Toronto · Youth Group

Our latest project is a **TEEN MAGAZINE**!

Who will produce the magazine?

YOU! We need editors, artists, photographers, ...

Who will write the articles?

YOU! Send an article. If it's interesting, we'll publish it!

What can you write about?

That's up to **YOU!** Write about the things that **YOU** like. Send photos and drawings too.

⊙ SPORTS

Did your team win the cup?
Did you win a medal? Tell us about it ...

⊙ HOBBIES

Have you got an interesting hobby?
We want to know about it!

⊙ MUSIC

What are your Top 3 songs?
Who's your favourite singer?

⊙ MOVIES

How about a profile of your favourite movie star? What's your favourite movie?

⊙ FASHION

What's cool this summer?
We need some tips!

1 👥 **Talking about a photo**

Choose one of the photos and talk about it.

– There's a boy/... in the photo.
– There are two girls/... in the photo.
– She's/He's/They're at home/at school/...
– In the foreground/background there is/are ...
– He/She is wearing/holding/...

▶ *SF Describing pictures (p. 132)*

2 **Now you**

What do you like to read in teen mags?

> articles about famous people •
> problem pages • love stories •
> tips about fashion • quizzes •
> articles about sport/music/...

3 **A chat** 🎧

a) Read the questions, then listen.

1 Who wants to write an article? Asif or Robert?
2 Who has these ideas for an article?
   Asif? Robert? Asif and Robert?
   – favourite songs
   – favourite singer
   – favourite films
   – favourite music films
   – a music quiz
3 Which idea do Robert and Asif like best?

b) 👥 Check. You can listen again.

c) Look quickly at pp. 90–91. Find out what Robert wrote in the end.

▶ *P 1 (p. 94) • WB 1 (p. 60)*

1 The teen mag

Skim the four articles on pp. 90–91. In which section of the mag would you find them?

Article A/B/… would be in the … section.

fashion • hobby • movie • music • sport

A What are people wearing this summer?
by Lena Gomez and Jade Delamere

Lena and Jade went out with a camera and found some interesting (??) summer fashions.

Surfer clothes are popular again this year. John likes long shorts and **BRIGHT** colours. Hmm … not sure about the shorts, but the T-shirt is **COOL!**

You have to have sunglasses, but what kind? We found **VERY BIG** sunglasses and **VERY SMALL** ones. We thought they both were pretty cool. What do you think??

▶ *Right or wrong?* **A** *Lena and Jade liked John's T-shirt.* **B** *They liked the small sunglasses best.*

B The Teen Mag Quiz
by Sam Chan

1 Match these sports to the pictures:
American football – basketball – cricket – lacrosse – rugby

2 How many players are there on a basketball team?
Ⓐ 5 Ⓑ 11 Ⓒ 15

3 How many players are there on an ice hockey team?
Ⓐ 5 Ⓑ 6 Ⓒ 10

▶ P 2–3 (pp. 94–95)

C My top three favourite songs   by Robert 'DJ Bobby' Smith

3 **'School's out' by Alice Cooper**
School is finishing for the summer soon so this had to be on the list. You always hear it on the radio just before summer vacation – and I think it's great.

'The sound of San Francisco' by Global Deejays
2
Summer is the time to travel. This great mix takes you to London, Paris ... and San Francisco. And if you can't go that far, at least you can get up and dance!

1 **'Summer in the city' by the Lovin' Spoonful**
Are you staying in the city this summer? Well, this is a great song for city people in the summer.

> *What are Robert's songs all about?*   A *school*   B *summer*   C *cities*   D *love*

▶ P 4–5 (pp. 95–96) • WB 3 (p. 61)

D A profile   by Emily Kumar and Jessica Browne

Name	Johnny Depp
Real name	John Christopher Depp
Born	June 9, 1963
Where	Kentucky, USA
Career	First he played in rock bands, then he became an actor.
Homes	Los Angeles and France
1st film	Nightmare on Elm Street
Other films	Pirates of the Caribbean, Charlie and the Chocolate Factory
Family	He has two children with French singer, Vanessa Paradis.

One of his most famous roles – Captain Jack Sparrow

> *Right or wrong?*   A *Johnny Depp is French.*   B *Depp isn't his real name.*

▶ P 6–7 (pp. 96–97) • WB 4–8 (pp. 61–64)

2   👥 Now you

Which of the four articles do you like best/like least? Why?
What kind of article would you write for a mag?
Make notes, then talk to your partner.

– I think article A/B/... is interesting/boring/fun.
– I'm (not) interested in sport/fashion/...
– I think it's a good article for a teen mag.
– Lots of people like quizzes/profiles/...
– I'd write about ...

▶ **Text File 10** (pp. 124–127) • **Checkpoint 5** WB (p. 65)

Extra **Project: Our mag**

In this project you will write an article for your own teen magazine.

1 Step 1: Choose your topic

a) *What do you want in your mag? Brainstorm ideas. Make notes. Use a list or a mind map. When you have finished, choose the best idea.*

> * *A profile of a pop star / film star / ...*
> * *My favourite sport*
> * *A quiz about music / sport / films / ...*
> * *My top 3 summer songs / sports films / ...*
> * *A report about a match / a competition / a concert / a film / ...*
> * *Fashion / make-up tips*
> * *...*

b) 👥 *Talk about all your ideas. Then make a chart like this:*

Who?	What?	When?
Youssef	profile of Podolski	next Tuesday
Laura	pop music quiz	
Tansu	...	

▶ *SF Brainstorming (p. 139)*

2 Step 2: Collect information

a) 👥 *Where can you get information? Complete the chart on the right.*

b) *Look for information for your article.*

> **Tipp**
>
> *Drucke nicht einfach Artikel aus dem Internet aus. Gib alles in deinen eigenen Worten wieder.*
>
> *Und achte darauf, dass deine Informationen auch glaubwürdig und richtig sind.*

Sources of information	Good for
encyclopedia	facts about people, places and things
internet	song lyrics, groups ...
magazines	interviews, photos, ...
library	...
other people, teachers, ...	...

3 Step 3: Write and correct your article

a) *Write your article and get it ready to show your group.*

b) 👥 *Correct each other's work in your group.*

▶ *Writing course: The steps of writing (p. 78)* •
Writing course: Correcting your work (p. 97)

4 👥 Step 4: Publish your mag

a) *Agree how you will publish your mag.*
– Let's write the articles on paper/on the computer.
– Let's make a poster/a real mag.
– We can put our mag on the school website.

b) *What are the different jobs? Decide who will do what. Make a list.*

Finish article – EVERYBODY!
Look for pictures – EVERYBODY!
Layout pages on computer – Aisha and Elias
Design front page – Laura
Make photocopies – Oleg

1 WORDS All about your interests

a) 〇 👥 *Work in groups of four. Each group member takes one topic. Write down the words and phrases from the green box that belong to your subject. Add more words if you can.*

fashion	films	music	sport
– colour your hair	– movie	– piano	– sport things
– clothes		– concert hall	

action film • actor • baggy jeans • band • beat • camera • cartoon • choir • cinema • cinema ticket • clothes • club • coach • colour your hair • comedy • competition • concert hall • cup final • design • DJ • dress • fashion show • film star • guitar • goalkeeper • half-time • hat • make-up • match • microphone • mix • model • MP3 player • old-fashioned • outfit • piano • piercing • pitch • player • popcorn • rap • rehearsal • score • series • singer • sport things • stadium • team • trainers • training session • trendy • violin • ...

b) 👥 *Tell your group the words you wrote down. Can the group find more words?*

c) *Look at the words in the green box again and find as many answers as you can.*

What can you wear?	Who can you see?
What can you play?	What can you watch?
What can you buy?	What can you listen to?
Where can you go to?	What can be trendy/old-fashioned/modern/...?

2 👥 LISTENING Numbers and spelling 🎧

a) *Listen to **part 1** on the CD. Write down the numbers. Swap with your partner. Listen again and check his/her numbers.*

b) *Listen to **part 2** on the CD. Write down the names. Swap with your partner. Do you think the spelling is correct? Listen again and check.*

c) **Extra** *Take turns. Choose a name from this book. Write it down. Then dictate it to your partner, as in b). Check.*

My name is Anna. That's A, double N, A ...

My number is zero, one, seven, double six ...

Sam 01

3 Extra STUDY SKILLS Research on the internet (Using key words and phrases)

a) What key words can you use to answer the following questions? Write down the key words.

1 How many players are there on a cricket team? *"how many players" cricket team*

2 When and where was Elvis Presley born? *"Elvis Presley" born*

3 What is Madonna's real name?

4 What was Kylie Minogue's first hit single?

5 What is the name of Manchester United's coach?

6 Is there a German „Bundesliga" for American football? Name five teams.

b) Try your key words from a) in an online search engine. Can you find the answers? Has everybody in the class got the same answers?

> **Tipps für Internetsuche**
>
> - Tippe ein oder mehrere Schlüsselwörter als Suchbegriffe in die Suchmaschine.
> - Wenn das Ergebnis nicht gut genug ist oder wenn du als Antwort zu viele Webseiten genannt bekommst:
>   – füge mehr Suchbegriffe hinzu oder
>   – probier andere Schlüsselwörter.
> - Wenn du nach zusammenhängenden Suchbegriffen suchst, schreibe sie in Anführungsstrichen, z. B. "interview with Shakira".
>
> **Beachte: Du kannst nicht immer sicher sein, ob die gefundenen Informationen stimmen!**

4 //○ REVISION What are their plans? (Present progressive / future meaning) ▶ D p. 109

a) What are these people doing this summer? Complete the sentences.

is/isn't are/aren't	+ ing

1 Robert *is staying* (stay) at home this summer.
He *isn't going* (go) to England this year.

2 Jill ... (go) on holiday. She ... (move) to the US with her family. Jill ... (start) a new school in September.

3 In August John ... (visit) Germany with his family. They ... (fly) to Frankfurt. Then they ... (go) to Berlin.

4 Lena ... (go) to the sea with her family in August. They ... (go) camping. They ... (stay) in a nice house near the beach.

b) 👥👥👥 What are your plans for the summer? Talk to people in your group.

> I'm staying at home.

> I'm visiting my grandparents/aunt/...

> What are you doing this summer?

> I'm going to France/Turkey/ the north of Germany/...

EVERYDAY ENGLISH

5 SPEAKING Working with a partner 🎧

a) ⊙ *Some students are writing an article about their top 3 sports films.*
Listen and find out which film is their number 1, number 2 and number 3.

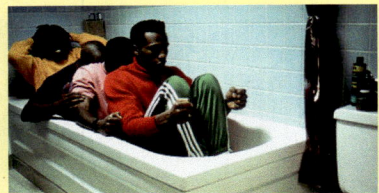

Rocky Balboa
Rocky is back! Can the old man beat the young champion?

Cool Runnings
The Jamaican team isn't very good at this sport, but the guys are very funny!

Bend it like Beckham
Two girls want to play football. Their parents don't think that's a good idea.

b) 👥 *Write down your four favourite films or songs. Compare your list with your partner's.*
Together make a list of your top 3 favourite films or songs. Talk like this.

A: My favourite film/song is ... Let's make it number one.

B: OK. I like ... Let's make that number 2.   B: What about ...? That's great too.

A: OK. We can make ... number one and ... number two.

B: What about our number 3? I think ... is really great.

A: OK. Good idea.   A: Oh no, you must be mad. ... is much better.

B: OK. So our top 3 is number 1 ..., number 2 ... and number 3 ...

6 MEDIATION Information from the internet

a) *Vanessa wants to write a profile of Mika. Does this text have the information that she needs for the profile? What's missing?*

Mika wurde am 18. August 1983 als Michael Penniman in Beirut, Libanon geboren. Sein Vater ist aus Amerika, seine Mutter aus dem Libanon. Bald nach seiner Geburt zog die Familie nach Paris. Mika war neun, als die Familie erneut umzog – diesmal nach London. Dort wohnt er noch heute.
Nach etlichen Versuchen, im Musikbusiness Fuß zu fassen, z. B. durch das Schreiben eines Werbesongs für eine Kaugummi-Marke oder von Flugzeug-Musik für eine bekannte britische Fluglinie, veröffentlichte er 2006 seine Debütsingle "Relax, take it easy". Im Jahr 2007 konnte Mika mit dem Song "Grace Kelly" überraschend Platz 1 der britischen Single-Charts erklimmen.

b) *Now complete the profile of Mika in English.*

Tipp

Versuch nicht bei einem deutschen Text alles zu übersetzen. Konzentriere dich auf das Wichtige!

Profile
Real Name: ＿＿＿＿   Lives: ＿＿＿＿＿＿＿
Born: ＿＿＿＿＿＿   1st single: ＿＿＿＿＿＿
Where: ＿＿＿＿＿＿   1st album: ＿＿＿＿＿
Family: ＿＿＿＿＿＿   1st No 1 single: ＿＿＿＿

7 WRITING Correcting your work

a) 👥 *Correct the mistakes in these sentences.*

1 The film is <u>exiting</u>.	spelling
2 Everybody in our class likes surfer <u>cloths</u>.	spelling
3 My sister <u>like</u> the singer Shakira very much.	verb
4 Last Friday I <u>go</u> to a big concert in Berlin.	verb
5 Yesterday <u>watched I</u> a new film.	word order
6 Nobody likes baggy jeans because they <u>old-fashioned are</u>.	word order

> **Tipp**
>
> *Alles, was du aufschreibst, solltest du auf sprachliche Richtigkeit überprüfen. Aber es ist nicht immer einfach, eigene Fehler zu finden:*
> **Rechtschreibung (spelling)**
>   *z. B. exciting (NOT ~~exiting~~)*
> **Verbformen (verb)**
>   *z. B. aufpassen beim* **simple present**:
>   *He, she, it, das „s" muss mit!*
> **Wortstellung (word order)**
>   *z. B. Gestern* ging *er ins Kino.*
>   *Yesterday he* went *to the cinema.*

b) *Look at some of your texts that your teacher has corrected. Find the mistakes that you made. Write a list like this for your mistakes:*

> **Tipp**
>
> *Führe eine Liste der Fehler, die du oft machst, und nutze sie beim Schreiben als persönliche Checkliste. Ergänze sie immer dann, wenn dein Lehrer/deine Lehrerin dich auf weitere Fehler aufmerksam macht.*

My mistakes

spelling	verb	word order
– bigger – making (NOT mak~~ei~~ing)	go, past = went (NOT ~~goed~~) she / he / it like<u>s</u> English Every day / On Mondays I play ... BUT: Now I'm playing ...	Yesterday I went ... (NOT ~~went I~~)

c) *Write Shakira's profile. Correct the mistakes.*

<u>Shakira</u>

Born: In 1977 in Colombia, South <u>america</u>.	spelling
Family: father <u>american</u>, mother Columbian.	spelling
She <u>have</u> six brothers and sisters.	verb
Languages: She <u>speak</u> Spanish and English.	verb
Early career: She <u>write</u> her first song when she was eight.	verb – past!
First album: `Magia´.	
First hit <u>singel</u>: Whenever, wherever	spelling

d) **Extra** 🔘 *Write a profile of a star. It can be a pop star, a film star, a sports star, ... – Write about:*
– when and where your star was born
– about his/her family
– about his/her school days
– how his/her career started
– about his/her first CD/film/medal/...
Correct your text.

How am I doing? – Units 1–5

This page will help you to check what you have learned in the whole of this book, not just in the last unit.

a) Find or choose the correct answers.

Facts about Britain

> Tube • Scotland • Wales • Manchester • London • Thames

1 The three countries of Great Britain are England, Scotland and ...
2 The capital of Great Britain is ... It's on the River ...
3 The other name for the underground in London is the ...
4 The Orkney Islands are north of ...
5 Old Trafford is the name of a football stadium in the English city of ...

Words

> the country • electronic media • music • sport • the town • transport

Name the word fields below:

6 ticket, train, ferry, tunnel, ...
7 mobile phone, download, website, ...
8 car park, theatre, traffic, ...
9 training, fan, score, stadium, ...
10 gig, DJ, hip-hop, ...
11 forest, river, mountain, bear, ...

Add at least one word to each of the word fields.

Writing

12 The main idea of a paragraph is usually in the ... sentence.
 Ⓐ first Ⓑ second Ⓒ last
13 What are the 5 Ws?

Everyday English

14 Frag, ob du eine Nachricht hinterlassen kannst.
 Can I leave a ...?
15 Frag, ob du eine Tageskarte kaufen kannst.
 Can I buy a ...?
16 Sag, dass du satt bist.
 I'm ...

Grammar

17 If we are late for school, our teacher ... very cross.
 Ⓐ has Ⓑ are Ⓒ will be Ⓓ were
18 I haven't read the book ... you gave me.
 Ⓐ who Ⓑ that
19 My sister and I aren't allowed to ride our bikes in the street because my mum is afraid we'll hurt ...
 Ⓐ us. Ⓑ ourselves. Ⓒ each other.

Study Skills

Welche Study Skills benutzt du?

> brainstorming • paraphrasing • skimming

20 Du willst schnell wissen, worum es in einem Text geht.
21 Dir fällt das passende englische Wort nicht ein.
22 Du sammelst Ideen – allein oder in der Gruppe.

b) Check your answers and the number of points for each correct answer on p. 215. Add up your points.

c) If you had 23 or more points, well done! Where did you make mistakes? The chart below will tell you what you can do to improve your English.

No.	Areas	Find out more	Exercises
1– 5	Britain facts	Units 1–4	–
6–11	Word fields	pp. 6, 11, 14, 20, 32, 38, 56, 63	WB pp. 3, 4, 9, 10, 14, 21, 24, 39, 40, 47, 63
12–13	Writing	Writing course, pp. 22, 39, 64, 78, 97	WB pp. 12, 22, 42, 50, 62
14–16	Everyday English	Units 1–3, pp. 25, 41, 65	WB pp. 16, 24, 61
20–24	Grammar	GF 3, 4, 6, (pp. 144, 145, 147)	WB pp. 25, 26, 27, 38, 48, 49
12–15	Study Skills	SF (pp. 135, 138, 139)	WB pp. 9, 28, 39, 60

Unit 2

13 Extra Loch Ness and Edinburgh ▶ *Unit 2 (p. 43)*

a) Read the box on the right. Then listen to your partner's text about Loch Ness.
*When you hear a mistake say **Stop**! Correct the sentence with facts from the box.*

Facts about Loch Ness
1. It is one of the most famous places in Scotland.
2. The word loch [lɒx] means lake.
3. Loch Ness is 37 kilometres long.
4. Some people say that there is a monster in the lake.
5. Every year thousands of tourists come to Loch Ness.

b) A student has written this text about Edinburgh. There are five mistakes in it. Read it through quietly. Then read it out to your partner. He/She will correct the mistakes.

Edinburgh

Edinburgh is the capital of Britain. More than a million tourists from all over the world visit Edinburgh every year. Visitors come to see the famous old buildings like Buckingham Palace.
   Some famous people came from Edinburgh. There was Alexander Graham Bell. He had the idea for the first computer. And J. K. Rowling wrote the first Harry Potter computer game in a café in Edinburgh.

Unit 3 Lösung, p. 60

1 👥 WORDS Rooms

c) Check your picture.

Unit 3

Who needs legs? 🎧 ▶ Unit 3 (p. 66)

> Birthday boy Nathan was fighting for his life yesterday after a two-hour operation. His mother Helen is by his bed where last night he was very very ill.

5 That was the report in the newspaper, on 13th April 1997.

Three months later, in July 1997, Nathan learned to walk again, this time with artificial legs. And soon after that he was back at
10 school!

'Yes, Nathan has lost his legs, but he's still mad about sport,' his mum said a few months later. 'He still goes riding. And he plays football at school: he sits in the goal and stops the
15 ball.'

When he was ten years old Nathan started to play sledge hockey – ice hockey for the disabled.

Then when he was 14, Nathan also started to
20 do athletics in the summer. A year later he won three gold medals at the Junior British Championships.

When Nathan was sixteen, in April 2004, he played for Great Britain at the World Sledge
25 Hockey Championships – he was the youngest player. In 2006 he represented Wales at the Melbourne Commonwealth Games and Great Britain at the Winter Paralympics in Turin.

The BBC asked Nathan Stephens what his
30 hopes were. His answer: I hope I can be in the next Summer and Winter Paralympics.
I hope we win more medals than before.

Working with the text

1 Who is Nathan Stephens?

a) Read the text and complete these notes:

> Nathan learned to walk again in _____.
> The sport that he started when he was ten: _____.
> He won his first athletics medals when he was _____.
> Nathan hopes _____.

b) 👥 *Ask your partner about Nathan's earlier life.*
– Where and when was Nathan born?
– What sports did he do as a little boy?
– Where did he go on his ninth birthday?
– What happened?
Take notes.
Then answer your partner's questions.

2 👥 Timeline

a) Copy and complete this timeline with your partner. Scan both texts again if necessary.

> Nathan born
>
> | 1988 | 1993 | 1997 | 1998 | 2002 | 2004 | 2006 | After 2006 |

b) **Extra** *What did Nathan do after 2006? Find out with the help of the internet.*

DOSSIER Timeline for ...

Find out about an interesting person (a sports star, a film star, ...). Draw a timeline for him/her.

Unit 3 Lösung, p. 61

4   A quiz (Relative clauses)

1 (A) Philipp
2 (B) The London Eye
3 (B) steel drums
4 (B) Harry Potter

5 (A) Keira Knighley
6 (A) Wayne Rooney
7 (B) Great Britain
8 (A) Sir Arthur Conan Doyle

Unit 3

5   👥 STUDY SKILLS Paraphrasing   ▶ Unit 3 (p. 62)

a) Listen to your partner and guess his/her words.

Oh, do you mean a ...?

b) Explain the words in the green box to your partner. Match the sentence halves.

teacher • map • crocodile • pea • bakery

1 It's a person who ...
2 It's something that you use to ...
3 It's an animal that ...
4 It's a vegetable that ...
5 It's a place where ...

... is small, round and green.
... helps students to learn things.
... you can buy bread.
... lives in water and has a long mouth with lots of teeth.
... find your way.

Unit 4

8   Plans for the week (Present progressive with future meaning)   ▶ Unit 4 (p. 79)

a) Talk to your partner about your plans for the week. Your partner will start.

A: On Monday evening I'm visiting my Grandad. What about you?
B I'm going swimming. On Tuesday evening I'm ... What about you?
A: I'm going ...

b) When are you doing the same things?
We're doing the same thing on ... and ...

	morning ☀	afternoon ☀	evening ☽
MON			going swimming
TUE			going to basketball training
WED		help sister with her homework	
THU			watching favourite TV programme
FRI			meeting my friends at a party
SAT	getting up early	going shopping	

Unit 1

4 //● REVISION A visit to the London Eye (Simple past) ▶ Unit 1 (p. 21)

Put the verbs in the simple past and complete the text.

Asif and Robert *had* (have) a really great time yesterday. In the morning Robert and his parents ... (take) the Tube to Waterloo. When they ... (arrive) at the London Eye, they *didn't see* (~~see~~) Asif. But then Asif ... (call) Robert on his mobile and they ... (find) him quickly. Luckily there ... (~~be~~) too many tourists there that day, so they ... (wait) very long. Soon they ... (be) up on the big wheel. The view ... (be) fantastic. They ... (~~see~~) Asif's house, but they ... (see) lots of famous London sights. After the ride, Asif and Robert ... (~~stay~~) with Robert's parents. They ... (go) to Asif's part of London and then to the Trocadero.

WRITING COURSE Part 1

6 WRITING A holiday postcard ▶ Unit 1 (p. 22)

d) more help

Put the sentences in the right order and write a postcard from an imaginary holiday in London.

– Start with a greeting.
– Say where you are.
– Say what the weather is like.
– Say what the place is like.
– Say what you usually do there.
– Say what you did yesterday.
– Say what you are going to do.
– Finish with a closing phrase.

> Our hotel isn't great, but the city is brilliant.

> See you soon,

> The weather is great – hot and sunny every day.

> Every day we go sightseeing.

> Hello from London!

> Dear Laura

> Yesterday afternoon we visited Buckingham Palace.

> This afternoon I'm going to visit the Tower of London.

Unit 1

9 | // ● | **REVISION**   **The Feely family**   (Present perfect)   ▶ *Unit 1 (p. 23)*

Write sentences about the Feely family.

 **1** Mrs Feely
– angry

 **2** Mo and Jo
– happy

 **3** Julie Feely
– proud

 **4** Kitty Feely
– scared

kids – not tidy room

they – have bath

she – write nice story

she – see big dog

 **5** Tommy Feely
– ill

 **6** Jill and Jenny Feely
– cold

 **7** Grandpa Feely
– sad

 **8** Mr Feely
– tired

he – eat too many
sweets

they – not close door

parrot – die

he – not sleep enough

1   Mrs Feely is angry because her kids haven't …
2   Mo and Jo Feely are happy because they …

Only a game   Working with the text   ▶ *Unit 1 (p. 28)*

2 | // ● | **How Robert felt**

Find at least one point in the story when Robert felt …

A nervous   I think Robert felt nervous when … (l. 19).
B excited
C scared
D shocked

Unit 2

2 //● WORDS Electronic media ▸ Unit 2 (p. 38)

a) Complete the text with the words in the box.

> chat • computer • download (2x) • logo •
> plays • ringtone • send • surf • text messages

b) Choose four words and make your own sentences.

Katrina has got her own ... in her room at home. She uses it to ... with friends and to ... the internet. It's cheaper for her to ... instant messages to her friends than to send ... on her mobile.
Katrina loves music, so she often spends her pocket money to ... her favourite songs. She hasn't got an MP3 player, but her mobile ... MP3s. Her ... on her mobile is a picture of a fiddle, and of course her ... is fiddle music. But it isn't a ... – it's her on her own fiddle!

Part 2

WRITING COURSE

4 WRITING An e-mail to a friend ▸ Unit 2 (p. 39)

d) more help Now write an e-mail to one of your friends about a real or imaginary day out. Maybe these words and phrases will help you

Remember:

Start with an interesting opening sentence.

> Dear Emily
> I had a great day last Saturday. I went to ... with ...

> Hi Will
> Guess what I did yesterday – I went to ...!

Start a new paragraph for each new idea.

> I had a great (fantastic / amazing ...) time.

> It is a really interesting (cool / fun / ...) place.

> I went with ... and ... They are always good fun.

> The best part of the day was (the morning / lunch / the afternoon).

> The weather was good – (hot and sunny / cold and sunny / only a bit of rain in the morning) – so we were able to do lots of things.

> First we ...   Then we ...   It was great.   Mum / ... bought me a ...

Finish with a general or personal statement.

> Must stop now.   Please write back soon.

> Write soon and tell me your news.

> Love, ...   Bye for now! ...

Unit 2

10   `// ●`   **Fiona's dreams**   (Conditional sentences type 2)   ▶ Unit 2 (p. 42)

> **Tipp**
>
> **If** clause + **simple past**   => *If I lived in London,*
>
> Main clause + **would/'d**   => *I'd be very happy.*

Fiona often dreams about what it would be like if she lived in London. Finish the sentences.

1   If I lived in London, (I'd be/I was) very happy.

2   If my parents visited me, (we'd go/we went) on the London Eye.

3   If I waited outside Buckingham Palace, perhaps (I'd see/I saw) the Queen.

4   If (I was/I'd be) a film star, I'd wear beautiful clothes.

5   If (I missed/I'd miss) my friends, I'd chat with them on the internet.

6   If (I wanted/I'd want) to see my family at home, I'd go by plane.

Orkney Star   Working with the text   ▶ Unit 2 (p. 46)

1   `// ●`   **What's the story about?**

a) Here are headings for the different parts of the story. Put them in the right order.

Page 44– 45

The journey to school
Katrina will be a star
At home on Monday morning
Katrina and the 'Beauties'
Katrina meets Sheena
The filming starts
The film crew
On Friday on Hoy
'Clones, maybe, but not beauties.'

b) Write one sentence about each part.

1   Katrina picked up her things and went …
2   In the car Katrina felt …
3   The head teacher told the school the news about …
4   The 'Beauties' wanted to help Katrina but she said …
5   Sheena, the director's assistant, looked just like …
6   The film crew were …
7   Bill asked Katrina …
8   Sheena didn't think the 'Beauties' were …
9   On Friday evening …

Working with the text ▸ *Unit 2 (p. 46)*

2 **The interview** more help

These questions and answers are part of an interview with Katrina.
Put them in the right order.

Director___ Katrina, where are you from?

Do you like it in the hostel?

How do you get to school?

Why is home better? | Where are you from?

Where do you stay from Monday to Friday?

Is it boring on a small island like Hoy?

Katrina___ ...

My family is there and it's quiet and beautiful there.

It's OK, but I like home better.

No, it isn't. I chat with my friends, and I play the fiddle with my dad.

I'm from Hoy. It's another island.

I come by ferry on Monday and go home on Friday. | I stay in the school hostel.

Unit 3

3 //● **What would you like?** (Relative clauses) ▸ *Unit 3 (p. 61)*

a) *Write sentences. Use who for people and that for things.*

| I'd like | a teacher
a car
a computer
a friend
a camera
an aunt | who
that | takes good pictures.
listens to my problems.
is fun to drive.
is really fast and easy to use.
gives me lots of nice presents.
explains things well and is funny. |

9 //● **REVISION Hobbies** (Word order in subordinate clauses) ▸ *Unit 3 (p. 63)*

Remember						
	S	V	O	S	V	O
English:	Latisha wears a red shirt when she plays football.					
German:	Latisha trägt ein rotes Hemd, wenn sie Fußball spielt.					
	S	V	O	S	O	V

a) *Complete these sentences.*
1 Latisha likes football because (it / an exciting game / is).
2 Latisha is unhappy when (a match / her team / loses).
3 Philipp doesn't usually go to football matches because (he / football / doesn't like).
4 Philipp had a good time when (went / he / to Latisha's match).
5 Latisha was happy because (to her match / came / Philipp).
6 Latisha was very happy when (a goal / she / scored).

b) *Write two sentences about your hobbies and free time activities.*
I like … because … • I often do / play / go … because … • I'm happy / sad when …

Unit 3

10   WRITING A report (Collecting and organizing ideas)   ▶ Unit 3 (p. 64)

d) [more help] *Complete the report in the blue box. Use the information in the chart.*

Who?	What?	Where?	When?	How?
• Manchester United U14s against Stoke U14s • best player: Latisha Byrd	• girls' football • cup final • final score 2–1	• in Manchester	• on Sunday afternoon	• fast start half-time 0–1 for Stoke • Stoke: 1st half – played well 2nd half – mistakes • after break – Manchester stronger • Byrd scored two goals

Manchester United U14 girls' football team played _____ last Sunday in _____. It was a cup final, so both teams made a _____ start. Stoke played well in the _____ half. At _____ the score was 0–1 for Stoke.

But after the break Stoke made _____. In the end Manchester won because they were ___. The final _____ was Manchester _____ Stoke 1. The _____ player on the pitch was Manchester's Latisha Byrd. She scored _____ goals in the second half.

Unit 4

4   [// ●]   School rules (*have to* and *allowed to*)   ▶ Unit 4 (p. 77)

a) *Write the rules at Robert's school.*
Students have to …
They aren't allowed to …

– arrive on time for school
– wear caps and jackets in class
– cycle or skate in the school building
– turn off phones in the classroom
– clean the tables after lunch
– smoke in the school yard or building
– be friendly to other students
– eat in the classrooms

Unit 4

5 🎧⬤ **What are they saying?** (Reflexive pronouns) ▸ Unit 4 (p. 77)

Complete the sentences under the pictures with words from the green box.

> myself • yourself (2×) • herself • himself •
> itself • ourselves • yourselves

1 Don't cut ...!

2 Please help ...

3 Look. It's cleaning ...

4 She taught ... to paint.

5 We really enjoyed ...

6 Did you hurt ...?

7 I'm going to buy ... something nice.

8 Look, he's looking at ...

6 🎧⬤ **Mum and Dad are on strike** (Reflexive pronouns) ▸ Unit 4 (p. 77)

Complete the sentences with the reflexive pronouns myself, yourself, himself, herself, ourselves, yourselves, themselves.

1 Mr and Mrs Jones are on strike. They want to enjoy **themselves**.
2 Mrs Jones usually makes Jack's lunch, but today he has to make it ...
3 Mr Jones usually looks after Jill in the afternoon, but today she has to look after ...
4 Jill doesn't understand. 'Why do I have to look after ... today?'
5 Mrs Jones usually teaches Jack the guitar in the evening, but today she says, 'Sorry, Jack, but you'll have to teach ...
6 Jack says to Jill, 'Mum and Dad don't want to cook for us today. We have to cook for ...'
7 'Don't blame us,' the parents say. 'You were terrible yesterday. You two can only blame ...!'

Unit 4

7   WRITING Telling a story (The steps of writing)   ▶ Unit 4 (p. 78)

more help | **Step 3** | **Revising**

Check this final paragraph.
1 First look at the <u>blue</u> verbs. They should all be in the
simple past. You need to correct three of them.
2 Then check the spelling of the words in <u>green</u>. You
need to correct one.

> After that it <u>started</u> to <u>rain</u>. Everybody <u>leave</u> the fun park. But the <u>grils</u> <u>stayed.</u> They <u>have</u> a great time <u>because</u> the fun park <u>is</u> <u>empty</u>.

Unit 5

4   // ●   REVISION What are their plans? (Present progressive for plans)   ▶ Unit 5 (p. 95)

a) *Write about these people's plans for the summer.*

1   Robert is staying at home. He isn't …

1   Robert – stay at home – this summer.
He – not go – England – this year.

2   Jill – not go – on holiday.
She – move – the US – with her family.
Jill – start – a new school – September.

3   August – John – visit – Germany – with family.
They – fly – Frankfurt. Then – they – go – Berlin.

4   Lena – go – the sea – with family – August.
They – not go – camping. They – stay – nice house – near beach.

Text File
Inhalt

> Tipp
>
> *In diesem **Text File** findest du zusätzliche Lesetexte.
> Die Fußnoten (am Ende jeder Seite) helfen dir, die
> wichtigsten neuen Wörter zu verstehen. Viel Spaß
> beim Lesen!*

▶ *SF Understanding new words (p. 128)*

TF 1 Pull In Emergency[1]   (adapted from 'Children's London', The Times)

Too young to rock? Never! The band Pull in Emergency (13 and 14 years old) tell you how.

☆ # Faith Bale

13, lead singer of the band **Pull In Emergency** from North London

'We try to wear cool clothes *and* sound good. Old, second-hand clothes are best, but you sometimes have to look at a lot of rubbish.'

☆ # Alice Costelloe

13, guitarist in P.I.E.

'I think it's good at 13 to try to go to as many gigs as you can. There's the Tin Pan Alley Festival in Denmark Street (www.tinpanalleyfestival.co.uk). It's free – and for all ages.'

 # Dylan Holmes

13, bass guitarist in P.I.E.

'If you can't get a studio, you can still make OK recordings[2] – on a computer or with a cheap microphone.'

1 Young bands

a) *Finish this sentence. Find different endings.*
As a young band you have to/you need …

b) *What young bands do you know in Germany? Tell your class about them.*

2 The song 🎧

Listen to the song by P.I.E. How do you like it?
I like/don't like that kind of music.
They play/sing well/badly.
They sound good/OK/terrible.
I'd like/I wouldn't like to be in that band.

---

[1] (to) pull in emergency [ɪˈmɜːdʒənsi] *(Notbremse) im Notfall ziehen*   [2] recording [rɪˈkɔːdɪŋ] *Aufnahme*

TF 2　Two Elizabeths　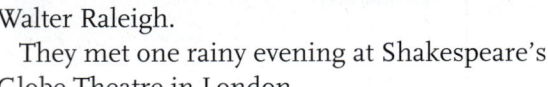

England has had two Queen Elizabeths.

Our first story is about Elizabeth I.
5　She became Queen in 1558, when she was 25 years old. She never married, but had a lot of
10　'favourites'. One of these 'favourites' was Walter Raleigh.

They met one rainy evening at Shakespeare's Globe Theatre in London.
15　The Queen wanted to get out of her carriage when she saw a very big puddle. Raleigh saw the puddle too. He took off his very expensive new cloak and threw it onto the puddle.

The Queen smiled. She went into the theatre
20　with dry[1] feet and Raleigh became her new 'favourite'.

A few years later Sir Walter Raleigh went to America. He brought back a dirty vegetable
25　called 'the potato' and a dry leaf[2] called 'tobacco'.

Our second story is about Queen Elizabeth II. She was also very young
30　when she became Queen in 1952 – just 26 years old.

One night in 1982, a man called Michael Fagan climbed into Buckingham Palace. The
35　Queen woke up in the middle of the night and found a man by her bed.

Queen Elizabeth II is famous for being very calm[3]. And that night was an example. She asked the man to sit down and started to talk
40　to him. After a few minutes she asked him, 'Would you like a drink?' He said, 'Yes, please.' So she picked up the phone.

'I'd like two gin and tonics, please. Oh, and my cigarettes,' she said.
45

The person on the other end of the phone knew something was wrong, because the Queen has never smoked!

In a few minutes the police were there and took Mr Fagan away.
50

▶ *What did Sir Walter Raleigh bring back from America? Which of these things do you find in the second story?*

---

[1] dry [draɪ] *trocken*　[2] leaf [liːf] *Blatt*　[3] calm [kɑːm] *ruhig*

TF 3 Online safety

: ru alone
  when u
  meet online
  m8s in
  real life?

: smart online
  safe offline_
  www.thinkuknow.co.uk

Home Office

1   The people

a) Look at the poster: 'm8s' is short for 'mates'. What does 'mates' mean?

b) Who are the two people in the poster? What do you think is going to happen?

c) Why is the person on the stairs wearing a mask?

1 He's playing a trick on his friend.
2 It's Halloween.
3 He wants to hide his face.

2   The message

a) What is the poster saying?

1 Send lots of text messages.
2 Be careful when you meet people online.
3 Be smart: Tell your online mates as much as possible about yourself!

b) Where would you put the poster?
I would put it in schools/libraries/...

3 Keep safe online

Do you know the online safety rules[1]? They are very important! Try this quiz.

Online Safety Quiz

Question 1

When you are online do you use ...?
- A: Your real name, age and address?
- B: A nickname[2]?
- C: Your best friend's name?

Question 2

Somebody says: Don't tell your parents about me. What should you do?
- A: Tell your parents quickly.
- B: Don't tell your parents.
- C: Ask why.

Question 3

What information can you get from somebody's real name online?
- A: Only their address.
- B: Only their age.
- C: Their age, address and telephone number.

Question 4

You have met someone online. You want to meet them. What do you do?
- A: Go alone.
- B: Go with a friend.
- C: Go with a parent.

Question 5

How do you stay safe on the internet?
- A: Wear gloves[3].
- B: Don't use the internet.
- C: Be careful and follow safety rules.

The answers are at the bottom of this page. For more on online safety go to ... www.EnglishG.de

Answers to Online Safety QUIZ

Q 1 A NEVER NEVER use your real name. And NEVER give your address!
B YES!
C NO, don't do this.

Q 2 A YES, tell your parents QUICKLY!
B and C NO, tell your parents!

Q 3 A and B NO! You can get more than that!
C You can find out ALL these things about somebody if you know their real name. So NEVER use your real name online.

Q 4 A and B NEVER do this alone or even with a friend.
C YES, DON'T GO if your parents can't come with you!

Q 5 A NO! If you want to stay WARM, wear gloves!
B If you don't want to use the internet, that's OK.
C The internet is cool, BUT you must be careful and follow the rules!

---

[1] rule [ruːl] *Regel*   [2] nickname ['nɪkneɪm] *Spitzname*   [3] glove [ɡlʌv] *(Finger-)Handschuh*

TF 4 **My blog**[1] ○ **Scotch pancakes**

Monday November 11

Was a bit bored this weekend and the weather was HORRIBLE!

Luckily some mates came round. We decided to make some Scotch pancakes. They are really easy and VERY GOOD!

1. Put 120 g self-raising flour[2] and 30 g sugar into a bowl.
2. Mix an egg and 150 ml milk in another bowl.
3. Mix the egg and milk mixture into the flour. Now you have to work QUICKLY or your pancakes will be flat[3]!
4. Melt butter in a HOT frying pan. Now put the pancake mixture into the pan with a spoon.
5. When there are lots of bubbles on the pancakes, turn them over.
6. Eat with butter, or butter and jam. If there are some left over[4], you can eat them cold too. BUT we ate them all!

POSTED by Tom at 5.15 pm

COMMENTS

Sugarmonster said ...

Hi Tom! I like your blog! I'm German.
I want to make your pancakes. What is self-raising flour??

Tom Scotland said ...

Hi Sugarmonster. You use self-raising flour when you want things to rise (go up). You can use normal flour and baking powder (about a teaspoon). My dictionary says that baking powder is 'Backpulver' in German. Does that sound right?

Sugarmonster said ...

Thanks, Tom! I tried the pancakes. They ARE GOOD! Would you like a German recipe[5]? What about my favourite 'Schokoladenpudding'?

Tom Scotland said ...

Can u do it in English?? My German isn't gr8!

ABOUT ME
TOM Scotland
View my profile

1 **What do you need?**
If you want to make Scotch pancakes, what do you need? Write a list.

2 **Your favourite easy recipe**
Write your favourite recipe in English. Choose an easy recipe and explain what to do in a simple way. Use a dictionary if you don't know a word. You can use pictures too.

---

[1] blog [blɒg] *Weblog (Online-Tagebuch)*   [2] flour ['flaʊə] *Mehl*   [3] flat [flæt] *flach*   [4] (be) left over [ˌleft 'əʊvə] *übrig sein*   [5] recipe ['resəpi] *Rezept*

TF 5 Girls and boys – together or not?

Minnie wants to play with the boys

Minnie Cruttwell has a problem. She plays in a mixed football team. Minnie is a very good player and she wants to stay with her team. But in England girls have to join a girls' team when they are 12. Minnie says, 'It's really unfair. I like my team. I don't want to change[1].'

Vote[2]

- Girls and boys should do sport together if they want to.
- Girls should do sport with girls, and boys should do sport with boys.

vote

1   What do you think?

a) 👥 *Discuss with your partner.*
– I think girls and boys should do sport in mixed teams/in different teams.
– Girls'/Boys'/Mixed teams are boring/ better/ more fun/...
– Girls are/aren't as good as boys.
– Boys/girls are stronger/bigger/quicker/ better team players/...

b) Vote in your class. Collect the girls' votes first. Then the boys' votes. Are the results different?

2   What about Germany?
Can girls and boys play in the same team in Germany?

---

[1] (to) change [tʃeɪndʒ] *wechseln*   [2] (to) vote (on sth.); vote (n) [vəʊt] *(über etwas) abstimmen; Stimme (bei Abstimmungen)*

TF 6   Football songs 🎧

You'll never walk alone

When you walk through a storm
Hold your head up high
And don't be afraid of the dark.
At the end of the storm
Is a golden sky
And the sweet, silver song of a lark[1].

Walk on through the wind,
Walk on through the rain,
Though your dreams be tossed and blown[2].
Walk on, walk on with hope in your heart,
And you'll never walk alone,
You'll never walk alone.

by Oscar Hammerstein

We are the champions

We are the champions, my friends
And we'll keep on fighting[3] till the end
We are the champions
We are the champions
No time for losers
'Cause we are the champions
Of the world

by Freddie Mercury

1   The songs
a) *Listen to the songs and read the words.*
Which song do you like better? Why?
– The music is better/nicer/ …
– The singer sounds more excited/happier/…
– The song is about support for others/ …

b) *Imagine you are at a match and your team is winning. Which song would you sing? Why?*

2   Now you
Which football songs (German or English) do you know? Have you been to a football stadium? How did you like it?

---

[1] lark [lɑːk] *Lerche*   [2] though your dreams be tossed and blown [tɒst] *etwa: auch wenn deine Träume in Gefahr geraten*   [3] (to) keep on fighting ['faɪtɪŋ] *weiterkämpfen*

TF 7 Tim, a rock and a rope[1] (adapted from Jacqueline Wilson's novel *Cliffhanger*) 🎧

Tim is on an adventure[2] holiday for children. There's just one problem. Tim hates sports – all sports. Here's what Tim wrote in one of his postcards:

▶ *Do you think Tim is enjoying his holiday? Do you think he wants to go abseiling? Why/ Why not? Look at the pictures. What do you think happens?*

Now read on.

Speech bubbles: "Poor Tim!" "AAARGH!!!" "Me... perhaps!!"

Thought bubble: "I wish I was somewhere else!" TIM

Tim. You next.'
  'No!'
  'Yes,' said Jake, our team leader[4].
  'No,' I said.
  'You all have to go sooner or later,' said Jake.
  'Later,' I said.
  'No. Sooner,' said Jake.
  'I can't,' I said.   10
  'Yes, you can, Tim,' said Jake.
'He's scared,' said Giles.
  'We're all scared,' said Jake. 'But you'll see it's easy, Tim. Believe me. Now. Into the harness[5].'   15
  Jake put me into the harness before I could get away. He was telling me things about this rope in this hand, that rope in that hand, but I couldn't listen. All I could hear was this terrible noise inside my head.   20
  'Don't let go of[6] the rope, OK?' said Jake.
  The noise in my head got louder and louder.
  This couldn't be real.   25
I closed my eyes.
  'Tim?' said Jake.
'Open your eyes! Now, your friend Biscuits is waiting for you down   30
there. Come on. Start to walk backwards.'
  I walked backwards one step. Then another. Then I stopped.   35
  'I can't!'
  'Yes, you can,' said Jake. 'You'll see. Don't worry. You can't fall.

POST CARD

Dear Mum and Dad
I promised to write you lots of postcards. But maybe this will be the last postcard you will get. Because we are going abseiling[3] today. It is very dangerous. I could easily fall to my death. I hope you'll see your only son again alive and well.

From Tim

Mr and Mrs R. Parsons,
10 Rainbow Street,
Didcot,
Oxon

---

[1] rope [rəʊp] *Seil*   [2] adventure [əd'ventʃə] *Abenteuer*   [3] (to) abseil ['æbseɪl] *(sich) abseilen*   [4] team leader ['tiːmliːdə] *Gruppenleiter*
[5] harness ['hɑːnɪs] *(Kletter-)Gurt*   [6] (to) let go of sth. *etwas loslassen*

40 You just have to remember, you *don't* let go of the rope.'

I looked at him and started to go back some more. I slipped[1] and suddenly ... I was hanging.

45 'Help!'

I was desperate[2].

I grabbed at[3] the rock.

I let go of the rope!

Suddenly I was sliding[4] backwards,
50 backwards, backwards.

I screamed[5].

I grabbed the rock. I was crying[6].

I heard them up above[7] me. They were shouting.

55 'He's fallen!'

'He's let go of the rope.'

'I *knew* he would'

'Of course Tim had to do it wrong!'

'He's *stuck*[8].'

60 'Don't stop, Tim!' Biscuits called from below.

I turned my head and tried to look at him.

'Help!'

65 'It's OK, Tim. Don't panic,' Jake called down. 'Now. Tim. Listen. You've let go of the rope.'

'I know!'

'But it's OK. You can't fall. You're safe.
70 Believe me.'

'I don't feel safe. I feel *sick*.[9]'

'Well, you can get down in a few seconds. All you have to do is grab the
75 rope.'

'How???'

'Just let go of the rock and ...'

'I can't!' Was Jake
80 mad? I *couldn't* let go.

'You're safe in your harness,' Jake called. 'You needn't hold on to the rock. You just have to grab the rope. See the rope?

I wish I was somewhere else!

TIM

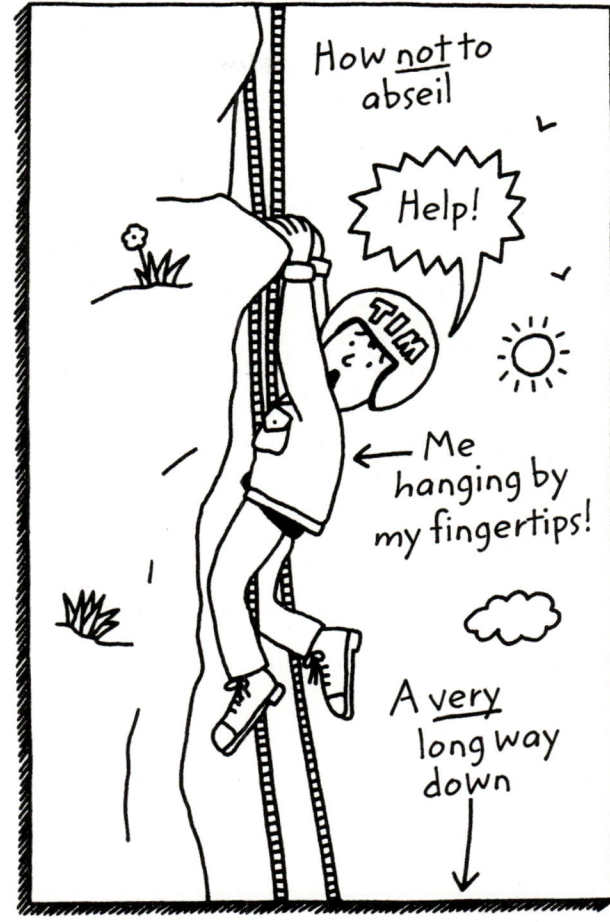

How <u>not</u> to abseil

Help!

← Me hanging by my fingertips!

A <u>very</u> long way down

Tim! Open your eyes!' 85

'I can't look down.'

'Look up. At me,' said Jake.

I opened my eyes a little. Jake was leaning right over the edge, not too terribly far away. He gave me a thumbs-up sign. 90

'That's good. Now. It's OK. Have a break if you like. It's not so bad now, is it?'

'Yes!'

'You can hang there all day if you really 95 want,' said Jake.

'No!'

'Or you can grab that rope and walk down. Mmm?'

I looked up at him. 100

'Can't you pull me up? Please?' I asked.

---

[1] (to) slip [slɪp] *(aus)rutschen* [2] desperate ['despərət] *verzweifelt* [3] (to) grab (at) sth. [græb] *etw. ergreifen* [4] (to) slide, slid, slid [slaɪd], [slɪd] *rutschen, gleiten* [5] (to) scream [skriːm] *(auf)schreien* [6] (to) cry [kraɪ] *weinen* [7] above [ə'bʌv] *über* [8] (to) be stuck [stʌk] *festsitzen*
[9] I feel sick. [sɪk] *Mir ist schlecht.*

'We're trying to get you down, Tim, not up!' said Jake. 'You can do it, Tim.'

He had to be joking![1]

105 'So just grab the rope …' Jake said.

I thought about it. My fingers were hurting terribly. *I couldn't* hang there forever. So I let go of the rock …

I swung round and it was so scary that 110 I closed my eyes and grabbed the rock again.

Jake didn't give up. 'Almost. Try again. Go on.'

So I tried again. My hand was wet with sweat[2] but I got the rope!

115 'Well done!' Jake called. 'There! I knew you could. Just hold on to it this time, eh? Now walk down. One step[3].'

I tried to move my feet. I couldn't feel them inside my boots. I made a little mouse's step.

120 'Great!' said Jake. 'Now another step.'

My other leg moved. And I moved too. I was going down.

'There we go,' said Jake. 'That's it. You're getting it now.'

'I'm doing it!' I said. 125

'That's right. You're doing it, Tim,' Jake called. 'You're almost halfway down[4]. Doing just great. Go on. Nice and easy. Good boy. Well done.'

'I'm doing it,' I whispered, 'I'm doing it. I'm 130 doing it. It's awful. But I'm doing it.'

I went down quicker and quicker – and then suddenly I was at the bottom and Biscuits hit me on the back.

'You did it, you did it, you did it!' Biscuits 135 sang.

Jake was cheering me from right up at the top of the rock.

'Well done, Tim! It wasn't so bad, was it? Do you want to do it again, eh?' 140

I shook[5] my head so hard that my helmet moved.

'Never ever ever again!'

1 Scary

a) Write Tim's next postcard back to his parents.
– Yesterday was great. I went down the cliff …
– Yesterday we went abseiling. It was awful …

b) What's the scariest thing that you've ever done? Make notes (what? where? when? who? how?) and tell the class about it.

POST CARD

Dear Mum and Dad

Mr and Mrs R. Parsons,

10 Rainbow Street,

Didcot,

Oxon

With love from Tim
xxxxxxxx to Mum
x to Dad

---

[1] He had to be joking! *Das war doch wohl nicht sein Ernst!*   [2] wet with sweat [wet], [swet] *schweißnass*   [3] step [step] *Schritt*
[4] halfway down [ˌhɑːfˈweɪ] *auf dem halben Wege nach unten*   [5] (to) shake, shook, shaken [ʃeɪk], [ʃʊk], [ˈʃeɪkən] *schütteln*

TF 8 If you meet a bear …

Safety in bear country

If you are in the mountain parks, you are in bear country. **Parks Canada** looks after the grizzly and black bears that live here.

Here are our bear safety tips.

AVOID[1] BEARS if you can

Here's how…

- Walk in a group of four or more.
- Make noise. Let the bears know that you are coming.
- Watch for fresh bear signs: paw prints, droppings[2], diggings[3].
- Never go near a bear. Stay at least 100 metres away.
- Be extra careful from late July to mid-September. The bears are looking for berries[4] then.

If you meet a bear …

- Never run.
- Stay calm[5] and move carefully.
- If you are in a group, stay together.
- If you have bear spray, get it ready.
- Talk to the bear.
- Leave the area. If this is impossible, wait until the bear moves away.

1 What to do in bear country

Read the tips. Two are wrong. Correct them.

1 To avoid bears be very quiet.
2 Stay away from bears as far as you can.
3 If you meet a bear, don't run.
4 Talk to the bear.
5 In June be extra careful.

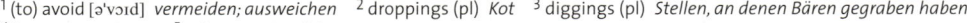

[1] (to) avoid [ə'vɔɪd] *vermeiden; ausweichen*   [2] droppings (pl) *Kot*   [3] diggings (pl) *Stellen, an denen Bären gegraben haben*
[4] berry ['beri] *Beere*   [5] calm [kɑːm] *ruhig*

TF 9   Poems – the four seasons[1]   🎧

1   Before you read

a) *Write down the names of the four seasons of the year. Add five words that go with each season.*

b) 👥 *Swap and compare with a partner.*

c) *Now read the poems. Which poem goes with which season?*

Who has seen the wind?

Who has seen the wind?
　　Neither I nor you[2] ;
But when the leaves hang trembling[3]
　　The wind is passing through.

Who has seen the wind?
　　Neither you nor I;
But when the trees bow down[4] their heads
　　The wind is passing by.

by Christina Rossetti

August heat

In August when the days are hot,
I like to find a shady spot[5],
And hardly[6] move a single bit

　　And sit –

　　　　And sit –

　　　　　　And sit!

anonymous

---

[1] season ['siːzn] *Jahreszeit*　[2] neither I nor you ['naɪðə … nɔː, 'niːðə … nɔː] *weder ich noch du*　[3] when the leaves hang trembling ['tremblɪŋ] *wenn die Blätter zitternd herabhängen*　[4] (to) bow down [ˌbaʊ 'daʊn] *senken*　[5] a shady spot [ˌʃeɪdi 'spɒt] *ein schattiger Platz*　[6] hardly ['hɑːdli] *kaum*

The winter is past

For, lo [1], the winter is past,
The rain is over and gone;
The flowers appear on the earth [2],
The time of the singing of birds is come,
And the voice of the turtle [3]
   Is heard in our land.

from The Song of Solomon

Snow storm

Oh, I am the King of Snowmen,
I've lived here for years and for years.
I've never been slushy [4]
Or melted, or mushy [5],
Or changed to a puddle of tears [6].

Oh, I am the King of Snowmen,
I'm jolly [7] and shiny and fat.
My home, small yet [8] classy,
Has skies blue and glassy
And snowstorms that swirl [9] round my hat

Oh, I am the King of Snowmen,
I've never been known to complain [10],
But sometimes my world shakes
With TERRIBLE earthquakes [11] –
Take cover! [12] They've started again!

by Clare Bevan

2 Your favourite

a) Which poem did you like best? Why?
I liked ... best, because I like the summer/it rhymes/it's funny/easy/...

b) Learn your favourite poem. Recite it to the class.

3 Write your own poem

a) Write a poem like the one below about one of the seasons. You can use a dictionary.
  Wind
   Ice
  November, December
  Tea and biscuits
  Enjoy the season and
  Relax!

b) Read your poem to the class. You can add a picture and put it in your DOSSIER.

---

[1] lo [ləʊ] *siehe! seht!* [2] earth [ɜːð] *Erde* [3] turtle ['tɜːtl] *(Wasser-)Schildkröte* [4] slushy ['slʌʃi] *matschig* [5] mushy ['mʌʃi] *breiig* [6] a puddle of tears ['pʌdl], [tɪəz] *eine Tränenpfütze* [7] jolly ['dʒɒli] *fröhlich* [8] yet [jet] *aber* [9] (to) swirl [swɜːl] *wirbeln* [10] I've never been known to complain [kəm'pleɪn] *etwa: ich habe mich noch nie beschwert* [11] earthquake ['ɜːθkweɪk] *Erdbeben* [12] Take cover! ['kʌvə] *Geh(t) in Deckung!*

TF 10 FANS – a play (adapted from Ann Cartwright's play *Fans*) 🎧

1 Before you read

Look at the photo. What are the four teenagers doing?
The girls are looking at … The boy is …

What else can you say about them?
The girls are friends/… / They like …
The boy likes … / He is …

Now read the play.

Scene:
Four friends are sitting in their form room.
The girls are looking at teen magazines.
Tim is reading a computer magazine.

Kaz __ He's lovely.
5 *Shaz* __ He's got lovely hair.
Jaz __ Lovely eyes.
Kaz ⌉
Shaz ⌋ Ah!
Jaz ⌋
10 *Tim* __ Are you talking about me again?
Kaz ⌉
Shaz ⌋ No!
Jaz ⌋
Tim __ Now you know you are really.
15 *Kaz* ⌉
Shaz ⌋ We're not!
Jaz ⌋
Tim __ Well, who ARE you on about[1], then?
Shaz __ Dermot Devlin!

Jaz __ From the band 20
Celtic Nomads.
Tim __ Oh. Him. He's
rubbish.
Kaz __ He is not!
Tim __ He looks like a girl. 25
Shaz __ He does not!
Tim __ He wears a dress!
Jaz __ It's a kaftan,
actually. It's ethnic[2].
Tim __ You mean hippy. He's stupid. 30
AND he can't sing.
Kaz __ I wish he'd walk into the room.[3]
Shaz __ I wish he'd walk into the room right
now.
Jaz __ I wish he'd walk into the room right 35
now – and I'd – and I'd scream[4].
Kaz ⌉
Shaz ⌋ Oo, and *I* would.

---

[1] (to) be on about … *reden von/über …*   [2] ethnic ['eθnɪk] *exotisch*   [3] I wish he'd walk into the room. [wɪʃ] *etwa: Wenn er (jetzt) hier hereinkäme!*   [4] (to) scream [skriːm] *schreien*

Tim ___ What for?

40   Kaz ___ Because he's lovely.

Shaz ___ You just don't understand, Tim. Read your computer magazine.

Jaz ___ Yeah. All those hard-drives and mega-nothings.

45   Tim ___ There's more point to this than[1] what you do.

Jaz ___ There isn't!

Tim ___ There is. At least I can look at these pictures and buy something. You can't

50   look at a picture of Dermot Drill-Head and buy him, can you?

Kaz ___ Oo!

Shaz ___ Buy Dermot Devlin!

Kaz ___ I'd pay anything[2].

55   Tim ___ But you can't! That's the point. You can't buy him.

Jaz ___ We can buy his music.

Shaz ___ And videos.

Kaz ___ Did you see his latest one?

60   Shaz ___ With him in the boat?

Jaz ___ Sailing towards that woman with the flowers in her hair?

Kaz ___ And the stars above their heads.

Jaz ___ And he moves that oil-drum out of the

65   way and that big bag of rubbish so that he can get to her.

Kaz ___ He's so strong!

Shaz ___ He's so romantic!

Jaz ___ And singing to her at the same time!

Kaz ___ ⎫

Shaz ___ ⎬ Wow!   70

Jaz ___ ⎭

Tim ___ I feel ill.

Kaz ___ Oh, shut up.

Shaz ___ Have you heard his latest song?   75

Jaz ___ Oh, you mean 'Siren Dream'?

Shaz ___ No, no, that was his last one.

Kaz ___ Oh, I know the one! 'Tidal Wave Sensation'?

Shaz ___ No! That's the CD album. I mean his   80 very latest, 'Flowing From The Heart'.

Kaz ___ Oh, yeah! I've heard that one! It's ever so romantic.

Tim ___ You do waste your money on that sad singer.   85

Jaz ___ He's not a sad singer! He's THE BUSINESS[3]!

Tim ___ It's such a shame[4].

Kaz ___ What is?

Tim ___ You're just sad and totally obsessed[5].   90

Shaz ___ Let's have a look at YOUR magazine, then.

Tim ___ Give us that back!

---

[1] there's more point to this than … *das macht mehr Sinn als …*   [2] anything *hier: alles*   [3] the business ['bɪznəs] *etwa: er ist DER HIT*
[4] such a shame [ˌsʌtʃ_ə ˈʃeɪm] *so ein Jammer, so eine Schande*   [5] obsessed [əbˈsest] *besessen*

Kaz — Yeah. Let's see how wonderful it is. Two
95   pounds fifty?! Oh, you do waste your
            money on this sad computer stuff!

Tim — It's not sad! A madman singer in
            a dress singing a song to his girlfriend
            whilst[1] sitting on an oil-drum! Now
100   THAT'S sad!

Jaz — Look at this! Page 14! Wow! New
            games!

Kaz — 'Deadliest Mortality Blood-Spurt
            Revenge'[2]? What kind of game's that?

105 Tim — A really good one.

Jaz — What do you have to do?

Tim — I'm not telling you.

Jaz — Why not?

Tim — 'Cause you'll make fun of me, that's
110   why not.

Kaz — Now why should we make fun of your
            very serious computer magazine?

Shaz — We wouldn't do that, would we?

Jaz — Certainly not. We're mature[3].

115 Kaz — So go on, Tim.

Tim — All right, but you'd better not make fun
            of it 'cause it's really serious.

Jaz — We won't.

Tim — Well – There's two gangs – The Bloods
120   and the Spurts – and you get to be in
            one of the gangs and fight the other
            one.

Kaz —
Shaz — What a load of rubbish!
Jaz —   125

Tim — I knew it! Shut up!

Kaz — Sounds really boring.

Tim — Boring?! It's brilliant! I've got the whole
            series.

Shaz — Series? There's more of them?   130

Tim — Yeah! There's 'Deadliest Mortality
            Blood-Spurt Revenge: The Beginning'
            followed by –

Jaz — Oh, don't tell me any more!

Kaz — How dreary[4]!   135

Tim — I'm getting the next one for my
            birthday! You should see all the stuff
            I've got. And the posters! And what
            I really want is a virtual-reality set-up
            where I can really INTERACT with the   140
            gangs!

Pause.

Kaz — Shame, isn't it?

Shaz — Yeah. Sad.

Kaz — He's just totally obsessed.   145

Tim — Look who's talking![5]

---

[1] whilst [waɪlst] *während*   [2] Deadliest Mortality Blood-Spurt Revenge *Name eines Computerspiels, in dem viel Blut vergossen wird*
[3] mature [məˈtʃʊə] *reif, vernünftig*   [4] dreary [ˈdrɪərɪ] *öde, langweilig*   [5] Look who's talking! *Das musst du/müsst ihr gerade sagen!*

Kaz __ Look out. Teacher's coming.

Shaz __ She'll be in here with her X-Files
magazine again.

150 *Jaz* __ She's on about that stuff all the time.

Shaz __ Now she IS obsessed.

Kaz __
Shaz __
Jaz __ She's such a fanatic!
Tim __

2 Right or wrong?

*Are the statements right or wrong? Correct the
wrong statements.*

1 Kaz, Shaz and Jaz are talking about Tim at
the beginning of the scene.
2 Tim likes Dermot Devlin.
3 Dermot Devlin is a film star.
4 Kaz, Shaz and Jaz think computer
magazines are interesting.
5 Tim thinks the girls are obsessed with
Dermot Devlin.
6 Tim likes video games.
7 The girls don't make fun of Tim.
8 All four make fun of the teacher.

3 Act out the play

*Make groups of eight. Four students learn the first
half of the play (pp. 124–125), four learn the second
half (pp. 126–127). Perform the play for your class.*

Skills File – Inhalt

Im **Skills File** findest du Hinweise zu Arbeits- und Lerntechniken. Was du in den Skills-Kästen der Units gelernt hast, wird hier näher erläutert.

Was du bereits aus Band 2 von English G 21 kennst, ist mit **REVISION** gekennzeichnet, z. B.
– **REVISION Understanding new words**, Seite 128
– **REVISION Learning words**, Seite 129.

Viele neue Hinweise helfen dir bei der Arbeit mit Hör- und Lesetexten, beim Sprechen, beim Schreiben von eigenen Texten, bei der Sprachmittlung und beim Lernen von Methoden.

Manchmal gibt es auch Aufgaben dazu.

STUDY AND LANGUAGE SKILLS

SF REVISION   Understanding new words

Immer gleich im Wörterbuch nachschlagen?

Das Nachschlagen unbekannter Wörter im Wörterbuch kostet Zeit und nimmt auf Dauer den Spaß am Lesen. Oft geht es auch ohne Wörterbuch!

Was hilft mir, unbekannte Wörter zu verstehen?

1. Bilder sind eine große Hilfe. Sie zeigen oft die Dinge, die du im Text nicht verstehst. Schau sie dir deshalb vor dem Lesen genau an.

2. Oft hilft dir der Textzusammenhang, also die Wörter, die vor oder nach dem unbekannten Wort stehen,
   z. B. *We must hurry. Our train* **departs** *in ten minutes.*

3. Viele englische Wörter werden ähnlich wie im Deutschen geschrieben oder klingen ähnlich, z. B. **wonderful**, **electrician**, **president**.

4. Manchmal stecken in neuen Wörtern bekannte Teile,
   z. B. **arrival**, **friendly**, **snowshoes**.

Hmm, *culture* sieht so aus wie das deutsche Wort „Kultur", oder?

> • Alles klar? Dann überlege, was diese Wörter bedeuten:
> **hilly • head of state • a winning shot • useful • canal • material • realistic • colony • official**

Super! Das ist es!

SF REVISION   Learning words

Worauf solltest du beim Lernen und Wiederholen von Vokabeln achten?

– Führe dein Vokabelverzeichnis, dein Vokabelheft oder deinen Karteikasten aus Klasse 6 weiter.

– Lerne immer 7–10 Vokabeln auf einmal.

– Lerne neue und wiederhole alte Vokabeln regelmäßig – am besten jeden Tag 5–10 Minuten.

– Lerne mit jemandem zusammen. Fragt euch gegenseitig ab oder übt die Wörter mit Lernspielen (z.B. Vokabel-Domino, Schiffe versenken, Quartett, *Vocabulary Action Sheets*).

– Du weißt nach zwei Jahren Englischlernen wahrscheinlich, mit welchen Methoden du am besten Vokabeln lernst: durch Hören und Nachsprechen, durch Bilder, am Computer (z.B. mit deinem *e-Workbook* oder dem *English Coach*) – oder indem du dir eigene Geschichten um die neuen Vokabeln ausdenkst, sie in Texte einbaust oder dich beim Vokabellernen in deinem Zimmer oder der Wohnung bewegst.

– Schreib die neuen Wörter auch immer auf und überprüfe die Schreibweise mithilfe des *Dictionary* oder *Vocabulary*.

Wie kannst du Wörter besser behalten?

Wörter und Wendungen kannst du besser behalten, wenn du sie in Wortgruppen sammelst und ordnest. Dazu gibt es verschiedene Möglichkeiten.

Du kannst …

– **Gegensatzpaare** sammeln, z.B.
old-fashioned – modern
spicy – mild
forget – remember

old-fashioned   modern   spicy   mild

– Wörter mit **gleicher Bedeutung** sammeln, z.B.
(to) train – (to) practise; film – movie

– Wörter in **Wortfamilien** sammeln, z.B.
  – **shop, shopper, shopping, shopping list, shop assistant**
  – **(to) ride (a horse/bike), (to) go riding, a bike ride, riding boots, riding hat**

– Wörter in **Wortnetzen** (*networks*) sammeln und ordnen.

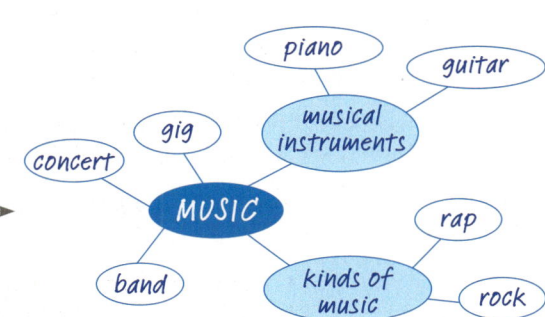

SF **Using an English-German dictionary** ▶ *Unit 1 (p. 26)*

Wann brauche ich ein englisch-deutsches Wörterbuch?

Du verstehst einen Text nicht, weil er zu viele Wörter enthält, die dir unbekannt sind? Dann hilft dir ein englisch-deutsches Wörterbuch weiter.
Im Text „Only a game" (S. 26–28) kommen auch Wörter vor, die du nicht kennst und die auch nicht in den EG 21-Wörterverzeichnissen aufgeführt sind, z. B. *danger, experimental, at your own risk, Roman London, rat, everywhere, voice*. Einige dieser Wörter kannst du sicherlich ableiten oder aus dem Zusammenhang erschließen. Wenn das nicht geht, hilft dir ein englisch-deutsches Wörterbuch.

Play at your own risk.

**Something ran over his foot.
A rat!**

'They started the fire! Stop them!' another voice shouted.

Wie benutze ich ein englisch-deutsches Wörterbuch?

– Die **Leitwörter** (*running heads*) oben auf der Seite helfen dir, schneller zu finden, was du suchst. Auf der linken Seite steht das erste Stichwort, auf der rechten Seite das letzte Stichwort der Doppelseite.

– **rise** ist das **Stichwort** (*headword*). Stichwörter sind alphabetisch geordnet: **r** vor **s**, **ra** vor **re**, **rhe** vor **rhi** usw.

– Die *kursiv* gedruckten Hinweise helfen dir, die für deinen Text passende Bedeutung zu finden.

– Die **Ziffern 1, 2** usw. zeigen, dass ein Stichwort unterschiedlichen Wortarten angehören kann (z. B. Adjektiv, Nomen, Verb).

– **Beispielsätze** und **Redewendungen** sind dem Stichwort zugeordnet. In den Beispielsätzen und Redewendungen ersetzt eine **Tilde** (~) das Stichwort.

– Die **Lautschrift** gibt Auskunft darüber, wie das Wort ausgesprochen und betont wird (→ *English sounds, p. 166*).

– **Unregelmäßige Verbformen**, **besondere Pluralformen**, die **Steigerungsformen der Adjektive** und ähnliche Hinweise stehen in Klammern.

> **riveting**

rink [rɪŋk] Eisbahn
rinse [rɪns] **1** *Nomen*; *für Haare* Tönung **2** *Verb mit Obj*; *Kleidung, Haare* ausspülen; *Geschirr* (ab)spülen

rise [raɪz] **1** *Verb ohne Obj* (**rose, risen**) *aus Stuhl o. Ä.* aufstehen, sich erheben; *von Sonne* aufgehen; *von Rakete* aufsteigen; *von Preis, Temperatur* ansteigen; *von Wasseroberfläche* (an)steigen **2** *Nomen*; *von Preis, Temperatur* Anstieg; *von Wasseroberfläche* (An)Steigen; *von Sozialismus* Aufstieg; *von Gehalt* Gehaltserhöhung; **give ~ to** verursachen
risen [ˈrɪzn] *Part. Perf.* ☞ **rise**
riser [ˈraɪzə]: **be an early / late ~** ein Frühaufsteher / Langschläfer sein
risk [rɪsk] **1** *Nomen* Risiko; **take a ~** ein Risiko eingehen; **at one's own ~** auf eigene Gefahr **2** *Verb mit Obj* riskieren; **let's ~ it** das Risiko gehen wir ein!
risky [ˈrɪski] (**-ier, -iest**) riskant
ritual [ˈrɪtjʊəl] **1** *Nomen* Ritual **2** *Adj* rituell
rival [ˈraɪvl] **1** *Nomen* Rivale, Rivalin; *von Firma, Mannschaft* Konkurrent(in) **2** *Verb mit Obj* (**-ll-**, *AE* **-l-**) *Person* rivalisieren mit; *Firma, Mannschaft* konkurrieren mit; **I can't ~ that** da kann ich nicht mithalten
rivalry [ˈraɪvlri] (*Pl* **-ies**) Rivalität; *zwi-*

• Finde nun heraus, was die folgenden Wörter und Wendungen bedeuten:
1. *at your own risk*
2. *'rose'* in *'The rocket rose into the sky.'*
3. *'rises'* in *'The sun rises in the east.'*
4. *rat*
5. *everywhere*
6. *voice*

• In deinem Wörterbuch werden vermutlich viele Abkürzungen und Symbole verwendet, wie z. B.
jn.
Obj
Pl
USA
Finde heraus, was sie bedeuten.

SF **Using a German-English dictionary** ▶ *Unit 2 (p. 35)*

Wann brauche ich ein deutsch-englisches Wörterbuch?

Stell dir vor, du sollst einen Text über Katrina schreiben. Du findest, dass die
Situation im Internat schwer für sie ist. Aber wie drückt man das auf Englisch
aus? Was heißt „schwer" in diesem Fall?
Hier hilft dir ein deutsch-englisches Wörterbuch.

Wie benutze ich ein deutsch-englisches Wörterbuch?

Viele Dinge sind dir wahrscheinlich vom
English-German dictionary vertraut:

Schwester

– **Leitwörter** (*running heads*) oben auf den Seiten helfen dir, das gesuchte Wort
  schneller zu finden.

– Die **Stichwörter** (*headwords*) sind alphabetisch
  geordnet. **Beispielsätze** und **Redewendungen**
  sind den Stichwörtern zugeordnet. Die **Tilde** (~)
  ersetzt das Stichwort.

– Die *kursiv gedruckten* Hinweise helfen dir, die
  für deinen Text passende Bedeutung zu finden.

– Die **Ziffern 1, 2** usw. zeigen, dass ein Stichwort
  unterschiedlichen Wortarten angehören kann
  (z.B. Adjektiv, Nomen, Verb).

– Bei schwierig auszusprechenden Wörtern stehen
  auch Hinweise zu Aussprache und Betonung.

– Bei kniffligen Wörtern gibt es in vielen
  Wörterbüchern weitere Hilfen und Hinweise.

schwer 1 *Adj; gewichtsmäßig* heavy
['hevi] (*auch Musik, Parfüm*); *schwierig*
difficult, hard (*auch Arbeit*); *Wein, Zigar-*
re strong; *Essen* rich; *Krankheit, Fehler,*
Unfall, Schaden serious ['sɪərɪəs]; *Strafe*
severe; *Gewitter, Kämpfe, Ausschreitun-*
gen heavy, violent; **schwere Zeiten** hard
times; **100 Pfund ~ sein** weigh [weɪ] 100
pounds; **es ~ haben** have a hard time;
das ist ~ zu sagen it's hard to say **2** *Adv*:
~ arbeiten work hard; **~ beschädigt**
Haus o.Ä. severely damaged; **ich bin ~**
erkältet I've got a bad cold; **er ist ~ zu**
verstehen it's hard to understand what
he's saying; **~ enttäuscht sein** be* bit-
terly disappointed; **das will ich ~ hoffen**
I really hope so; ☞ **schwerfallen,**
schwertun

Schwerkraft
☞ **schwer ma**
ancholy ['mel
Schwerpunkt
gen (main) er
Schwert sword
schwertun: sic
culty with sth.
Schwerverbrec
offender
schwerverwun
schwerwiegend
['sɪərɪəs]
Schwester sist
als Anrede

schwer krank

schwer

Das deutsche **schwer** hat drei Hauptbedeutungen:
1) *schwer von Gewicht*: **heavy**;
2) *schwerwiegend, ernst*: **serious**, **bad**;
3) *schwierig*: **difficult**, **hard**, **tough**.

Welche Entsprechung von **schwer** brauchst du in diesen Sätzen?
1. Das Leben im Internat ist schwer für Katrina.
2. Schultaschen sind für jüngere Schüler häufig zu schwer.
3. Heute Morgen war ein schwerer Unfall auf der Autobahn.
4. Die Matheaufgabe ist sehr schwer.
5. Letzte Nacht gab es ein schweres Gewitter.

Tipp

Lies immer erst den **gesamten Wörterbucheintrag**, bevor du dich für eine
bestimmte Übersetzung entscheidest. Nimm nicht einfach die erste
Übersetzung, die dir angeboten wird!

SF **REVISION**   Describing pictures

Wie kann ich Bilder beschreiben?

Wo?
– Um zu sagen, wo etwas abgebildet ist, benutze:
at the top/bottom • **in the foreground/background** •
in the middle • **on the left/right**
– Du kannst diese *phrases* auch kombinieren:
at the bottom on the left • **at the top on the right**
– Diese Präpositionen sind auch hilfreich:
behind • **between** • **in front of** • **next to** • **under**

Wie?
Geh bei der Beschreibung in einer bestimmten
Reihenfolge vor, z. B. von links nach rechts, von oben nach
unten oder vom Vordergrund zum Hintergrund.

Wie kann ich beschreiben, was die Personen auf dem Bild tun?

Um zu sagen, was die Personen auf dem Bild tun, benutze das **present
progressive**.
Robert and Asif <u>are standing</u> inside the London Eye. Robert <u>is taking</u> a photo.

SF **REVISION**   Giving a presentation

Wie mache ich eine gute Präsentation?

Vorbereitung
– Schreib die wichtigsten Gedanken gut geordnet als
Notizen auf, z. B. auf nummerierte Karteikarten oder als
Mindmap.
– Bereite ein Poster oder eine Folie vor. Schreib groß und
für alle gut lesbar.
– Übe deine Präsentation zu Hause vor einem Spiegel.
Sprich laut, deutlich und langsam, mach Pausen.

Durchführung
– Bevor du beginnst, häng das Poster auf bzw. leg deine Folie auf den
ausgeschalteten Projektor und sortiere deine Vortragskarten.
– Warte, bis es ruhig ist. Schau die Zuhörer an.
– Erkläre zu Anfang, worüber du sprechen wirst. Lies nicht von deinen Karten ab,
sondern sprich frei.

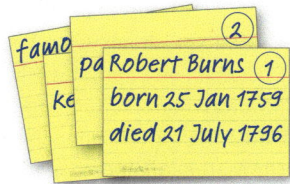

My presentation is about …
First, I'd like to talk about …
Second, …

This picture/photo/…
shows …

Schluss
– Sag, dass du fertig bist.
– Frag die Zuhörenden, ob sie Fragen haben. Bedanke dich fürs Zuhören.

That's the end of my
presentation. Have you got
any questions?

LISTENING AND READING SKILLS

SF REVISION   Listening   ▶ *Unit 1 (p. 13)*

Was muss ich beim *listening* beachten?

Vor dem Hören

– Überlege, worum es in dem Hörtext gehen wird. Frag dich, was du schon über das Thema weißt.
– Lies die Aufgabe gut durch, damit du weißt, worauf du achten sollst – auf die Hauptgedanken oder auf bestimmte Informationen wie z.B. einen Namen, eine Uhrzeit, eine Jahreszahl.
– Bereite dich darauf vor, Notizen zu machen. Leg z.B. eine Tabelle oder Liste an.

Beim Hören

– Keine Panik! Du musst nicht alles verstehen. Konzentriere dich auf das Wesentliche. Oft werden wichtige Informationen auch wiederholt.
– Achte auf Geräusche und unterschiedliche Stimmen. Was ein Sprecher/eine Sprecherin besonders betont, das ist wichtig!
– Wenn du gezielt Informationen suchst, denk an die Aufgabe und lass dich nicht von anderen Einzelheiten ablenken.
  Aufgepasst! Die Informationen, die du suchst, kommen vielleicht in einer anderen Reihenfolge vor, als du sie erwartest.
– Mach nur kurze Notizen, z.B. Anfangsbuchstaben, Symbole oder Stichworte, keine ganzen Sätze.

Nach dem Hören

– Vervollständige deine Notizen sofort.
– Konzentriere dich beim erneuten Hören auf das, was du nicht sicher verstanden hast.

London Eye	Trocadero

SF REVISION   Multiple-choice exercises

Worauf sollte ich bei Multiple-Choice-Aufgaben achten?

– Lies die Frage oder den Satz sehr genau durch.
– Manchmal fällt dir die Lösung sofort ein. Dann findest du die Bestätigung in den Auswahlantworten.
– Lies in jedem Fall alle vorgegebenen Lösungen, bevor du dich entscheidest.
– Sprich die Sätze mit den verschiedenen Lösungsmöglichkeiten leise nach. Oft hört man heraus, was richtig ist.
– Achte darauf, dass du nur **eine** der Antworten ankreuzt.
– Mach erst alle Aufgaben und geh zum Schluss zu den Fragen zurück, bei denen du unsicher bist.

1 Which is a famous London sight?
  A Brandenburg Gate
  B Eiffel Tower
  C Buckingham Palace
  D the Orkney Islands

2 What did Robert and Asif do at the Trocadero?
  A play football
  B eat Indian food
  C visit Asif's family
  D play a new game

SF REVISION Scanning

Lesen, um nach Informationen zu suchen

Du brauchst einen Text nicht genau zu lesen, wenn du nur bestimmte Informationen benötigst. Suche den Text nach Schlüsselwörtern (**key words**) ab und lies nur dort genauer, wo du sie findest.

Wie gehe ich vor?

Schritt 1:
Bevor du auf den Text schaust
Denk an das Schlüsselwort, nach dem du suchst. Es hilft dir, wenn du es aufschreibst.

Schritt 2:
Das Schlüsselwort finden
Geh mit deinen Augen sehr schnell durch den Text. Dabei hast du das Schriftbild oder das Bild des Wortes, nach dem du suchst, vor Augen. Das gesuchte Wort wird dir sofort „ins Auge springen".
Du kannst auch mit dem Finger durch den Text gehen: in breiten Schlingen oder Bewegungen wie bei einem „S", einem „Z" oder einem „U".
Wenn du das Schlüsselwort gefunden hast, lies nur dort weiter, um Näheres zu erfahren.

Schritt 3:
Gegebenenfalls neue Schlüsselwörter finden
Es kann passieren, dass das Schlüsselwort, nach dem du suchst, im Text nicht vorkommt. Dann musst du überlegen, welche anderen Wörter mit der benötigten Information zu tun haben, und nach diesen suchen.
Stell dir z. B. vor, du suchst auf einer Speisekarte ein Gericht mit Fleisch. Das Wort *meat* steht aber nirgends. Dann versuch es z. B. mit *lamb*, *chicken* oder *pork*.

SF Skimming ▶ *Unit 5 (p. 90)*

Lesen, um sich einen Überblick zu verschaffen

Skimming bedeutet, dass du in kurzer Zeit einen Text überfliegst, um dir einen ersten Überblick zu verschaffen, worum es geht. Das ist z. B. sehr nützlich, wenn du herausfinden willst, ob ein Text, den du im Internet oder in einem Buch gefunden hast, die Informationen enthält, nach denen du (z. B. für ein Referat) suchst.

Wie gehe ich vor?

Wichtige Informationen über den Text geben dir

– die **Überschrift**

– **hervorgehobene** Wörter oder Sätze

– die **Bilder** und **Bildunterschriften**

– die **Zwischenüberschriften**

– der **erste Satz** jedes Absatzes

– der **letzte Satz** des Textes

– **Grafiken** und **Statistiken**

– die **Quelle** des Textes

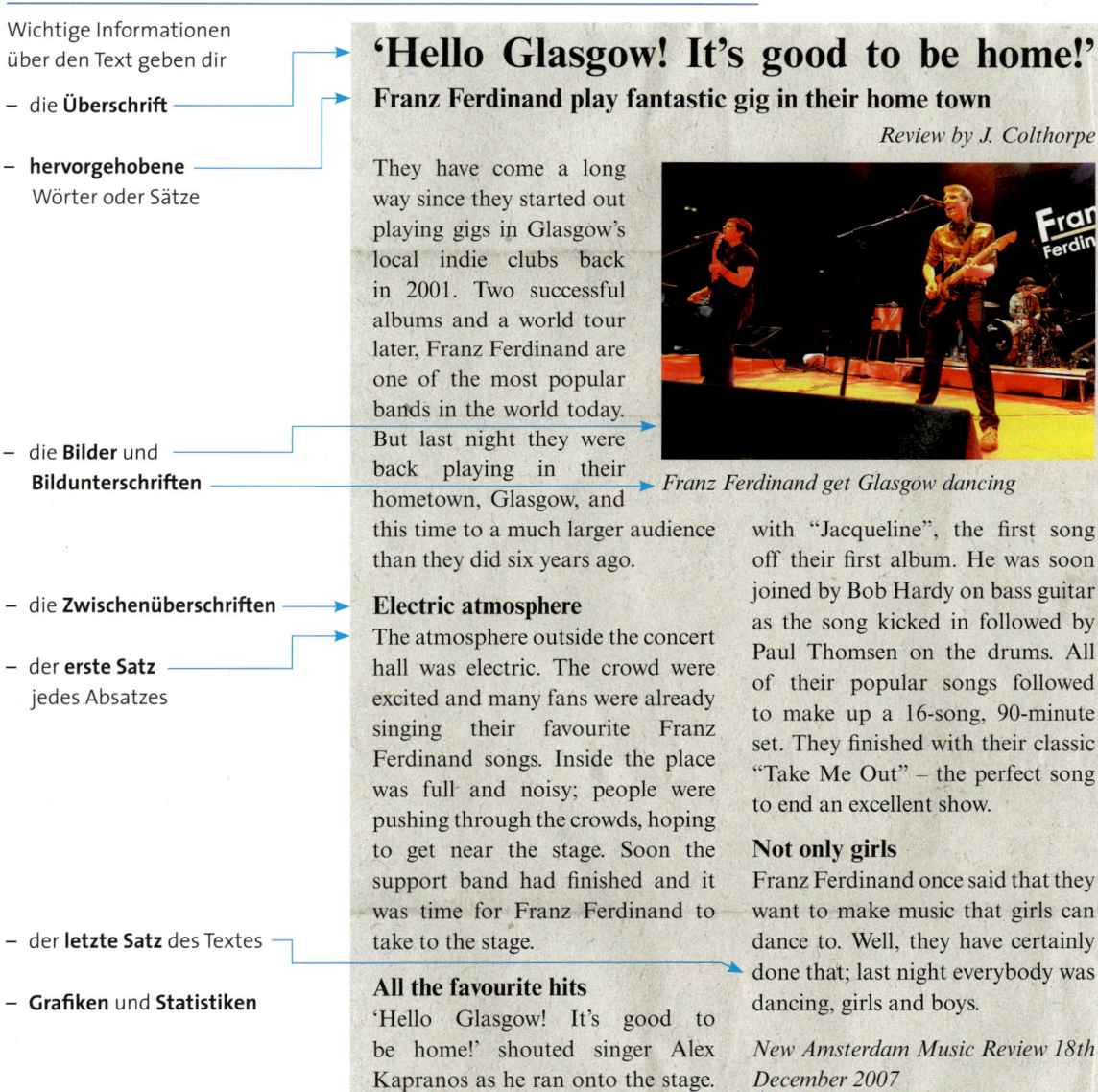

'Hello Glasgow! It's good to be home!'
Franz Ferdinand play fantastic gig in their home town

Review by J. Colthorpe

They have come a long way since they started out playing gigs in Glasgow's local indie clubs back in 2001. Two successful albums and a world tour later, Franz Ferdinand are one of the most popular bands in the world today. But last night they were back playing in their hometown, Glasgow, and this time to a much larger audience than they did six years ago.

Franz Ferdinand get Glasgow dancing

Electric atmosphere
The atmosphere outside the concert hall was electric. The crowd were excited and many fans were already singing their favourite Franz Ferdinand songs. Inside the place was full and noisy; people were pushing through the crowds, hoping to get near the stage. Soon the support band had finished and it was time for Franz Ferdinand to take to the stage.

All the favourite hits
'Hello Glasgow! It's good to be home!' shouted singer Alex Kapranos as he ran onto the stage. The crowd cheered as Alex started with "Jacqueline", the first song off their first album. He was soon joined by Bob Hardy on bass guitar as the song kicked in followed by Paul Thomsen on the drums. All of their popular songs followed to make up a 16-song, 90-minute set. They finished with their classic "Take Me Out" – the perfect song to end an excellent show.

Not only girls
Franz Ferdinand once said that they want to make music that girls can dance to. Well, they have certainly done that; last night everybody was dancing, girls and boys.

New Amsterdam Music Review 18th December 2007

- Überflieg den Artikel, um herauszufinden, worum es darin geht.
- Dann löse die Aufgabe 1 auf Seite 90.

SF REVISION Taking notes

Worum geht es beim Notizenmachen?

Wenn du beim Lesen oder Zuhören Notizen machst, kannst du dich später besser daran erinnern, wenn du etwas vortragen, nacherzählen oder einen Bericht schreiben sollst.

Wie mache ich Notizen?

In Texten oder Gesprächen gibt es immer wichtige und unwichtige Wörter. Die wichtigen Wörter werden Schlüsselwörter (**key words**) genannt und nur die solltest du notieren. Meist sind das Substantive und Verben, manchmal auch Adjektive oder Zahlen.

Hmm, da hab ich wohl ein paar Symbole zu viel benutzt ...

> **Tipp**
> - Verwende Ziffern (z. B. „7" statt „seven").
> - Verwende Symbole und Abkürzungen, z. B. ✔ (für Ja) und **+** (für und) oder GB für Great Britain, K. für Katrina.
>   Du kannst auch eigene Symbole erfinden.
> - Verwende **not** oder ✕ statt „doesn't" oder „don't".

SF REVISION Marking up a text

Wann sollte ich einen Text markieren?

Du hast einen Text mit vielen Fakten vor dir liegen und sollst später über bestimmte Dinge berichten. Dann wird es dir helfen, die für dich wichtigen Informationen im Text zu markieren.

Wie gehe ich am besten vor?

Lies den Text und markiere nur die für dein Thema wichtigen Informationen. Nicht jeder Satz enthält für deine Aufgabe wichtige Wörter und oft reicht es aus, nur ein oder zwei Wörter in einem Satz zu markieren.

– Du kannst wichtige Wörter einkreisen.

– Du kannst sie unterstreichen.

– Du kannst sie mit einem Textmarker hervorheben.

ABER:
Markiere nur auf Fotokopien von Texten oder in deinen eigenen Büchern.

The **British Museum** has one of the largest and most fascinating collections of ⟨mummies⟩ in the world outside of Cairo. The collection of mummies shows the visitor the unusual way the Egyptian people ⟨prepared the dead Pharaoh⟩s before they

The **British Museum** has one of the largest and most fascinating collections of mummies in the world outside of Cairo. The collection of mummies shows the visitor the unusual way the Egyptian people prepared the dead Pharaohs before they

The **British Museum** has one of the largest and most fascinating collections of mummies in the world outside of Cairo. The collection of mummies shows the visitor the unusual way the Egyptian people prepared the dead Pharaohs before they

MEDIATION SKILLS

SF REVISION   Mediation

Wann muss ich zwischen zwei Sprachen vermitteln?

Manchmal musst du zwischen zwei Sprachen vermitteln. Das nennt
man **mediation**.

1. Du gibst englische Informationen auf Deutsch weiter:
   Du fährst z. B. mit deiner Familie nach Großbritannien und deine
   Eltern oder Geschwister wollen wissen, was jemand in einem
   Café gesagt hat oder was an einer Informationstafel steht.

2. Du gibst deutsche
   Informationen auf
   Englisch weiter:
   Vielleicht ist bei dir zu
   Hause eine
   Austauschschülerin
   aus England
   oder Dänemark zu Gast,
   die kein Deutsch spricht
   und Hilfe braucht.

3. In schriftlichen Prüfungen musst du
   manchmal in einem englischen Text
   gezielt nach Informationen suchen
   und diese auf Deutsch wiedergeben.

Worauf muss ich bei *mediation* achten?

Übersetze nicht alles wörtlich, gib nur das Wesentliche weiter.
Du kannst Unwichtiges weglassen und Sätze anders formulieren.

Well, let's go to the show by car. We can't walk there because of the children. They can't walk so far.

Er will mit dem Auto fahren. Die Kinder können nicht so weit laufen.

Tipp

Verwende kurze und einfache Sätze.
Wenn du ein Wort nicht kennst,
– ersetze es durch ein anderes mit ähnlicher Bedeutung oder
– umschreibe es.   ▶ *Paraphrasing (S. 138)*

SPEAKING AND WRITING SKILLS

SF Paraphrasing ▸ *Unit 3 (p. 55)*

Worum geht es beim Paraphrasing?

Paraphrasing bedeutet, etwas mit anderen Worten zu erklären. Man kann vieles umschreiben, z. B. einen Gegenstand, eine Tätigkeit oder eine Person.

Wie gehe ich beim Paraphrasing vor?

– Man kann mit einem Wort umschreiben, das dieselbe Bedeutung hat:
  to ride a bike is the same as to cycle
  Oder man sagt das Gegenteil:
  to win is the opposite of to lose

– Manchmal braucht man mehrere Wörter, z. B. wenn man etwas beschreibt oder erklären will, wie man es verwendet:
  A pitch is a place for a football match.

– Oder du beginnst mit **It's like …:**
  It's like a house, but it's only for horses.
  (*a riding stable*)

A swimsuit is something that …

– Du kannst zum Umschreiben auch ein allgemeines Wort nehmen (z. B. **a person**, **something**) und das wird mit einem durch **who**, **that** oder **where** eingeleiteten Satz näher erklärt:
  A coach is a person who trains sports teams.
  A swimsuit is something that girls wear when they go swimming.
  A bakery is a place where people can buy bread and rolls.

---

1. Umschreibe ein Wort aus der linken Spalte mit einem Wort aus der rechten Spalte. Benutze **the same as** oder **the opposite of**:
sad is the opposite of … / white is …

sad	parents
white	happy
clean	black
brilliant	dirty
mother/father	great

2. Findest du ein passendes Wort für diese Umschreibungen?
  – **It's a man or woman who looks funny and works in a circus.**
  – **It's something you put food on.**
  – **It's a place where you watch films.**
  – **It's something that you use to play table tennis.**

3. What's wrong here? Correct the sentences.
  – **A horse is a place where lots of football fans go to watch a match.**
  – **A stadium is a meal that you eat in the evening.**
  – **Dinner is an animal you can ride on.**

SF Brainstorming   ▶ *Unit 4 (p. 72)*

Wofür ist Brainstorming gut?

Write a text about a great weekend oder *Prepare a presentation on …* – so oder so ähnlich lauten viele Aufgaben, die dir im Unterricht gestellt werden. Immer wenn du selbst etwas schreiben oder präsentieren sollst, ist es nützlich, wenn du im ersten Schritt möglichst viele Ideen zum Thema sammelst. Dabei hilft dir das Brainstorming.

Wie gehe ich beim Brainstorming vor?

Brainstorming erfolgt in zwei Schritten:

Schritt 1:
Schreib alle Ideen so auf, wie sie dir einfallen. Es ist zunächst völlig egal, ob die Ideen gut sind oder nicht. Du kannst die Ideen durcheinander auf einen Zettel schreiben oder schon etwas geordnet, z. B. jede Idee auf eine neue Zeile.

Schritt 2:
Wenn du fertig bist, lies alle deine Ideen durch und wähle die besten aus. Sortiere deine Ideen und fasse sie sinnvoll zusammen.
Beim Sortieren und Zusammenfassen kannst du z. B. die folgenden Techniken anwenden. Sie kommen dir sicher bekannt vor:

Making a mind map

1. Schreib das Thema in die Mitte eines leeren, unlinierten Blattes Papier. Male einen Kreis oder eine Wolke drum herum.

2. Überleg dir, welche Oberbegriffe zu deiner Sammlung von Ideen passen. Verwende unterschiedliche Farben.

3. Ergänze jede Idee, die zu einem Oberbegriff passt, auf einem Nebenast. Nimm dafür nur wichtige Schlüsselwörter. Du kannst auch Symbole verwenden und Bilder ergänzen.

no homework
sleep – every morning
watch DVDs
disco / party with friends
swimming pool
no jobs for parents
parents not at home
hang out

The 5 Ws
Schreib die 5 W-Fragen **Who? What? When? Where? Why?** in eine Tabelle.
Schreib deine Ideen zu jeder Frage darunter.

who	what	when	where	why
I + friends no parents	do sports go to disco chat	Friday Saturday	at home at friends' swimming pool	no homework no jobs to do have fun

WRITING COURSE – ZUSAMMENFASSUNG

The steps of writing

1. Brainstorming – erst Ideen sammeln, dann sortieren (s. S.139).
2. Schreiben. Dabei achte darauf,
   – deine Sätze zu verbinden und auszubauen (*Writing better sentences*)
   – deinen Text gut zu strukturieren (*Using paragraphs*)
   – bei einem Bericht die 5 Ws abzudecken (*Writing a report*).
3. Deinen Text inhaltlich und sprachlich überprüfen (*Correcting your text*).

Writing better sentences ▶ *Unit 4, Step 2 (p. 78)*

REVISION Linking words

Eine Geschichte klingt interessanter, wenn man die Sätze mit **linking words** miteinander verbindet. Dazu gehören:

– **Time phrases** wie **at 7 o'clock, every morning, later, suddenly, then, next** ...
– **Konjunktionen** wie **and, because, but, so, when, while**
– **Relativpronomen** wie **that** und **who**. ▶ *Unit 3 (p. 54)*

Adjektive und Adverbien

– Mit Adjektiven kannst du Personen, Orte oder Erlebnisse genauer und interessanter beschreiben. Vergleiche: **The man looked into the room.**
   ▶ **The young man looked into the empty room.**
– Mit Adverbien kannst du beschreiben, **wie** jemand etwas macht:
   The young man looked nervously into the empty room.

Using paragraphs ▶ *Unit 2 (p. 39)*

REVISION Structuring a text

Ein Text ist viel besser zu verstehen, wenn er mehrere Absätze enthält:
– eine Einleitung (**beginning**) – hier schreibst du, worum es geht
– einen Mittelteil (**middle**) – hier schreibst du mehr über dein Thema
– einen Schluss (**end**) – hier bringst du den Text zu einem interessanten Ende.

REVISION Topic sentences

Beginne einen Absatz mit kurzen, einleitenden Sätzen (**topic sentences**), weil sie den Lesern sofort sagen, worum es geht, z.B.
1. Orte: **My trip to ... was fantastic. / ... is famous for ... / ... is a great place**.
2. Personen: **... is great/funny/interesting/clever ...**
3. Aktivitäten: **... is great fun. / Lots of people ... every day.**

Wie kann ich meine Absätze interessant gestalten?

– Beginne mit einem interessanten Einstiegssatz:
   Guess what happened to me today! / Did I tell you that ...?
– Fang für jeden neuen Aspekt einen neuen Absatz an.
– Beende deinen Text mit einer Zusammenfassung oder etwas Persönlichem.

Writing a report – collecting and organizing ideas ▶ *Unit 3 (p. 64)*

Worauf kommt es bei einem Bericht an?

Wenn du einen Bericht (z. B. über ein Spiel, einen Ausflug) schreibst, beachte:
– Gib dem Leser **eine schnelle Orientierung**, was passiert ist.
– Beginne mit **wichtigen Informationen** und gib erst dann Detailinformationen.
– Ein Bericht gibt immer Antworten auf die **5 Ws**:
  Who? What? When? Where? Why? und manchmal auch How?

Correcting your text ▶ *Unit 5 (p. 97)*

Ein Text ist noch nicht „fertig", wenn du ihn zu Ende geschrieben hast. Du solltest ihn immer mehrmals durchlesen:
– einmal, um zu sehen, ob er vollständig und gut verständlich ist
– noch einmal, um ihn auf Fehler zu überprüfen.

tomato [təˈmɑːtəʊ], *pl*
tomatoes Tomate II

wife [waɪf], *pl* wives [waɪvz]
Ehefrau II

drop (-pp-) [drɒp] fallen lassen I

forget (-tt-) [fəˈget] vergessen I

Spelling mistakes

Lies deinen Text langsam, Wort für Wort, Buchstabe für Buchstabe. Wenn du unsicher bist, hilft dir ein Wörterbuch. Beachte folgende Regeln:

> **Tipp**
>
> – Manche Wörter haben Buchstaben, die man nicht spricht, aber schreibt, z. B. walk, know.
>
> – Manchmal ändert sich die Schreibweise, wenn ein Wort eine Endung erhält, z. B. take → taking, grumble → grumbled, fly → flies, run → running, plan → planned.

Grammar mistakes

> **Tipp**
>
> – Im **simple present** merke: *He, she, it* – das „s" muss mit! z. B. she knows.
>
> – **Unregelmäßige Verben**: Manche Verben bilden das *simple past* und das Partizip Perfekt (*past participle*) unregelmäßig. Lerne diese Formen. Die Liste steht auf S. 214–215: go – went – gone; buy – bought – bought.
>
> – **Verneinung bei Vollverben**: Im *simple present* mit don't/doesn't, im *simple past* mit didn't, z. B. He doesn't speak French, he didn't learn it at school.
>
> – **Satzstellung**: Im Englischen gilt immer (auch im Nebensatz):
> a) subject – verb – object (SVO) ...   when I saw my brother.
>   als ich meinen Bruder sah.
> b) Orts- vor Zeitangabe I bought a nice book in the city yesterday.

> **Tipp**
>
> Führe eine Liste der Fehler, die du oft machst und nutze sie beim Schreiben als persönliche Checkliste. Ergänze sie wenn dein Lehrer/deine Lehrerin dich auf weitere Fehler aufmerksam macht. –
> Ein Beispiel findest du in ▶ *Unit 5 (p. 97)*

Grammar File – Inhalt

Im **Grammar File** (S. 142–149) wird zusammengefasst, was du in den fünf Units **über die englische Sprache** lernst.

In der **linken Spalte** findest du **Beispielsätze** und **Übersichten**, z.B.

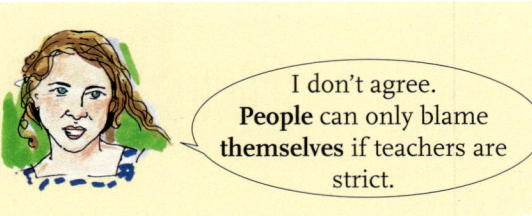

> I don't agree. **People** can only blame **themselves** if teachers are strict.

Reflexive pronouns

Singular

myself	(ich) mir/mich
yourself	(du) dir/dic̶
himself	(er) si̶c̶
herself	(s̶

In der **rechten Spalte** stehen **Erklärungen** und nützliche **Hinweise**. Das **rote Ausrufezeichen** (**!**) macht dich auf besondere Fehlerquellen aufmerksam.

Hinweise wie ▶ *Unit 1 (p. 15)* • *P 4–5 (p. 21)* zeigen dir, zu welcher Unit und welcher Seite ein **Grammar-File-**Abschnitt gehört und welche Übungen du dazu im *Practice*-Teil findest.

Die **grammatischen Fachbegriffe** (*grammatical terms*) kannst du auf Seite 149 nachschlagen.

Am Ende der Abschnitte stehen wieder kleine Aufgaben zur Selbstkontrolle. Schreib die Lösungen in dein Heft. Überprüfe sie dann auf Seite 148.

Unit 1

GF 1 The present perfect and the simple past

Das *present perfect* und das *simple past*

---

a) REVISION The simple past

Last weekend Robert **went** to London with his parents.

In the afternoon they **visited** the Tower, and then they **took** the Tube to Waterloo.

Asif **met** them at the London Eye and they all **had** a great time.

▶ *Unit 1 (p.15)* • *P 4–5 (p.21)*

Die einfache Form der Vergangenheit

Mit dem *simple past* berichtest du über Vergangenes – z.B., wenn du eine Geschichte erzählst.
Das *simple past* drückt aus, dass etwas zu einem **bestimmten Zeitpunkt** oder **in einem bestimmten abgeschlossenen Zeitraum** in der Vergangenheit geschah. (Frage: **Wann?**)
Daher findest du in *simple past*-Sätzen oft **genaue Zeitangaben** wie *last weekend, yesterday, a week ago, in 2005.*

---

b) REVISION The present perfect

Asif **has** already **visited** the London Trocadero.
… hat schon mal … besucht

He **has** always **wanted** to go on the London Eye, but he **hasn't done** that yet.
… hat schon immer … gehen wollen
… hat … noch nicht getan

He and his friends **have** often **been** to Brick Lane Market.
… sind schon oft … gewesen

▶ *Unit 1 (p.16)* • *P 8–9 (p.23)*

Das *present perfect*

Mit dem *present perfect* drückst du aus, dass etwas **irgendwann** in der Vergangenheit geschehen ist.
Daher findest du oft **Adverbien der unbestimmten Zeit** in *present perfect*-Sätzen, z.B.

already	schon (mal)	*always*	(schon) immer
just	gerade (eben)	*never*	(noch) nie
not … yet	noch nicht	*often*	(schon) oft
ever?	jemals?	*yet?*	schon?

! Beim *present perfect* ist der genaue Zeitpunkt des Geschehens nicht wichtig oder nicht bekannt.

---

c) Extra Present perfect or simple past?

1 Have you **ever** tried Turkish food?

Yes, I have.

2 And **when did** you **try** it?

3 We **went** to a Turkish restaurant **last Saturday**.

▶ *Unit 1 (p.17)* • *P 11 (p.24)*

***Present perfect* oder *simple past*?**

◀ 1 Asif fragt, ob Robert **überhaupt schon mal** türkisch gegessen hat – also *present perfect*:

Have you *ever* **tried** Turkish food?

◀ 2 Dann möchte er wissen, **wann** das war, und er fragt daher im *simple past*:

*And when **did** you **try** it?*

◀ 3 Robert antwortet im *simple past*, weil er den **genauen Zeitpunkt** nennt:

*We **went** to a Turkish restaurant last Saturday.*

Unit 2

GF 2 REVISION The *will*-future Das Futur mit *will*

Katrina's mum (**Vorhersage**)	Hurry up, Katrina! We**'ll be** late for the ferry.
Katrina (**Vermutung**)	No, we **won't**. I'm ready now. And I think the ferry **will be** a few minutes late anyway.

▶ *Unit 2 (p. 33)* • *P 5 (p. 40)*

Mit *will* + Infinitiv kannst du über die Zukunft sprechen. Du verwendest es für Vorhersagen und Vermutungen.

Die Kurzform von *will not* heißt *won't*.

GF 3 Conditional sentences   Bedingungssätze

a) REVISION Conditional sentences (type 1)

Alison	If they **choose** you, you**'ll be** a star. Wenn sie dich wählen, bist du … / Wenn sie dich wählen, wirst du … sein.
Linda	If I **don't get** to the shop soon, they **won't have** those trendy new bags any more.

▶ *Unit 2 (p. 34)* • *P 9 (p. 42)*

Bedingungssätze (Typ 1)

Du kennst bereits Bedingungssätze vom Typ 1 („**Was** ist**, wenn …**"-Sätze).
Sie sagen aus, was unter bestimmten Bedingungen geschieht oder nicht geschieht:

if-Satz (Bedingung)	Hauptsatz (Folge)
If they **choose** *you,*	*you***'ll be** *a star.*
simple present	**will-future**

b) Conditional sentences (type 2)

If a film-maker **chose** me for one of his films, I **would be** famous.

Wenn ein Filmemacher mich für einen seiner Filme auswählen würde, wäre ich berühmt / würde ich berühmt.

I **wouldn't live** here if I **was** rich and famous.

Ich würde nicht hier wohnen, wenn ich reich und berühmt wäre.

▶ *Unit 2 (p. 35)* • *P 10–11 (p. 42)*

Bedingungssätze (Typ 2)

Bedingungssätze vom Typ 2 sind
„**Was** wäre**, wenn …**"-Sätze.
Sie drücken aus, was unter bestimmten Bedingungen **sein würde**, aber doch eher unwahrscheinlich ist (oder sogar unmöglich):
Es ist unwahrscheinlich, dass Fiona von einem Filmemacher ausgewählt werden wird. Also wird sie wahrscheinlich auch nicht berühmt.

if-Satz (Bedingung)	Hauptsatz (Folge)
If a film-maker **chose** *me,*	*I* **would be** *famous.*
simple past	**would + infinitive**

(Kurzform von *I/you/he/…* would: *I'd / you'd / he'd / …*)

❗ Im *if*-Satz steht **kein *would***. Also nicht:
If a film-maker ~~would choose~~ *me, …*

If I **had** enough money, I **could** buy a new bike.
…, könnte ich mir ein neues Rad kaufen.

Im Hauptsatz kann auch *could* („könnte") stehen.

Vervollständige die Sätze in deinem Heft. Achte auf die richtige Form der Verben.

1 If the other girls … (call) Latisha names, she wouldn't listen.
2 Latisha would forget the girls if she … (be) Katrina.
3 If people … (call) you Fishface, you … (be) upset too. Right?
4 What would you do if classmates … (call) you names?

Unit 3

GF 4 **Relative clauses**   Relativsätze

Mit Relativsätzen sagst du genauer,
wen oder was du meinst.

The girl who plays for United U14s is Latisha.
Das Mädchen, das für die U14 von *United* spielt, …

◄ In Relativsätzen, die **Personen** beschreiben,
verwendest du **who**:
  the man / the woman / people who …
  der Mann, der … / die Frau, die … / Leute, die …

Banglaboy is **a boy** who Latisha knows from the festival in Birmingham.
… ein Junge, den Latisha vom Festival … kennt.

Are there **things** that you don't like?
… Sachen, die du nicht magst?

◄ In Relativsätzen, die **Dinge** (und Tiere) beschreiben,
verwendest du **that**:
  things / the dish / an animal that …
  Sachen, die … / das Gericht, das … / ein Tier, das …

Mrs Byrd has cooked **a dish** that Philipp likes.
… ein Gericht, das Philipp mag.

… **things** which you don't like
The girl that plays for United U14s …

Für Dinge (und Tiere) wird auch *which* verwendet.
Und manchmal findest du auch *that* für Personen.

The girl   **who plays**   football …

Das Mädchen, **das** Fußball **spielt** …

! Beachte die unterschiedliche Wortstellung in englischen und deutschen Relativsätzen.

▶ *Unit 3 (p. 54)* • *P 3–4 (p. 61)*

Wo brauchst du who, wo brauchst du that?

1 Philipp is the German boy … is staying with Latisha.
2 Latisha thinks football is a sport … is really hard work.
3 What's the name of the player … scored two goals in United U14s' last match?

Unit 4

GF 5 Modals and their substitutes Modale Hilfsverben und ihre Ersatzverben

Wenn du sagen willst, dass jemand etwas tun **kann, darf** oder **muss**, dann verwendest du *can, may, must* oder ihre **Ersatzverben**:

a) „können": *can – (to) be able to*

Katrina can play the fiddle.
Robert doesn't play an instrument,
but he's able to DJ. kann auflegen

Robert was ill last Saturday,
so he wasn't able to DJ. konnte nicht auflegen

Do you think he'll be able to DJ
next Saturday? wird auflegen können

I could hear music, but I couldn't see anybody.
Ich konnte Musik hören, aber ich konnte niemanden sehen.

„können": *can – (to) be able to*

– **Gegenwart** (wenn jemand etwas tun **kann**):
  can und *am/is/are able to*

– **Vergangenheit** (wenn jemand etwas tun **konnte**):
  was/were able to

– **Zukunft** (wenn jemand etwas tun **können wird**):
  will be able to

Zu *can* gibt es auch die Vergangenheitsform *could*. Sie steht vor allem in verneinten Sätzen und Fragen und mit Verben der Wahrnehmung *(see, hear, ...)*.

b) „dürfen": *can, may – (to) be allowed to*

Can/May I go to Ashley's party, Mum?
Are you allowed to go to Ashley's
party on Saturday? Darfst du ... gehen?

Emily wasn't allowed to go to the
youth centre last month. durfte nicht gehen

But she'll be allowed to go to Ashley's
party on Saturday. wird gehen dürfen

„dürfen": *can, may – (to) be allowed to*

– **Gegenwart** (wenn jemand etwas tun **darf**):
  can, may und *am/is/are allowed to*

– **Vergangenheit** (wenn jemand etwas tun **durfte**):
  was/were allowed to

– **Zukunft** (wenn jemand etwas tun **dürfen wird**):
  will be allowed to

c) „müssen": *must – (to) have to*

'OK, you can go. But you must be back by ten.'
Emily can go to the party,
but she has to be back by ten. muss zurück sein

Emily was allowed to go to the party, but
she had to be back by ten. musste zurück sein

Emily will have to stay at home tomorrow
evening. wird bleiben müssen

▶ *Unit 4 (p. 70) • P 3–4 (pp. 76–77)*

„müssen": *must – (to) have to*

– **Gegenwart** (wenn jemand etwas tun **muss**):
  must und *has/have to*

– **Vergangenheit** (wenn jemand etwas tun **musste**):
  had to

– **Zukunft** (wenn jemand etwas tun **müssen wird**):
  will have to

Vervollständige den Dialog. Es geht um Ashleys Party am kommenden Wochenende.

*Emily*___ My parents are so strict. I'm sure I ... (not be allowed to) go to Ashley's party.
*Jessica*___ Well, I'm sure I ... (have to) be home by ten again, as always.
*Robert*___ I ... (not be able to) go to the party.

GF 6 **Reflexive pronouns**   Reflexivpronomen

Teachers are too strict. I often ask **myself** why we need a dress code.

I don't agree. **People** can only blame **themselves** if teachers are strict.

Reflexivpronomen *(myself, themselves, …)* bezeichnen dieselbe Person oder Sache wie das Subjekt *(I, people, …)*:

Subjekt		Reflexivpronomen
I	*often ask*	*myself* …
People	*can only blame*	*themselves* …

Ich frage mich oft, …
Die Leute können sich nur selbst die Schuld geben, …

Reflexive pronouns

Singular			Plural		
myself	(ich) mir/mich			**ourselves**	(wir) uns
yourself	(du) dir/dich			**yourselves**	(ihr) euch
himself	(er) sich			**themselves**	(sie) sich
herself	(sie) sich				
itself	(er/sie/es) sich				

Relax! What are you **arguing** about? Some of us **feel** OK in a school uniform, others like jeans and T-shirts better.

! Es gibt eine Reihe von Verben, die im Deutschen mit „sich" gebraucht werden, im Englischen aber ohne Reflexivpronomen.

Beispiele:
(to) argue	<u>sich</u> streiten
(to) feel	<u>sich</u> fühlen
(to) meet	<u>sich</u> treffen
(to) move	<u>sich</u> bewegen
(to) relax	<u>sich</u> entspannen
(to) remember	<u>sich</u> erinnern

Did you **enjoy yourselves** at the party? Habt ihr **euch** gut **amüsiert** auf der Party?

The food is on the table – just **help yourself**. Das Essen steht auf dem Tisch – **bedien dich** einfach.

! Merke dir die Wendungen
– *Enjoy yourself.*
  „Viel Spaß!" / „Amüsier dich gut!"

– *Help yourself.*
  „Greif zu!" / „Bedien dich!"

▶ *Unit 4 (p. 71)* • *P 5–6 (p. 77)*

Schreib die Sätze in dein Heft. In welchen Sätzen brauchst du ein Reflexivpronomen?

1 Hurry … up or you'll be late for the party.
2 The food is over there. Help …
3 Did you enjoy … at the party?
4 I had a great time, but I felt … very tired the next day.

GF 7 The present progressive with future meaning

Das *present progressive* mit futurischer Bedeutung

I can't come to the phone. I**'m washing** my hair.
... Ich wasche mir gerade die Haare.

Das *present progressive* verwendest du, wenn jemand gerade dabei ist, etwas zu tun.

Robert **is doing** a gig on Friday, and he and his parents **are driving** to their cabin on Saturday morning.

So Robert **isn't going** to Ashley's party at the weekend.

Robert hat am Freitag einen Auftritt, und er und seine Eltern fahren am Samstagmorgen zu ihrer Hütte.

Daher wird Robert am Wochenende nicht zu Ashleys Party gehen.

▶ Unit 4 (p. 72) • P 8 (p. 79)

Du kannst mit dem *present progressive* auch über **feste Pläne** und **Verabredungen** sprechen.

Dabei muss klar sein, dass es sich um etwas Zukünftiges handelt, z.B. durch eine Zeitangabe wie *on Friday, next week, at the weekend, tomorrow.*

Welche festen Verabredungen hat Robert am Wochenende?

1 On Friday night I ... (DJ).
2 On Saturday morning I ... (drive) to our cabin with my parents.
3 And on Sunday morning I ... (go) fishing with my dad.

Lösungen der Grammar-File-Aufgaben

p.148   1 On Friday night I**'m DJ**ing.
2 On Saturday morning I**'m driving** to our cabin with my parents.
3 And on Sunday morning I**'m going** fishing with my dad.

p.147   1 Hurry up or you'll be late for the party.
2 The food is over there. Help yourself/**yourselves.**
3 Did you enjoy yourself/**yourselves** at the party?
4 I had a great time, but I felt very tired the next day.

p.146   My parents are so strict. I'm sure I **won't be allowed to** go to Ashley's party.
Well, I'm sure I **will have to** be home by ten again, as always.
I **won't be able to** go to the party.

p.145/2 1 Philipp is the German boy **who** is staying with Latisha.
2 Latisha thinks football is a sport **that** is really hard work.
3 What's the name of the player **who** scored two goals in United U14s' last match?

p.145/1 1 If the other girls **called** Latisha names, she wouldn't listen.
2 Latisha would forget the girls if she **was** Katrina.
3 If people **called** you 'Fishface', you **would be** upset too. Right?
4 What would you do if classmates **called** you names?

Grammatical terms (Grammatische Fachbegriffe)

adjective ['ædʒɪktɪv]	Adjektiv	good, red, new, boring, ...
adverb ['ædvɜ:b]	Adverb	always, badly, here, really, today
adverb of frequency ['fri:kwənsi]	Häufigkeitsadverb	always, often, never, ...
adverb of indefinite time [ɪn,defɪnət 'taɪm]	Adverb der unbestimmten Zeit	already, ever, just, never, ...
adverb of manner ['mænə]	Adverb der Art und Weise	badly, happily, quietly, well, ...
comparison [kəm'pærɪsn]	Steigerung	old – older – oldest
conditional sentence [kən,dɪʃənl 'sentəns]	Bedingungssatz	I'd call him if I knew his number.
conjunction [kən'dʒʌŋkʃn]	Konjunktion	and, or, but; because, before, ...
going to-**future**	Futur mit *going to*	I'**m going to watch** TV tonight.
if-**clause** ['ɪf klɔːz]	*if*-Satz, Nebensatz mit *if*	**If I see Robert,** I'll tell him.
imperative [ɪm'perətɪv]	Imperativ (Befehlsform)	Open your books. Don't talk.
infinitive [ɪn'fɪnətɪv]	Infinitiv (Grundform des Verbs)	(to) open, (to) see, (to) read, ...
irregular verb [ɪ,regjələ 'vɜ:b]	unregelmäßiges Verb	(to) go – went – gone
modal ['məʊdl]	modales Hilfsverb, Modalverb	can, could, may, must, ...
negative statement [,negətɪv 'steɪtmənt]	verneinter Aussagesatz	I don't like bananas.
noun [naʊn]	Nomen, Substantiv	Sophie, girl, brother, time, ...
object ['ɒbdʒɪkt]	Objekt	My sister is writing **a letter**.
object form ['ɒbdʒɪkt fɔːm]	Objektform (der Personalpronomen)	me, you, him, her, it, us, them
past participle [,pɑːst 'pɑːtɪsɪpl]	Partizip Perfekt	cleaned, planned, gone, seen, ...
past progressive [,pɑːst prə'gresɪv]	Verlaufsform der Vergangenheit	At 7.30 I **was having** dinner.
personal pronoun [,pɜːsənl 'prəʊnaʊn]	Personalpronomen (persönliches Fürwort)	I, you, he, she, it, we, they; me, you, him, her, it, us, them
plural ['plʊərəl]	Plural, Mehrzahl	
positive statement [,pɒzətɪv 'steɪtmənt]	bejahter Aussagesatz	I like oranges.
possessive determiner [pə,zesɪv dɪ'tɜːmɪnə]	Possessivbegleiter (besitzanzeigender Begleiter)	my, your, his, her, its, our, their
possessive form [pə,zesɪv fɔːm]	s-Genitiv	Jo's brother; my sister's room
possessive pronoun [pə,zesɪv 'prəʊnaʊn]	Possessivpronomen	mine, yours, his, hers, ours, theirs
preposition [,prepə'zɪʃn]	Präposition	after, at, in, next to, under, ...
present perfect [,preznt 'pɜːfɪkt]	*present perfect*	We'**ve made** a cake for you.
present progressive [,preznt prə'gresɪv]	Verlaufsform der Gegenwart	The Byrds **are having** lunch.
pronoun ['prəʊnaʊn]	Pronomen, Fürwort	
question tag ['kwestʃən tæg]	Frageanhängsel	This place is great, **isn't it?**
question word ['kwestʃən wɜːd]	Fragewort	what?, when?, where?, how?, ...
regular verb [,regjələ 'vɜːb]	regelmäßiges Verb	(to) help – helped – helped
reflexive pronoun [rɪ,fleksɪv 'prəʊnaʊn]	Reflexivpronomen	myself, yourself, themselves, ...
relative clause [,relətɪv 'klɔːz]	Relativsatz	There's the girl **who helped me.**
relative pronoun [,relətɪv 'prəʊnaʊn]	Relativpronomen	who, that, which
short answer [,ʃɔːt_'ɑːnsə]	Kurzantwort	Yes, I am. / No, I don't. / ...
simple past [,sɪmpl 'pɑːst]	einfache Form der Vergangenheit	Jo **wrote** two letters yesterday.
simple present [,sɪmpl 'preznt]	einfache Form der Gegenwart	I always **go** to school by bike.
singular ['sɪŋgjələ]	Singular, Einzahl	
spelling ['spelɪŋ]	Schreibweise, Rechtschreibung	
subject ['sʌbdʒɪkt]	Subjekt	**My sister** is writing a letter.
subject form ['sʌbdʒɪkt fɔːm]	Subjektform (der Personalpronomen)	I, you, he, she, it, we, they
subordinate clause [sə,bɔːdɪnət 'klɔːz]	Nebensatz	I like Scruffy **because I like dogs**.
verb [vɜːb]	Verb	hear, open, help, go, ...
will-**future**	Futur mit *will*	I think it **will be** cold tonight.
word order ['wɜːd_,ɔːdə]	Wortstellung	
yes/no question	Entscheidungsfrage	Are you 13? Do you like comics?

Diese Wörterverzeichnisse findest du in deinem Englischbuch:

- Das **Vocabulary** (Vokabelverzeichnis – S.150–166) enthält alle Wörter und Wendungen, die du lernen musst. Sie stehen in der Reihenfolge, in der sie in den Units vorkommen.
- Das **Dictionary** besteht aus zwei alphabetischen Wörterlisten zum Nachschlagen:
Englisch – Deutsch: S.167–188
Deutsch – Englisch: S.189–208.

So ist das Vocabulary aufgebaut:

- Hier siehst du, wo die Wörter vorkommen.
p.56/A 5 = Seite 56, Abschnitt 5
p.60/P 2 = Seite 60, Übung 2

- Die Lautschrift zeigt dir, wie ein Wort ausgesprochen und betont wird.
(→ Englische Laute: S.166)

- Eingerückte Wörter lernst du am besten zusammen mit dem vorausgehenden Wort, weil die beiden zusammengehören.

- Diese Kästen solltest du dir besonders gut ansehen.

Tipps zum Wörterlernen findest du im Skills File auf der Seite 129.

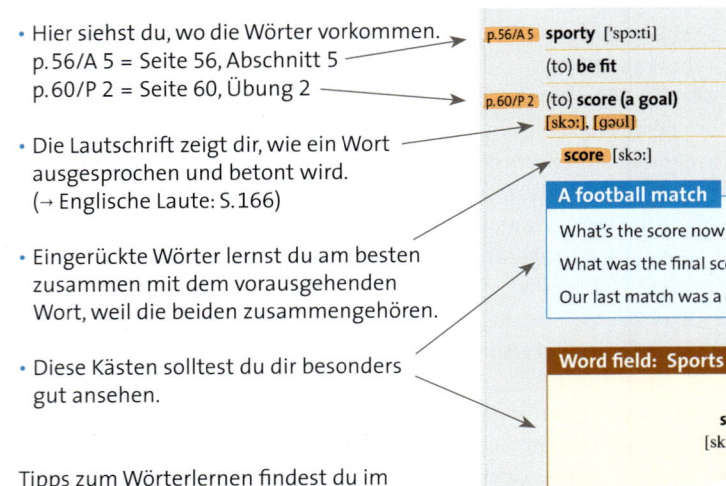

p.56/A 5	sporty ['spɔːti]	sportlich	
	(to) be fit	fit sein	
p.60/P 2	(to) score (a goal) [skɔː], [gəʊl]	ein Tor schießen, einen Treffer erzielen	We won – Smith
	score [skɔː]	Spielstand; Punktestand	

A football match

What's the score now? – 2–0. *(you say: two nil)* ____ Wie steht es
What was the final score? – Chelsea 2, Arsenal 1. ____ Wie war der En
Our last match was a draw, 2–2. *(you say: two all)* ____ Unser let

Word field: Sports

skis
[skiːz]

Abkürzungen:

n	= *noun*	*v*	= *verb*
adj	= *adjective*	*adv*	= *adverb*
prep	= *preposition*	*conj*	= *conjunction*
pl	= *plural*	*no pl*	= *no plural*
p.	= *page*	*pp.*	= *pages*
sb.	= *somebody*	*sth.*	= *something*
jn.	= *jemanden*	*jm.*	= *jemandem*
AE	= *American English*	*BE*	= *British English*

infml = *informal* (umgangssprachlich, informell)

Symbole:

! Hier stehen Hinweise auf Besonderheiten, bei denen man leicht Fehler machen kann.

◄► ist das „Gegenteil"-Zeichen: **slow** ◄► **fast** (**slow** ist das Gegenteil von **fast**)

~ Die **Tilde** in den Beispielsätzen steht für das neue Wort.
Beispiel: **youth** – In her ~ my grandma was very beautiful.

Introduction

p.6	**introduction (to)** [ˌɪntrəˈdʌkʃn]	Einführung (in)	This book is a good ~ **to** a difficult topic.
	youth [juːθ]	Jugend	the time when you are young In her ~ my grandma was very beautiful.
	national [ˈnæʃnəl]	national	**national** ◄► **international**
	festival [ˈfestɪvl]	Fest, Festival, Festspiele	At a ~ you can see lots of bands.
	the United Kingdom (UK) [juˌnaɪtɪd ˈkɪŋdəm], [juː ˈkeɪ]	das Vereinigte Königreich	**!** **the UK** = Great Britain (England, Scotland, Wales) and Northern Ireland *(Nordirland)*
	from **all over** the UK / the world / England	aus dem gesamten Vereinigten Königreich / aus der ganzen Welt / aus ganz England	Madonna is famous **all over** the world. (= auf der ganzen Welt)

Numbers

Im Englischen steht oft ein **Komma** in Zahlen, die größer als 1 000 sind.	**10,000**	= ten thousand
	10,400	= ten thousand four hundred
❗	**10.4**	= ten **point** four (*deutsch:* 10,4 = zehn **Komma** vier)
	1,100,000	= one million one hundred thousand
❗	**1.1 million**[1]	= one **point** one million (*deutsch:* 1,1 Millionen)

[1] ['mɪljən]

	brilliant ['brɪliənt]	toll, genial, großartig	
	kind (of) [kaɪnd]	Art	What **~ of** music do you like? – Rock music. ❗ Was für ein Auto ...? = What **kind of** car ...?
	classical ['klæsɪkl]	klassisch	Do you like Mozart? – Oh yes! I love **~** music.
	concert ['kɒnsət]	Konzert	❗ Betonung auf der 1. Silbe: **concert** ['kɒnsət]
	workshop ['wɜːkʃɒp]	Workshop, Lehrgang	
	(to) DJ ['diː dʒeɪ]	(Musik/CDs/Platten) auflegen *(in der Disko)*	noun: **DJ (disc jockey)** – verb: (to) **DJ**
	steel drum [ˌstiːl 'drʌm]	Steeldrum	**steel drums**
	steel [stiːl]	Stahl	
	drum [drʌm]	Trommel	❗ (to) **play** the **drums** *(pl)* = Schlagzeug spielen
p.7	**fiddle** ['fɪdl] *(infml)*	Fiedel, Geige	❗ (to) **play** the **fiddle** = Geige spielen
	north [nɔːθ]	Norden; nach Norden; nördlich	

north [nɔːθ]
north-west [ˌnɔːθ'west]   **north-east** [ˌnɔːθ'iːst]
west [west]   **east** [iːst]
south-west [ˌsaʊθ'west]   **south-east** [ˌsaʊθ'iːst]
south [saʊθ]

p.8	**hostel** ['hɒstl]	Herberge, Wohnheim	A **youth ~** is usually cheaper than a hotel.
	instrument ['ɪnstrəmənt]	Instrument	
	boss [bɒs]	Chef/in, Boss	
	gig [gɪg] *(infml)*	Gig, Auftritt	❗ (to) **do a gig** = einen Auftritt haben, ein Konzert geben
p.9	**mixture** ['mɪkstʃə]	Mischung	
	western ['westən]	westlich, West-	France is one of the biggest countries in **~** Europe.
p.10	**the United States (US)** [juˌnaɪtɪd 'steɪts], [juː_'es]	die Vereinigten Staaten (von Amerika)	
	How about ...?	Wie wär's mit ...?	= What about ...?
	hungry ['hʌngri]	hungrig	❗ Ich habe **Hunger.** = I'm **hungry.**
	Nice to meet you.	Nett, dich kennenzulernen.	
p.11	**half an hour** [ˌhɑːf_ən_'aʊə]	eine halbe Stunde	❗ Word order: **half an hour** – **eine halbe Stunde**
	half [hɑːf], *pl* **halves** [hɑːvz]	Hälfte	I felt ill and spent **~** of the day in bed.

Personen-, Orts- und Ländernamen → S. 210–211 · Unregelmäßige Verben → S. 212–213 · Classroom English → S. 216

(to) **mail** [meɪl]	schicken, senden *(per Post oder E-Mail)*	Julie **~ed** her friends some photos of her birthday party.
(to) **keep in touch** [ˌkiːp ɪn ˈtʌtʃ], **kept, kept** [kept]	in Verbindung bleiben, Kontakt halten	It was nice to meet you. – Yes, let's **keep in ~**.
Wait and see!	Wart's ab!	What's for dinner this evening? – **Wait and ~!**
recording [rɪˈkɔːdɪŋ]	Aufnahme, Aufzeichnung	
(to) **go with**	gehören zu, passen zu	The first text **goes ~** the third picture.
electric [ɪˈlektrɪk]	elektrisch, Elektro-	
flute [fluːt]	Querflöte	
recorder [rɪˈkɔːdə]	Blockflöte	
saxophone [ˈsæksəfəʊn]	Saxophon	
trumpet [ˈtrʌmpɪt]	Trompete	
violin [ˌvaɪəˈlɪn]	Violine, Geige	

saxophone

electric guitar

recorder

flute

violin

trumpet

Unit 1: My London

p.12 **capital** [ˈkæpɪtl]	Hauptstadt	Berlin is the **~** of Germany.
PS [ˌpiːˈes] **(postscript** [ˈpəʊstskrɪpt]**)**	PS *(Nachschrift unter Briefen)* (Postskript)	
big wheel [ˌbɪg ˈwiːl]	Riesenrad	
wheel [wiːl]	Rad	A bike has two **~s**.
parliament [ˈpɑːləmənt]	Parlament	❗ Schreibung: **parliament** Betonung auf der 1. Silbe: **parliament** [ˈpɑːləmənt]

Buildings and places in a town

In London:

cathedral [kəˈθiːdrəl]	Kathedrale, Dom	**St Paul's Cathedral** [sənt ˈpɔːlz]
circus [ˈsɜːkəs]	(runder) Platz	**Piccadilly Circus** [ˌpɪkədɪli ˈsɜːkəs]
lane [leɪn]	Gasse, Weg	**Brick Lane** [ˌbrɪk ˈleɪn]
palace [ˈpæləs]	Palast, Schloss	**Buckingham Palace** [ˌbʌkɪŋəm ˈpæləs]
square [skweə]	Platz	**Leicester Square** ❗ [ˌlestə ˈskweə] **Trafalgar Square** [trəˌfælgə ˈskweə]

sound file [ˈsaʊnd faɪl]	Tondatei, Soundfile	

second-hand [ˌsekənd ˈhænd]	gebraucht; aus zweiter Hand	❗ I bought it **second-hand**. = ... <u>aus</u> zweiter Hand

Tipps zum Wörterlernen → S.129 · Englische Laute → S.166 · Alphabetische Wörterverzeichnisse → S.167– 188 / S.189–208

p.13	**queen** [kwiːn]	Königin	**Queen** Elizabeth II (you say: **Queen** Elizabeth the second)
	(to) **record** [rɪˈkɔːd]	*(Musik / einen Film) aufnehmen*	Let's ~ that film. Then we can watch it later.
p.14/A 1	**single (ticket)** [ˈsɪŋgl]	einfache Fahrkarte *(nur Hinfahrt)*	**single (ticket)** ◄► **return (ticket)**
	Travelcard [ˈtrævlkɑːd]	Tagesfahrkarte *(der Londoner Verkehrsbetriebe)*	a one-day ticket
	adult [ˈædʌlt]	Erwachsene(r)	Children pay 50 p, **~s** £ 1.50.
	central [ˈsentrəl]	Zentral-, Mittel-	❗ Betonung auf der 1. Silbe: <u>**central**</u> [ˈsentrəl]
	line [laɪn]	(U-Bahn-)Linie	
	(to) **change** [tʃeɪndʒ]	umsteigen	Take the Central line and ~ to the Bakerloo line at Oxford Circus.
	the Tube *(no pl)* [tjuːb] *(BE)*	die Londoner U-Bahn	the underground (in London)
p.15/A 3	**high** [haɪ]	hoch	This mountain is very ~.
p.16/A 5	**twice** [twaɪs]	zweimal	❗ **once** (1x) − **twice** (2x) − **three times** (3x)
	once [wʌns]	einmal	
	(once/twice) **a week**	(einmal/zweimal) pro Woche	Our band practises once ~ week.
	curry [ˈkʌri]	Curry(gericht)	Would you like a **curry** or a pizza?
	spicy [ˈspaɪsi]	würzig, scharf gewürzt	
	mild [maɪld]	mild	❗ Aussprache: **mild** [maɪld] **spicy** ◄► **mild**
	dish [dɪʃ]	Gericht *(Speise)*	What's your favourite ~? – Spaghetti Napoli.
p.20/P 2	**transport** [ˈtrænspɔːt]	Beförderung, Transport	

Word field: Transport

1 **bus stop** [ˈbʌs stɒp]
2 **gate** [geɪt] Flugsteig
3 **taxi** [ˈtæksi]
4 **tram** [træm]
5 **airport** [ˈeəpɔːt]
6 **ferry** [ˈferi]
7 **lorry** [ˈlɒri]

	ground [graʊnd]	(Erd-)Boden	This railway tunnel is 20 metres under the ~. ❗ <u>Erd</u>boden = **ground** − <u>Fuß</u>boden = **floor**
p.22/P 6	**course** [kɔːs]	Kurs, Lehrgang	My mum does an English ~ on Friday evenings.
p.24/P 10	**butter** [ˈbʌtə]	Butter	
	vegetable [ˈvedʒtəbl]	*(ein)* Gemüse	❗ **Vegetables <u>are</u>** good for me. = **Gemüse <u>ist</u>** gut ...

Word field: Food

turkey ['tɜːki]
Truthahn,
Pute/Puter

pig   pork

pork [pɔːk]
Schweine-
fleisch

cow   beef

beef [biːf]
Rindfleisch

lamb

lamb [læm]
Lamm(fleisch)

 2

 3

 4

1

1 steak [steɪk]

2 pea [piː]

3 onion ❗ ['ʌnjən]

4 mushroom ['mʌʃrʊm, -ruːm]

butcher ['bʊtʃə]	Fleischer/in, Metzger/in	A ~ sells meat.
bakery ['beɪkəri]	Bäckerei	At a ~ you can buy bread and rolls.

at the butcher's / to the doctor's / …

Wenn der **Ort** gemeint ist, an dem jemand seinen Beruf ausübt – z.B. eine Fleischerei oder eine Arztpraxis – wird oft der **s-Genitiv** benutzt:

Please buy some meat **at the butcher's**.	Kauf bitte etwas Fleisch beim Metzger.
She felt ill and went **to the doctor's**.	Sie fühlte sich krank und ging zum Arzt.
I met Grandpa **at the chemist's** this morning.	Ich habe Opa heute Morgen beim Apotheker getroffen.

p.25/P 12	**everyday** *(adj)* ['evrideɪ]	Alltags-; alltägliche(r, s)	Are you going to wear anything special tonight? – No, just my ~ clothes: jeans and a T-shirt.
	(to) break a journey [breɪk], ['dʒɜːni], **broke** [brəʊk], **broken** ['brəʊkən]	eine Reise unterbrechen	
	journey ['dʒɜːni]	Fahrt, Reise	

Please get on the bus now!

p.25/P 13	**announcement** [ə'naʊnsmənt]	Durchsage, Ansage; Ankündigung, Bekanntgabe	

Only a game

helmets

p.26	**helmet** ['helmɪt]	Helm	
	sign [saɪn]	Schild; Zeichen	The ~ says it's only a mile to the city centre. Give me a ~ when I can come in.
	danger ['deɪndʒə]	Gefahr	

around		
herum... / umher...	We <u>walked</u> **around** till we found a nice café.	herumlaufen, umherspazieren
	It's fun to <u>run</u> and <u>jump</u> **around** in the park after school.	herumrennen; herumspringen
in ... umher, durch	We walked **around** <u>the town</u> and looked at the sights.	in der Stadt umher, durch die Stadt
	They rode their bikes **around** <u>the village</u>.	im Dorf umher, durch das Dorf
um ... (herum)	There was water all **around** them.	ganz um sie herum
	Let's run **around** the lake and see who is fastest.	um den See (herum)
!	*(auch zeitlich:)* I'll see you **around** six.	um sechs Uhr herum, gegen sechs

excited [ɪkˈsaɪtɪd]	begeistert, aufgeregt	**!** He was **excit<u>ed</u>**. = Er war aufgeregt.
		It was **excit<u>ing</u>**. = Es war aufreg**end**.

button [ˈbʌtn]	Knopf	**buttons**

moment [ˈməʊmənt]	Moment	Wait a ~!
p.27 **yuck** [jʌk]	igitt	**Yuck!** This soup is really awful!
realistic [ˌriːəˈlɪstɪk]	realistisch, wirklichkeitsnah	I want to see all the sights in London. – Be ~. We've only got two days.
friendly [ˈfrendli]	freundlich	noun: **friend** – adjective: **friendly**
shocked [ʃɒkt]	schockiert	Mr Brown was ~ when he saw his daughter's green hair.

plug [plʌg]	Stecker	a German **plug** / a British **plug**
p.28 **flash** [flæʃ]	Lichtblitz	
ending [ˈendɪŋ]	Ende, (Ab-)Schluss *(einer Geschichte, eines Films usw.)*	Not every story can have a happy ~.

How am I doing?

p.29 **How am I doing?**	Wie komme ich voran? *(Wie sind meine Fortschritte?)*	
area [ˈeəriə]	Bereich; Gebiet, Gegend	Grammar is my problem ~. I live in an ~ with a lot of restaurants.
fact [fækt]	Tatsache, Fakt	I've found lots of interesting ~s for my essay on the Music for Youth Festival.

Unit 2: Island girl

p.30	**coast** [kəʊst]	Küste	Cuxhaven is on the ~, but Hamburg isn't.
			❗ **an** der Küste = **on** the **coast**

big – large – huge

big / large	**big** und **large** sind oft austauschbar.		a **big/large** family; a **big/large** house
	big ist umgangssprachlicher als **large**, daher solltest du in eher förmlichen Texten besser **large** schreiben.		
	large wird in der Regel nicht verwendet, um Menschen zu beschreiben.		a very **big** man
huge [hjuːdʒ]	**huge** bedeutet „riesig", „sehr groß".		a **huge** suitcase

rocks

rock [rɒk]	Fels, Felsen	
oil [ɔɪl]	Öl	
oil rig [ˈɔɪl rɪg]	(Öl-)Bohrinsel	
ceilidh [ˈkeɪli]	*Musik- und Tanzveranstaltung, vor allem in Schottland und Irland*	

p.32/A 1	**electronic** [ɪˌlekˈtrɒnɪk]	elektronisch	
	media (pl) [ˈmiːdiə]	Medien	It's faster to use ~ like the phone or e-mail than to write letters.
	text message [ˈtekst ˌmesɪdʒ]	SMS	
	message [ˈmesɪdʒ]	Nachricht	
	(to) **text** sb. [tekst]	jm. eine SMS schicken	Have a good trip. And ~ me when you get there.
p.32/A 2	**mate** [meɪt] *(infml)*	Freund/in, Kumpel	a good friend
	(to) **surf the internet** [sɜːf]	im Internet surfen	
	(to) **download** [ˌdaʊnˈləʊd]	runterladen, downloaden	You can ~ music or pictures from the internet.
	(to) **mix** [mɪks]	mischen, mixen	If you ~ blue and yellow, you get green.
	mix [mɪks]	Mix, Mischung	
	instant messages (pl) [ˌɪnstənt ˈmesɪdʒɪz]	*Nachrichten, die man im Internet austauscht (in Echtzeit)*	
	ringtone [ˈrɪŋtəʊn]	Klingelton	
p.33/A 3	(to) **take** [teɪk], **took** [tʊk], **taken** [ˈteɪkən]	dauern, *(Zeit)* brauchen	It ~s about 15 minutes to get home from here. How long does the journey to Lyness ~?
	(to) **pick** sb. **up** [ˌpɪk ˈʌp]	jn. abholen	He's ~ing up Mr Brown.
	arrival (arr) [əˈraɪvl]	Ankunft	verb: (to) **arrive** – noun: **arrival**
	departure (dep) [dɪˈpɑːtʃə]	Abfahrt, Abflug; Abreise	**arrival** ◄► **departure**

	until [ən'tɪl]	bis	= till
p.33/A 5	(to) **be able to** do sth. ['eɪbl]	etwas tun können; fähig sein / in der Lage sein, etwas zu tun	Sarah **wasn't ~ to** come to my party last Friday. (= Sarah **couldn't** come ...)
p.34/A 6	**trendy** ['trendi]	modisch, schick	
	type [taɪp] *(infml)*	Typ	
	rucksack ['rʌksæk]	Rucksack	
	(to) **expect** [ɪk'spekt]	erwarten	How many guests are you **~ing** to your party?
p.35/A 8	**upset** [ˌʌp'set]	aufgebracht, gekränkt, mitgenommen	John was **~** because his sister didn't remember his birthday.
	(to) **upset** sb. **(-tt-)** [ʌp'set], **upset, upset**	jn. ärgern, kränken, aus der Fassung bringen	It **~s** me when people are rude to me.
	(to) **turn on/off** [tɜːn]	ein-/ausschalten	
	glad [glæd]	froh, dankbar	Tim is a good friend. I'm really **~** that I met him.
	beauty ['bjuːti]	Schönheit	adjective: **beautiful** – noun: **beauty**
	(to) **call** sb. **names**	jn. mit Schimpfwörtern hänseln, jm. Schimpfwörter nachrufen	He felt upset because the other kids always **~ed him names** like Carrot-Nose or Rabbit-Ears.
	I/you/... **would** ... [wəd, wʊd]	ich würde / du würdest ...	I don't want to leave my hometown. I **~** miss all my friends.
	bully ['bʊli]	(Schul-)Tyrann	verb: (to) **bully** – noun: **bully**
	exactly [ɪg'zæktli]	genau	You think that man is a thief? – **Exactly**.
	advice *(no pl)* [əd'vaɪs]	Rat, Ratschläge	Take my **~**: go and see a doctor.

Word field: Town and country

p.38/P 1

hilly ['hɪli] hügelig

car park ['kɑː pɑːk]

busy ['bɪzi] belebt, verkehrsreich; hektisch

canal [kə'næl]

a **busy** street

p.39/P 4	(to) **guess** [ges]	raten, erraten, schätzen	How old are you? – **Guess.** – 13? – No, I'm 14.
	general ['dʒenrəl]	allgemeine(r, s)	❗ Betonung auf der 1. Silbe: **general** ['dʒenrəl]
	personal ['pɜːsənl]	persönliche(r, s)	
	statement ['steɪtmənt]	Aussage, Feststellung	I'm afraid I don't agree with that **~**.
	monitor ['mɒnɪtə]	Monitor, Bildschirm	
p.41/P 7	(to) **press** [pres]	drücken	
	(to) **lock** [lɒk]	abschließen; sperren	Please **~** the door when you leave the house.
	(to) **unlock** [ˌʌn'lɒk]	aufschließen; entsperren	I lost the key, so I couldn't **~** the suitcase.

Orkney Star

p.44	**light** [laɪt]	Licht	**a cup of tea**
	a **cup of** tea [kʌp]	eine Tasse Tee	
	scarf [skɑːf], *pl* **scarves** [skɑːvz]	Schal	
	Assembly [ə'sembli]	Versammlung *(morgendliche Schulversammlung, oft mit Andacht)*	
	head teacher [ˌhed 'tiːtʃə]	Schulleiter/in	
	news *(no pl)* [njuːz]	Neuigkeit(en), Nachricht(en)	❗ Das **sind** gute **Nachrichten**!= That**'s** good **news**! (singular) *Never*: The news a̶r̶e̶ … or a̶ ̶n̶e̶w̶s̶.
	surprise [sə'praɪz]	Überraschung	You're here? That's a ~.
	across [ə'krɒs]	(quer) über	a bridge ~ a river
	anorak ['ænəræk]	Anorak, Windjacke	
p.45	**microphone** ['maɪkrəfəʊn]	Mikrofon	
	(to) **go well**	gut (ver)laufen, gutgehen	Was the test difficult? – Yes, but it **went ~**.
	bell [bel]	Klingel, Glocke	bells / The **bell** rang. = Es klingelte.
	clone [kləʊn]	Klon	
	jealous (of) ['dʒeləs]	neidisch (auf); eifersüchtig (auf)	You get so much pocket money! I'm really ~. Sarah is ~ **of** her baby brother. She thinks her parents love him more.
	community hall [kə'mjuːnəti]	Gemeinschaftshalle, -saal, Gemeindehalle, -saal	

How am I doing?

p.47	(to) **translate (from … into)** [træns'leɪt]	übersetzen (aus … ins)	We had to ~ the text **from** English **into** German.
	translation [træns'leɪʃn]	Übersetzung	
	(to) **look** sth. **up** [ˌlʊk ̱'ʌp]	etwas nachschlagen	
	meaning ['miːnɪŋ]	Bedeutung	Look up the ~ of 'stew' in your dictionary.

Unit 3: Sport and more

p.52	**final** ['faɪnl]	Finale, Endspiel	❗ Betonung und Aussprache: **final** ['faɪnl]
	final ['faɪnl]	letzte(r, s); End-	The young man saved the girl in the ~ minute of the film.
	semi-final [ˌsemi'faɪnl]	Halbfinale	
	training session ['seʃn]	Trainingsstunde, -einheit	
p.53	**profile** ['prəʊfaɪl]	Porträt, Steckbrief	

Tipps zum Wörterlernen → S.129 · Englische Laute → S.166 · Alphabetische Wörterverzeichnisse → S.167– 188 / S.189–208

	age [eɪdʒ]	Alter	What ~ are you? = How old are you?

What sex is it?

male   **female**

	sex [seks]	Geschlecht	
	female ['fiːmeɪl]	weiblich	
	male [meɪl]	männlich	
	location [ləʊ'keɪʃn]	Wohn-/Standort, Lage	

(to) **enter** a room ◄► (to) **leave** a room

p.54/A 1	(to) **enter** ['entə]	betreten; eintreten (in)	
	exchange student [ɪks'tʃeɪndʒ ˌstjuːdnt]	Austauschschüler/in	
p.54/A 2	**appetite** ['æpɪtaɪt]	Appetit	❗ Manchmal sagt man **Enjoy!**, wenn man gemeinsam isst. Aber nie ~~Good appetite!~~
	(to) **bet** [bet] **(-tt-), bet, bet**	wetten	I ~ that you can't stand on your head.
	liver ['lɪvə]	Leber	What's for dinner? – **Liver**. – Yuck. I don't like ~.
p.55/A 3	**quay** [kiː]	Kai, Kaimauer	Lots of people were waiting on the ~ to watch the big ship.
	stadium ['steɪdiəm]	Stadion	
	onto ['ɒntə, 'ɒntu]	auf (... hinauf)	The cat saw the dog and jumped ~ the table.
	pitch [pɪtʃ]	Fußball-/Hockeyplatz	
	(to) **be interested (in)** ['ɪntrəstɪd]	interessiert sein (an), sich interessieren (für)	❗ I'm **interested in** music. = Ich interessiere mich für Musik. an **interesting** CD = eine interessante CD
	(to) **paraphrase** ['pærəfreɪz]	umschreiben, anders ausdrücken	
p.56/A 5	**sporty** ['spɔːti]	sportlich	
	(to) **be fit**	fit sein	
	against [ə'genst]	gegen	Manchester United won ~ Rochdale.
	(to) **score (a goal)** [skɔː], [gəʊl]	ein Tor schießen, einen Treffer erzielen	We won 3–2. – Oh, great! Who **scored**? – Smith **scored** all three ~s.
	score [skɔː]	Spielstand; Punktestand	
	goal [gəʊl]	Tor (im Sport)	

A football match

What's the score now? – 2–0. (you say: **two nil**)   Wie steht es jetzt? – 2:0.

What was the final score? – Chelsea 2, Arsenal 1.   Wie war der Endstand? – 2:1.

	competition [ˌkɒmpəˈtɪʃn]	Wettbewerb, Wettkampf	There was a maths ~ at our school last week.
	(to) **train** [treɪn]	trainieren	
	coach [kəʊtʃ]	Trainer/in	
p.57/A 8	(to) **beat** [biːt], **beat, beaten** [ˈbiːtn]	schlagen; besiegen	I **beat** my brother at tennis last Sunday.
	in the end	schließlich, zum Schluss	No bus came, so **in the ~** we walked home. **!** **at the end** of the lesson = am Ende / am Schluss der Stunde
	(to) **mean** [miːn], **meant, meant** [ment]	bedeuten	What does 'forest' **mean**? – It **means** 'Wald'. **!** *Never:* What means …?

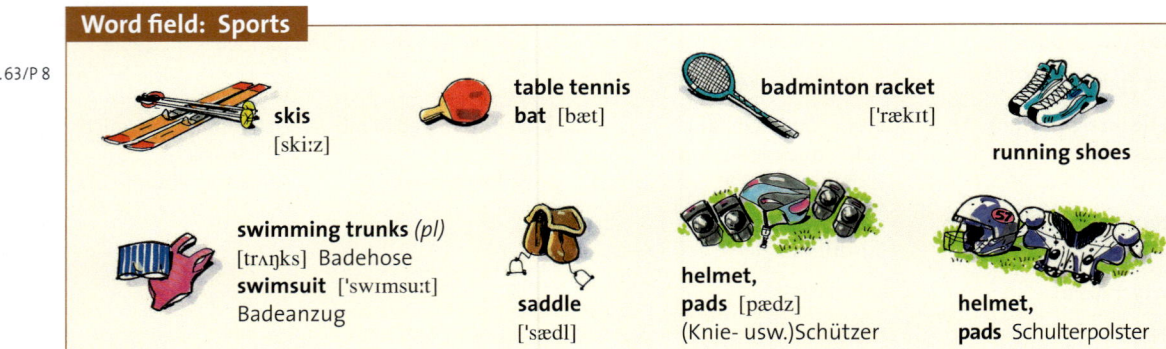

cups

	cup [kʌp]	Pokal	

goalkeeper

	goalkeeper [ˈgəʊlkiːpə]	Torwart, Torfrau	
p.60/P 2	**stress** [stres]	Betonung	
p.62/P 6	**kidney** [ˈkɪdni]	Niere	

Word field: Sports

p.63/P 8

skis [skiːz]

table tennis bat [bæt]

badminton racket [ˈrækɪt]

running shoes

swimming trunks *(pl)* [trʌŋks] Badehose **swimsuit** [ˈswɪmsuːt] Badeanzug

saddle [ˈsædl]

helmet, pads [pædz] (Knie- usw.)Schützer

helmet, pads Schulterpolster

p. 64/P 10	(to) **organize** [ˈɔːgənaɪz]	ordnen, organisieren	
	thought [θɔːt]	Gedanke	verb: (to) **think** – noun: **thought**
	half-time [ˌhɑːf ˈtaɪm]	Halbzeit(pause)	the break between the first and the second half of a match **!** the **first half** = die **erste Halbzeit**
p.65/P 11	**meal** [miːl]	Mahlzeit, Essen	Breakfast, lunch and dinner are **~s**.
	mashed potatoes [ˌmæʃt pəˈteɪtəʊz]	Kartoffelbrei, Kartoffelpüree	
	Help yourself!	Bedien dich! / Greif zu!	

Who needs legs?

p.66	(to) **grow up** [ˌɡrəʊ_ˈʌp], **grew up** [ˌɡruː_ˈʌp], **grown up** [ˌɡrəʊn_ˈʌp]	erwachsen werden; aufwachsen	Dave wants to be a doctor when he **~s up**. When my grandparents were **~ing up**, they didn't have a television.
	not (…) any more	nicht mehr	The Greens do**n't** live here **any more**. They moved to London.
	(to) **cut** sth. **off (-tt-)** [kʌt], **cut, cut**	etwas abschneiden, abtrennen	
	ambulance [ˈæmbjələns]	Krankenwagen	❗ Betonung und Aussprache: **ambulance** [ˈæmbjələns]
	athletics [æθˈletɪks]	Leichtathletik	I'm an **~** fan, I love sports like running and jumping.
	medal [ˈmedl]	Medaille	❗ Betonung auf der 1. Silbe: <u>**medal**</u> [ˈmedl]
	hope [həʊp]	Hoffnung	noun: **hope** – verb: (to) **hope**
p.100	(to) **fight (for)** [faɪt], **fought** [fɔːt], **fought**	kämpfen (für, um)	Nathan had to **~ for** his life after his accident.
	operation (on) [ˌɒpəˈreɪʃn]	Operation (an)	He had an **~ on** his knee after he was hurt in the match.
	artificial [ˌɑːtɪˈfɪʃl]	künstlich, Kunst-	Are those flowers real or **~**?
	(to) **be mad about** sth. [mæd]	verrückt nach/auf etwas sein	He **is mad ~** chocolate ice cream.
	sledge [sledʒ]	Schlitten	a **sledge**
	disabled [dɪsˈeɪbld]	(körper)behindert	
	championship [ˈtʃæmpiənʃɪp]	Meisterschaft	
	(to) **represent** [ˌreprɪˈzent]	repräsentieren, vertreten	There were groups from all over Europe at the festival. A group from Frankfurt **~ed** Germany.
	the Commonwealth [ˈkɒmənwelθ]	*Gemeinschaft der Länder des ehemaligen Britischen Weltreichs*	
	Paralympics [ˌpærəˈlɪmpɪks]	Paralympische Spiele *(Olympische Spiele für Sportler/innen mit körperlicher Behinderung)*	

Unit 4: Growing up in Canada

p.69	(to) **go camping** [ˈkæmpɪŋ]	zelten gehen	We **went ~** last summer.
	(to) **camp** [kæmp]	zelten	We **~ed** near a lake.
	(to) **go canoeing** [kəˈnuːɪŋ]	Kanu fahren gehen	canoe They **went canoeing.**
	(to) **canoe** [kəˈnuː]	Kanu fahren	
	(to) **go hunting** [ˈhʌntɪŋ]	jagen gehen	
	(to) **hunt** [hʌnt]	jagen	Do people still **~** lions in Africa?

Verbs and nouns with the same form

(to) **canoe**	paddeln, Kanu fahren	(to) **drive**	*(Auto)* fahren	(to) **link**	verbinden, verknüpfen
canoe	Kanu, Paddelboot	**drive**	(Auto-)Fahrt	**link**	Verbindung, Verknüpfung
(to) **colour**	kolorieren, färben	(to) **fish**	fischen, angeln	(to) **ski**	Ski fahren
	bunt an-, ausmalen	**fish**	Fisch	**ski**	Ski
colour	Farbe				
(to) **cook**	kochen	(to) **hunt**	jagen	(to) **sleep**	schlafen
cook	Koch/Köchin	**hunt**	Jagd	**sleep**	Schlaf

(to) **go snowshoeing** ['snəʊʃuːɪŋ]	Schneeschuhwandern gehen	two pairs of **snowshoes**
(to) **have sleepovers** ['sliːpəʊvəz]	Schlafpartys veranstalten	We often **have sleepovers** at Sally's. She has got a very big room.
(to) **hang out** (with friends) [ˌhæŋ_'aʊt], **hung** [hʌŋ], **hung** *(infml)*	rumhängen, abhängen (mit Freunden/Freundinnen)	
cabin ['kæbɪn]	Hütte	
(to) **shoot** [ʃuːt], **shot** [ʃɒt], **shot**	schießen, erschießen	
p.70/A1 **mom** [mɒm, *AE:* mɑm] *(AE)*	Mama, Mutti; Mutter	= *BE* mum
(to) **be allowed to do** sth. [ə'laʊd]	etwas tun dürfen	

„können" und „dürfen"

Du kennst bereits **can** für „können" und für „dürfen":

Ananda **can** play hockey very well.	Ananda kann sehr gut Hockey spielen.
You **can** go to the disco, but be home at 10, please.	Du darfst in die Disko gehen, …

Wenn es um die **Vergangenheit** oder die **Zukunft** geht, verwende

– für **„können"** eine Form von **be able to** und
– für **„dürfen"** eine Form von **be allowed to**.

(to) **be able to**:	The museum was closed on Friday, but we **were able to** go on Saturday.[1]	…, aber wir konnten am Samstag hingehen.
	I **won't be able to** meet you tomorrow.	Ich werde dich morgen nicht treffen können.
(to) **be allowed to**:	**Were** you **allowed to** watch the film last night?	Durftest du den Film gestern Abend sehen?
	When I'm 18 I**'ll be allowed to** drive.	Wenn ich 18 bin, werde ich Auto fahren dürfen.

[1] Es gibt auch eine Vergangenheitsform **could** („konnte"): It was so dark that we **couldn't** really see the sea.

bill [bɪl]	Rechnung	*at a restaurant:* Could we have the ~, please?
It's not my fault. [fɔːlt]	Es ist nicht meine Schuld.	
strict [strɪkt]	streng	Peter's parents are very ~. He isn't allowed to watch TV after 8 o'clock.
(to) **be grounded** ['graʊndɪd]	Ausgehverbot/Hausarrest haben	I can't hang out with my friends. I**'m ~** for a week because I didn't do my homework.

Tipps zum Wörterlernen → S.129 · Englische Laute → S.166 · Alphabetische Wörterverzeichnisse → S.167–188 / S.189–208

(to) **do badly/well (in)**	schlecht/gut abschneiden (in)	Karen **did** very **well in** her English test.
old-fashioned [ˌəʊldˈfæʃnd]	altmodisch	
modern [ˈmɒdən]	modern	❗ Betonung auf der 1. Silbe: <u>**modern**</u> [ˈmɒdən]
p.71/A 3 **dress code** [ˈdres kəʊd]	Kleiderordnung, Bekleidungsvorschrift	
rule [ruːl]	Regel, Vorschrift	I don't understand the game. Can you explain the **~s**, please?
jewellery [ˈdʒuːəlri]	Schmuck	I've got some earrings, but no other **~**.

Reflexive pronouns (Reflexivpronomen)

I've hurt **myself**.	Ich habe	**mir**	wehgetan /	**mich** verletzt.
You've hurt **yourself**.	Du ...	**dir**	...	/ **dich** ...
He's hurt **himself**.	Er ...	**sich**	...	/ **sich** ...
She's hurt **herself**.	Sie ...	**sich**	...	/ **sich** ...
It's hurt **itself**.	Es ...	**sich**	...	/ **sich** ...
We've hurt **ourselves**.	Wir ...	**uns**	...	/ **uns** ...
You've hurt **yourselves**.	Ihr ...	**euch**	...	/ **euch** ...
They've hurt **themselves**.	Sie ...	**sich**	...	/ **sich** ...

❗ Aussprache/Betonung:
-self [-ˈse<u>lf</u>]
-selves [-ˈse<u>lvz</u>]

tight ◄► baggy

baggy [ˈbægi]	weit (geschnitten)	
tight [taɪt]	eng	
(to) **blame** sb. **(for)** [bleɪm]	jm. die Schuld geben (an); jm. Vorwürfe machen (wegen)	Don't **~** me. It wasn't my fault.
p.71/A 4 **underwear** [ˈʌndəweə]	Unterwäsche	
stomach [ˈstʌmək]	Bauch; Magen	
p.72/A 5 **guys** (pl) [gaɪz] (AE, infml)	Leute	Hey, you **~**! Wait for me. I'll come with you.
by ten (o'clock)	bis (spätestens) zehn Uhr	Please be home **~** ten. (= not later than ten)

German „bis"

until / till („bis")

I can stay up **until / till** eleven o'clock tonight.
We lived in Scotland **until / till** I was 12.

by („bis spätestens", „nicht später als")

We need your report **by** Friday (= on or before Friday).
You must be home **by** 5.30 (= at or before 5.30).

from ... to („von ... bis")

We're open **from** Mondays **to** Saturdays.

p.72/A 6 (to) **brainstorm** [ˈbreɪnstɔːm]	brainstormen (so viele Ideen wie möglich sammeln)	
p.73/A 8 **leader** [ˈliːdə]	Leiter/in, (An-)Führer/in	

Personen-, Orts- und Ländernamen → S.210–211 · Unregelmäßige Verben → S.212–213 · Classroom English → S.216

each other [iːtʃ‿ˈʌðə]	einander, sich (gegenseitig)	Paul likes Linda and Linda likes Paul. = Paul and Linda like **each other**.

each other – themselves

each other

Robert and Asif are taking photos of **each other**.
*Robert und Asif fotografieren **sich gegenseitig**. / Robert und Asif machen Fotos **voneinander**. (Robert fotografiert Asif, und Asif fotografiert Robert.)*

sich = sich <u>gegenseitig</u>, einander → **each other**

themselves

Robert and Asif are taking photos of **themselves**.
*Robert und Asif machen Fotos **von sich (selbst)**. (Robert fotografiert sich, und Asif fotografiert sich.)*

sich = sich <u>selbst</u> → **themselves**

	stage [steɪdʒ]	Bühne	
p.73/A 9	**chorus** [ˈkɔːrəs]	Refrain	❗ German „Chor" = English **choir** [ˈkwaɪə]
p.76/P 1	**per cent (%)** [pəˈsent]	Prozent	Twenty **per ~** of two hundred is forty.
	per [pɜː, pə]	pro	50 miles **~** hour = 50 miles an hour
	kilometre (km) [ˈkɪləmiːtə]	Kilometer	1,000 metres = 1 **~**
	centimetre (cm) [ˈsentɪmiːtə]	Zentimeter	100 **~s** = 1 **metre**
	kilogram [ˈkɪləgræm], **kilo** [ˈkiːləʊ] **(kg)**	Kilogramm, Kilo (kg)	We need two **kilograms/kilos of** oranges for the orange juice.

a 150-kilogram bear / a 14-hour flight / …

a **150-kilogram** bear	ein 150 Kilogramm schwerer Bär	❗ Im Englischen steht das Nomen im Singular:
a **ten-kilometre** walk	eine Zehn-Kilometer-Wanderung	
a **14-hour** flight	ein 14-stündiger Flug, ein 14-Stunden-Flug	a **14-<u>hour</u>** flight
a **24-hour** supermarket	ein Supermarkt, der 24 Stunden geöffnet ist	(*nicht:* a 14-~~hours~~ flight)
a **two-week** holiday	ein zweiwöchiger Urlaub	

a sixteen-year-old	ein/e Sechzehnjährige/r	
a sixteen-year-old girl	ein sechzehnjähriges Mädchen	
million [ˈmɪljən]	Million	❗ one **million** cars (eine Million Autos) – two **million** cars (zwei Million<u>en</u> Autos) *But:* **million<u>s</u> of** cars (Millionen von Autos)

p.77/P 4	**(to) smoke** [sməʊk]	rauchen	**smoke**
	smoke	Rauch	**No smoking!**
p.77/P 6	**strike** [straɪk]	Streik	❗ (to) **be on strike** = streiken, sich im Streik befinden (to) **go on strike** = streiken, in den Streik treten

Tipps zum Wörterlernen → S.129 · Englische Laute → S.166 · Alphabetische Wörterverzeichnisse → S.167–188 / S.189–208

p.78/P 7	**wet** [wet]	feucht, nass	They got **~** when they walked through the rain.
	(to) **revise** [rɪ'vaɪz]	überarbeiten; wiederholen	**!** (to) **revise** = **1.** überarbeiten – (to) **~** a text, a story, … **2.** wiederholen – (to) **~** vocabulary, grammar, …
	spelling ['spelɪŋ]	(Recht-)Schreibung, Schreibweise	Remember to check your **~** when you write a text.
p.80/P 12	**dialogue** ['daɪəlɒg]	Dialog	

Two newspaper articles

p.81	**article** ['ɑːtɪkl]	(Zeitungs-)Artikel	There was an **~** in the school magazine about the World Cup.
	knife [naɪf], *pl* **knives** [naɪvz]	Messer	**!** stummes „k": **knife** [naɪf] **spoon** [spuːn] **knife** **teaspoon** **fork** [fɔːk]
	(to) **attack** [ə'tæk]	angreifen	
	attack [ə'tæk]	Angriff	
	while [waɪl]	während	Somebody stole my bike **~** I was in the shop.
	victim ['vɪktɪm]	Opfer	
	latest ['leɪtɪst]	neueste(r,s)	The Kooks are great. Have you heard their **~** CD?
	(to) **escape (from** sb./sth.**)** [ɪ'skeɪp]	fliehen (vor jm./aus etwas); entkommen	A lion **~d from** its cage at London Zoo last night. The thief **~d** in a fast sports car.

Unit 5: A teen magazine

p.88	(to) **produce** [prə'djuːs]	produzieren, herstellen	Germany **~s** millions of cars every year.
	editor ['edɪtə]	Redakteur/in	
	artist ['ɑːtɪst]	Künstler/in; Grafiker/in	**!** Betonung auf der 1.Silbe: <u>**ar**tist</u> ['ɑːtɪst] **artist** = Künstler/in (*nicht:* ~~Ar**tist**/in~~)
	photographer [fə'tɒgrəfə]	Fotograf/in	
	(to) **publish** ['pʌblɪʃ]	veröffentlichen	J. K. Rowling **~ed** her first Harry Potter book in 1997.
	That's up to you.	Das liegt bei dir. / Das kannst/musst du (selbst) entscheiden.	Will I be on the football team? – **That's up ~ you**. If you practise hard, you'll have a good chance.
	drawing ['drɔːɪŋ]	Zeichnung	
	(to) **draw** [drɔː], **drew** [druː], **drawn** [drɔːn]	zeichnen	I'll **~** a little map to help you to find my flat. verb: (to) **draw** – noun: **drawing**
p.89	**movie** ['muːvi]	Film	= film
	(to) **like** sth. **best/least** [liːst]	etwas am meisten/wenigsten mögen	Which article do you **like best**, and which do you **like least**?
p.90/A 1	(to) **skim** a text **(-mm-)** [skɪm]	einen Text überfliegen (*um den Inhalt grob zu erfassen*)	
	section ['sekʃn]	Abschnitt, Teil, (Themen-)Bereich	**!** Betonung auf der 1. Silbe: <u>**sec**tion</u> ['sekʃn]

Personen-, Orts- und Ländernamen → S.210–211 · Unregelmäßige Verben → S.212–213 · Classroom English → S.216

	popular ['pɒpjələ]	beliebt, populär	
p.91/A1	**vacation** [və'keɪʃn, *AE*: veɪ'keɪʃn] *(AE)*	Urlaub, Ferien	= *BE* holiday
	that far/good/bad/...	so weit/gut/schlecht/...	I knew you could sing, but I didn't know you were ~ good. (= so good)
	career [kə'rɪə]	Karriere	
	role [rəʊl]	Rolle	What's your ~ in the play? – I'm the detective.
	captain ['kæptɪn]	Kapitän/in	
p.94/P1	**interest** ['ɪntrəst]	Interesse	

English sounds (Englische Laute)

Die Lautschrift in den eckigen Klammern zeigt dir, wie ein Wort ausgesprochen wird.
In der folgenden Übersicht findest du alle Lautzeichen.

Vokale (Selbstlaute)

[iː]	gr**ee**n	[eɪ]	sk**a**te
[i]	happ**y**	[aɪ]	t**i**me
[ɪ]	**i**n	[ɔɪ]	b**oy**
[e]	y**e**s	[əʊ]	**o**ld
[æ]	bl**a**ck	[aʊ]	n**ow**
[ɑː]	p**a**rk	[ɪə]	h**ere**
[ɒ]	s**o**ng	[eə]	wh**ere**
[ɔː]	m**o**rning	[ʊə]	t**our**
[uː]	bl**ue**		
[ʊ]	b**oo**k		
[ʌ]	m**u**m		
[ɜː]	T-sh**ir**t		
[ə]	**a** partn**er**		

Konsonanten (Mitlaute)

[b]	**b**ox	[f]	**f**ull
[p]	**p**lay	[v]	**v**ery
[d]	**d**ad	[s]	**s**ister
[t]	**t**en	[z]	plea**s**e
[g]	**g**ood	[ʃ]	**sh**op
[k]	**c**at	[ʒ]	televi**s**ion
[m]	**m**um	[tʃ]	**t**eacher
[n]	**n**o	[dʒ]	**G**ermany
[ŋ]	si**ng**	[θ]	**th**anks
[l]	**h**ello	[ð]	**th**is
[r]	**r**ed	[h]	**h**e
[w]	**w**e		
[j]	**y**ou		

The English alphabet (Das englische Alphabet)

a [eɪ]	**h** [eɪtʃ]	**o** [əʊ]	**v** [viː]
b [biː]	**i** [aɪ]	**p** [piː]	**w** ['dʌbljuː]
c [siː]	**j** [dʒeɪ]	**q** [kjuː]	**x** [eks]
d [diː]	**k** [keɪ]	**r** [ɑː]	**y** [waɪ]
e [iː]	**l** [el]	**s** [es]	**z** [zed]
f [ef]	**m** [em]	**t** [tiː]	
g [dʒiː]	**n** [en]	**u** [juː]	

Das Dictionary besteht aus zwei alphabetischen Wörterlisten:

Englisch – Deutsch (S. 167–188)
Deutsch – Englisch (S. 189–208).

Das **English – German Dictionary** enthält den Wortschatz der Bände 1 bis 3 von *English G 21*.
Wenn du wissen möchtest, was ein Wort bedeutet, wie man es ausspricht oder wie es genau geschrieben wird, kannst du hier nachschlagen.

Im **English – German Dictionary** werden folgende **Abkürzungen** und **Symbole** verwendet:

jm. = jemandem	sb. = somebody	*pl* = *plural* (Mehrzahl)	*AE* = *American English*
jn. = jemanden	sth. = something	*no pl* = *no plural*	*infml* = *informal*

° Mit diesem Kringel sind Wörter markiert, die nicht zum Lernwortschatz gehören.
▶ Der Pfeil verweist auf Kästchen im Vocabulary (S. 150–166), in denen du weitere Informationen zu diesem Wort findest.

Die **Fundstellenangaben** zeigen, wo ein Wort zum ersten Mal vorkommt.
Die Ziffern in Klammern bezeichnen Seitenzahlen:

Ⅰ = Band 1 • Ⅱ = Band 2 • Ⅲ = Band 3
Ⅲ Intro (6) = Band 3, Introduction, Seite 6
Ⅲ Intro (6/151) = Band 3, Introduction, Seite 151 (im Vocabulary, zu Seite 6)
Ⅲ 1 (12) = Band 3, Unit 1, Seite 12
Ⅲ 1 (12/152) = Band 3, Unit 1, Seite 152 (im Vocabulary, zu Seite 12)

Tipps zur Arbeit mit dem Dictionary findest du im Skills File auf Seite 130.

A

a [ə]
1. ein, eine Ⅰ
2. once/twice a week einmal/zweimal pro Woche Ⅲ 1 (16)
a bit ein bisschen, etwas Ⅱ • **a few** ein paar, einige Ⅱ • **a lot (of)** eine Menge, viel, viele Ⅱ • **He likes her a lot.** Er mag sie sehr. Ⅰ
able ['eɪbl]**: able to do sth.** etwas tun können; fähig sein / in der Lage sein, etwas zu tun Ⅲ 2 (33)
▶ S. 162 „können" und „dürfen"
about [ə'baʊt]
1. über Ⅰ
2. ungefähr Ⅱ
ask about sth. nach etwas fragen Ⅰ • **How about …?** Wie wär's mit …? Ⅲ Intro (10) • **This is about Mr Green.** Es geht um Mr Green. Ⅰ **What about …? 1.** Was ist mit …? / Und …? Ⅰ; **2.** Wie wär's mit …? Ⅰ **What are you talking about?** Wovon redest du? Ⅰ • **What was the best thing about …?** Was war das Beste an …? Ⅱ
accent ['æksənt] Akzent Ⅱ
accident ['æksɪdənt] Unfall Ⅱ
across [ə'krɒs] (quer) über Ⅲ 2 (44)
act [ækt] aufführen, spielen Ⅰ
°**Act out …** Spiele/Spielt … vor.

activity [æk'tɪvəti] Aktivität, Tätigkeit Ⅰ
actor ['æktə] Schauspieler/in Ⅱ
add (to) [æd] hinzufügen, ergänzen, addieren (zu) Ⅰ
address [ə'dres] Adresse, Anschrift Ⅱ
adult ['ædʌlt] Erwachsene(r) Ⅲ 1 (14)
advice *(no pl)* [əd'vaɪs] Rat, Ratschläge Ⅲ 2 (35)
afraid [ə'freɪd]
1. be afraid (of) Angst haben (vor) Ⅰ
2. I'm afraid leider Ⅱ
after ['ɑːftə] nach *(zeitlich)* Ⅰ
after that danach Ⅰ
after ['ɑːftə] nachdem Ⅱ
afternoon [ˌɑːftə'nuːn] Nachmittag Ⅰ • **in the afternoon** nachmittags, am Nachmittag Ⅰ • **on Friday afternoon** freitagnachmittags, am Freitagnachmittag Ⅰ
again [ə'gen] wieder; noch einmal Ⅰ
against [ə'genst] gegen Ⅲ 3 (56)
age [eɪdʒ] Alter Ⅲ 3 (53)
ago [ə'gəʊ]**: a minute ago** vor einer Minute Ⅰ
agree (on) [ə'griː] sich einigen (auf) Ⅰ • **agree with sb./sth.** jm./etwas zustimmen; mit jm./etwas übereinstimmen Ⅱ

airport ['eəpɔːt] Flughafen Ⅲ 1 (20/153)
all [ɔːl] alle; alles Ⅰ • **all day** den ganzen Tag (lang) Ⅰ • **all over the world** auf der ganzen Welt Ⅲ Intro (6/150) • **all right** gut, in Ordnung Ⅱ • **all the time** die ganze Zeit Ⅰ • **from all over the UK/the world/England** aus dem gesamten Vereinigten Königreich/ aus der ganzen Welt/aus ganz England Ⅲ Intro (6) • **This is all wrong.** Das ist ganz falsch. Ⅰ
allowed [ə'laʊd]**: be allowed to do sth.** etwas tun dürfen Ⅲ 4 (70)
▶ S. 162 „können" und „dürfen"
°**almost** ['ɔːlməʊst] fast, beinahe
alone [ə'ləʊn] allein Ⅰ
along the street [ə'lɒŋ] entlang der Straße / die Straße entlang Ⅱ
alphabet ['ælfəbet] Alphabet Ⅰ
°**alphabetical** [ˌælfə'betɪkl] alphabetisch
already [ɔːl'redi] schon, bereits Ⅱ
also ['ɔːlsəʊ] auch Ⅱ
always ['ɔːlweɪz] immer Ⅰ
am [eɪ 'em]**: 7 am** 7 Uhr morgens/ vormittags Ⅰ
amazing [ə'meɪzɪŋ] erstaunlich, unglaublich Ⅱ
ambulance ['æmbjələns] Krankenwagen Ⅲ 3 (66)

American football [əˌmerɪkən ˈfʊtbɔːl] Football I
an [ən] ein, eine I
and [ənd, ænd] und I
angel [ˈeɪndʒl] Engel II
angry (about sth./with sb.) [ˈæŋɡri] wütend, böse (über etwas/auf jn.) II
animal [ˈænɪml] Tier II
announcement [əˈnaʊnsmənt] Durchsage, Ansage; Ankündigung, Bekanntgabe III 1 (25)
anorak [ˈænəræk] Anorak, Windjacke III 2 (44)
another [əˈnʌðə] ein(e) andere(r, s); noch ein(e) I • **another 45 p** weitere 45 Pence, noch 45 Pence II
answer [ˈɑːnsə] antworten; beantworten I
answer (to) [ˈɑːnsə] Antwort (auf) I
any [ˈeni]: **any …?** (irgend)welche …? I • **not (…) any** kein, keine I • **not (…) any more** nicht mehr III 3 (66)
anybody [ˈenibɒdi] (irgend)jemand II • **not (…) anybody** niemand II
anything [ˈeniθɪŋ] (irgend)etwas II • **not (…) anything** nichts II
anyway [ˈeniweɪ]
  1. sowieso I
  2. trotzdem II
anywhere [ˈeniweə] irgendwo(hin) II • **not (…) anywhere** nirgendwo(hin) II
appetite [ˈæpɪtaɪt] Appetit III 3 (54)
apple [ˈæpl] Apfel I
appointment [əˈpɔɪntmənt] Termin, Verabredung I
April [ˈeɪprəl] April I
are [ɑː] bist; sind; seid I • **How are you?** Wie geht es dir/Ihnen/euch? II • **The pencils are 35 p.** Die Bleistifte kosten 35 Pence. I **You're joking, aren't you?** Du machst Witze, nicht wahr? / Das ist nicht dein Ernst, oder? II
area [ˈeəriə] Bereich; Gebiet, Gegend III 1 (29)
argue [ˈɑːɡjuː] sich streiten, sich zanken I
arm [ɑːm] Arm I
armchair [ˈɑːmtʃeə] Sessel I
around [əˈraʊnd] um … (herum); in … umher, durch III 1 (26/155) **around six** um sechs herum, gegen sechs III 1 (26/155) • **around the lake** um den See herum III 1 (26/155) • **around the town** in der Stadt umher, durch die Stadt III 1 (26/155) • **run around** herumrennen III 1 (26/155) • **jump around** herumspringen III 1 (26/155) • **walk around** herumgehen, umher-

spazieren III 1 (26/155)
▶ S.155 around
arrival (arr) [əˈraɪvl] Ankunft III 2 (33)
arrive [əˈraɪv] ankommen, eintreffen III
art [ɑːt] Kunst I
article [ˈɑːtɪkl] (Zeitungs-)Artikel III 4 (81)
artificial [ˌɑːtɪˈfɪʃl] künstlich, Kunst- III 3 (100)
artist [ˈɑːtɪst] Künstler/in; Grafiker/in III 5 (88)
as [əz, æz]
  1. als, während II
  2. as old/big as so alt/groß wie II
ask [ɑːsk] fragen I • **ask about sth.** nach etwas fragen I • **ask questions** Fragen stellen I • **ask sb. the way** jn. nach dem Weg fragen II
asleep [əˈsliːp]: **be asleep** schlafen I
Assembly [əˈsembli] Versammlung (morgendliche Schulversammlung, oft mit Andacht) III 2 (44)
°**assistant** [əˈsɪstənt] Assistent/in
at [ət, æt]: **at 7 Hamilton Street** in der Hamiltonstraße 7 I • **at 8.45** um 8.45 I • **at break** in der Pause (zwischen Schulstunden) II • **at home** daheim, zu Hause I • **at last** endlich, schließlich I • **at least** zumindest, wenigstens I • **at night** nachts, in der Nacht I • **at school** in der Schule I • **at that table** an dem Tisch (dort) / an den Tisch (dort) I • **at the bottom (of)** unten, am unteren Ende (von) I • **at the butcher's / at the chemist's** beim Metzer/beim Apotheker III 1 (24/154) • **at the end (of)** am Ende (von) I • **at the Shaws' house** im Haus der Shaws / bei den Shaws zu Hause I • **at the station** am Bahnhof I • **at the top (of)** oben, am oberen Ende, an der Spitze (von) I • **at the weekend** am Wochenende I • **at work** bei der Arbeit / am Arbeitsplatz I
ate [et, eɪt] siehe **eat**
athletics [æθˈletɪks] Leichtathletik III 3 (66)
attack [əˈtæk] angreifen III 4 (81)
attack [əˈtæk] Angriff III 4 (81/165)
audience [ˈɔːdɪəns] Publikum; Zuschauer/innen, Zuhörer/innen II
August [ˈɔːɡəst] August I
aunt [ɑːnt] Tante I • **auntie** [ˈɑːnti] Tante II
autumn [ˈɔːtəm] Herbst I
away [əˈweɪ] weg, fort I
awful [ˈɔːfl] furchtbar, schrecklich II

B

baby [ˈbeɪbi] Baby I • **have a baby** ein Baby/Kind bekommen II
back (to) [bæk] zurück (nach) I
back door [ˌbæk ˈdɔː] Hintertür II
background [ˈbæɡraʊnd] Hintergrund II • **background file** etwa: Hintergrundinformation II
bacon [ˈbeɪkən] Schinkenspeck II
bad [bæd] schlecht, schlimm I **do badly (in)** schlecht abschneiden (in) III 4 (70)
badminton [ˈbædmɪntən] Badminton, Federball I • **badminton racket** [ˈrækɪt] Badmintonschläger III 3 (63/160)
bag [bæɡ] Tasche, Beutel, Tüte I
baggy [ˈbæɡi] weit (geschnitten) III 4 (71)
bakery [ˈbeɪkəri] Bäckerei III 1 (24)
ball [bɔːl] Ball II
banana [bəˈnɑːnə] Banane I
band [bænd] Band, (Musik-)Gruppe I
bank [bæŋk] Bank, Sparkasse I **bank robber** [ˈbæŋk ˌrɒbə] Bankräuber/in I
bar [bɑː] Bar II
baseball [ˈbeɪsbɔːl] Baseball I **baseball cap** Baseballmütze II
basket [ˈbɑːskɪt] Korb I • **a basket of apples** ein Korb Äpfel I
basketball [ˈbɑːskɪtbɔːl] Basketball I
bat [bæt]: **table tennis bat** Tischtennisschläger III 3 (63/160)
bath [bɑːθ] Bad, Badewanne II **have a bath** baden, ein Bad nehmen II
bathroom [ˈbɑːθruːm] Badezimmer I
be [biː], **was/were, been** sein I
beach [biːtʃ] Strand II • **on the beach** am Strand II
bear [beə] Bär II
beat [biːt], **beat, beaten** schlagen; besiegen III 3 (57)
beaten [ˈbiːtn] siehe **beat**
beautiful [ˈbjuːtɪfl] schön I
beauty [ˈbjuːti] Schönheit III 2 (35)
became [bɪˈkeɪm] siehe **become**
because [bɪˈkɒz] weil I
become [bɪˈkʌm], **became, become** werden II
bed [bed] Bett I • **Bed and Breakfast (B&B)** [ˌbed ən ˈbrekfəst] Frühstückspension (wörtlich: Bett und Frühstück) I • **go to bed** ins Bett gehen I
bedroom [ˈbedruːm] Schlafzimmer I

beef [biːf] Rindfleisch III 1 (24/154)

been [biːn] *siehe* **be**

before [bɪˈfɔː] vor *(zeitlich)* I

before [bɪˈfɔː] bevor II

beginning [bɪˈgɪnɪŋ] Beginn, Anfang; Einleitung II

behind [bɪˈhaɪnd] hinter II

bell [bel] Klingel, Glocke III 2 (45) **The bell rang.** Es klingelte. III 2 (45/158)

°**below** [bɪˈləʊ] unten

best [best] am besten II • **the best ...** der/die/das beste ...; die besten ... I • **like sth. best** etwas am meisten mögen III 5 (89) **What was the best thing about ...?** Was war das Beste an ...? II

bet (-tt-) [bet], **bet, bet** wetten III 3 (54)

better [ˈbetə] besser I • **like sth. better** etwas lieber mögen II

between [bɪˈtwiːn] zwischen II

big [bɪg] groß I • **big wheel** [ˌbɪg ˈwiːl] Riesenrad III 1 (12)

▶ S.156 big – large – huge

bike [baɪk] Fahrrad I • **bike ride** (Rad-)Fahrt II • **ride a bike** Rad fahren I

bill [bɪl] Rechnung III 4 (70)

°**billiards** [ˈbɪliədz] Billiard I

bin [bɪn] Mülltonne II

biology [baɪˈɒlədʒi] Biologie I

bird [bɜːd] Vogel I

birdcage [ˈbɜːdkeɪdʒ] Vogelkäfig III 3 (60)

birthday [ˈbɜːθdeɪ] Geburtstag I **Happy birthday.** Herzlichen Glückwunsch zum Geburtstag. I • **My birthday is in May.** Ich habe im Mai Geburtstag. I • **My birthday is on 13th June.** Ich habe am 13. Juni Geburtstag. I • **When's your birthday?** Wann hast du Geburtstag? I

biscuit [ˈbɪskɪt] Keks, Plätzchen I

bit: a bit [ə ˈbɪt] ein bisschen, etwas II

black [blæk] schwarz I

blame sb. (for) [bleɪm] jm. die Schuld geben (an); jm. Vorwürfe machen (wegen) III 4 (71)

bleep [bliːp] piepsen II

bleep [bliːp] Piepton II

°**bloody** [ˈblʌdi] blutig

blue [bluː] blau I

board [bɔːd] (Wand-)Tafel I **on the board** an der/die Tafel I **notice board** Anschlagtafel, schwarzes Brett I

boat [bəʊt] Boot, Schiff I

°**boater** [ˈbəʊtə] Bootsführer/in

body [ˈbɒdi] Körper I

book [bʊk] Buch I

boot [buːt] Stiefel I

boring [ˈbɔːrɪŋ] langweilig I

born [bɔːn]: **be born** geboren sein/werden II

boss [bɒs] Chef/in, Boss III Intro (8)

both [bəʊθ] beide I

bottle [ˈbɒtl] Flasche I • **a bottle of milk** eine Flasche Milch I

bottom [ˈbɒtəm] unteres Ende II **at the bottom (of)** unten, am unteren Ende (von) II

bought [bɔːt] *siehe* **buy**

bowl [bəʊl] Schüssel I • **a bowl of cornflakes** eine Schale Cornflakes I

box [bɒks] Kasten, Kästchen, Kiste I • **sandwich box** Brotdose I

°**boxercise** [ˈbɒksəsaɪz] *Sportart, die auf den Fitnessübungen des Boxsports basiert*

boy [bɔɪ] Junge I

brainstorm [ˈbreɪnstɔːm] brainstormen *(so viele Ideen wie möglich sammeln)* III 4 (72)

bread *(no pl)* [bred] Brot I

break a journey [ˌbreɪk ə ˈdʒɜːni], **broke, broken** eine Reise unterbrechen III 1 (25)

break [breɪk] Pause I • **at break** in der Pause *(zwischen Schulstunden)* II

breakfast [ˈbrekfəst] Frühstück I **have breakfast** frühstücken I

bridge [brɪdʒ] Brücke I

bright [braɪt] hell, leuchtend II

brilliant [ˈbrɪliənt] toll, genial, großartig III Intro (6)

bring [brɪŋ], **brought, brought** (mit-, her)bringen I

British [ˈbrɪtɪʃ] britisch; Brite, Britin II

brochure [ˈbrəʊʃə] Prospekt, Broschüre II

broke [brəʊk] *siehe* **break**

broken [ˈbrəʊkən] *siehe* **break**

broken *(adj)* [ˈbrəʊkən] gebrochen; zerbrochen, kaputt II

brother [ˈbrʌðə] Bruder I

brought [brɔːt] *siehe* **bring**

brown [braʊn] braun I

°**budget** [ˈbʌdʒɪt]: **be on a budget** mit wenig Geld auskommen müssen

budgie [ˈbʌdʒi] Wellensittich I

°**buffet** [ˈbʊfeɪ] Büfett I

build [bɪld], **built, built** bauen II

building [ˈbɪldɪŋ] Gebäude II

built [bɪlt] *siehe* **build**

bully [ˈbʊli] einschüchtern, tyrannisieren II

bully [ˈbʊli] (Schul-)Tyrann III 2 (35)

bunk (bed) [bʌŋk] Etagenbett, Koje II

bus [bʌs] Bus I • **bus stop** [ˈbʌs stɒp] Bushaltestelle III 1 (20/153)

business [ˈbɪznəs]: **Mind your own business.** Das geht dich nichts an! / Kümmere dich um deine eigenen Angelegenheiten! II

busy [ˈbɪzi] belebt, verkehrsreich; hektisch III 2 (38/157)

but [bət, bʌt] aber I

butcher [ˈbʊtʃə] Fleischer/in, Metzger/in III 1 (24) • **at the butcher's** beim Metzger III 1 (24/154)

butter [ˈbʌtə] Butter III 1 (24)

button [ˈbʌtn] Knopf III 1 (26)

buy [baɪ], **bought, bought** kaufen I

°**buzz** [bʌz] *hier:* den Summer/die Glocke betätigen

by [baɪ]
1. von I
2. an; (nahe) bei II
3. by car/train/bike/... mit dem Auto/Zug/Rad/... II
4. bis spätestens, nicht später als III 4 (72/163) • **by ten o'clock** bis (spätestens) zehn Uhr III 4 (72)
5. by the way übrigens II
▶ S.163 German „bis"

Bye. [baɪ] Tschüs! I

C

cabin [ˈkæbɪn] Hütte III 4 (69)

café [ˈkæfeɪ] *(kleines)* Restaurant, Imbissstube, Café II

cage [keɪdʒ] Käfig I

cake [keɪk] Kuchen, Torte I

calendar [ˈkælɪndə] Kalender I

call [kɔːl] rufen; anrufen; nennen I **call sb. names** jn. mit Schimpfwörtern hänseln, jm. Schimpfwörter nachrufen III 2 (35)

call [kɔːl] Anruf, Telefongespräch I

calm down [ˌkɑːm ˈdaʊn] sich beruhigen II

came [keɪm] *siehe* **come**

camel [ˈkæml] Kamel II

camera [ˈkæmərə] Kamera, Fotoapparat I

°**cameraman** [ˈkæmrəmən] Kameramann

camp [kæmp] zelten III 4 (69/161)

can [kən, kæn]
1. können I
2. dürfen I
Can I help you? Kann ich Ihnen helfen?/ Was kann ich für Sie tun? *(im Geschäft)* I
▶ S.162 „können" und „dürfen"

canal [kəˈnæl] Kanal III 2 (38/157)

canoe [kə'nuː] Kanu III 4 (162)

canoe [kə'nuː] Kanu fahren III 4 (69/162)

canteen [kæn'tiːn] Kantine, Schulmensa II

cap [kæp] Mütze, Kappe II

capital ['kæpɪtl] Hauptstadt III 1 (12)

captain ['kæptɪn] Kapitän/in III 5 (91)

°**caption** ['kæpʃn] Bildunterschrift

car [kɑː] Auto I • **car park** ['kɑː pɑːk] Parkplatz III 2 (38/157)

caravan ['kærəvæn] Wohnwagen II

card [kɑːd] (Spiel-, Post-)Karte I

career [kə'rɪə] Karriere III 5 (91)

careful ['keəfl]
1. vorsichtig II
2. sorgfältig II

caretaker ['keəteɪkə] Hausmeister/in II

carrot ['kærət] Möhre, Karotte I

cartoon [kɑː'tuːn] Cartoon (Zeichentrickfilm; Bilderwitz) II

case [keɪs] Fall I

castle ['kɑːsl] Burg, Schloss II

cat [kæt] Katze I

catch [kætʃ], **caught, caught** fangen; erwischen II

cathedral [kə'θiːdrəl] Kathedrale, Dom III 1 (12/152)

caught [kɔːt] *siehe* **catch**

CD [ˌsiː'diː] CD I • **CD player** CD-Spieler I

ceilidh ['keɪli] *Musik- und Tanzveranstaltung, vor allem in Schottland und Irland* III 2 (30/31)

cent (c) [sent] Cent I

centimetre (cm) ['sentimiːtə] Zentimeter III 4 (76/164)

central ['sentrəl] Zentral-, Mittel- III 1 (14)

centre ['sentə] Zentrum, Mitte I
city centre Stadtzentrum, Innenstadt I • **sports centre** Sportzentrum I

century ['sentʃəri] Jahrhundert II

chair [tʃeə] Stuhl I

°**chain** [tʃeɪn] Kette

champion ['tʃæmpiən] Meister/in, Champion I

championship ['tʃæmpiənʃɪp] Meisterschaft III 3 (100)

change [tʃeɪndʒ] umsteigen III 1 (14)

change [tʃeɪndʒ] Wechselgeld I

°**charity** ['tʃærəti] Wohltätigkeitsorganisation

°**chart** [tʃɑːt] Schaubild, Diagramm, Tabelle

chat (-tt-) [tʃæt] plaudern; chatten II

chat room ['tʃæt ruːm] Chatroom III 2 (32)

cheap [tʃiːp] billig I

check [tʃek] (über)prüfen, kontrollieren I

checkpoint ['tʃekpɔɪnt] Kontrollpunkt *(hier: zur Selbstüberprüfung)* I

cheer [tʃɪə] jubeln, Beifall klatschen II

cheese [tʃiːz] Käse I

chemist ['kemɪst] Drogerie, Apotheke II • **at the chemist's** beim Apotheker III 1 (24/154)

cherry ['tʃeri] Kirsche II

chicken ['tʃɪkɪn] Huhn; (Brat-)Hähnchen I

child [tʃaɪld], *pl* **children** ['tʃɪldrən] Kind I

chips (pl) [tʃɪps] Pommes frites I

chocolate ['tʃɒklət] Schokolade I

choir ['kwaɪə] Chor I

choose [tʃuːz], **chose, chosen** (sich) aussuchen, (aus)wählen I

chorus ['kɔːrəs] Refrain III 4 (73)

chose [tʃəʊz] *siehe* **choose**

chosen ['tʃəʊzn] *siehe* **choose**

Christmas ['krɪsməs] Weihnachten I

church [tʃɜːtʃ] Kirche I

cinema ['sɪnəmə] Kino I • **go to the cinema** ins Kino gehen II

°**circle** ['sɜːkl] Kreis • °**double circle** Doppelkreis, „Kugellager" *(als Kommunikationsform)*

circus ['sɜːkəs] (runder) Platz III 1 (12/152)

city ['sɪti] (Groß-)Stadt I • **city centre** Stadtzentrum, Innenstadt I

class [klɑːs] (Schul-)Klasse I • **class teacher** Klassenlehrer/in I

classical ['klæsɪkl] klassisch III Intro (6)

classmate ['klɑːsmeɪt] Klassenkamerad/in, Mitschüler/in I

classroom ['klɑːsruːm] Klassenzimmer I

clean [kliːn] sauber II

clean [kliːn] sauber machen, putzen I • **I clean my teeth.** Ich putze mir die Zähne. I

cleaner ['kliːnə] Putzfrau, -mann II

clear [klɪə] klar, deutlich I

°**clerk** [klɑːk] Angestellte/(r)

clever ['klevə] schlau, klug I

click on sth. [klɪk] etwas anklicken II

climb [klaɪm] klettern; hinaufklettern (auf) I • **Climb a tree.** Klettere auf einen Baum. I

clinic ['klɪnɪk] Klinik II

clock [klɒk] (Wand-, Stand-, Turm-)Uhr I

clone [kləʊn] Klon III 2 (45)

close [kləʊs]: **That was close.** Das war knapp. II

close [kləʊz] schließen, zumachen I

closed [kləʊzd] geschlossen II

°**closing phrase** ['kləʊzɪŋ freɪz] Grußformel *(am Briefende)*

clothes (pl) [kləʊðz, kləʊz] Kleider, Kleidung(sstücke) II

cloud [klaʊd] Wolke II

cloudy ['klaʊdi] bewölkt II

clown [klaʊn] Clown/in II

club [klʌb] Klub; Verein I

coach [kəʊtʃ] Trainer/in III 3 (56)

coast [kəʊst] Küste III 2 (30) • **on the coast** an der Küste III 2 (30/156)

cola ['kəʊlə] Cola I

cold [kəʊld] kalt I • **be cold** frieren I

cold [kəʊld] Erkältung II • **have a cold** erkältet sein, eine Erkältung haben II

collect [kə'lekt] sammeln I

collector [kə'lektə] Sammler/in II

colour ['kʌlə] färben III 4 (162)

colour ['kʌlə] Farbe I • **What colour is ...?** Welche Farbe hat ...? I

°**combine** [kəm'baɪn] kombinieren, verbinden

come [kʌm], **came, come** kommen I • **come home** nach Hause kommen I • **come in** hereinkommen I • **Come on.**
1. Na los, komm. II; **2.** Ach komm! / Na hör mal! II

comic ['kɒmɪk] Comic-Heft I

Commonwealth ['kɒmənwelθ]: **the Commonwealth** *Gemeinschaft der Länder des ehemaligen Britischen Weltreichs* III 3 (100)

°**compare** [kəm'peə] vergleichen

comparison [kəm'pærɪsn] Steigerung; Vergleich II

°**competition** [ˌkɒmpə'tɪʃn] Wettbewerb, Wettkampf III 3 (56)

°**complete** [kəm'pliːt] vervollständigen, ergänzen

computer [kəm'pjuːtə] Computer I

community [kə'mjuːnəti]: **community hall** Gemeinschaftshalle, -saal, Gemeindehalle, -saal III 2 (45)

concert ['kɒnsət] Konzert III Intro (6)

°**context** ['kɒntekst]: **from the context** aus dem Zusammenhang, aus dem Kontext

cook [kʊk] kochen, zubereiten II

cook [kʊk] Koch/Köchin III 4 (162)

cooker ['kʊkə] Herd I

cool [kuːl]
1. kühl II
2. cool I

copy ['kɒpi] kopieren; abschreiben II

copy ['kɒpi] Kopie II

corner ['kɔːnə] Ecke I • **on the corner of Green Street and London Road** Green Street, Ecke London Road II

cornflakes ['kɔːnfleɪks] Cornflakes I

correct [kə'rekt] berichtigen, korrigieren II

°**correct** [kə'rekt] richtig, korrekt II

could [kəd, kʊd]: **he could …** er konnte … II
▶ S.162 „können" und „dürfen"

count [kaʊnt] zählen II

°**counter** ['kaʊntə] Spielstein I

country ['kʌntri] Land *(auch als Gegensatz zur Stadt)* II • **in the country** auf dem Land II

course [kɔːs] Kurs, Lehrgang III 1 (22)

course: of course [əv 'kɔːs] natürlich, selbstverständlich I

cousin ['kʌzn] Cousin, Cousine I

cover ['kʌvə]
1. (CD-)Hülle I
2.°**inside cover** [ˌɪnsaɪd 'kʌvə] Umschlaginnenseite I

cow [kaʊ] Kuh II

°**crew** [kruː] Crew, (Schiffs-)Mannschaft, Team • °**film crew** Filmcrew, Filmteam I

°**cricket** ['krɪkɪt] Kricket I

crisps *(pl)* [krɪsps] Kartoffelchips I

crocodile ['krɒkədaɪl] Krokodil II

cross [krɒs] überqueren II

cross [krɒs]: **be cross (with)** böse, sauer sein (auf) I

°**culture** ['kʌltʃə] Kultur I

cup [kʌp]
1. Tasse III 2 (44) • **a cup of tea** eine Tasse Tee III 2 (44)
2. Pokal III 3 (57)

cupboard ['kʌbəd] Schrank I

°**curling** ['kɜːlɪŋ] Eisstockschießen, Curling I

curry ['kʌri] Curry(gericht) III 1 (16)

customer ['kʌstəmə] Kunde, Kundin II

cut (-tt-) [kʌt], **cut, cut** schneiden III 3 (66) • **cut sth. off** etwas abtrennen, abschneiden III 3 (66)

cycle ['saɪkl] (mit dem) Rad fahren II • **cycle path** Radweg II

D

dad [dæd] Papa, Vati; Vater I

dance [dɑːns] tanzen I

dance [dɑːns] Tanz I

dancer ['dɑːnsə] Tänzer/in II

dancing ['dɑːnsɪŋ] Tanzen I
dancing lessons Tanzstunden, Tanzunterricht I

danger ['deɪndʒə] Gefahr III 1 (26)

dangerous ['deɪndʒərəs] gefährlich II

dark [dɑːk] dunkel I

date [deɪt] Datum I

daughter ['dɔːtə] Tochter I

day [deɪ] Tag I • °**a day out** ein Tagesausflug • **one day** eines Tages I • **days of the week** Wochentage I • **one-day ticket** Tageskarte III 1 (14/153)

dead [ded] tot I

dear [dɪə] Schatz, Liebling I
Oh dear! Oje! II

dear [dɪə]: **Dear Jay …** Lieber Jay, … I

December [dɪ'sembə] Dezember I

°**decide (on)** [dɪ'saɪd] sich entscheiden (für), beschließen II

deer, *pl* **deer** [dɪə] Reh, Hirsch II

degree [dɪ'griː] Grad II

delicious [dɪ'lɪʃəs] köstlich, lecker II

department store [dɪ'pɑːtmənt stɔː] Kaufhaus II

departure (dep) [dɪ'pɑːtʃə] Abfahrt, Abflug; Abreise III 2 (33)

describe sth. (to sb.) [dɪ'skraɪb] (jm.) etwas beschreiben II

description [dɪ'skrɪpʃn] Beschreibung II

design [dɪ'zaɪn] entwerfen, gestalten II

desk [desk] Schreibtisch I

detail ['diːteɪl] Detail, Einzelheit II

detective [dɪ'tektɪv] Detektiv/in I

dialogue ['daɪəlɒg] Dialog III 4 (80)

diary ['daɪəri] Tagebuch; Terminkalender I • °**keep a diary** ein Tagebuch führen II

dice, *pl* **dice** [daɪs] Würfel II

dictionary ['dɪkʃənri] Wörterbuch, *(alphabetisches)* Wörterverzeichnis I

did [dɪd] *siehe* **do** • **Did you go …?** Bist du … gegangen? / Seid ihr … gegangen? I • **we didn't sing** ['dɪdnt] wir sangen nicht / wir haben nicht gesungen I

die (of) *(-ing form:* **dying***)* [daɪ] sterben (an) II

°**difference** ['dɪfrəns] Unterschied I

different (from) ['dɪfrənt] verschieden, unterschiedlich; anders (als) I

difficult ['dɪfɪkəlt] schwierig, schwer I

dining room ['daɪnɪŋ ruːm] Esszimmer I

dinner ['dɪnə] Abendessen, Abendbrot I • **have dinner** Abendbrot essen I

°**dinosaur** ['daɪnəsɔː] Dinosaurier I

°**director** [də'rektə] Regisseur/in I

dirty ['dɜːti] schmutzig I

disabled [dɪs'eɪbld] (körper)behindert III 3 (100)

°**disagree** [ˌdɪsə'griː] nicht zustimmen; anderer Meinung sein I

disappear [ˌdɪsə'pɪə] verschwinden II

disco ['dɪskəʊ] Disko I

°**discuss** [dɪ'skʌs] besprechen; diskutieren (über) I

discussion [dɪ'skʌʃn] Diskussion II

dish [dɪʃ] Gericht *(Speise)* III 1 (16)

dishwasher ['dɪʃwɒʃə] Geschirrspülmaschine I

disc jockey (DJ) ['dɪsk dʒɒki] Diskjockey III Intro (6/151)

°**divide (into)** [dɪ'vaɪd] auf-, einteilen (in) I

divorced [dɪ'vɔːst] geschieden I

DJ ['diːdʒeɪ] (Musik/CDs/Platten) auflegen *(in der Disko)* III Intro (6)

DJ ['diːdʒeɪ] Diskjockey III Intro (6/151)

do [duː], **did, done** tun, machen I **Do you like …?** Magst du …? I **do a gig** einen Auftritt haben, ein Konzert geben III Intro (8/151) • **do a good job** gute Arbeit leisten II **do a project** ein Projekt machen, durchführen II • **do an exercise** eine Übung machen II • **do badly/well (in)** schlecht/gut abschneiden (in) III 4 (70) • **do sport** Sport treiben I

°**docklands** ['dɒkləndz] Hafenviertel I

doctor ['dɒktə] Doktor; Arzt/Ärztin II • **to the doctor's** zum Arzt III 1 (24/154)

°**documentary** [ˌdɒkju'mentri] Dokumentarfilm, -beitrag I

dog [dɒg] Hund I

done [dʌn] *siehe* **do**

don't [dəʊnt]: **Don't listen to Dan.** Hör/Hört nicht auf Dan. I • **I don't know.** Ich weiß es nicht. I • **I don't like …** Ich mag … nicht. / Ich mag kein(e) … I

door [dɔː] Tür I • °**next door** nebenan I

doorbell ['dɔːbel] Türklingel I

dossier ['dɒsieɪ] Mappe, Dossier *(des Sprachenportfolios)* I

double ['dʌbl] zweimal, doppelt, Doppel- I • °**double circle** ['sɜːkl] Doppelkreis, „Kugellager" *(als Gesprächskreis)* I

down [daʊn] hinunter, herunter, nach unten I • **down there** dort unten II • **fall down** hinfallen II

download [ˌdaʊn'ləʊd] runterladen, downloaden III 2 (32)

downstairs [ˌdaʊn'steəz] unten; nach unten I

°**dragon** ['dræɡən] Drachen

drama ['drɑːmə] Schauspiel, darstellende Kunst I

drank [dræŋk] *siehe* **drink**

draw [drɔː], **drew, drawn** zeichnen III 5 (88/165)

drawing ['drɔːɪŋ] Zeichnung III 5 (88)

drawn [drɔːn] *siehe* **draw**

dream [driːm] Traum I • **dream house** Traumhaus I

dress [dres] Kleid I

dress code ['dres kəʊd] Kleiderordnung, Bekleidungsvorschrift III 4 (71)

dressed [drest]: **get dressed** sich anziehen I

drew [druː] *siehe* **draw**

drink [drɪŋk] Getränk I

drink [drɪŋk], **drank, drunk** trinken I

drive [draɪv] Fahrt III 4 (69/162)

drive [draɪv], **drove, driven** *(ein Auto/mit dem Auto)* fahren II

driven ['drɪvn] *siehe* **drive**

driver ['draɪvə] Fahrer/in II

drop (-pp-) [drɒp] fallen lassen I

drove [drəʊv] *siehe* **drive**

drum [drʌm] Trommel III Intro (6)

drums *(pl)* [drʌmz] Schlagzeug III Intro (6/151) • **play the drums** Schlagzeug spielen III Intro (6/151)

drunk [drʌŋk] *siehe* **drink**

dustbin ['dʌstbɪn] Mülltonne II

DVD [ˌdiː viː' diː] DVD I

E

each [iːtʃ] jeder, jede, jedes (einzelne) I

each other [iːtʃ‿'ʌðə] einander, sich (gegenseitig) III 4 (73)
  ▶ S.164 each other – themselves

ear [ɪə] Ohr I

earache ['ɪəreɪk] Ohrenschmerzen II

early ['ɜːli] früh I

earring ['ɪərɪŋ] Ohrring I

°**earth** [ɜːθ] Erde I

east [iːst] Osten; nach Osten; östlich III Intro (7/151)

easy ['iːzi] leicht, einfach I

eat [iːt], **ate, eaten** essen I

eaten ['iːtn] *siehe* **eat**

editor ['edɪtə] Redakteur/in III 5 (88)

egg [eɡ] Ei II

electric [ɪ'lektrɪk] elektrisch, Elektro- III Intro (11)

°**electrician** [ɪˌlek'trɪʃn] Elektriker/in

electronic [ɪˌlek'trɒnɪk] elektronisch III 2 (32)

elephant ['elɪfənt] Elefant I

elevator ['elɪveɪtə] *(AE)* Fahrstuhl, Aufzug II

°**else** [els]: **What else can you do?** Was kannst du sonst noch machen?

e-mail ['iːmeɪl] E-Mail I

empty ['empti] leer I

°**encyclopedia** [ɪnˌsaɪklə'piːdiə] Enzyklopädie, Lexikon

end [end] Ende, Schluss I • **at the end (of)** am Ende (von) I • **in the end** schließlich, zum Schluss III 3 (57)

ending ['endɪŋ] Ende, (Ab-)Schluss *(einer Geschichte, eines Films usw.)* III 1 (28)

enemy ['enəmi] Feind/in II

engineer [ˌendʒɪ'nɪə] Ingenieur/in II

English ['ɪŋɡlɪʃ] Englisch; englisch I

enjoy [ɪn'dʒɔɪ] genießen II • **Enjoy yourself.** Viel Spaß! / Amüsier dich gut! III 4 (147)

enough [ɪ'nʌf] genug I

enter ['entə] betreten; eintreten (in) III 3 (54)

°**entry** ['entri] Eintrag, Eintragung *(im Wörterbuch, Tagebuch)*

escape (from sb./sth.) [ɪ'skeɪp] fliehen (vor jm./aus etwas); entkommen III 4 (81)

essay (about, on) ['eseɪ] Aufsatz (über) I

°**etc.** [et'setərə] usw.

euro (€) ['jʊərəʊ] Euro I

even ['iːvn] sogar II

evening ['iːvnɪŋ] Abend I • **in the evening** abends, am Abend I **on Friday evening** freitagabends, am Freitagabend I

ever? ['evə] je? / jemals? / schon mal? II

every ['evri] jeder, jede, jedes I

everybody ['evribɒdi] jeder, alle II

everyday *(adj)* ['evrideɪ] Alltags-; alltägliche(r, s) III 1 (25)

°**everyone** ['evriwʌn] jeder, alle

everything ['evriθɪŋ] alles I

exactly [ɪɡ'zæktli] genau III 2 (35)

°**example** [ɪɡ'zɑːmpl] Beispiel °**for example** zum Beispiel

°**except** [ɪk'sept] außer, bis auf

exchange student [ɪks'tʃeɪndʒ ˌstjuːdnt] Austauschschüler/in III 3 (54)

excited [ɪk'saɪtɪd] begeistert, aufgeregt III 1 (26)

exciting [ɪk'saɪtɪŋ] aufregend, spannend I

Excuse me, … [ɪk'skjuːz miː] Entschuldigung, … / Entschuldigen Sie, … I

exercise ['eksəsaɪz] Übung, Aufgabe I • **exercise book** Schulheft, Übungsheft I

expect [ɪk'spekt] erwarten III 2 (34)

expensive [ɪk'spensɪv] teuer I

explain sth. to sb. [ɪk'spleɪn] jm. etwas erklären, erläutern II

explanation [ˌeksplə'neɪʃn] Erklärung II

explore [ɪk'splɔː] erkunden, erforschen I

explorer [ɪk'splɔːrə] Entdecker/in, Forscher/in II

extra ['ekstrə] zusätzlich I

eye [aɪ] Auge I

F

face [feɪs] Gesicht I

fact [fækt] Tatsache, Fakt III 1 (29)

factory ['fæktri] Fabrik II

fair [feə] fair, gerecht II

fall [fɔːl], **fell, fallen** fallen, stürzen; hinfallen II • **fall down** hinfallen II • **fall off** herunterfallen (von) II

fallen ['fɔːlən] *siehe* **fall**

family ['fæməli] Familie I • **family tree** (Familien-)Stammbaum I

famous (for) ['feɪməs] berühmt (für, wegen) II

fan [fæn] Fan I

fantastic [fæn'tæstɪk] fantastisch, toll I

far [fɑː] weit (entfernt) II

farm [fɑːm] Bauernhof, Farm II

°**farmhouse** ['fɑːmhaʊs] Bauernhaus

fashion ['fæʃn] Mode II

fast [fɑːst] schnell II • **fast food** [ˌfɑːst 'fuːd] Fastfood III 2 (40)

father ['fɑːðə] Vater I

fault [fɔːlt]: **It's not my fault.** Es ist nicht meine Schuld. III 4 (70)

favourite ['feɪvərɪt] Lieblings- I **my favourite colour** meine Lieblingsfarbe I

February ['februəri] Februar I

fed [fed] *siehe* **feed** • **be fed up (with sth.)** [ˌfed‿'ʌp] die Nase voll haben (von etwas) II

feed [fiːd], **fed, fed** füttern I

feel [fiːl], **felt, felt** sich fühlen; fühlen; sich anfühlen I

feet [fiːt] *Plural von „foot"* I

fell [fel] *siehe* **fall**

felt [felt] *siehe* **feel**

felt tip ['felt tɪp] Filzstift I

female ['fiːmeɪl] weiblich III 3 (53)

ferry ['feri] Fähre III 1 (20/153)

festival ['fɛstɪvl] Fest, Festival, Festspiele III Intro (6)

few [fjuː]: **a few** ein paar, einige II

fiddle ['fɪdl] (infml) Fiedel, Geige III Intro (7) • **play the fiddle** Geige, Fiedel spielen III Intro (7/151)

field [fiːld] Feld, Acker, Weide II **in the field** auf dem Feld II

fight [faɪt], **fought, fought**
1. kämpfen III 3 (100) • **fight for** kämpfen (für, um) III 3 (100)
°2. streiten

file [faɪl]: **background file** etwa: Hintergrundinformation(en) II **grammar file** Grammatikanhang I **skills file** Anhang mit Lern- und Arbeitstechniken I • **sound file** ['saʊnd faɪl] Tondatei, Soundfile III 1 (12)

°**fill in** [,fɪl_'ɪn]
1. einsetzen
2. ausfüllen

film [fɪlm] Film I • °**film crew** [kruː] Filmcrew, Filmteam • **film star** Filmstar I • °**film researcher** [rɪ'sɜːtʃə] Filmrechercheur/in

°**filming** ['fɪlmɪŋ] Dreharbeiten

final ['faɪnl] Finale, Endspiel III 3 (52)

final ['faɪnl] letzte(r, s); End- III 3 (52/158) • **final score** Endstand (beim Sport) III 3 (56/159)
▶ S.159 A football match

find [faɪnd], **found, found** finden I **find out (about)** herausfinden (über) I

finder ['faɪndə] Finder I

fine [faɪn]
1. gut, schön; in Ordnung II
2. (gesundheitlich) gut II
I'm/He's fine. Es geht mir/ihm gut. II

finger ['fɪŋgə] Finger I

finish ['fɪnɪʃ] beenden, zu Ende machen; enden I

fire ['faɪə] Feuer, Brand II

fireman/-woman ['faɪəmən, 'faɪə,wʊmən] Feuerwehrmann/ -frau II

first [fɜːst]
1. erste(r, s) I
2. zuerst, als Erstes I
be first der/die Erste sein I • **the first half** die erste Halbzeit III 3 (64/160)

°**First Nations** [,fɜːst 'neɪʃnz] indianische Ureinwohner/innen Kanadas

fish [fɪʃ] fischen, angeln III 4 (69/162)

fish, pl fish [fɪʃ] Fisch I

fit (-tt-) [fɪt] passen I

fit: be fit [fɪt] fit sein III 3 (56)

°**flag** [flæg] Fahne, Flagge

flash [flæʃ] Lichtblitz III 1 (28)

flat [flæt] Wohnung I

flew [fluː] siehe **fly**

flight [flaɪt] Flug II • **a 14-hour flight** ein 14-stündiger Flug, ein 14-Stunden-Flug III 4 (76/164)

floor [flɔː] Fußboden II

°**flow chart** ['fləʊ tʃɑːt] Flussdiagramm

flown [fləʊn] siehe **fly**

flute [fluːt] Querflöte III Intro (11)

fly [flaɪ], **flew, flown** fliegen II

fog [fɒg] Nebel II

foggy ['fɒgi] neblig II

folk music ['fəʊk ,mjuːzɪk] Folk (englische, schottische, irische oder nordamerikanische Volksmusik des 20. Jahrhunderts) III Intro (6)

follow ['fɒləʊ] folgen; verfolgen I
°**the following ...** die folgenden ...

food [fuːd]
1. Essen; Lebensmittel I
2. Futter I

foot [fʊt], pl **feet** [fiːt] Fuß I

football ['fʊtbɔːl] Fußball I **football boots** Fußballschuhe, -stiefel I

for [fə, fɔː] für I • **for breakfast/lunch/dinner** zum Frühstück/Mittagessen/Abendbrot I • °**for example** zum Beispiel • **for lots of reasons** aus vielen Gründen I **for miles** meilenweit II • **for three days** drei Tage (lang) I °**for the festival** wegen des Festivals • **just for fun** nur zum Spaß I • **What for?** Wofür? II **What's for homework?** Was haben wir als Hausaufgabe auf? I

foreground ['fɔːgraʊnd] Vordergrund II

forest ['fɒrɪst] Wald II

forget (-tt-) [fə'get], **forgot, forgotten** vergessen I

forgot [fə'gɒt] siehe **forget**

forgotten [fə'gɒtn] siehe **forget**

fork [fɔːk] Gabel III 4 (81/165)

form [fɔːm]
1. (Schul-)Klasse I • **form teacher** Klassenlehrer/in I
°2. Form

°**form** [fɔːm] bilden

fought [fɔːt] siehe **fight**

found [faʊnd] siehe **find**

°**found** [faʊnd] gründen

fox [fɒks] Fuchs II

free [friː]
1. frei I • **free time** Freizeit, freie Zeit I
2. kostenlos I

French [frentʃ] Französisch I

Friday ['fraɪdeɪ, 'fraɪdi] Freitag I

fridge [frɪdʒ] Kühlschrank I

friend [frend] Freund/in I

friendly ['frendli] freundlich III 1 (27)

frog [frɒg] Frosch II

from [frəm, frɒm]
1. aus I
2. von I
from all over the UK/the world/England aus dem gesamten Vereinigten Königreich/aus der ganzen Welt/aus ganz England III Intro (6)
from Monday to Friday von Montag bis Freitag III 4 (72/163) • **I'm from ...** Ich komme aus ... / Ich bin aus ... I • **Where are you from?** Wo kommst du her? I
▶ S.163 German „bis"

front [frʌnt]: **in front of** vor (räumlich) I • **front door** [,frʌnt 'dɔː] Wohnungstür, Haustür I

°**front page** [,frʌnt 'peɪdʒ] Titelseite I

fruit [fruːt] Obst, Früchte; Frucht I **fruit salad** ['fruːt ,sæləd] Obstsalat I

full [fʊl] voll I

fun [fʌn] Spaß I • **have fun** Spaß haben, sich amüsieren I • **Have fun!** Viel Spaß! I • **just for fun** nur zum Spaß I • **Riding is fun.** Reiten macht Spaß. I

funny ['fʌni] witzig, komisch I

°**fusion** ['fjuːʒn] aus der Verschmelzung verschiedener Musikrichtungen entstandener Musikstil

°**future** ['fjuːtʃə] Zukunft

G

game [geɪm] Spiel I

°**gap** [gæp] Lücke

garage ['gærɑːʒ] Garage II

garden ['gɑːdn] Garten I

gate [geɪt] Flugsteig III 1 (20/153)

gave [geɪv] siehe **give**

general ['dʒenrəl] allgemeine(r, s) III 2 (39)

geography [dʒi'ɒgrəfi] Geografie, Erdkunde I

German ['dʒɜːmən] Deutsch; deutsch; Deutsche(r) I

Germany ['dʒɜːməni] Deutschland I

get (-tt-) [get], **got, got**
1. bekommen, kriegen II
2. holen, besorgen II
3. gelangen, (hin)kommen I
4. **get angry/hot/...** wütend/heiß/... werden II
5. **get off (the train/bus)** (aus dem Zug/Bus) aussteigen I • **get on (the train/bus)** (in den Zug/Bus) einsteigen I

6. get up aufstehen I
get dressed sich anziehen I
get ready (for) sich fertig machen (für), sich vorbereiten (auf) I
get things ready Dinge fertig machen, vorbereiten I
getting by in English [ˌgetɪŋ ˈbaɪ] *etwa:* auf Englisch zurechtkommen I
°**gherkin** [ˈgɜːkɪn] (Essig-)Gurke
ghost [gəʊst] Geist, Gespenst II
°**gift** [gɪft] Geschenk
gig [gɪg] *(infml)* Gig, Auftritt III Intro (8) • **do a gig** einen Auftritt haben, ein Konzert geben III Intro (8/151)
giraffe [dʒəˈrɑːf] Giraffe II
girl [gɜːl] Mädchen I
give [gɪv], **gave, given** geben I
given [ˈgɪvn] *siehe* **give**
glad [glæd] froh, dankbar III 2 (35)
glass [glɑːs] Glas I • **a glass of water** ein Glas Wasser I
glasses (pl) [ˈglɑːsɪz] (eine) Brille I
glue [gluː] (auf-, ein)kleben II
glue [gluː] Klebstoff I • **glue stick** [ˈgluː stɪk] Klebestift I
go [gəʊ], **went, gone** gehen I; fahren II • **go by car/train/bike/...** mit dem Auto/Zug/Rad/... fahren II • **go for a walk** spazieren gehen, einen Spaziergang machen II • **go home** nach Hause gehen I • **go on** weitermachen I • °**How does the story go on?** Wie geht die Geschichte weiter? • **go on a trip** einen Ausflug machen II • **go on holiday** in Urlaub fahren II • **go riding** reiten gehen I • **go shopping** einkaufen gehen I • **go surfing** wellenreiten gehen, surfen gehen II • **go swimming** schwimmen gehen I • **go to bed** ins Bett gehen I • **go to the cinema** ins Kino gehen II • **go together** zusammenpassen, -gehören II • **go well** gut (ver)laufen, gutgehen III 2 (45) • **go with** gehören zu, passen zu III Intro (11) • **Let's go.** Auf geht's! *(wörtlich:* Lass uns gehen.) I
goal [gəʊl] Tor *(im Sport)* III 3 (56)
goalkeeper [ˈgəʊlkiːpə] Torwart, Torfrau III 3 (57)
go-kart [ˈgəʊkɑːt] Gokart III 4 (78)
gone [gɒn] *siehe* **go**
good [gʊd]
1. gut I • **Good afternoon.** Guten Tag. *(nachmittags)* I • **Good luck (with ...)!** Viel Glück (bei/mit ...)! I **Good morning.** Guten Morgen. I
2. brav II

Goodbye. [ˌgʊdˈbaɪ] Auf Wiedersehen. I • **say goodbye** sich verabschieden I
got [gɒt] *siehe* **get**
got [gɒt]: **I've got ...** Ich habe ... I **I haven't got a chair.** Ich habe keinen Stuhl. I
grammar [ˈgræmə] Grammatik I **grammar file** *Grammatikanhang* I
°**grandad** [ˈgrændæd] *(infml)* Opa
grandchild [ˈgræntʃaɪld], *pl* **grandchildren** [ˈ-tʃɪldrən] Enkel/in I
grandfather [ˈgrænfɑːðə] Großvater I
grandma [ˈgrænmɑː] Oma I
grandmother [ˈgrænmʌðə] Großmutter I
grandpa [ˈgrænpɑː] Opa I
grandparents [ˈgrænpeərənts] Großeltern I
granny [ˈgræni] Oma II
great [greɪt] großartig, toll I
°**Greater Manchester/Berlin/...** Großraum Manchester/Berlin/...
green [griːn] grün I
°**greeting** [ˈgriːtɪŋ] Gruß, Begrüßung I
grew [gruː] *siehe* **grow**
grey [greɪ] grau II
ground [graʊnd] (Erd-)Boden III 1 (20)
grounded [ˈgraʊndɪd]: **be grounded** Ausgehverbot/Hausarrest haben III 4 (70)
group [gruːp] Gruppe I • **group word** Oberbegriff II
grow [grəʊ], **grew, grown**
1. *(Getreide usw.)* anbauen, anpflanzen II
2. grow up erwachsen werden; aufwachsen III 3 (66)
grown [grəʊn] *siehe* **grow**
grumble [ˈgrʌmbl] murren, nörgeln I
guess [ges] raten, erraten, schätzen III 2 (39)
guest [gest] Gast I
°**guide book** [ˈgaɪd bʊk] Reiseführer I
guinea pig [ˈgɪni pɪg] Meerschweinchen I
guitar [gɪˈtɑː] Gitarre I • **play the guitar** Gitarre spielen I
guys (pl) [gaɪz] *(AE, infml)* Leute III 4 (72)

H

had [hæd] *siehe* **have** *und* **have got**
°**haggis** [ˈhægɪs] *gefüllter Schafsmagen*
hair *(no pl)* [heə] Haar, Haare I

half [hɑːf], *pl* **halves** [hɑːvz]
1. Hälfte III Intro (11/151)
2. Halbzeit III 3 (64/160)
the first half die erste Halbzeit III 3 (64/160)
half [hɑːf]: **half an hour** eine halbe Stunde III Intro (11) • **half past 11** halb zwölf (11.30 / 23.30) I • °**half-price** zum halben Preis • °**half the size** halb so groß
half-time [ˌhɑːf ˈtaɪm] Halbzeit(pause) III 3 (64)
hall [hɔːl] Flur, Diele I
halves [hɑːvz] *Plural von „half"*
hamburger [ˈhæmbɜːgə] Hamburger I
hamster [ˈhæmstə] Hamster I
hand [hænd] Hand I
handball [ˈhændbɔːl] Handball III 3 (53)
hang out (with friends) [ˌhæŋ ˈaʊt], *(infml)* **hung, hung** rumhängen, abhängen (mit Freunden/Freundinnen) III 4 (69)
happen (to) [ˈhæpən] geschehen, passieren (mit) I
happy [ˈhæpi] glücklich, froh I **Happy birthday.** Herzlichen Glückwunsch zum Geburtstag. I **happy ending** Happyend II
harbour [ˈhɑːbə] Hafen II
hard [hɑːd] hart; schwer, schwierig II • **work hard** hart arbeiten II
hat [hæt] Hut II
hate [heɪt] hassen, gar nicht mögen I
have [həv, hæv], **had, had** haben, besitzen II • **have a baby** ein Baby/Kind bekommen II • **have a bath** baden, ein Bad nehmen II **have a cold** erkältet sein, eine Erkältung haben II • **have a picnic** ein Picknick machen I • **have a sauna** in die Sauna gehen II **have a shower** (sich) duschen I **have a sore throat** Halsschmerzen haben II • **have a temperature** Fieber haben II • **have breakfast/dinner** frühstücken/Abendbrot essen I • **have ... for breakfast** ... zum Frühstück essen/trinken I **have fun** Spaß haben, sich amüsieren I • **have sleepovers** Schlafpartys veranstalten III 4 (69) • **have to do** tun müssen I
have got: I've got ... [aɪv ˈgɒt] Ich habe ... I • **I haven't got a chair.** Ich habe keinen Stuhl. I
he [hiː] er I
head [hed] Kopf I • °**head of state** Staatsoberhaupt • **head teacher** Schulleiter/in III 2 (44)

headache ['hedeɪk] Kopfschmerzen II

°**heading** ['hedɪŋ] Überschrift, Titel

healthy ['helθi] gesund II

hear [hɪə]**, heard, heard** hören I

heard [hɜːd] *siehe* **hear**

heart [hɑːt] Herz II

hedgehog ['hedʒhɒg] Igel II

held [held] *siehe* **hold**

helicopter ['helɪkɒptə] Hubschrauber, Helikopter II

Hello. [hə'ləʊ] Hallo. / Guten Tag. I

helmet ['helmɪt] Helm III 1 (26)

help [help] helfen I • **Help yourself!** Bedien dich! / Greif zu! III 3 (65) • **Can I help you?** Kann ich Ihnen helfen? / Was kann ich für Sie tun? *(im Geschäft)* I

help [help] Hilfe I

her [hə, hɜː]
1. ihr, ihre I
2. sie; ihr I

here [hɪə]
1. hier I
2. hierher I
Here you are. Bitte sehr. / Hier bitte. I

hers [hɜːz] ihrer, ihre, ihrs II

herself [hə'self, hɜː'self] sich (selbst) III 4 (71/163)

Hey. [heɪ] Hallo! III Intro (8)

Hi! [haɪ] Hallo! I • **Say hi to Dilip for me.** Grüß Dilip von mir. I

hid [hɪd] *siehe* **hide**

hidden ['hɪdn] *siehe* **hide**

hide [haɪd]**, hid, hidden** sich verstecken; *(etwas)* verstecken I

high [haɪ] hoch III 1 (15)

°**Highland** ['haɪlənd] Hochland-

hill [hɪl] Hügel II

hilly ['hɪli] hügelig III 2 (38/157)

him [hɪm] ihn; ihm I

himself [hɪm'self] sich (selbst) III 4 (71/163)

hip hop ['hɪp hɒp] Hip Hop III Intro (6)

hippo ['hɪpəʊ] Flusspferd II

his [hɪz]
1. sein, seine I
2. seiner, seine, seins II

history ['hɪstri] Geschichte I

hit (-tt-) [hɪt]**, hit, hit** schlagen II

hobby ['hɒbi] Hobby I

hockey ['hɒki] Hockey I • **hockey shoes** Hockeyschuhe I

hold [həʊld]**, held, held** halten II
°**hold up** hochhalten

holiday(s) ['hɒlədeɪ(z)] Ferien I
holiday flat Ferienwohnung II
°**be on holiday** in Urlaub sein; Ferien haben/machen • **go on holiday** in Urlaub fahren II

a two-week holiday ein zweiwöchiger Urlaub III 4 (76/164)

home [həʊm] Heim, Zuhause I
at home daheim, zu Hause I
come home nach Hause kommen I • **get home** nach Hause kommen I • **go home** nach Hause gehen I

°**homeless** ['həʊmləs] obdachlos

homework *(no pl)* ['həʊmwɜːk] Hausaufgabe(n) I • **do homework** die Hausaufgabe(n) machen I
What's for homework? Was haben wir als Hausaufgabe auf? I

Hooray! [hu'reɪ] Hurra! II

hope [həʊp] hoffen II

hope [həʊp] Hoffnung III 3 (66)

horrible ['hɒrəbl] scheußlich, grauenhaft II

horse [hɔːs] Pferd I

hospital ['hɒspɪtl] Krankenhaus II

°**host** [həʊst] Gastgeber/in • °**host family** Gastfamilie

hostel ['hɒstl] Herberge, Wohnheim III Intro (8) • **youth hostel** ['juːθ ˌhɒstl] Jugendherberge III Intro (8/151)

hot [hɒt] heiß I • **hot chocolate** heiße Schokolade I

hotel [həʊ'tel] Hotel II

hotline ['hɒtlaɪn] Hotline II

hour ['aʊə] Stunde II • **half an hour** [ˌhɑːf_ən_'aʊə] eine halbe Stunde III Intro (11) • **a 14-hour flight** ein 14-stündiger Flug, ein 14-Stunden-Flug III 4 (76/164) • **a 24-hour supermarket** ein Supermarkt, der 24 Stunden geöffnet ist III 4 (76/164)

house [haʊs] Haus I • **at the Shaws' house** im Haus der Shaws / bei den Shaws zu Hause I

how [haʊ] wie I • **How about …?** Wie wär's mit …? III Intro (10)
How am I doing? Wie komme ich voran? *(Wie sind meine Fortschritte?)* III 1 (29) • **How are you?** Wie geht es dir/Ihnen/euch? II
How do you know …? Woher weißt/kennst du …? I • **how many?** wie viele? I • **how much?** wie viel? I • **How much is/are …?** Was kostet/kosten …? / Wie viel kostet/kosten …? I • **How old are you?** Wie alt bist du? I • **How was …?** Wie war …? I

huge [hjuːdʒ] riesig, sehr groß III 2 (30/156)
► S.156 big – large – huge

hundred ['hʌndrəd] hundert I

hung out [ˌhʌŋ_'aʊt] *siehe* **hang out**

hungry ['hʌŋgri] hungrig III Intro (10) • **be hungry** Hunger haben, hungrig sein III Intro (10)

hunt [hʌnt] jagen III 4 (69/161)

hunt [hʌnt] Jagd III 4 (69/162)
°**hunting knife** Jagdmesser

°**hunter** ['hʌntə] Jäger/in

hurry ['hʌri] eilen; sich beeilen II
hurry up sich beeilen I

hurry ['hʌri]**: be in a hurry** in Eile sein, es eilig haben I

hurt [hɜːt]**, hurt, hurt** wehtun; verletzen I

hurt [hɜːt] verletzt II

husband ['hʌzbənd] Ehemann II

hutch [hʌtʃ] (Kaninchen-)Stall I

I

I [aɪ] ich I • **I'm** [aɪm] ich bin I
I'm from … Ich komme aus … / Ich bin aus … I • **I'm … years old.** Ich bin … Jahre alt. I • **I'm sorry.** Entschuldigung. / Tut mir leid. I

ice: ice cream [ˌaɪs 'kriːm] (Speise-)Eis I • **ice hockey** ['aɪs hɒki] Eishockey • **ice rink** ['aɪs rɪŋk] Schlittschuhbahn II

idea [aɪ'dɪə] Idee, Einfall I

if [ɪf]
1. falls, wenn II
2. ob II

ill [ɪl] krank II

°**imaginary** [ɪ'mædʒɪnəri] imaginär, *(nur in der Vorstellung vorhanden, nicht wirklich)*

°**imagine sth.** [ɪ'mædʒɪn] sich etwas vorstellen

important [ɪm'pɔːtnt] wichtig II

impossible [ɪm'pɒsəbl] unmöglich II

°**improve** [ɪm'pruːv] verbessern

in [ɪn] in I • **in … Street** in der … straße I • **in English** auf Englisch I • **in front of** vor *(räumlich)* I
in here hier drinnen I • **in the afternoon** nachmittags, am Nachmittag I • **in the country** auf dem Land II • **in the end** schließlich, zum Schluss III 3 (57) • **in the evening** abends, am Abend I • **in the field** auf dem Feld II • **in the morning** am Morgen, morgens I • **in the photo** auf dem Foto I • **in the picture** auf dem Bild I • **in the yard** auf dem Hof II • **in time** rechtzeitig II

°**include** [ɪn'kluːd] beinhalten

°**Indian** ['ɪndiən] *indianische* Ureinwohner/in Kanadas

infinitive [ɪnˈfɪnətɪv] Infinitiv (*Grundform des Verbs*) I

information (about/on) *(no pl)* [ˌɪnfəˈmeɪʃn] Information(en) (über) II • °**information point** Informationsstelle

inline skating [ˈɪnlaɪn ˌskeɪtɪŋ] Inlineskaten III 3 (63)

inside [ˌɪnˈsaɪd]
1. innen (drin), drinnen I
2. nach drinnen II
3. inside the car ins Auto (hinein), ins Innere des Autos II
°**inside cover** [ˌɪnsaɪd ˈkʌvə] Umschlaginnenseite

install [ɪnˈstɔːl] installieren, einrichten II

instant messages *(pl)* [ˌɪnstənt ˈmesɪdʒɪz] *Nachrichten, die man im Internet austauscht (in Echtzeit)* III 2 (32)

instructions *(pl)* [ɪnˈstrʌkʃnz] (Gebrauchs-)Anweisung(en), Anleitung(en) II

instrument [ˈɪnstrəmənt] Instrument III Intro (8)

interest [ˈɪntrəst] Interesse III 5 (94)

interested: be interested (in) [ˈɪntrəstɪd] interessiert sein (an), sich interessieren (für) III 3 (55)

interesting [ˈɪntrəstɪŋ] interessant I

international [ˌɪntəˈnæʃnəl] international III Intro (6/150)

internet [ˈɪntənet] Internet III 2 (32)
surf the internet [sɜːf] im Internet surfen III 2 (32)

interview [ˈɪntəvjuː] Interview I

interview [ˈɪntəvjuː] interviewen, befragen II

into [ˈɪntə, ˈɪntʊ] in ... (hinein) I

introduction (to) [ˌɪntrəˈdʌkʃn] Einführung (in) III Intro (6)

°**Inuit** [ˈɪnuɪt, ˈɪnjuɪt] Inuit *(eskimoische Volksgruppe in Zentral- und Nordostkanada und Grönland)*

°**invent** [ɪnˈvent] erfinden

°**invention** [ɪnˈvenʃn] Erfindung

invitation (to) [ˌɪnvɪˈteɪʃn] Einladung (zu) I

invite (to) [ɪnˈvaɪt] einladen (zu) I

°**irregular** [ɪˈregjələ] unregelmäßig

is [ɪz] ist I

island [ˈaɪlənd] Insel II

°**issue** [ˈɪʃuː] (Streit-)Frage, Thema, Angelegenheit

it [ɪt] er/sie/es I • **It's £1.** Er/Sie/Es kostet 1 Pfund. I • **It says here: ...** Hier steht: ... / Es heißt hier: ... II

its [ɪts] sein/seine; ihr/ihre I

itself [ɪtˈself] sich (selbst) III 4 (71/163)

J

jacket [ˈdʒækɪt] Jacke, Jackett II

January [ˈdʒænjuəri] Januar I

jazz [dʒæz] Jazz III Intro (6)

jealous (of) [ˈdʒeləs] neidisch (auf); eifersüchtig (auf) III 2 (45)

jeans *(pl)* [dʒiːnz] Jeans I

jewellery [ˈdʒuːəlri] Schmuck III 4 (71)

job [dʒɒb] Aufgabe, Job I

join sb. [dʒɔɪn] sich jm. anschließen; bei jm. mitmachen II

joke [dʒəʊk] Witz I

joke [dʒəʊk] scherzen, Witze machen II

journey [ˈdʒɜːni] Fahrt, Reise III 1 (25)

judo [ˈdʒuːdəʊ] Judo I • **do judo** Judo machen I

jug [dʒʌg] Krug I • **a jug of milk** ein Krug Milch I

juice [dʒuːs] Saft I

July [dʒuˈlaɪ] Juli I

°**jumble** [ˈdʒʌmbl] gebrauchte Sachen, Trödel

jumble sale [ˈdʒʌmbl seɪl] Wohltätigkeitsbasar II

jump [dʒʌmp] springen II • **jump around** herumspringen III 1 (26/155)

June [dʒuːn] Juni I

junior [ˈdʒuːniə] Junioren-, Jugend- I

just [dʒʌst]
1. (einfach) nur, bloß I
2. gerade (eben), soeben II

K

kangaroo [ˌkæŋgəˈruː] Känguru II

keep [kiːp], **kept, kept:**
°**keep a diary** ein Tagebuch führen
keep fit fit bleiben • **keep in touch** [ˌkiːp ɪn ˈtʌtʃ] in Verbindung bleiben, Kontakt halten III Intro (11) • **keep sth. warm/cool/open/...** etwas warm/kühl/offen/... halten II

kept [kept] *siehe* **keep**

key [kiː]
1. Schlüssel
°**2.** Taste
key ring Schlüsselring II • **key word** Stichwort, Schlüsselwort I

keyboard [ˈkiːbɔːd] Keyboard *(elektronisches Tasteninstrument)* III Intro (7)

kid [kɪd] Kind, Jugendliche(r) I

kidney [ˈkɪdni] Niere III 3 (62)

kill [kɪl] töten I

kilogram (kg) [ˈkɪləgræm], **kilo** [ˈkiːləʊ] Kilogramm, Kilo (kg)

III 4 (76) • **two kilos of oranges** zwei Kilo Orangen III 4 (76/164)
a 150-kilogram bear ein 150 Kilogramm schwerer Bär III 4 (76/164)

kilometre (km) [ˈkɪləmiːtə] Kilometer III 4 (76) • **a ten-kilometre walk** eine Zehn-Kilometer-Wanderung III 4 (76/164)

°**kilt** [kɪlt] Kilt, Schottenrock

kind (of) [kaɪnd] Art III Intro (6) • **What kind of car...?** Was für ein Auto III Intro (6/151)

king [kɪŋ] König I

kitchen [ˈkɪtʃɪn] Küche I

kite [kaɪt] Drachen I

kiwi [ˈkiːwiː] Kiwi II

knee [niː] Knie I

knew [njuː] *siehe* **know**

knife [naɪf], *pl* **knives** [naɪvz] Messer III 4 (81) • °**hunting knife** Jagdmesser

know [nəʊ], **knew, known**
1. wissen I
2. kennen I
know about sth. von etwas wissen; über etwas Bescheid wissen II • **How do you know ...?** Woher weißt du ...? / Woher kennst du ...? I • **I don't know.** Ich weiß es nicht. I • **..., you know.** ..., wissen Sie. / ..., weißt du. I • **You know what, Sophie?** Weißt du was, Sophie? I

known [nəʊn] *siehe* **know**

L

°**lacrosse** [ləˈkrɒs] Lacrosse *(Sportart)*

°**label** [ˈleɪbl] beschriften, etikettieren

laid [leɪd] *siehe* **lay**

lake [leɪk] (Binnen-)See II

lamb [læm] Lamm(fleisch) III 1 (24/154)

lamp [læmp] Lampe I

land [lænd] landen II

land [lænd] Land, Grund und Boden II

lane [leɪn] Gasse, Weg III 1 (12/152)

language [ˈlæŋgwɪdʒ] Sprache I

large [lɑːdʒ] groß II
▶ S.156 big – large – huge

lasagne [ləˈzænjə] Lasagne I

last [lɑːst] letzte(r, s) I • **the last day** der letzte Tag I • **at last** endlich, schließlich I

late [leɪt] spät; zu spät I • **be late** zu spät sein/kommen I • °**sleep late** ausschlafen • **Sorry, I'm late.** Entschuldigung, dass ich zu spät bin/komme. I

later [ˈleɪtə] später I
latest [ˈleɪtɪst] neueste(r, s) III 4 (81)
laugh [lɑːf] lachen I
laughter [ˈlɑːftə] Gelächter II
lay [leɪ], **laid, laid: lay the table** den Tisch decken I
°**layout** [ˈleɪaʊt] Layout, Seitengestaltung
°**lazy** [ˈleɪzi] faul
leader [ˈliːdə] (An-)Führer/in, Leiter/in, III 4 (73)
°**leaf** [liːf], pl **leaves** [liːvz] Blatt
learn [lɜːn] lernen I • **learn sth. about sth.** etwas über etwas erfahren, etwas über etwas herausfinden II
least [liːst]: **at least** zumindest, wenigstens I • **like sth. least** etwas am wenigsten mögen III 5 (89)
leave [liːv]**, left, left**
1. (weg)gehen; abfahren II
2. verlassen II
3. zurücklassen II
left [left] siehe **leave**
left [left] linke(r, s) II • **look left** nach links schauen II • **on the left** links, auf der linken Seite II • **turn left** (nach) links abbiegen II
leg [leg] Bein I
°**legend** [ˈledʒənd] Legende
leisure centre [ˈleʒə sentə] Freizeitzentrum, -park II
lemonade [ˌleməˈneɪd] Limonade I
lesson [ˈlesn] (Unterrichts-)Stunde I • **lessons** (pl) [ˈlesnz] Unterricht I
let [let]**, let, let** lassen II • **Let's ...** Lass uns ... / Lasst uns ... I • **Let's go.** Auf geht's! (wörtlich: Lass uns gehen.) I • **Let's look at the list.** Sehen wir uns die Liste an. / Lasst uns die Liste ansehen. I
letter [ˈletə]
1. Buchstabe I
2. letter (to) Brief (an) II
lettuce [ˈletɪs] (Kopf-)Salat II
library [ˈlaɪbrəri] Bibliothek, Bücherei I
life [laɪf], pl **lives** [laɪvz] Leben I
lift [lɪft] Fahrstuhl, Aufzug II
light [laɪt] Licht III 2 (44)
like [laɪk] wie I • **What was the weather like?** Wie war das Wetter? II
like [laɪk] mögen, gernhaben I
like sth. best/least etwas am meisten/wenigsten mögen III 5 (89) • **like sth. better** etwas lieber mögen II • **I like swimming/dancing.** Ich schwimme/tanze gern. I • **I'd like ... (= I would**

like ...) Ich hätte gern ... / Ich möchte gern ... I • **I'd like to talk about ... (= I would like to talk about ...)** Ich möchte/würde gern über ... reden I • **Would you like ...?** Möchtest du ...? / Möchten Sie ...? I • **Would you like some?** Möchtest du etwas/ein paar? / Möchten Sie etwas/ein paar? I
line [laɪn]
1. Zeile II
2. (U-Bahn-)Linie III 1 (14)
link [lɪŋk] verbinden, verknüpfen I
link [lɪŋk] Verbindung, Verknüpfung III 4 (69/162)
linking word [ˈlɪŋkɪŋ wɜːd] Bindewort II
lion [ˈlaɪən] Löwe II
list [lɪst] Liste I
list [lɪst] auflisten, aufzählen II
listen (to) [ˈlɪsn] zuhören; sich etwas anhören I
listener [ˈlɪsnə] Zuhörer/in II
little [ˈlɪtl] klein I
live [lɪv] leben, wohnen I
live music [laɪv] Livemusik II
liver [ˈlɪvə] Leber III 3 (54)
lives [laɪvz] Plural von „life" I
living room [ˈlɪvɪŋ ruːm] Wohnzimmer I
local [ˈləʊkl] Orts-, örtlich II
location [ləʊˈkeɪʃn] Wohn-/Standort, Lage III 3 (53)
lock [lɒk] abschließen; sperren III 2 (41)
long [lɒŋ] lang I
look [lʊk]
1. schauen, gucken I
2. look different/great/old anders/toll/alt aussehen I
look after sth./sb. auf etwas/jn. aufpassen; sich um etwas/jn. kümmern II • **look at** ansehen, anschauen I • **look for** suchen II
look left/right nach links/rechts schauen II • **look round** sich umsehen I • **look sth. up** etwas nachschlagen III 2 (47) **look up (from)** hochsehen, aufschauen (von) II
°**loon** [luːn] Seetaucher
lorry [ˈlɒri] Lastwagen III 1 (20/153)
lose [luːz]**, lost, lost** verlieren II
lost [lɒst] siehe **lose**
lot [lɒt]: **a lot (of)** eine Menge, viel, viele II • **Thanks a lot!** Vielen Dank! I • **He likes her a lot.** Er mag sie sehr. I • **lots more** viel mehr I • **lots of** eine Menge, viele, viel I
loud [laʊd] laut I
love [lʌv] lieben, sehr mögen II

love [lʌv]
1. Liebe II
°**2.** Liebes, Liebling
Love ... Liebe Grüße, ... (Briefschluss) I
luck [lʌk]: **Good luck (with ...)!** Viel Glück (bei/mit ...)! I
luckily [ˈlʌkɪli] zum Glück, glücklicherweise II
lunch [lʌntʃ] Mittagessen I
lunch break Mittagspause I
°**lunchtime** Mittagszeit
°**lyrics** (pl) [ˈlɪrɪks] Liedtext(e)

M

°**machine** [məˈʃiːn] Maschine I
°**macintosh** [ˈmækɪntɒʃ] wasserdichter Regenmantel benannt nach dem schottischen Erfinder Macintosh
mad [mæd] verrückt I • **be mad about sth.** verrückt nach/auf etwas sein III 3 (100)
made [meɪd] siehe **make**
°**mag** [mæg] Abkürzung für **magazine**
magazine [ˌmægəˈziːn] Zeitschrift, Magazin I
mail [meɪl] schicken, senden (per Post oder E-Mail) III Intro (11) • **mail sb.** jn. anmailen II
mail [meɪl] Mail III 2 (38)
°**main** [meɪn] Haupt-
make [meɪk]**, made, made** machen; bauen I • **make a mess** alles durcheinanderbringen, alles in Unordnung bringen I • °**make notes** sich Notizen machen • °**What makes a game a good game?** Was macht ein Spiel zu einem guten Spiel?
make-up [ˈmeɪkʌp] Make-up II
°**make-up tip** Schminktipp
male [meɪl] männlich III 3 (53/159)
man [mæn], pl **men** [men] Mann I
many [ˈmeni] viele I • **how many?** wie viele? I
map [mæp] Landkarte, Stadtplan II
March [mɑːtʃ] März I
mark sth. up [ˌmɑːk ˈʌp] etwas markieren, kennzeichnen II
market [ˈmɑːkɪt] Markt II
marmalade [ˈmɑːməleɪd] (Orangen-)Marmelade I
married (to) [ˈmærɪd] verheiratet (mit) I
mashed potatoes [ˌmæʃt pəˈteɪtəʊz] Kartoffelbrei, Kartoffelpüree III 3 (65)
match [mætʃ] Spiel, Wettkampf I

°**match** [mætʃ]
1. passen zu
2. zuordnen
°**Match the letters and numbers.**
Ordne die Buchstaben den Zahlen
zu.
mate [meɪt] *(infml)* Freund/in,
Kumpel III 2 (32)
°**material** [məˈtɪəriəl] Material
maths [mæθs] Mathematik I
matter [ˈmætə]: **What's the matter?**
Was ist los? / Was ist denn? II
May [meɪ] Mai I
may [meɪ] dürfen III 4 (146)
maybe [ˈmeɪbi] vielleicht I
me [miː] mir; mich I • **Me too.** Ich
auch. I • **more than me** mehr als
ich II • **That's me.** Das bin ich. I
Why me? Warum ich? I
meal [miːl] Mahlzeit, Essen III 3 (65)
mean [miːn]**, meant, meant**
1. bedeuten III 3 (57) • **What does
'forest' mean?** Was bedeutet
„forest"? III 3 (57/160)
2. meinen *(sagen wollen)* II
meaning [ˈmiːnɪŋ] Bedeutung
III 2 (47)
meant [ment] *siehe* **mean**
meat [miːt] Fleisch I
medal [ˈmedl] Medaille III 3 (66)
media *(pl)* [ˈmiːdiə] Medien III 2 (32)
mediation [ˌmiːdiˈeɪʃn] Vermittlung,
Sprachmittlung, Mediation II
medium [ˈmiːdiəm] mittel(groß) II
meet [miːt]**, met, met**
1. treffen; kennenlernen I
2. sich treffen I
Nice to meet you. Nett, dich
kennenzulernen. III Intro (10)
°**memory** [ˈmeməri] Memory
men [men] *Plural von „man"* I
menu [ˈmenjuː] Speisekarte I
mess [mes]: **be a mess** sehr unordentlich sein; fürchterlich aussehen II • **make a mess** alles
durcheinanderbringen, alles in
Unordnung bringen I
message [ˈmesɪdʒ] Nachricht
III 2 (32/156) • **text message** [ˈtekst
ˌmesɪdʒ] SMS III 2 (32)
met [met] *siehe* **meet**
metre [ˈmiːtə] Meter II
mice [maɪs] *Plural von „mouse"* I
microphone [ˈmaɪkrəfəʊn] Mikrofon
III 2 (45)
middle (of) [ˈmɪdl] Mitte I;
Mittelteil II
mild [maɪld] mild III 1 (16)
mile [maɪl] Meile *(= ca. 1,6 km)* II
for miles meilenweit II
milk [mɪlk] Milch I
million [ˈmɪljən] Million III 4 (76)

mime [maɪm] pantomimisch darstellen, vorspielen II
°**mime** [maɪm] Pantomime
mind map [ˈmaɪnd mæp] Mindmap
(„Gedankenkarte", „Wissensnetz")
I
Mind your own business. [ˌmaɪnd
jərˌəʊn ˈbɪznəs] Das geht dich
nichts an! / Kümmere dich um
deine eigenen Angelegenheiten! II
mine [maɪn] meiner, meine, meins
II
mints *(pl)* [mɪnts] Pfefferminzbonbons I
minute [ˈmɪnɪt] Minute I • **Wait a
minute.** Warte mal! / Moment
mal! II
mirror [ˈmɪrə] Spiegel II
miss [mɪs]
1. vermissen II
2. Miss a turn. Einmal aussetzen.
II
Miss White [mɪs] Frau White *(unverheiratet)* I
missing [ˈmɪsɪŋ]: **be missing** fehlen
II • °**the missing information/
words** die fehlenden Informa-
tionen/Wörter
mistake [mɪˈsteɪk] Fehler I
mix [mɪks] mischen, mixen III 2 (32)
mix [mɪks] Mix, Mischung
III 2 (32/156)
mixture [ˈmɪkstʃə] Mischung
III Intro (9)
°**mix up** [ˌmɪksˈʌp] durcheinanderbringen
°**mobile** [ˈməʊbaɪl] Mobile
mobile (phone) [ˈməʊbaɪl] Mobiltelefon, Handy I
model [ˈmɒdl] Modell(-flugzeug,
-schiff usw.) I; (Foto-)Modell II
modern [ˈmɒdən] modern
III 4 (70/163)
mole [məʊl] Maulwurf II
mom [mɒm, *AE* mɑm] *(AE)* Mama,
Mutti; Mutter III 4 (70)
moment [ˈməʊmənt] Moment
III 1 (26)
Monday [ˈmʌndeɪ, ˈmʌndi] Montag
I • **Monday morning** Montagmorgen I
money [ˈmʌni] Geld I
monitor [ˈmɒnɪtə] Monitor, Bildschirm III 2 (39)
monkey [ˈmʌŋki] Affe II
monster [ˈmɒnstə] Ungeheuer,
Monster II
month [mʌnθ] Monat I
moon [muːn] Mond II
more [mɔː] mehr I • **lots more**
viel mehr I • **more than** mehr als
II • **more than me** mehr als ich II

more boring (than) langweiliger
(als) II • **no more music** keine
Musik mehr I • **not (...) any more**
nicht mehr III 3 (66)
morning [ˈmɔːnɪŋ] Morgen, Vormittag I • **in the morning** morgens, am Morgen I • **Monday
morning** Montagmorgen I • **on
Friday morning** freitagmorgens,
am Freitagmorgen I
most [məʊst] (der/die/das) meiste ...; am meisten II • **most people**
die meisten Leute I • **(the) most
boring** der/die/das langwei-
ligste ...; am langweiligsten II
mother [ˈmʌðə] Mutter I
mountain [ˈmaʊntən] Berg II
mouse [maʊs], *pl* **mice** [maɪs] Maus
I
mouth [maʊθ] Mund I
move [muːv]
1. bewegen; sich bewegen II
Move back one space. Geh ein
Feld zurück. II • **Move on one
space.** Geh ein Feld vor. II
2. move (to) umziehen (nach, in)
II • **move in** einziehen II • **move
out** ausziehen II
movement [ˈmuːvmənt] Bewegung
II
movie [ˈmuːvi] Film III 5 (89)
MP3 player [ˌempiːˈθriː ˌpleɪə] MP3-
Spieler I
Mr ... [ˈmɪstə] Herr ... I
Mrs ... [ˈmɪsɪz] Frau ... I
Ms ... [mɪz, məz] Frau ... II
much [mʌtʃ] viel I • **how much?**
wie viel? I • **How much is/are ...?**
Was kostet/kosten ...? / Wie viel
kostet/kosten ...? I • **like/love sth.
very much** etwas sehr mögen/
sehr lieben II
°**multicultural** [ˌmʌltiˈkʌltʃərəl]
multikulturell
multiple choice [ˌmʌltɪpl ˈtʃɔɪs]
Multiple-Choice I
mum [mʌm] Mama, Mutti; Mutter
I
°**mummy** [ˈmʌmi] Mumie
museum [mjuːˈziːəm] Museum I
mushroom [ˈmʌʃrʊm] Pilz
III 1 (24/154)
music [ˈmjuːzɪk] Musik I
musical [ˈmjuːzɪkl] Musical I
°**musician** [mjuːˈzɪʃn] Musiker/in
must [mʌst] müssen I
mustn't do [ˈmʌsnt] nicht tun
dürfen II
my [maɪ] mein/e I
myself [maɪˈself] mir/mich
(selbst) III 4 (71/163)

N

name [neɪm] Name I • **My name is …** Ich heiße … / Mein Name ist … I • **What's your name?** Wie heißt du? I

name [neɪm] nennen; benennen II

°**national** ['næʃnəl] national III Intro (6)

°**natural history** [ˌnætʃrəl 'hɪstri] Naturkunde

near [nɪə] in der Nähe von, nahe (bei) I

neat [niːt] gepflegt II • **neat and tidy** schön ordentlich II

need [niːd] brauchen, benötigen I

needn't do ['niːdnt] nicht tun müssen, nicht zu tun brauchen II

neighbour ['neɪbə] Nachbar/in I

nervous ['nɜːvəs] nervös, aufgeregt I

°**netball** ['netbɔl] Korbball

°**network** ['netwɜːk] (Wörter-)Netz

never ['nevə] nie, niemals I

new [njuː] neu I

news (no pl) [njuːz] Nachrichten, Neuigkeiten III 2 (44) • **That's good news.** Das sind gute Nachrichten. III 2 (44/158)

newspaper ['njuːspeɪpə] Zeitung I

next [nekst]: **be next** der/die Nächste sein I • **the next morning/day** am nächsten Morgen/Tag I **What have we got next?** Was haben wir als Nächstes? I • °**next door** [ˌnekst 'dɔː] nebenan

next to [nekst] neben II

nice [naɪs] schön, nett I • **Nice to meet you.** Nett, dich kennenzulernen. III Intro (10)

night [naɪt] Nacht, später Abend I **at night** nachts, in der Nacht I **on Friday night** freitagnachts, Freitagnacht I

°**nightmare** ['naɪtmeə] Alptraum

nil [nɪl] null III 3 (56/159)
▶ S.159 A football match

no [nəʊ] nein I

no [nəʊ] kein, keine I • **no more music** keine Musik mehr I • **No smoking.** Rauchen verboten. III 4 (77/164) • **No way!** Auf keinen Fall! / Kommt nicht in Frage! II

nobody ['nəʊbədi] niemand II

nod (-dd-) [nɒd] nicken (mit) II

noise [nɔɪz] Geräusch; Lärm I

noisy ['nɔɪzi] laut, lärmend II

north [nɔːθ] Norden; nach Norden; nördlich III Intro (7)

north-east [ˌnɔːθ'iːst] Nordosten; nach Nordosten; nordöstlich III Intro (7/151)

north-west [ˌnɔːθ'west] Nordwesten; nach Nordenwesten; nordwestlich III Intro (7/151)

nose [nəʊz] Nase I

not [nɒt] nicht I • **not (…) any** kein, keine I • **not (…) any more** nicht mehr III 3 (66) • **not (…) anybody** niemand • **not (…) anything** nichts II • **not (…) anywhere** nirgendwo(hin) II • **not (…) yet** noch nicht II

note [nəʊt] Mitteilung, Notiz I °**make notes** sich Notizen machen **take notes** sich Notizen machen I

nothing ['nʌθɪŋ] nichts II

°**notice** ['nəʊtɪs] Notiz, Mitteilung **notice board** Anschlagtafel, schwarzes Brett I

November [nəʊ'vembə] November I

now [naʊ] nun, jetzt I

number ['nʌmbə] Zahl, Ziffer, Nummer I

O

o [əʊ] null I

°**och** [ox] ach (besonders in Schottland und Irland gebräuchlich)

o'clock [ə'klɒk]: **eleven o'clock** elf Uhr I

October [ɒk'təʊbə] Oktober I

°**odd** [ɒd]: **What word is the odd one out?** Welches Wort passt nicht dazu / gehört nicht dazu?

of [əv, ɒv] von I • **two kilos of oranges** zwei Kilo Orangen III 4 (76/164)

of course [əv 'kɔːs] natürlich, selbstverständlich I

off [ɒf]: **cut sth. off** etwas abtrennen, abschneiden III 3 (66) • **fall off** herunterfallen (von) II • **get off (the train/bus)** (aus dem Zug/Bus) aussteigen I • **take sth. off** etwas ausziehen (Kleidung) II • **take 10 c off** 10 Cent abziehen I • **turn on/off** ein-/ausschalten III 2 (35)

°**official** [ə'fɪʃl] offiziell

often ['ɒfn] oft, häufig I

Oh dear! [əʊ 'dɪə] Oje! II

Oh well … [əʊ 'wel] Na ja … / Na gut … I

oil [ɔɪl] Öl III 2 (30) • **oil rig** ['ɔɪl rɪg] (Öl-)Bohrinsel III 2 (30)

OK [əʊ'keɪ] okay, gut, in Ordnung I

old [əʊld] alt I • **a sixteen-year-old** ein/e Sechzehnjährige/r III 4 (76) • **a sixteen-year-old girl** ein sechzehnjähriges Mädchen III 4 (76/164)

old-fashioned [ˌəʊld'fæʃnd] altmodisch III 4 (70)

on [ɒn]
1. auf I
2. be on eingeschaltet sein, an sein (Radio, Licht usw.) II • °**on a team** in einem Team • **on 13th June** am 13. Juni I • **on Friday** am Freitag I • **on Friday afternoon** freitagnachmittags, am Freitagnachmittag I • **on Friday evening** freitagabends, am Freitagabend I • **on Friday morning** freitagmorgens, am Freitagmorgen I • **on Friday night** freitagnachts, Freitagnacht I • **on the beach** am Strand II • **on the board** an die Tafel I • **on the bus** im Bus III 1 (14) • **on the coast** an der Küste III 2 (30/156) • **on the corner of Green Street and London Road** Green Street, Ecke London Road II • **on the left** links, auf der linken Seite II • **on the phone** am Telefon I • **on the plane** im Flugzeug II **on the radio** im Radio I • **on the right** rechts, auf der rechten Seite II • °**on the river** am Fluss • **on the train** im Zug I **on TV** im Fernsehen I • **What page are we on?** Auf welcher Seite sind wir? I • **go on holiday** in Urlaub fahren II • **straight on** geradeaus weiter II

once [wʌns] einmal III 1 (16/153) **once a week** einmal pro Woche III 1 (16/153)

one [wʌn] eins, ein, eine I • **one day** eines Tages I • **one-day ticket** Tageskarte III 1 (14/153) • **a new one** ein neuer / eine neue / ein neues II • **my old ones** meine alten II

onion ['ʌnjən] Zwiebel III 1 (24/154)

online [ˌɒn'laɪn] online, Online- III 2 (35)

only ['əʊnli]
1. nur, bloß I
2. the only guest der einzige Gast I

onto ['ɒntə, 'ɒntu] auf (… hinauf) III 3 (55)

open ['əʊpən] öffnen, aufmachen I

open ['əʊpən] offen, geöffnet II

°**opening sentence** [ˌəʊpənɪŋ 'sentəns] Einleitungssatz

operation (on) [ˌɒpə'reɪʃn] Operation (an) III 3 (100)

opposite ['ɒpəzɪt] Gegenteil I

or [ɔː] oder I

orange ['ɒrɪndʒ] orange(farben) I

orange ['ɒrɪndʒ] Orange, Apfelsine I • **orange juice** ['ɒrɪndʒ dʒuːs] Orangensaft I

°**order** ['ɔːdə]
1. Reihenfolge • **in the right order** in der richtigen Reihenfolge **word order** Wortstellung
2. Befehl

organize ['ɔːgənaɪz] ordnen, organisieren III 3 (64)

other ['ʌðə] andere(r, s) • **the others** die anderen I • **the other way round** anders herum II

Ouch! [aʊtʃ] Autsch! I

our ['aʊə] unser, unsere I

ours ['aʊəz] unserer, unsere, unseres II

ourselves [aʊə'selvz] uns (selbst) III 4 (71/163)

out [aʊt] heraus, hinaus; draußen II **out of ...** aus ... (heraus/hinaus) I
°**a day out** ein Tagesausflug

outfit ['aʊtfɪt] Outfit (Kleidung; Ausrüstung) II

outside [,aʊt'saɪd]
1. draußen I
2. nach draußen II
3. outside his room vor seinem Zimmer; außerhalb seines Zimmers I

over ['əʊvə]
1. über, oberhalb von I
2. be over vorbei/zu Ende sein I **all over the world** auf der ganzen Welt III Intro (6/150) • **from all over the UK/the world/England** aus dem gesamten Vereinigten Königreich/aus der ganzen Welt/aus ganz England III Intro (6) • **over there** da drüben, dort drüben II **over to ...** hinüber zu/nach ... II

own [əʊn]: **our own pool** unser eigenes Schwimmbad II

P

pack [pæk] packen, einpacken II

packet ['pækɪt] Päckchen, Packung, Schachtel I • **a packet of mints** ein Päckchen/eine Packung Pfefferminzbonbons I

pads (pl) [pædz] (Knie- usw.)Schützer (für Inlineskater); Schulterpolster (beim American Football) III 3 (63/160)

page [peɪdʒ] (Buch-, Heft-)Seite I **What page are we on?** Auf welcher Seite sind wir? I

paid [peɪd] siehe **pay**

paint [peɪnt] (an)malen I

painter ['peɪntə] Maler/in II

pair [peə]: **a pair (of)** ein Paar II

palace ['pæləs] Palast, Schloss III 1 (12/152)

°**pancake** ['pænkeɪk] Pfannkuchen

paper ['peɪpə]
1. Papier I
2. Zeitung I

paragraph ['pærəgrɑːf] Absatz (in einem Text) I

Paralympics [,pærə'lɪmpɪks] Paralympische Spiele (Olympische Spiele für Sportler/innen mit körperlicher Behinderung) III 3 (100)

paramedic [,pærə'medɪk] Sanitäter/in II

paraphrase ['pærəfreɪz] umschreiben, anders ausdrücken III 3 (55)

parcel ['pɑːsl] Paket I

parents ['peərənts] Eltern I

park [pɑːk] Park I

parliament ['pɑːləmənt] Parlament III 1 (12)

parrot ['pærət] Papagei I

part [pɑːt] Teil I

partner ['pɑːtnə] Partner/in I

party ['pɑːti] Party I

pass [pɑːs] (herüber)reichen, weitergeben I • **pass round** herumgeben I

past [pɑːst] Vergangenheit I

past [pɑːst] vorbei (an), vorüber (an) II • **half past 11** halb zwölf (11.30/23.30) I • **quarter past 11** Viertel nach elf (11.15/23.15) I

path [pɑːθ] Pfad, Weg II

pay (for) [peɪ], **paid, paid** bezahlen II

PE [,piː'iː], **Physical Education** [,fɪzɪkəl_edʒu'keɪʃn] Turnen, Sportunterricht I

pea [piː] Erbse III 1 (24/154)

pen [pen] Kugelschreiber, Füller I

pence (p) (pl) [pens] Pence (Plural von „penny") I

pencil ['pensl] Bleistift I • **pencil case** ['pensl keɪs] Federmäppchen I • **pencil sharpener** ['pensl ʃɑːpnə] Bleistiftanspitzer I

penny ['peni] kleinste britische Münze I

people ['piːpl] Menschen, Leute I

per [pɜː, pə] pro III 4 (76/164)

per cent (%) [pə' sent] Prozent III 4 (76)

°**perhaps** [pə'hæps] vielleicht I

person ['pɜːsn] Person II

personal ['pɜːsənl] persönliche(r, s) III 2 (39)

pet [pet] Haustier I • **pet shop** Tierhandlung I

phone [fəʊn] Telefon I • **on the phone** am Telefon I • **phone call** Anruf, Telefongespräch I • **phone number** Telefonnummer I

phone [fəʊn] telefonieren, anrufen I

photo ['fəʊtəʊ] Foto I • **in the photo** auf dem Foto I • **take photos** Fotos machen, fotografieren I

photographer [fə'tɒgrəfə] Fotograf/in III 5 (88)

°**phrase** [freɪz] Ausdruck, (Rede-)Wendung

piano [pi'ænəʊ] Klavier, Piano I **play the piano** Klavier spielen I

pick up [,pɪk_'ʌp]: **pick sb. up** jn. abholen III 2 (33) • **pick sth. up** etwas hochheben, aufheben II

picnic ['pɪknɪk] Picknick I • **have a picnic** ein Picknick machen I

picture ['pɪktʃə] Bild I • **in the picture** auf dem Bild I

pie [paɪ] Obstkuchen; Pastete II

piece [piːs]: **a piece of** ein Stück I **a piece of paper** ein Stück Papier I

piercing ['pɪəsɪŋ] Piercing III 4 (70)

pig [pɪg] Schwein III 1 (24/154)

pink [pɪŋk] pink(farben), rosa I

pirate ['paɪrət] Pirat, Piratin I

pitch [pɪtʃ] Fußball-/Hockeyplatz III 3 (55)

pizza ['piːtsə] Pizza I

place [pleɪs] Ort, Platz I

°**placemat** ['pleɪsmæt] Set, Platzdeckchen

plan [plæn] Plan I

plan (-nn-) [plæn] planen I

plane [pleɪn] Flugzeug II • **on the plane** im Flugzeug II

planet ['plænɪt] Planet II

plate [pleɪt] Teller I • **a plate of chips** ein Teller Pommes frites I

°**platform** ['plætfɔːm] Bahnsteig, Gleis I

play [pleɪ] spielen I • **play football** Fußball spielen I • **play the drums (pl)** Schlagzeug spielen III Intro (6/151) • **play the fiddle** Geige, Fiedel spielen III Intro (7/151) **play the guitar** Gitarre spielen I **play the piano** Klavier spielen I

play [pleɪ] Theaterstück I

player ['pleɪə] Spieler/in I

please [pliːz] bitte (in Fragen und Aufforderungen) I

plug [plʌg] Stecker III 1 (27)

pm [,piː_'em]: **7 pm** 7 Uhr abends/ 19 Uhr II

pocket ['pɒkɪt] Tasche (an einem Kleidungsstück) II • **pocket money** Taschengeld II

poem ['pəʊɪm] Gedicht I

point [pɔɪnt] Punkt II • **10.4 (ten point four)** 10,4 (zehn Komma vier) III Intro (6/151)
▶ S.151 Numbers
point (at/to sth.) [pɔɪnt] zeigen, deuten (auf etwas) II
police *(pl)* [pə'liːs] Polizei I
police station Polizeiwache, Polizeirevier II
policeman [pə'liːsmən] Polizist II
policewoman [pə'liːswʊmən] Polizistin II
poltergeist ['pəʊltəgaɪst] Poltergeist I
poor [pɔː, pʊə] arm I • **poor Sophie** (die) arme Sophie I
pop [pɒp] Pop(musik) III Intro (6)
popcorn ['pɒpkɔːn] Popcorn II
popular ['pɒpjələ] beliebt, populär III 5 (90)
°**population** [ˌpɒpju'leɪʃn] Bevölkerung
pork [pɔːk] Schweinefleisch III 1 (24/154)
possible ['pɒsəbl] möglich II
postcard ['pəʊstkɑːd] Postkarte II
poster ['pəʊstə] Poster I
post office ['pəʊst ˌɒfɪs] Postamt II
postscript (PS) ['pəʊstskrɪpt] Postskript *(Nachschrift unter Briefen)* III 1 (12)
potato [pə'teɪtəʊ], *pl* **potatoes** Kartoffel I
pound (£) [paʊnd] Pfund *(britische Währung)* I
practice ['præktɪs] *hier:* Übungsteil I
practise ['præktɪs] üben; trainieren I
prepare [prɪ'peə] vorbereiten; sich vorbereiten II • **prepare for** sich vorbereiten auf II
present ['preznt]
1. Gegenwart I
2. Geschenk I
°**present sth. (to sb.)** [prɪ'zent] (jm.) etwas präsentieren, vorstellen
presentation [ˌprezn'teɪʃn] Präsentation, Vorstellung I
presenter [prɪ'zentə] Moderator/in II
°**president** ['prezɪdənt] Präsident I
press [pres] drücken III 2 (41)
pretty ['prɪti] hübsch I
pretty healthy/good/... ['prɪti] ziemlich gesund/gut/... II
price [praɪs] (Kauf-)Preis I
°**half-price** zum halben Preis
prize [praɪz] Preis, Gewinn I
probably ['prɒbəbli] wahrscheinlich II
problem ['prɒbləm] Problem II
produce [prə'djuːs] produzieren, herstellen III 5 (88)

profile ['prəʊfaɪl] Porträt, Steckbrief III 3 (53)
programme ['prəʊgræm] Programm I
project (about, on) ['prɒdʒekt] Projekt (über, zu) I • **do a project** ein Projekt machen, durchführen II
promise ['prɒmɪs] versprechen II
°**pronounce** [prə'naʊns] aussprechen
pronunciation [prəˌnʌnsi'eɪʃn] Aussprache I
proof *(no pl)* [pruːf] Beweis(e) II
proud (of sb./sth.) [praʊd] stolz (auf jn./etwas) II
°**province** ['prɒvɪns] Provinz
PS [ˌpiː'es] **(postscript** ['pəʊstskrɪpt]**)** PS (Postskript; *Nachschrift unter Briefen)* III 1 (12)
pub [pʌb] Kneipe, Lokal II
publish ['pʌblɪʃ] veröffentlichen III 5 (88)
pull [pʊl] ziehen I
pullover ['pʊləʊvə] Pullover II
purple ['pɜːpl] violett; lila I
purse [pɜːs] Geldbörse II
push [pʊʃ] drücken, schieben, stoßen I
put (-tt-) [pʊt]**, put, put** legen, stellen, *(etwas wohin)* tun I • **put sth. on** etwas anziehen *(Kleidung)* II • °**Put up your hand.** Heb deine Hand. / Hebt eure Hand.
puzzled ['pʌzld] verwirrt II
pyjamas *(pl)* [pə'dʒɑːməz] Schlafanzug II

Q

quarter ['kwɔːtə]: **quarter past 11** Viertel nach 11 (11.15 / 23.15) I
quarter to 12 Viertel vor 12 (11.45 / 23.45) I
quay [kiː] Kai, Kaimauer III 3 (55)
queen [kwiːn] Königin III 1 (13)
question ['kwestʃn] Frage I • **ask questions** Fragen stellen I
°**question word** Fragewort
quick [kwɪk] schnell I
quiet ['kwaɪət] leise, still, ruhig I
quite bad/quick/good ... [kwaɪt] ziemlich schlimm/schnell/gut/... II
quiz [kwɪz]**,** *pl* **quizzes** ['kwɪzɪz] Quiz, Ratespiel I

R

rabbit ['ræbɪt] Kaninchen I
racket ['rækɪt]: **badminton racket** Badmintonschläger III 3 (63/160)

radio ['reɪdiəʊ] Radio I • **on the radio** im Radio I
railway ['reɪlweɪ] Eisenbahn II
rain [reɪn] Regen II
rain [reɪn] regnen II
rainy ['reɪni] regnerisch II
ran [ræn] *siehe* **run**
rang [ræŋ] *siehe* **ring**
rap [ræp] Rap *(rhythmischer Sprechgesang)* I
RE [ˌɑːr'iː]**, Religious Education** [rɪˌlɪdʒəs ˌedʒu'keɪʃn] Religion, Religionsunterricht I
read [riːd]**, read, read** lesen I • °**read out** vorlesen • °**Read out loud.** Lies laut vor. • °**Read the poem to a partner.** Lies das Gedicht einem Partner/einer Partnerin vor.
read [red] *siehe* **read**
reader ['riːdə] Leser/in I
ready ['redi] bereit, fertig I • **get ready (for)** sich fertig machen (für), sich vorbereiten (auf) I • **get things ready** Dinge fertig machen, vorbereiten I
real [rɪəl] echt, wirklich I
realistic [ˌriːə'lɪstɪk] realistisch, wirklichkeitsnah III 1 (27)
really ['rɪəli] wirklich I
reason ['riːzn] Grund, Begründung I • **for lots of reasons** aus vielen Gründen I
°**recipe** ['resəpi] Rezept
record [rɪ'kɔːd] *(Musik/einen Film)* aufnehmen III 1 (13)
recorder [rɪ'kɔːdə] Blockflöte III Intro (11)
recording [rɪ'kɔːdɪŋ] Aufnahme, Aufzeichnung III Intro (11)
recycled [ˌriː'saɪkld] wiederverwertet, wiederverwendet, recycelt II
recycling [ˌriː'saɪklɪŋ] Wiederverwertung, Recycling II
red [red] rot I
reggae ['regeɪ] Reggae III Intro (6)
rehearsal [rɪ'hɜːsl] Probe *(am Theater)* I
rehearse [rɪ'hɜːs] proben *(am Theater)* I
relax [rɪ'læks] (sich) entspannen, sich ausruhen II
remember sth. [rɪ'membə]
1. sich erinnern (an etwas) I
2. sich etwas merken I
°**Remember ...** Denk dran, ...
°**repeat** [rɪ'piːt] wiederholen I
report (on) [rɪ'pɔːt] Bericht, Reportage (über) I
report (to sb.) [rɪ'pɔːt] (jm.) berichten II

represent [ˌreprɪˈzent] repräsentieren, vertreten III 3 (100)

rescue helicopter [ˈreskjuːˌhelɪkɒptə] Rettungshubschrauber II

°**research** [rɪˈsɜːtʃ, ˈriːsɜːtʃ] Recherche

°**researcher** [rɪˈsɜːtʃə]: **film researcher** Filmrechercheur/in

°**reserve** [rɪˈzɜːv] Reservat, Schutzgebiet (in Kanada)

rest [rest] Rest II

restaurant [ˈrestrɒnt] Restaurant II

result [rɪˈzʌlt] Ergebnis, Resultat I

return ticket [rɪˈtɜːn ˌtɪkɪt] Rückfahrkarte II

revise [rɪˈvaɪz]
1. überarbeiten III 4 (78)
2. wiederholen III 4 (78)

revision [rɪˈvɪʒn] Wiederholung (des Lernstoffs) I

rhino [ˈraɪnəʊ] Nashorn II

rich [rɪtʃ] reich II

ridden [ˈrɪdn] siehe **ride**

ride [raɪd], **rode, ridden** reiten I • **go riding** [ˈraɪdɪŋ] reiten gehen I • **ride a bike** Rad fahren I

ride [raɪd]: **(bike) ride** (Rad-)Fahrt II

°**riding stable** [ˈraɪdɪŋ ˌsteɪbl] Reitstall

right [raɪt] richtig I • **all right** [ɔːl ˈraɪt] gut, in Ordnung II • **be right** Recht haben I • **That's right.** Das ist richtig. / Das stimmt. I • **You need a school bag, right?** Du brauchst eine Schultasche, stimmt's? / nicht wahr? I

right [raɪt] rechte(r, s) II • **look right** nach rechts schauen II • **on the right** rechts, auf der rechten Seite II • **turn right** (nach) rechts abbiegen II

right [raɪt]: **right now** jetzt sofort; jetzt gerade I

ring [rɪŋ] Ring II

ring [rɪŋ], **rang, rung** klingeln, läuten II • **The bell rang.** Es klingelte. III 3 (45/158)

ringtone [ˈrɪŋtəʊn] Klingelton III 2 (32)

river [ˈrɪvə] Fluss II

RnB [ˌɑːr_ənˈbiː] RnB (Rhythm and Blues; Form des Blues, in der Rhythmus eine große Rolle spielt) III Intro (6)

road [rəʊd] Straße I • **Park Road** [ˌpɑːk ˈrəʊd] Parkstraße I

°**roadie** [ˈrəʊdi] Roadie (Helfer einer Band, zuständig für Auf- und Abbau der Anlage)

rock [rɒk] Fels, Felsen III 2 (30/31)

rock (music) [rɒk] Rock(musik) III Intro (6

rode [rəʊd] siehe **ride**

role [rəʊl] Rolle III 5 (91)

role play [ˈrəʊl pleɪ] Rollenspiel II

roll [rəʊl] Brötchen I

Roman [ˈrəʊmən] römisch; Römer, Römerin I

room [ruːm] Raum, Zimmer I

round [raʊnd] rund II

round [raʊnd] um … (herum); in … umher II • **the other way round** anders herum II

rubber [ˈrʌbə] Radiergummi I

rubbish [ˈrʌbɪʃ] (Haus-)Müll, Abfall II

rucksack [ˈrʌksæk] Rucksack III 2 (34)

rude [ruːd] unhöflich, unverschämt II

rule [ruːl] Regel, Vorschrift III 4 (71)

ruler [ˈruːlə] Lineal I

run [rʌn] (Wett-)Lauf II

run (-nn-) [rʌn], **ran, run** laufen, rennen I • **run around** herumrennen II 1 (26/155)

rung [rʌŋ] siehe **ring**

runner [ˈrʌnə] Läufer/in II

running shoes [ˈrʌnɪŋ ʃuːz] Laufschuhe III 3 (63/160)

°**running track** [træk] Laufbahn (Sport)

°**rush hour** [ˈrʌʃ_aʊə] Hauptverkehrszeit

S

sad [sæd] traurig II

saddle [ˈsædl] Sattel III 3 (63/160)

safe (from) [seɪf] sicher, in Sicherheit (vor) II

said [sed] siehe **say**

sailor [ˈseɪlə] Seemann, Matrose II

salad [ˈsæləd] Salat (als Gericht oder Beilage) I

same [seɪm]: **the same …** der-/die-/dasselbe …; dieselben … I • **be/look the same** gleich sein/aussehen I

sandwich [ˈsænwɪtʃ] Sandwich, (zusammengeklapptes) belegtes Brot I • **sandwich box** Brotdose I

sang [sæŋ] siehe **sing**

sat [sæt] siehe **sit**

°**satellite** [ˈsætəlaɪt] Satellit I

Saturday [ˈsætədeɪ, ˈsætədi] Samstag, Sonnabend I

sauna [ˈsɔːnə] Sauna II • **have a sauna** in die Sauna gehen II

sausage [ˈsɒsɪdʒ] (Brat-, Bock-)Würstchen, Wurst I

save [seɪv]
1. retten II
2. sparen II

saw [sɔː] siehe **see**

saxophone [ˈsæksəfəʊn] Saxophon III Intro (11)

say [seɪ], **said, said** sagen I • **It says here: …** Hier steht: …/Es heißt hier: … II • **say goodbye** sich verabschieden I • **Say hi to Dilip for me.** Grüß Dilip von mir. I • **say sorry** sich entschuldigen II

scan a text (-nn-) [skæn] einen Text schnell nach bestimmten Wörtern/Informationen absuchen II

scared [skeəd] verängstigt II • **be scared (of)** Angst haben (vor) I

scarf [skɑːf], pl **scarves** [skɑːvz] Schal III 2 (44)

scary [ˈskeəri] unheimlich; gruselig I

scene [siːn] Szene I

school [skuːl] Schule I • **at school** in der Schule I • **school bag** Schultasche I • **school subject** Schulfach I

science [ˈsaɪəns] Naturwissenschaft I

°**scientist** [ˈsaɪəntɪst] (Natur-)Wissenschaftler/in

score (a goal) [skɔː], [gəʊl] ein Tor schießen, einen Treffer erzielen III 3 (56)

score [skɔː] Spielstand; Punktestand III 3 (56/159) • **final score** Endstand (beim Sport) III 3 (56/159) **What's the score? – 2–0 (two nil)** Wie steht es? (beim Sport) – 2:0. III 3 (56/159)
▶ S.159 A football match

sea [siː] Meer, (die) See I

°**search engine** [ˈsɜːtʃ_endʒɪn] Suchmaschine (im Internet)

second [ˈsekənd] zweite(r, s) I • **second-hand** [ˌsekənd ˈhænd] gebraucht; aus zweiter Hand III 1 (12)

section [ˈsekʃn] Abschnitt, Teil, (Themen-)Bereich III 5 (90)

see [siː], **saw, seen**
1. sehen I
2. see sb. jn. besuchen, jn. aufsuchen II
See? Siehst du? I • **See you.** Tschüs. / Bis bald. I • **Wait and see!** Wart's ab! III Intro (11)

°**seem (to do)** [siːm] (zu tun) scheinen

seen [siːn] siehe **see**

sell [sel], **sold, sold** verkaufen II

semi-final [ˌsemiˈfaɪnl] Halbfinale III 3 (52)

send (to) [send], **sent, sent** schicken, senden (an) II

sent [sent] siehe **send**

sentence [ˈsentəns] Satz I

September [sep'tembə] September I

series, *pl* **series** ['sɪəriːz] (Sende-)Reihe, Serie II

°**settle** ['setl] besiedeln, sich niederlassen

°**settler** ['setlə] Siedler/in

setup ['setʌp] Setup II

sex [seks] Geschlecht III 3 (53)

share sth. (with sb.) [ʃeə] sich etwas teilen (mit jm.) I

she [ʃiː] sie I

sheep, *pl* **sheep** [ʃiːp] Schaf II

shelf [ʃelf], *pl* **shelves** [ʃelvz] Regal(brett) I

shine [ʃaɪn], **shone, shone** scheinen (Sonne) II

ship [ʃɪp] Schiff I

shirt [ʃɜːt] Hemd I

shocked [ʃɒkt] schockiert III 1 (27)

shoe [ʃuː] Schuh I

shone [ʃɒn] *siehe* **shine**

shoot [ʃuːt], **shot, shot** schießen, erschießen III 4 (69)

shop [ʃɒp] Laden, Geschäft I
shop assistant ['ʃɒp_ə,sɪstənt] Verkäufer/in I • **shop window** Schaufenster II

shop (**-pp-**) [ʃɒp] einkaufen (gehen) I

shopping ['ʃɒpɪŋ] (das) Einkaufen I
go shopping einkaufen gehen I
shopping list Einkaufsliste I

short [ʃɔːt] kurz I

°**shortbread** ['ʃɔːtbred] schottischer Butterkeks

shorts (*pl*) [ʃɔːts] Shorts, kurze Hose I

shot [ʃɒt] *siehe* **shoot**

shoulder ['ʃəʊldə] Schulter I

shout [ʃaʊt] schreien, rufen I

show [ʃəʊ] Show, Vorstellung I

show [ʃəʊ], **showed, shown** zeigen I

shower ['ʃaʊə] Dusche I • **have a shower** (sich) duschen I

shown [ʃəʊn] *siehe* **show**

shut up [ˌʃʌt'ʌp], **shut, shut** den Mund halten II

shy [ʃaɪ] schüchtern, scheu II

side [saɪd] Seite II

sights (*pl*) [saɪts] Sehenswürdigkeiten II

sign [saɪn] Schild; Zeichen III 1 (26)

silent letter [ˌsaɪlənt 'letə] „stummer" Buchstabe (*nicht gesprochener Buchstabe*) I

silly ['sɪli] albern, dumm I

sing [sɪŋ], **sang, sung** singen I

singer ['sɪŋə] Sänger/in II

single ['sɪŋgl] ledig, alleinstehend I

single (ticket) ['sɪŋgl] einfache Fahrkarte (*nur Hinfahrt*) III 1 (14)

°**Sir** [sɜː, sə] *britischer Adelstitel*

sink [sɪŋk] Spüle, Spülbecken I

sister ['sɪstə] Schwester I

sit (-tt-) [sɪt], **sat, sat** sitzen; sich setzen I • **sit down** sich hinsetzen II • **Sit with me.** Setz dich zu mir. / Setzt euch zu mir. I

size [saɪz] Größe I • °**half the size** halb so groß

skate ['skeɪt] Inliner fahren I

skateboard ['skeɪtbɔːd] Skateboard I

°**skate park** ['skeɪt pɑːk] Skatepark I

skates (*pl*) [skeɪts] Inliner I

sketch [sketʃ] Sketch I

ski [skiː] Ski fahren/laufen III 4 (69/162)

ski [skiː] Ski III 3 (63/160) • °**ski slope** ['skiː sləʊp] Skipiste I

skills file ['skɪlz faɪl] Anhang mit Lern- und Arbeitstechniken I

skim a text (**-mm-**) [skɪm] einen Text überfliegen (*um den Inhalt grob zu erfassen*) III 5 (90)

skirt [skɜːt] Rock I

°**ski slope** ['skiː sləʊp] Skipiste I

sky [skaɪ] Himmel II

slave [sleɪv] Sklave, Sklavin II

sledge [sledʒ] Schlitten III 3 (100)

sleep [sliːp], **slept, slept** schlafen I °**sleep late** ausschlafen

sleep [sliːp] Schlaf III 4 (69/162)

sleepover ['sliːpəʊvə] Schlafparty III 4 (69)

slept [slept] *siehe* **sleep**

slow [sləʊ] langsam II

small [smɔːl] klein I

smart [smɑːt] clever, schlau II

smell [smel] riechen II

smell [smel] Geruch II

smile [smaɪl] lächeln I • **smile at sb.** jn. anlächeln II

smile [smaɪl] Lächeln II

smoke [sməʊk] rauchen III 4 (77) **no smoking** Rauchen verboten III 4 (77/164)

smoke [sməʊk] Rauch III 4 (77/164)

snack [snæk] Snack, Imbiss II

snake [sneɪk] Schlange I

snow [snəʊ] Schnee II

°**snowmobile** ['snəʊməbiːl] Schneemobil

snowshoe ['snəʊʃuː] Schneeschuh III 4 (69/162)

snowshoeing ['snəʊʃuːɪŋ] Schneeschuhwandern III 4 (69)

so [səʊ]
1. also; deshalb, daher I • **So?** Und? / Na und? II
2. so sweet so süß I

3. Do you really think so? Meinst du wirklich? / Glaubst du das wirklich? II

soap [səʊp] Seife I

sock [sɒk] Socke, Strumpf I

sofa ['səʊfə] Sofa I

software ['sɒftweə] Software II

sold [səʊld] *siehe* **sell**

some [səm, sʌm] einige, ein paar I **some cheese/juice** etwas Käse/Saft I

somebody ['sʌmbədi] jemand I **Find/Ask somebody who …** Finde/Frage jemanden, der … II

something ['sʌmθɪŋ] etwas II

sometimes ['sʌmtaɪmz] manchmal I

somewhere ['sʌmweə] irgendwo(hin) II

son [sʌn] Sohn I

song [sɒŋ] Lied, Song I

soon [suːn] bald I

sore [sɔː]: **have a sore throat** Halsschmerzen haben II

sorry ['sɒri]: **(I'm) sorry.** Entschuldigung. / Tut mir leid. I • **Sorry, I'm late.** Entschuldigung, dass ich zu spät bin/komme. I • **Sorry?** Wie bitte? I • **say sorry** sich entschuldigen II

sort [sɔːt] Art, Sorte II

sound [saʊnd] klingen, sich (*gut usw.*) anhören I

sound [saʊnd] Laut; Klang I °**sound assistant** ['saʊnd_ə,sɪstənt] Tonassistent/in • **sound file** ['saʊnd faɪl] Tondatei, Soundfile III 1 (12)

soup [suːp] Suppe II

°**sour** ['saʊə] sauer

°**source** [sɔːs] (Informations-)Quelle I

south [saʊθ] Süden; nach Süden; südlich III Intro (7/151)

south-east [ˌsaʊθ'iːst] Südosten; nach Südosten; südöstlich III Intro (7/151)

south-west [ˌsaʊθ'west] Südwesten; nach Südwesten; südwestlich III Intro (151)

°**souvenir** [ˌsuːvə'nɪə] Souvenir, Mitbringsel

space [speɪs]
°**1.** Weltraum
2. Move back one space. Geh ein Feld zurück. II • **Move on one space.** Geh ein Feld vor. II

spaghetti [spə'geti] Spaghetti II

speak (to) [spiːk], **spoke, spoken** sprechen (mit), reden (mit) II

special ['speʃl]: **a special day** ein besonderer Tag I

°**speech bubble** ['spiːtʃ ˌbʌbl] Sprech-blase

spell [spel] buchstabieren I

spelling ['spelɪŋ] (Recht-)Schreibung, Schreibweise III 4 (78)

spend [spend], **spent, spent: spend money (on)** Geld ausgeben (für) II • **spend time (on)** Zeit verbringen (mit) II

spent [spent] *siehe* **spend**

spicy ['spaɪsi] würzig, scharf gewürzt III 1 (16)

spoke [spəʊk] *siehe* **speak**

spoken ['spəʊkən] *siehe* **speak**

spoon [spuːn] Löffel III 4 (81/165)

sport [spɔːt] Sport; Sportart I
do sport Sport treiben I • **sports centre** Sportzentrum I • °**sports hall** Sporthalle

sporty ['spɔːti] sportlich III 3 (56)

spring [sprɪŋ] Frühling I

spy [spaɪ] Spion/in I

square [skweə] Platz III 1 (12/152)

squirrel ['skwɪrəl] Eichhörnchen II

stadium ['steɪdiəm] Stadion III 3 (55)

stage [steɪdʒ] Bühne III 4 (73)

stairs (pl) [steəz] Treppe; Treppenstufen I

stamp [stæmp] Briefmarke I

stand [stænd], **stood, stood** stehen; sich (hin)stellen II

star [stɑː]
1. Stern II
2. (Film-, Pop-)Star I

start [stɑːt] starten, anfangen, beginnen (mit) I

state [steɪt] Staat III Intro (10/151)
°**head of state** Staatsoberhaupt

statement ['steɪtmənt] Aussage, Feststellung III 2 (39)

station ['steɪʃn] Bahnhof I • **at the station** am Bahnhof I

statue ['stætʃuː] Statue II

stay [steɪ]
1. bleiben I
2. wohnen, übernachten II • °**stay with** wohnen bei

steak [steɪk] Steak III 1 (24/154)

steal [stiːl], **stole, stolen** stehlen II

steel [stiːl] Stahl III Intro (6) • **steel drum** [ˌstiːl 'drʌm] Steeldrum III Intro (6)

step [step] Schritt I

stereo ['steriəʊ] Stereoanlage I

still [stɪl] (immer) noch I

stole [stəʊl] *siehe* **steal**

stolen ['stəʊlən] *siehe* **steal**

stomach ['stʌmək]
1. Magen I
2. Bauch III 4 (71)
stomach ache Magenschmerzen, Bauchweh II

stone [stəʊn] Stein II

stood [stʊd] *siehe* **stand**

stop (-pp-) [stɒp]
1. aufhören I
2. anhalten I
Stop that! Hör auf damit! / Lass das! I

storm [stɔːm] Sturm; Gewitter II

stormy ['stɔːmi] stürmisch II

story ['stɔːri] Geschichte, Erzählung I

straight on [streɪt_'ɒn] geradeaus weiter II

strawberry ['strɔːbəri] Erdbeere II

street [striːt] Straße I • **at 7 Hamilton Street** in der Hamiltonstraße 7 I

°**stretch** [stretʃ] (sich) dehnen

stress [stres] Betonung III 3 (60)

°**stressed** [strest] betont

strict [strɪkt] streng III 4 (70)

strike [straɪk] Streik III 4 (77) • **be on strike** streiken, sich im Streik befinden III 4 (77/164) • **go on strike** streiken, in den Streik treten III 4 (77/164)

strong [strɒŋ] stark II

structure ['strʌktʃə] strukturieren, aufbauen II

student ['stjuːdənt] Schüler/in; Student/in I

study skills (pl) ['stʌdi skɪlz] Lern- und Arbeitstechniken I

stuff [stʌf] Zeug, Kram II

stupid ['stjuːpɪd] blöd, dämlich II

subject ['sʌbdʒɪkt]
1. Schulfach I
°**2.** Betreff in einer E-Mail

subway ['sʌbweɪ]: **the subway** (AE) die U-Bahn I

°**such** [sʌtʃ] so, solch

suddenly ['sʌdnli] plötzlich, auf einmal I

sugar ['ʃʊgə] Zucker II

suitcase ['suːtkeɪs] Koffer II

summer ['sʌmə] Sommer I

sun [sʌn] Sonne II

Sunday ['sʌndeɪ, 'sʌndi] Sonntag I

sung [sʌŋ] *siehe* **sing**

sunglasses (pl) ['sʌnglɑːsɪz] (eine) Sonnenbrille I

sunny ['sʌni] sonnig II

supermarket ['suːpəmɑːkɪt] Supermarkt II • **a 24-hour supermarket** ein Supermarkt, der 24 Stunden geöffnet ist III 4 (76/164)

sure [ʃʊə, ʃɔː]: **be sure** sicher sein II

surf the internet [sɜːf] im Internet surfen III 2 (32)

surfboard ['sɜːfbɔːd] Surfbrett II

surfing ['sɜːfɪŋ]: **go surfing** wellenreiten gehen, surfen gehen II

surprise [sə'praɪz] Überraschung III 2 (44)

survey (on) ['sɜːveɪ] Umfrage, Untersuchung (über) II

survive [sə'vaɪv] überleben II

swam [swæm] *siehe* **swim**

°**swap** (-pp-) [swɒp] tauschen

sweatshirt ['swetʃɜːt] Sweatshirt I

sweet [swiːt] süß I

sweetheart ['swiːthɑːt] Liebling, Schatz II

sweets (pl) [swiːts] Süßigkeiten I

swim (-mm-) [swɪm], **swam, swum** schwimmen I • **go swimming** schwimmen gehen I

swimmer ['swɪmə] Schwimmer/in II

swimming pool ['swɪmɪŋ puːl] Schwimmbad, Schwimmbecken I

swimming trunks (pl) ['swɪmɪŋ trʌŋks] Badehose III 3 (63/160)

swimsuit ['swɪmsuːt] Badeanzug III 3 (63/160)

swum [swʌm] *siehe* **swim**

syllable ['sɪləbl] Silbe I

T

table ['teɪbl] Tisch I

table tennis ['teɪbl tenɪs] Tischtennis I • **table tennis bat** [bæt] Tischtennisschläger III 3 (63/160)

°**tag** [tæg] *hier:* Stoffband • °**tag rugby** Tag Rugby

take [teɪk], **took, taken**
1. nehmen I
2. (weg-, hin)bringen I
3. dauern, (Zeit) brauchen III 2 (33)
take notes sich Notizen machen I • **take out** herausnehmen I • **take photos** Fotos machen, fotografieren I • **take sth. off** etwas ausziehen (Kleidung) II • **take 10 c off** 10 Cent abziehen I • °**Take turns.** Wechselt euch ab. • **We'll take them.** (beim Einkaufen) Wir nehmen sie. I

taken ['teɪkən] *siehe* **take**

talk [tɔːk]: **talk (about)** reden (über), sich unterhalten (über) I **talk (to)** reden (mit), sich unterhalten (mit) I

°**tall** [tɔːl] groß (Person)

taught [tɔːt] *siehe* **teach**

taxi ['tæksi] Taxi III 1 (20/153)

tea [tiː] Tee; (auch:) leichte Nachmittags- oder Abendmahlzeit I

teach [tiːtʃ], **taught, taught** unterrichten, lehren I

teacher ['tiːtʃə] Lehrer/in I • **head teacher** Schulleiter/in III 2 (44)

team [ti:m] Team, Mannschaft I
°**on a basketball team** in einem Basketballteam
teaspoon ['ti:spu:n] Teelöffel III 4 (81/165)
teddy ['tedi] Teddy III 2 (44)
teen [ti:n] Teenager-, Jugend- III 5 (88)
teenager ['ti:neɪdʒə] Teenager, Jugendliche(r) II
teeth [ti:θ] *Plural von „tooth"* I
telephone ['telɪfəʊn] Telefon I
telephone number Telefonnummer I • **What's your telephone number?** Was ist deine Telefonnummer? I
television (TV) ['telɪvɪʒn] Fernsehen I
tell (about) [tel], **told, told** erzählen (von), berichten (über) I • **Tell me your names.** Sagt mir eure Namen. I • **tell sb. the way** jm. den Weg beschreiben II
temperature ['temprətʃə] Temperatur II • **have a temperature** Fieber haben II
tennis ['tenɪs] Tennis I
term [tɜ:m] Trimester II
terrible ['terəbl] schrecklich, furchtbar I
°**territory** ['terətri] Territorium, Hoheitsgebiet
test [test] Test, Prüfung II
text [tekst] Text I
text sb. [tekst] jm. eine SMS schicken III 2 (32)
text message ['tekst ˌmesɪdʒ] SMS III 2 (32/156)
than [ðæn, ðən] als II • **more than** mehr als II • **more than me** mehr als ich II
thank [θæŋk]**: Thank you.** Danke (schön). I • **Thanks.** Danke. I **Thanks a lot!** Vielen Dank! I **Thanks very much!** Danke sehr! / Vielen Dank! II
that [ðət, ðæt]
1. das (dort) I
2. jene(r, s) I
That's me. Das bin ich. I • **That's right.** Das ist richtig. / Das stimmt. I • **That's up to you.** Das liegt bei dir. / Das kannst/musst du (selbst) entscheiden. III 5 (88) • **That was close.** Das war knapp. II
that [ðət, ðæt] der, die, das; die (Relativpronomen) III 3 (54)
that [ðət, ðæt] dass I
that far/good/bad/... [ðæt] so weit/gut/schlecht/... III 5 (91)
the [ðə, ði] der, die, das; die I
theatre ['θɪətə] Theater II

their [ðeə] ihr, ihre (Plural) I
theirs [ðeəz] ihrer, ihre, ihrs II
them [ðəm, ðem] sie; ihnen I
themselves [ðəm'selvz] sich (selbst) III 4 (71/163)
  ▶ S.164 each other – themselves
then [ðen] dann, danach I
there [ðeə]
1. da, dort I
2. dahin, dorthin I
down there dort unten II • **over there** da drüben, dort drüben I • **there are** es sind (vorhanden); es gibt I • **there's** es ist (vorhanden); es gibt I • **there isn't a ...** es ist kein/e ...; es gibt kein/e ... I
thermometer [θə'mɒmɪtə] Thermometer II
these [ði:z] diese, die (hier) I
they [ðeɪ] sie (Plural) I
thief [θi:f], *pl* **thieves** [θi:vz] Dieb/in II
thing [θɪŋ] Ding, Sache I • **What was the best thing about ...?** Was war das Beste an ...? II
think [θɪŋk], **thought, thought** glauben, meinen, denken I
think about 1. nachdenken über II; **2.** denken über, halten von II
think of 1. denken über, halten von II; **2.** denken an; sich ausdenken II
third [θɜ:d] dritte(r, s) I
this [ðɪs]
1. dies (hier) I
2. diese(r, s) I
This is Isabel. Hier spricht Isabel. / Hier ist Isabel. (am Telefon) II
this morning/afternoon/evening heute Morgen/Nachmittag/Abend I • **this way** hier entlang, in diese Richtung II
those [ðəʊz] die (da), jene (dort) I
thought [θɔ:t] *siehe* **think**
thought [θɔ:t] Gedanke III 3 (64)
thousand ['θaʊznd] tausend I
threw [θru:] *siehe* **throw**
throat [θrəʊt] Hals, Kehle II
through [θru:] durch II
throw [θrəʊ], **threw, thrown** werfen I
thrown [θrəʊn] *siehe* **throw**
Thursday ['θɜ:zdeɪ, 'θɜ:zdi] Donnerstag I
°**tick** [tɪk] Häkchen
°**tick** [tɪk] ankreuzen, ein Häkchen machen
ticket ['tɪkɪt]
1. Eintrittskarte I
2. Fahrkarte II • **return ticket** Rückfahrkarte II • **single ticket** einfache Fahrkarte (nur Hinfahrt) III 1 (14)

tidy ['taɪdi] aufräumen I
tidy ['taɪdi] ordentlich, aufgeräumt II
tiger ['taɪgə] Tiger II
tight [taɪt] eng III 4 (71/163)
till [tɪl] bis (zeitlich) I
  ▶ S.163 German „bis"
time [taɪm]
1. Zeit; Uhrzeit I
2. time(s) Mal(e); -mal II
in time rechtzeitig III 1 (16/153)
three times dreimal III 1 (16/153)
What's the time? Wie spät ist es? I • °**What time is the ferry ?** Um wie viel Uhr / Wann geht die Fähre?
timetable ['taɪmteɪbl]
1. Stundenplan I
2. Fahrplan II
tip [tɪp] Tipp II
tired ['taɪəd] müde I
title ['taɪtl] Titel, Überschrift I
to [tə, tu]
1. zu, nach I • **to Jenny's** zu Jenny I • **to the doctor's** zum Arzt III 1 (24/154) • °**to the front** nach vorn
2. an e-mail to eine E-Mail an I **write to** schreiben an I
3. quarter to 12 Viertel vor 12 (11.45 / 23.45) I • **from Monday to Friday** von Montag bis Freitag III 4 (72/163)
4. try to help/to play/... versuchen, zu helfen/zu spielen/... I
5. um zu II
  ▶ S.163 German „bis"
toast [təʊst] Toast(brot) I
tobacco [tə'bækəʊ] Tabak II
today [tə'deɪ] heute I
toe [təʊ] Zeh I
together [tə'geðə] zusammen I
toilet ['tɔɪlət] Toilette I
told [təʊld] *siehe* **tell**
tomato [tə'mɑ:təʊ], *pl* **tomatoes** Tomate II
tomorrow [tə'mɒrəʊ] morgen I
tomorrow's weather das Wetter von morgen II
°**tongue-twister** ['tʌŋtwɪstə] Zungenbrecher
tonight [tə'naɪt] heute Nacht, heute Abend I • **tonight's programme** das Programm von heute Abend; das heutige Abendprogramm II
too [tu:]**: from Bristol too** auch aus Bristol I • **Me too.** Ich auch. I
too much/big/... [tu:] zu viel/groß/... I
took [tʊk] *siehe* **take**
tooth [tu:θ], *pl* **teeth** [ti:θ] Zahn I

toothache ['tuːθeɪk] Zahn-schmerzen II

top [tɒp]
1. Spitze, oberes Ende I • **at the top (of)** oben, am oberen Ende, an der Spitze (von) I
2. Top, Oberteil I

topic ['tɒpɪk] Thema, Themen-bereich I • **topic sentence** *Satz, der in das Thema eines Absatzes einführt* II

tornado [tɔːˈneɪdəʊ] Tornado, Wirbelsturm II

tortoise ['tɔːtəs] Schildkröte I

°**tossing the caber** [ˌtɒsɪŋ ðə ˈkeɪbə] Baumstammwerfen

touch [tʌtʃ] berühren, anfassen II
keep in touch in Verbindung blei-ben, Kontakt halten III Intro (11)

tour (of the house) [tʊə] Rundgang, Tour (durch das Haus) I

tourist ['tʊərɪst] Tourist/in II
tourist information Fremden-verkehrsamt II

towards sb./sth. [təˈwɔːdz] auf jn./ etwas zu II

tower ['taʊə] Turm I

town [taʊn] (Klein-)Stadt I

°**traditional** [trəˈdɪʃənl] traditionell

traffic ['træfɪk] Verkehr II

train [treɪn] Zug I • **on the train** im Zug I

train [treɪn] trainieren III 3 (56)

trainers *(pl)* ['treɪnəz] Turnschuhe II

training session ['seʃn] Trainings-stunde, -einheit III 3 (52)

tram [træm] Straßenbahn III 1 (20/153)

translate (from ... into) [trænsˈleɪt] übersetzen (aus ... ins) III 2 (47)

translation [trænsˈleɪʃn] Überset-zung III 2 (47)

transport ['trænspɔːt] Beförderung, Transport III 1 (20)

travel (-ll-) ['trævl] reisen II

Travelcard ['trævlkɑːd] Tagesfahr-karte *(der Londoner Verkehrsbetrie-be)* III 1 (14)

tree [triː] Baum I

trendy ['trendi] modisch, schick III 2 (34)

trick [trɪk]
1. (Zauber-)Kunststück, Trick I • **do tricks** (Zauber-)Kunststücke machen I
2. Streich II

trip [trɪp] Reise; Ausflug I • **go on a trip** einen Ausflug machen II

trouble ['trʌbl] Schwierigkeiten, Ärger II • **be in trouble** in Schwie-rigkeiten sein; Ärger kriegen II

trousers *(pl)* ['traʊzəz] Hose II

true [truː] wahr II

trumpet ['trʌmpɪt] Trompete III Intro (11)

try [traɪ]
1. versuchen I
2. probieren, kosten I
try and do sth. / try to do sth. ver-suchen, etwas zu tun I • **try on** anprobieren *(Kleidung)* I

T-shirt ['tiːʃɜːt] T-Shirt I

tube: the Tube *(no pl)* [tjuːb] *(BE)* die Londoner U-Bahn III 1 (14)

Tuesday ['tjuːzdeɪ, 'tjuːzdi] Dienstag I

tunnel ['tʌnl] Tunnel II

turkey ['tɜːki] Truthahn III 1 (24/154)

turn [tɜːn]
1. sich umdrehen II • **turn left/ right** (nach) links/rechts abbiegen II • **turn to sb.** sich jm. zuwenden; sich an jn. wenden II
2. turn on/off ein-/ausschalten III 2 (35)

turn [tɜːn]: **It's your turn.** Du bist dran / an der Reihe. I • **Miss a turn.** Einmal aussetzen. II °**Take turns.** Wechselt euch ab. • **Whose turn is it?** Wer ist dran / an der Reihe? II

TV [tiːˈviː] Fernsehen I • **on TV** im Fernsehen I • **watch TV** fern-sehen I

twice [twaɪs] zweimal III 1 (16)
twice a week zweimal pro Woche III 1 (16/153)

twin [twɪn]: **twin brother** Zwillings-bruder I • **twins** *(pl)* Zwillinge I

type [taɪp] *(infml)* Typ III 2 (34)

U

uncle ['ʌŋkl] Onkel I

uncool [ˌʌnˈkuːl] *(infml)* uncool III 2 (34)

under ['ʌndə] unter I

underground [ˈʌndəɡraʊnd]: **the underground** die U-Bahn II

°**underline** [ˌʌndəˈlaɪn] unter-streichen

°**underlined** [ˌʌndəˈlaɪnd] unterstri-chen

understand [ˌʌndəˈstænd], **under-stood, understood** verstehen, begreifen II

understood [ˌʌndəˈstʊd] *siehe* **understand**

underwear ['ʌndəweə] Unter-wäsche III 4 (71)

unfair [ˌʌnˈfeə] unfair III 2 (40)

unfriendly [ʌnˈfrendli] unfreundlich III 2 (40)

unhappy [ʌnˈhæpi] unglücklich III 2 (40)

unhealthy [ʌnˈhelθi] ungesund III 2 (40)

uniform ['juːnɪfɔːm] Uniform I

unit ['juːnɪt] Lektion, Kapitel I

united: the United Kingdom (UK) [juˌnaɪtɪd ˈkɪŋdəm]**,** [juː ˈkeɪ] das Vereinigte Königreich *(Großbritan-nien und Nordirland)* III Intro (6)
United States (US) [juˌnaɪtɪd ˈsteɪts], [juːˈes] die Vereinigten Staaten *(von Amerika)* III Intro (10)

unlock [ˌʌnˈlɒk] aufschließen; ent-sperren III 2 (41)

unsafe [ʌnˈseɪf] nicht sicher, gefähr-lich III 2 (40)

untidy [ʌnˈtaɪdi] unordentlich III 2 (40)

until [ənˈtɪl] bis III 2 (33)
▶ S.163 German „bis"

up [ʌp] hinauf, herauf, nach oben I
up the hill den Hügel hinauf II
That's up to you. Das liegt bei dir. / Das kannst/musst du (selbst) entscheiden. III 5 (88)

upset [ʌpˈset] aufgebracht, ge-kränkt, mitgenommen III 2 (35)

upset sb. (-tt-) [ʌpˈset], **upset, upset** jn. ärgern, kränken, aus der Fas-sung bringen III 2 (35/157)

upstairs [ʌpˈsteəz] oben; nach oben I

us [əs, ʌs] uns I

use [juːz] benutzen, verwenden I

°**used** [juːzd] gebraucht

usually ['juːʒuəli] meistens, gewöhnlich, normalerweise I

V

vacation [vəˈkeɪʃn, *AE:* veɪˈkeɪʃn] *(AE)* Urlaub, Ferien III 5 (91)

valley ['væli] Tal II

vegetable ['vedʒtəbl] *(ein)* Gemüse III 1 (24)

very ['veri] sehr I • **like/love sth. very much** etwas sehr mögen/ sehr lieben II • **Thanks very much!** Danke sehr! / Vielen Dank! II

victim ['vɪktɪm] Opfer III 4 (81)

video ['vɪdiəʊ] Video III 1 (12)

view [vjuː] Aussicht, Blick II

°**Viking** ['vaɪkɪŋ] Wikinger/in

village ['vɪlɪdʒ] Dorf I

violin [ˌvaɪəˈlɪn] Violine, Geige III Intro (11)

°**virtual reality** [ˌvɜːtʃuəl riˈæləti] *durch Computerprogramme simu-lierte Realität*

visit ['vɪzɪt] besuchen II

visit ['vɪzɪt] Besuch II

visitor ['vɪzɪtə] Besucher/in, Gast I

vocabulary [və'kæbjələri] Vokabelverzeichnis, Wörterverzeichnis I

voicemail ['vɔɪsmeɪl] Voicemail III 2 (33)

volleyball ['vɒlibɔːl] Volleyball I

W

wait (for) [weɪt] warten (auf) I
Wait a minute. Warte mal! / Moment mal! II • **Wait and see!** Wart's ab! III Intro (11) • **I can't wait to see …** ich kann es kaum erwarten, … zu sehen I

waiter ['weɪtə] Kellner II

waitress ['weɪtrəs] Kellnerin II

walk [wɔːk] (zu Fuß) gehen I
walk around herumlaufen, umherspazieren III 1 (26/155) • **walk around the town** in der Stadt umhergehen, durch die Stadt gehen III 1 (26/155)

walk [wɔːk] Spaziergang II • **go for a walk** spazieren gehen, einen Spaziergang machen II
a ten-kilometre walk eine Zehn-Kilometer-Wanderung III 4 (76/164)

wall [wɔːl] Wand; Mauer II

°walrus ['wɔːlrəs] Walross I

want [wɒnt] (haben) wollen I
want to do tun wollen I

wardrobe ['wɔːdrəʊb] Kleiderschrank I

warm [wɔːm] warm II

was [wəz, wɒz]: (I/he/she/it) was *siehe* be

wash [wɒʃ] waschen I • **I wash my face.** Ich wasche mir das Gesicht. I

washing machine ['wɒʃɪŋ məˌʃiːn] Waschmaschine I

watch [wɒtʃ] beobachten, sich *etwas* ansehen; zusehen I
watch TV fernsehen I

watch [wɒtʃ] Armbanduhr I

water ['wɔːtə] Wasser I

wave [weɪv] winken II

way [weɪ]
1. Weg I • **ask sb. the way** jn. nach dem Weg fragen II • **on the way (to)** auf dem Weg (zu/nach) II • **tell sb. the way** jm. den Weg beschreiben II
2. Richtung II • **the other way round** anders herum II • **the wrong way** in die falsche Richtung II • **this way** hier entlang, in diese Richtung II • **which way?** in wel-

che Richtung? / wohin? II
3. by the way übrigens II
4. No way! Auf keinen Fall! / Kommt nicht in Frage! II

we [wiː] wir I

weak [wiːk] schwach II

wear [weə], **wore, worn** tragen, anhaben *(Kleidung)* I

weather ['weðə] Wetter II

°weather forecast ['weðə fɔːkɑːst] Wettervorhersage I

webcam ['webkæm] Webcam, Internetkamera III 3 (65)

website ['websaɪt] Website II

Wednesday ['wenzdeɪ, 'wenzdi] Mittwoch I

°wee [wiː] *(infml)* klein *(besonders in Schottland gebräuchlich)*

week [wiːk] Woche I • **days of the week** Wochentage I
a two-week holiday ein zweiwöchiger Urlaub III 4 (76/164)

weekend [ˌwiːk'end] Wochenende I
at the weekend am Wochenende I

welcome ['welkəm]
1. Welcome (to Bristol). Willkommen (in Bristol). I
2. You're welcome. Gern geschehen. / Nichts zu danken. I

welcome sb. (to) ['welkəm] jn. begrüßen, willkommen heißen (in) I
They welcome you to … Sie heißen dich in … willkommen I

well [wel]
1. gut II • **go well** gut (ver)laufen, gutgehen III 2 (45) • **do well (in)** gut abschneiden (in) III 4 (70/163) • **You did well.** Das hast du gut gemacht. II • **Oh well …** Na ja … / Na gut … I • **Well, …** Nun, … / Also, … I

°well-known [ˌwel'nəʊn] **bekannt**
2. *(gesundheitlich)* **gut; gesund, wohlauf** II

°wellies (pl) ['weliz] *(infml)* Gummistiefel *(Plural)*

Welsh [welʃ] walisisch; Walisisch II

went [went] *siehe* go

were [wə, wɜː]: **(we/you/they) were** *siehe* be

west [west] Westen; nach Westen; westlich III Intro (7/151)

western ['westən] westlich, West- III Intro (9)

wet [wet] feucht, nass III 4 (78)

what [wɒt]
1. was I
2. welche(r, s) I
What about …? **1.** Was ist mit …? / Und …? I; **2.** Wie wär's mit …? I
What are you talking about? Wo-

von redest du? I • **What colour is …?** Welche Farbe hat …? I
°**What else can you do?** Was kannst du sonst noch machen? I
What for? Wofür? II • **What have we got next?** Was haben wir als Nächstes? I • **What kind of car…?** Was für ein Auto…? III Intro (6/151)
What page are we on? Auf welcher Seite sind wir? I • **What's for homework?** Was haben wir als Hausaufgabe auf? I • °**What time?** Um wie viel Uhr? / Wann? I • **What's the matter?** Was ist los? / Was ist denn? II • **What's the time?** Wie spät ist es? I • **What's your name?** Wie heißt du? I
What's your telephone number? Was ist deine Telefonnummer? I
What was the weather like? Wie war das Wetter? II

wheel [wiːl] Rad III 1 (12/152) • **big wheel** [ˌbɪg 'wiːl] Riesenrad III 1 (12)

wheelchair ['wiːltʃeə] Rollstuhl I

when [wen] wann I • **When's your birthday?** Wann hast du Geburtstag? I

when [wen]
1. wenn I
2. als I

where [weə]
1. wo I
2. wohin I
Where are you from? Wo kommst du her? I

which [wɪtʃ]: **Which picture …?** Welches Bild …? I • **which way?** in welche Richtung? / wohin? II

which [wɪtʃ] der, die, das; die *(Relativpronomen)* III 3 (145)

while [waɪl] während III 4 (81)

whisky ['wɪski] Whisky II

whisper ['wɪspə] flüstern I

whistle ['wɪsl] pfeifen II

white [waɪt] weiß I

who [huː]
1. wer I
2. wen / wem II

who [huː] der, die, das; die *(Relativpronomen)* III 3 (54) • **Find/Ask somebody who …** Finde/Frage jemanden, der … II

whose? [huːz] wessen? II • **Whose are these?** Wem gehören diese? II
Whose turn is it? Wer ist dran / an der Reihe? II

why [waɪ] warum I • **Why me?** Warum ich? I

wife [waɪf], *pl* **wives** [waɪvz] Ehefrau II

wild [waɪld] wild II

will [wɪl]: **you'll be cold (= you will be cold)** du wirst frieren; ihr werdet frieren II • **you won't be cold** [wəʊnt] **(= you will not be cold)** du wirst nicht frieren; ihr werdet nicht frieren II

win (-nn-) [wɪn], **won, won** gewinnen I

wind [wɪnd] Wind I

window ['wɪndəʊ] Fenster I

windsurfing ['wɪndsɜːfɪŋ] Windsurfen III 1 (22)

windy ['wɪndi] windig I

winner ['wɪnə] Gewinner/in, Sieger/in II

winter ['wɪntə] Winter I

with [wɪð]
   1. mit I
   2. bei I
   go with gehören zu, passen zu III Intro (11) • **Sit with me.** Setz dich zu mir. / Setzt euch zu mir. I

without [wɪ'ðaʊt] ohne I

wives [waɪvz] Plural von „wife" II

wolf [wʊlf], pl **wolves** [wʊlvz] Wolf II

woman ['wʊmən], pl **women** ['wɪmɪn] Frau I

won [wʌn] siehe **win**

won't [wəʊnt]: **you won't be cold (= you will not be cold)** du wirst nicht frieren; ihr werdet nicht frieren II

wonder ['wʌndə] sich fragen, gern wissen wollen II

woodpecker ['wʊdpekə] Specht II

word [wɜːd] Wort I • **word building** Wortbildung II • °**word order** Wortstellung

wore [wɔː] siehe **wear**

work [wɜːk] arbeiten I • **work hard** hart arbeiten II • **work on sth.** an etwas arbeiten I

work [wɜːk] Arbeit I • **at work** bei der Arbeit/am Arbeitsplatz I

worker ['wɜːkə] Arbeiter/in II

worksheet ['wɜːkʃiːt] Arbeitsblatt I

workshop ['wɜːkʃɒp] Workshop, Lehrgang III Intro (6)

world [wɜːld] Welt I • **all over the world** auf der ganzen Welt III Intro (6/150) • **from all over the UK/the world/England** aus dem gesamten Vereinigten Königreich/aus der ganzen Welt/aus ganz England III Intro (6)

worn [wɔːn] siehe **wear**

worry ['wʌri] Sorge, Kummer II

worry (about) ['wʌri] sich Sorgen machen (wegen, um) I • **Don't worry.** Mach dir keine Sorgen. I

worse [wɜːs] schlechter, schlimmer II

worst [wɜːst]: **(the) worst** am schlechtesten, schlimmsten; der/die/das schlechteste, schlimmste ... II

would [wəd, wʊd]: **I/you/... would ...** ich würde/du würdest ... III 2 (35) **I'd like ... (= I would like ...)** Ich hätte/möchte gern ... I • **Would you like ...?** Möchtest du ...? / Möchten Sie ...? I • **Would you like some?** Möchtest du etwas/ein paar? / Möchten Sie etwas/ein paar? I • **I'd like to talk about ... (= I would like to talk about ...)** Ich möchte über ... reden / Ich würde gern über ... reden II

write [raɪt], **wrote, written** schreiben I • **write down** aufschreiben I • **write to** schreiben an I

writer ['raɪtə] Schreiber/in; Schriftsteller/in II

written ['rɪtn] siehe **write**

wrong [rɒŋ] falsch, verkehrt II **be wrong 1.** falsch sein I; **2.** sich irren, Unrecht haben II • **the wrong way** in die falsche Richtung II

wrote [rəʊt] siehe **write**

Y

°**ya** [jə] (infml) dich/dir

yard [jɑːd] Hof II • **in the yard** auf dem Hof II

yawn [jɔːn] gähnen II

year [jɪə]
   1. Jahr I
   2. Jahrgangsstufe I
   a sixteen-year-old ein/e Sechzehnjährige/r III 4 (76) **a sixteen-year-old girl** ein sechzehnjähriges Mädchen III 4 (76/164)

yellow ['jeləʊ] gelb I

yes [jes] ja I

yesterday ['jestədeɪ, 'jestədi] gestern I • **yesterday morning/afternoon/evening** gestern Morgen/Nachmittag/Abend I • **yesterday's homework** die Hausaufgaben von gestern II

yet [jet]: **not (...) yet** noch nicht II **yet?** schon? II

yoga ['jəʊgə] Yoga I

you [juː]
   1. du; Sie I
   2. ihr I • **you two** ihr zwei I
   3. dir; dich; euch I

young [jʌŋ] jung I

your [jɔː]
   1. dein/e I
   2. Ihr I
   3. euer/eure I

yours [jɔːz]
   1. deiner, deine, deins II
   2. Ihrer, Ihre, Ihrs II
   3. eurer, eure, eures II

yourself [jɔː'self] dir/dich (selbst) III 4 (71/163)

yourselves [jɔː'selvz] euch (selbst) III 4 (71/163)

youth [juːθ] Jugend, Jugend- III Intro (6) • **youth club** ['juːθ ˌklʌb] Jugendclub III 3 (56) • **youth hostel** ['juːθ ˌhɒstl] Jugendherberge III Intro (8/151)

yuck [jʌk] igitt III 1 (27)

Z

zebra ['zebrə] Zebra II

zero ['zɪərəʊ] null I

Das **German – English Dictionary** enthält den **Lernwortschatz** der Bände 1 bis 3 von *English G 21*. Es kann dir eine erste Hilfe sein, wenn du vergessen hast, wie etwas auf Englisch heißt.

Wenn du wissen möchtest, wo das englische Wort zum ersten Mal in *English G 21* vorkommt, dann kannst du im **English – German Dictionary** (S. 167–188) nachschlagen.

Im **German – English Dictionary** werden folgende **Abkürzungen** und **Symbole** verwendet:

jm. = jemandem	sb. = somebody	*pl* = *plural*	BE = *British English*	*infml* = *informal*
jn. = jemanden	sth. = something	*no pl* = *no plural*	AE = *American English*	

▶ Der Pfeil verweist auf Kästchen im Vocabulary (S. 150–166), in denen du weitere Informationen findest.

A

abbiegen: (nach) links/rechts abbiegen turn left/right [tɜːn]
Abend evening ['iːvnɪŋ]; *(später Abend)* night [naɪt] • **am Abend, abends** in the evening
Abendbrot, -essen dinner ['dɪnə] **Abendbrot essen** have dinner **zum Abendbrot** for dinner
aber but [bət, bʌt]
abfahren *(wegfahren)* leave [liːv]
Abfahrt *(Abreise)* departure (dep) [dɪ'pɑːtʃə]
Abfall rubbish ['rʌbɪʃ]
Abflug departure (dep) [dɪ'pɑːtʃə]
abhängen (mit Freunden/Freundinnen) *(rumhängen)* hang out (with friends) [ˌhæŋ_'aʊt]
abholen: jn. abholen pick sb. up [ˌpɪk_'ʌp]
Abreise departure (dep) [dɪ'pɑːtʃə]
Absatz *(in einem Text)* paragraph ['pærəɡrɑːf]
abschließen lock [lɒk]
Abschluss *(einer Geschichte, eines Films usw.)* ending ['endɪŋ]
abschneiden: etwas abschneiden cut sth. off [ˌkʌt_'ɒf]
Abschnitt section ['sekʃn]
abschreiben *(kopieren)* copy ['kɒpi]
abtrennen: etwas abtrennen *(abschneiden)* cut sth. off [ˌkʌt_'ɒf]
abziehen: 10 Cent abziehen take 10 c off [ˌteɪk_'ɒf]
Acker field [fiːld]
addieren (zu) add (to) [æd]
Adresse address [ə'dres]
Affe monkey ['mʌŋki]
Aktivität activity [æk'tɪvəti]
Akzent accent ['æksənt]
albern silly ['sɪli]
alle *(die ganze Gruppe)* all [ɔːl]
allein alone [ə'ləʊn]
alleinstehend single ['sɪŋɡl]
alles everything ['evriθɪŋ]; all [ɔːl]
allgemeine (r, s) general ['dʒenrəl]

alltägliche(r, s), Alltags- everyday ['evrideɪ]
Alphabet alphabet ['ælfəbet]
als 1. *(zeitlich)* when [wen]; *(während)* as [əz, æz]
2. größer/teurer als bigger/more expensive than [ðæn, ðən]
also *(daher, deshalb)* so [səʊ]
Also, ... Well, ... [wel]
alt old [əʊld]
Alter age [eɪdʒ]
altmodisch old-fashioned [ˌəʊld'fæʃnd]
am 1. am Bahnhof at the station **am oberen Ende (von)** at the top (of) • **am Strand** on the beach **am Telefon** on the phone • **am unteren Ende (von)** at the bottom (of) ['bɒtəm]
2. *(nahe bei)* **am Meer** by the sea
3. *(zeitlich)* **am 13. Juni** on 13th June • **am Morgen/Nachmittag/ Abend** in the morning/afternoon/ evening • **am Ende (von)** at the end (of) • **am Freitag** on Friday **am Freitagmorgen** on Friday morning • **am nächsten Morgen/ Tag** the next morning/day • **am Wochenende** at the weekend
amüsieren: sich amüsieren have fun [hæv 'fʌn] • **Amüsier dich gut!** Enjoy yourself.
an 1. an dem/den Tisch (dort) at that table • **an der Spitze** at the top (of) • **an der/die Tafel** on the board • **an jn. schreiben** write to sb.
2. *(nahe bei)* **an der See** by the sea
3. Was war das Beste an ...? What was the best thing about ...?
4. an sein *(Radio, Licht usw.)* be on
anbauen *(Getreide usw.)* grow [ɡrəʊ]
andere(r, s) other ['ʌðə] • **die anderen** the others
anders (als) different (from) ['dɪfrənt] **anders ausdrücken** *(umschreiben)* paraphrase ['pærəfreɪz] • **anders herum** the other way round

Anfang beginning [bɪ'ɡɪnɪŋ]
anfangen (mit) start [stɑːt]
anfassen touch [tʌtʃ]
anfühlen: sich gut anfühlen feel good [fiːl]
Anführer/in leader ['liːdə]
angeln fish [fɪʃ]
angreifen attack [ə'tæk]
Angriff attack [ə'tæk]
Angst haben (vor) be afraid (of) [ə'freɪd]; be scared (of) [skeəd]
anhaben *(Kleidung)* wear [weə]
anhalten stop [stɒp]
Anhänger/in *(Fan)* supporter [sə'pɔːtə]
anhören 1. sich etwas anhören listen to sth. ['lɪsn]
2. sich gut anhören sound good [saʊnd]
anklicken: etwas anklicken click on sth. [klɪk]
ankommen arrive [ə'raɪv]
Ankündigung announcement [ə'naʊnsmənt]
Ankunft arrival (arr) [ə'raɪvl]
anlächeln: jn. anlächeln smile at sb. [smaɪl]
Anleitung(en) *(Gebrauchsanweisungen)* instructions (pl) [ɪn'strʌkʃnz]
anmailen: jn. anmailen mail sb. [meɪl]
anmalen paint [peɪnt]; *(bunt ausmalen)* colour ['kʌlə]
Anorak anorak ['ænəræk]
anpflanzen *(Getreide usw.)* grow [ɡrəʊ]
anprobieren *(Kleidung)* try on [ˌtraɪ_'ɒn]
Anruf call; phone call ['fəʊn kɔːl]
anrufen call [kɔːl]; phone [fəʊn]
Ansage *(Durchsage)* announcement [ə'naʊnsmənt]
anschauen look at [lʊk]
Anschlagtafel notice board ['nəʊtɪs bɔːd]
anschließen: sich jm. anschließen join sb. [dʒɔɪn]
Anschrift address [ə'dres]

ansehen: sich etwas ansehen look at sth. [lʊk]; watch sth. [wɒtʃ]

Antwort (auf) answer (to) ['ɑːnsə]

antworten answer ['ɑːnsə]

Anweisung(en) (Gebrauchsanweisungen) instructions (pl) [ɪn'strʌkʃnz]

anziehen: etwas anziehen (Kleidung) put sth. on [ˌpʊt_'ɒn] • **sich anziehen** get dressed [get 'drest]

Apfel apple ['æpl]

Apfelsine orange ['ɒrɪndʒ]

Apotheke chemist ['kemɪst]

Apotheker: beim Apotheker at the chemist's
▶ S.154 at the butcher's / to the doctor's

April April ['eɪprəl]

Appetit appetite ['æpɪtaɪt] • **Guten Appetit** Enjoy! [ɪn'dʒɔɪ]

Arbeit work [wɜːk] • **bei der Arbeit / am Arbeitsplatz** at work • **gute Arbeit leisten** do a good job

arbeiten (an) work (on) [wɜːk]

Arbeiter/in worker ['wɜːkə]

Arbeitsblatt worksheet ['wɜːkʃiːt]

Arbeits- und Lerntechniken study skills ['stʌdi skɪlz]

Ärger (Schwierigkeiten) trouble ['trʌbl] • **Ärger kriegen** be in trouble

ärgern: jn. ärgern (kränken) upset sb. [ʌp'set]

arm poor [pɔː, pʊə]

Arm arm [ɑːm]

Armbanduhr watch [wɒtʃ]

Art 1. (Sorte) sort (of) [sɔːt]; kind (of) [kaɪnd]
2. Art und Weise way [weɪ]

Artikel article ['ɑːtɪkl]

Arzt/Ärztin doctor ['dɒktə] • **zum Arzt** to the doctor's
▶ S.154 at the butcher's / to the doctor's

auch: auch aus Bristol from Bristol too [tuː]; also from Bristol ['ɔːlsəʊ] • **Ich auch.** Me too.

auf on [ɒn] • **auf (... hinauf)** onto ['ɒntə, 'ɒntʊ] • **auf dem Bild/Foto** in the picture/photo • **auf dem Feld** in the field • **auf dem Hof** in the yard • **auf dem Land** (im Gegensatz zur Stadt) in the country; (nicht auf dem Wasser) on land • **auf dem Weg (zu/nach)** on the way (to) • **auf der ganzen Welt** all over the world • **auf einmal** suddenly ['sʌdnli] • **auf Englisch** in English • **Auf geht's!** Let's go. **auf jn./etwas zu** towards sb./sth. [tə'wɔːdz] • **Auf keinen Fall!** No way! • **Auf welcher Seite sind wir?** What page are we on? • **Auf Wiedersehen.** Goodbye. [ˌgʊd'baɪ]

aufbewahren keep [kiːp]

aufführen (Szene, Dialog) act [ækt]

Aufgabe (im Schulbuch) exercise ['eksəsaɪz]; (Job) job [dʒɒb]

aufgebracht (wegen) upset [ʌp'set]

aufgeräumt (ordentlich) tidy ['taɪdi]

aufgeregt (nervös) nervous ['nɜːvəs]; (begeistert) excited [ɪk'saɪtɪd]

aufheben: etwas aufheben (hochheben) pick sth. up [pɪk_'ʌp]

aufhören stop [stɒp]

auflegen (Musik/CDs/Platten; in der Disko) DJ ['diːdʒeɪ]

auflisten list [lɪst]

aufmachen open ['əʊpən]

Aufnahme (Aufzeichnung) recording [rɪ'kɔːdɪŋ]

aufnehmen (Musik / einen Film) record [rɪ'kɔːd]

aufpassen: auf etwas/jn. aufpassen look after sth./sb. [ˌlʊk_'ɑːftə]

aufräumen tidy ['taɪdi]

aufregend exciting [ɪk'saɪtɪŋ]

Aufsatz essay ['eseɪ]

aufschauen (von) look up (from) [ˌlʊk_'ʌp]

aufschließen unlock [ˌʌn'lɒk]

aufschreiben write down [ˌraɪt 'daʊn]

aufstehen get up [ˌget_'ʌp]

aufsuchen: jn. aufsuchen see sb. [siː]

Auftritt (Konzert) gig [gɪg] (infml) **einen Auftritt haben** (ein Konzert geben) do a gig

aufwachsen grow up [ˌgrəʊ_'ʌp]

aufzählen (auflisten) list [lɪst]

Aufzeichnung (Aufnahme) recording [rɪ'kɔːdɪŋ]

Aufzug lift [lɪft] (BE); elevator ['elɪveɪtə] (AE)

Auge eye [aɪ]

August August ['ɔːgəst]

aus: Ich komme/bin aus ... I'm from ... [frəm, frɒm] • **aus ... (heraus/hinaus)** out of ... ['aʊt_əv] • **aus der ganzen Welt** from all over the world • **aus dem Zug/Bus aussteigen** get off the train/bus **aus vielen Gründen** for lots of reasons • **aus zweiter Hand** (gebraucht) second-hand [ˌsekənd 'hænd]

ausdenken: sich etwas ausdenken think of sth. [θɪŋk]

ausdrücken: anders ausdrücken (umschreiben) paraphrase ['pærəfreɪz]

Ausflug trip [trɪp] • **einen Ausflug machen** go on a trip

ausgeben: Geld ausgeben (für) spend money (on) [spend]

Ausgehverbot haben be grounded ['graʊndɪd]

ausmalen (bunt anmalen, kolorieren) colour ['kʌlə]

ausruhen: sich ausruhen relax [rɪ'læks]

Aussage statement ['steɪtmənt]

ausschalten turn off [tɜːn]

aussehen: anders/toll/alt aussehen look different/great/old [lʊk] **fürchterlich aussehen** be a mess [mes]

außerhalb seines Zimmers outside his room [ˌaʊt'saɪd]

aussetzen: Einmal aussetzen. Miss a turn. [tɜːn]

Aussicht (auf) (Blick) view (of) [vjuː]

Aussprache pronunciation [prəˌnʌnsi'eɪʃn]

aussteigen (aus dem Zug/Bus) get off (the train/bus) [ˌget_'ɒf]

aussuchen: (sich) etwas aussuchen choose sth. [tʃuːz]

Austauschschüler/in exchange student [ɪks'tʃeɪndʒ ˌstjuːdnt]

auswählen choose [tʃuːz]

ausziehen 1. (aus Wohnung) move out [ˌmuːv_'aʊt] **2. etwas ausziehen** (Kleidung) take sth. off [ˌteɪk_'ɒf]

Auto car [kɑː]

Autofahrt drive [draɪv]

Autsch! Ouch! [aʊtʃ]

B

Baby baby ['beɪbi] • **ein Baby bekommen** have a baby

Bäckerei bakery ['beɪkəri]

Badeanzug swimsuit ['swɪmsuːt]

Badehose swimming trunks (pl) [trʌŋks]

baden (ein Bad nehmen) have a bath [bɑːθ]

Badewanne bath [bɑːθ]

Badezimmer bathroom ['bɑːθruːm]

Badminton badminton ['bædmɪntən]

Badmintonschläger badminton racket ['rækɪt]

Bahnhof station ['steɪʃn] • **am Bahnhof** at the station

bald soon [suːn] • **Bis bald.** See you. ['siː juː]

Ball ball [bɔːl]

Banane banana [bə'nɑːnə]

Band (Musikgruppe) band [bænd]

Bank (Sparkasse) bank [bæŋk]

Bankräuber/in bank robber ['rɒbə]

Bar bar [bɑː]

Bär bear [beə]

Baseball baseball ['beɪsbɔːl]

Baseballmütze baseball cap [kæp]

Basketball basketball ['bɑːskɪtbɔːl]

Bauchweh stomach ache [ˈstʌmək_eɪk]

bauen build [bɪld]

Bauernhof farm [fɑːm]

Baum tree [triː]

beantworten answer [ˈɑːnsə]

Becken *(Schwimmbecken)* pool [puːl]

bedeuten mean [miːn]

Bedeutung meaning [ˈmiːnɪŋ]

beeilen: sich beeilen hurry [ˈhʌri]; hurry up [ˌhʌri_ˈʌp]

beenden finish [ˈfɪnɪʃ]; end [end]

Beginn beginning [bɪˈɡɪnɪŋ]

Beförderung *(Transport)* transport [ˈtrænspɔːt]

begeistert *(aufgeregt)* excited [ɪkˈsaɪtɪd]

beginnen (mit) start [stɑːt]

begreifen understand [ˌʌndəˈstænd]

Begründung *(Grund)* reason [ˈriːzn]

behalten keep [kiːp]

behindert disabled [dɪsˈeɪbld]

bei: bei den Shaws zu Hause at the Shaws' house • **bei der Arbeit** at work • **Englisch bei Mr Kingsley** English with Mr Kingsley

beide both [bəʊθ]

Beifall klatschen cheer [tʃɪə]

Bein leg [leg] • **etwas auf die Beine stellen** get sth. off the ground

Beispiel example [ɪɡˈzɑːmpl] • **zum Beispiel** for example

Bekanntgabe announcement [əˈnaʊnsmənt]

Bekleidungsvorschrift dress code [ˈdres kəʊd]

bekommen get [get] • **ein Baby bekommen** have a baby

belebt *(Straße, Ort)* busy [ˈbɪzi]

beliebt popular [ˈpɒpjələ]

benennen name [kɔːl]

benötigen need [niːd]

benutzen use [juːz]

beobachten watch [wɒtʃ]

bereit ready [ˈredi]

Bereich area [ˈeəriə]; section [ˈsekʃn]

bereits already [ɔːlˈredi]

Berg mountain [ˈmaʊntən]

Bericht (über) report (on) [rɪˈpɔːt]

berichten (über) tell (about) [tel] **(jm.) etwas berichten** report sth. (to sb.) [rɪˈpɔːt]

berichtigen correct [kəˈrekt]

beruhigen: sich beruhigen calm down [ˌkɑːm ˈdaʊn]

berühmt famous [ˈfeɪməs]

berühren touch [tʌtʃ]

Bescheid: über etwas Bescheid wissen know about sth. [nəʊ]

beschreiben: (jm.) etwas beschrei- ben describe sth. (to sb.) [dɪˈskraɪb]

jm. den Weg beschreiben tell sb. the way

Beschreibung description [dɪˈskrɪpʃn]

besiegen beat [biːt]

besitzen have [həv, hæv]

besondere(r, s): ein besonderer Tag a special day [ˈspeʃl]

besorgen *(holen)* get [get]

besser better [ˈbetə]

beste: am besten (the) best [best] **der/die/das beste ...; die besten ...** the best ... • **Was war das Beste an ...?** What was the best thing about ...?

Besuch visit [ˈvɪzɪt]

besuchen: jn. besuchen visit sb. [ˈvɪzɪt]; see sb. [siː]

Besucher/in visitor [ˈvɪzɪtə]

Betonung stress [stres]

betreten enter [ˈentə]

Bett bed [bed] • **ins Bett gehen** go to bed

Beutel bag [bæɡ]

bevor before [bɪˈfɔː]

bewegen: sich bewegen move [muːv]

Bewegung movement [ˈmuːvmənt]

Beweis(e) proof *(no pl)* [pruːf]

bewölkt cloudy [ˈklaʊdi]

bezahlen: etwas bezahlen pay for sth. [peɪ]

Bibliothek library [ˈlaɪbrəri]

Bild picture [ˈpɪktʃə] • **auf dem Bild** in the picture

Bildschirm monitor [ˈmɒnɪtə]

billig cheap [tʃiːp]

Bindewort linking word [ˈlɪŋkɪŋ wɜːd]

Biologie biology [baɪˈɒlədʒi]

bis *(zeitlich)* until [ənˈtɪl]; till [tɪl] **Bis bald.** See you. [ˈsiː juː] • **bis (spätestens) zehn Uhr** by ten o'clock • **von Montag bis Freitag** from Mondays to Fridays
► S.163 German „bis"

bisschen: ein bisschen a bit [bɪt]

bitte 1. *(in Fragen und Aufforderun- gen)* please [pliːz]
2. Bitte sehr. / Hier bitte. Here you are.
3. Bitte, gern geschehen. You're welcome. [ˈwelkəm]
4. Wie bitte? Sorry? [ˈsɒri]

blau blue [bluː]

bleiben stay [steɪ] • **in Verbindung bleiben** keep in touch [ˌkiːp_ɪn ˈtʌtʃ]

Bleistift pencil [ˈpensl]

Bleistiftanspitzer pencil sharpener [ˈpensl ʃɑːpnə]

Blick *(Aussicht)* view [vjuː]

Blitz *(Lichtblitz)* flash [flæʃ]

Blockflöte recorder [rɪˈkɔːdə]

blöd stupid [ˈstjuːpɪd]

bloß just [dʒʌst]; only [ˈəʊnli]

Boden *(Erdboden)* ground [ɡraʊnd]

Bohrinsel *(Ölbohrinsel)* oil rig [ˈɔɪl rɪɡ]

Boot boat [bəʊt]

böse sein (auf jn.) be cross (with sb.) [krɒs]; be angry (with sb.) [ˈæŋɡri] • **böse sein (über etwas)** be angry (about sth.)

Boss boss [bɒs]

Brand fire [ˈfaɪə]

brainstormen *(so viele Ideen wie möglich sammeln)* brainstorm [ˈbreɪnstɔːm]

brauchen need [niːd]; *(Zeit brauchen, dauern)* take [teɪk] • **nicht zu tun brauchen** needn't do [ˈniːdnt]

braun brown [braʊn]

brav good [ɡʊd]

Brief (an) letter (to) [ˈletə]

Briefmarke stamp [stæmp]

Brille: (eine) Brille glasses *(pl)* [ˈɡlɑːsɪz]

bringen: (mit-, her)bringen bring [brɪŋ] • **(weg-, hin)bringen** take [teɪk] • **alles in Unordnung bringen** make a mess • **etwas auf den Weg bringen** get sth. off the ground

britisch; Brite, Britin British [ˈbrɪtɪʃ]

Broschüre brochure [ˈbrəʊʃə]

Brot bread *(no pl)* [bred]

Brötchen roll [rəʊl]

Brotdose sandwich box [ˈsænwɪtʃ bɒks]

Brücke bridge [brɪdʒ]

Bruder brother [ˈbrʌðə]

Buch book [bʊk]

Bücherei library [ˈlaɪbrəri]

Buchstabe letter [ˈletə]

buchstabieren spell [spel]

Bühne stage [steɪdʒ]

bunt an-, ausmalen colour [ˈkʌlə]

Burg castle [ˈkɑːsl]

Bus bus [bʌs]

Bushaltestelle bus stop [ˈbʌs stɒp]

Butter butter [ˈbʌtə]

C

Café café [ˈkæfeɪ]

Cartoon cartoon [kɑːˈtuːn]

CD CD [ˌsiːˈdiː] • **CD-Spieler** CD player [ˌsiːˈdiː ˌpleɪə]

Cent cent (c) [sent]

Chatroom chat room [ˈtʃæt ruːm]

chatten chat [tʃæt]

Chef/in boss [bɒs]

Chor choir [ˈkwaɪə]

clever clever [ˈklevə]; smart [smɑːt]

Clown/in clown [klaʊn]

Cola cola [ˈkəʊlə]

Comic-Heft comic [ˈkɒmɪk]

Computer computer [kəmˈpjuːtə]
cool cool [kuːl]
Cornflakes cornflakes [ˈkɔːnfleɪks]
Cousin, Cousine cousin [ˈkʌzn]
Curry(gericht) curry [ˈkʌri]

D

da, dahin *(dort, dorthin)* there [ðeə]
  da drüben over there [ˌəʊvə ˈðeə]
daheim at home [ət ˈhəʊm]
daher so [səʊ]
dämlich stupid [ˈstjuːpɪd]
danach *(zeitlich)* after that [ˌɑːftə ˈðæt]
dankbar thankful [ˈθæŋkfl]; *(froh)* glad [glæd]
Danke. Thank you. [ˈθæŋk juː]; Thanks. • **Danke sehr!** Thanks very much! • **Vielen Dank!** Thanks a lot!
dann then [ðen]
darstellende Kunst drama [ˈdrɑːmə]
das 1. *(Artikel)* the [ðə, ðiː]
  2. *(Relativpronomen)* **das Mädchen, das …** the girl who … / the girl that … • **das Auto, das …** the car that … / the car which …
das (dort) *(Singular)* that [ðət, ðæt]; *(Plural)* those [ðəʊz] • **Das bin ich.** That's me.
dass that [ðət, ðæt]
dasselbe the same [seɪm]
Datum date [deɪt]
dauern *(Zeit brauchen)* take [teɪk]
decken: den Tisch decken lay the table [ˌleɪ ðə ˈteɪbl]
dein(e) … your … [jɔː]
deiner, deine, deins yours [jɔːz]
denken think [θɪŋk] • **denken an** think of • **Was denkst du über …?** What do you think about/of …?
der 1. *(Artikel)* the [ðə, ðiː]
  2. *(Relativpronomen)* **der Mann, der …** the man who … / the man that … • **der Laden, der …** the shop that … / the shop which …
derselbe the same [seɪm]
deshalb so [səʊ]
Detail detail [ˈdiːteɪl]
Detektiv/in detective [dɪˈtektɪv]
deuten (auf etwas) *(zeigen)* point (at/to sth.) [pɔɪnt]
deutlich clear [klɪə]
Deutsch; deutsch; Deutsche(r) German [ˈdʒɜːmən]
Deutschland Germany [ˈdʒɜːməni]
Dezember December [dɪˈsembə]
Dialog dialogue [ˈdaɪəlɒg]
dich you [juː] • **dich (selbst)** *(Reflexivpronomen)* yourself [jɔːˈself]
  ▶ S.163 Reflexive pronouns

die 1. *(Artikel)* the [ðə, ðiː]
  2. *(Relativpronomen)* **die Frau, die …** the woman who … / the woman that … • **die Jacke, die …** the jacket that … / the jacket which …
die (dort) *(Singular)* that [ðət, ðæt]; *(Plural)* those [ðəʊz] • **die (hier)** *(Singular)* this [ðɪs]; *(Plural)* these [ðiːz]
Dieb/in thief [θiːf], *pl* thieves [θiːvz]
Diele hall [hɔːl]
Dienstag Tuesday [ˈtjuːzdeɪ, ˈtjuːzdi] *(siehe auch unter „Freitag")*
dies (hier); diese(r, s) *(Singular)* this [ðɪs]; *(Plural)* these [ðiːz]
dieselbe(n) the same [seɪm]
Ding thing [θɪŋ]
dir you [juː]
Diskjockey DJ [ˈdiːdʒeɪ]
Disko disco [ˈdɪskəʊ]
Diskussion discussion [dɪˈskʌʃn]
Doktor doctor [ˈdɒktə]
Dom cathedral [kəˈθiːdrəl]
Donnerstag Thursday [ˈθɜːzdeɪ, ˈθɜːzdi] *(siehe auch unter „Freitag")*
doppelt, Doppel- double [ˈdʌbl]
Dorf village [ˈvɪlɪdʒ]
dort, dorthin there [ðeə] • **dort drüben** over there [ˌəʊvə ˈðeə]
  dort unten down there
Dossier dossier [ˈdɒsieɪ]
downloaden *(runterladen)* download [ˌdaʊnˈləʊd]
Drachen kite [kaɪt]
dran: Ich bin dran. It's my turn. [tɜːn]
draußen outside [ˌaʊtˈsaɪd]; out [aʊt]
  nach draußen outside
dreimal three times
drinnen inside [ˌɪnˈsaɪd] • **hier drinnen** in here [ˌɪn ˈhɪə] • **nach drinnen** inside
dritte(r, s) third [θɜːd]
Drogerie chemist [ˈkemɪst]
drüben: da/dort drüben over there [ˌəʊvə ˈðeə]
drücken push [pʊʃ]; *(pressen)* press [pres]
du you [juː]
dumm *(albern)* silly [ˈsɪli]
dunkel dark [dɑːk]
durch through [θruː]; *(in…umher)* around [əˈraʊnd] • **durch die Stadt** around the town
  ▶ S.155 around
durcheinander: alles durcheinanderbringen make a mess [ˌmeɪk‿ə ˈmes]
durchführen: ein Projekt durchführen do a project
Durchsage *(Ansage)* announcement [əˈnaʊnsmənt]
dürfen can [kən, kæn]; may [meɪ]; be allowed to [əˈlaʊd] • **nicht dürfen**

mustn't [ˈmʌsnt]
  ▶ S.162 „können" und „dürfen"
Dusche shower [ˈʃaʊə]
duschen; sich duschen have a shower [ˈʃaʊə]
DVD DVD [ˌdiː viːˈ diː]

E

echt real [rɪəl]
Ecke corner [ˈkɔːnə] • **Green Street, Ecke London Road** on the corner of Green Street and London Road
Ehefrau wife [waɪf], *pl* wives [waɪvz]
Ehemann husband [ˈhʌzbənd]
Ei egg [eg]
Eichhörnchen squirrel [ˈskwɪrəl]
eifersüchtig (auf) jealous (of) [ˈdʒeləs]
eigene(r, s): unser eigenes Schwimmbad our own pool [əʊn]
eigentlich *(in Wirklichkeit)* actually [ˈæktʃuəli]
Eile: in Eile sein be in a hurry [ˈhʌri]
eilen *(sich beeilen)* hurry [ˈhʌri]
eilig: es eilig haben be in a hurry [ˈhʌri]
ein(e) a, an [ə, ən]; one [wʌn]
  ein(e) andere(r, s) … another … [əˈnʌðə] • **eine Menge** a lot (of) [lɒt]; lots (of) [lɒts] • **ein neuer / eine neue / ein neues** a new one [wʌn] • **ein paar** some [səm, sʌm]
eines Tages one day
einander *(sich gegenseitig)* each other [iːtʃ‿ˈʌðə]
  ▶ S.164 each other – themselves
einfach *(nicht schwierig)* easy [ˈiːzi]
  einfach nur just [dʒʌst] • **einfache Fahrkarte** *(nur Hinfahrt)* single (ticket) [ˈsɪŋgl]
Einfall *(Idee)* idea [aɪˈdɪə]
Einführung (in) introduction (to) [ˌɪntrəˈdʌkʃn]
eingeschaltet sein *(Licht usw.)* be on
einige some [səm, sʌm]; *(einige wenige)* a few [fjuː]
einigen: sich einigen (auf) agree (on) [əˈgriː]
einkaufen shop [ʃɒp] • **einkaufen gehen** go shopping; shop
Einkaufen shopping [ˈʃɒpɪŋ]
Einkaufsliste shopping list
einladen (zu) invite (to) [ɪnˈvaɪt]
Einladung (zu) invitation (to) [ˌɪnvɪˈteɪʃn]
einmal once [wʌns] • **einmal pro Woche** once a week • **auf einmal** suddenly [ˈsʌdnli] • **Einmal aussetzen.** Miss a turn. [tɜːn] • **früher einmal** once

einpacken pack [pæk]
eins, ein, eine one ['wʌn]
Einsatzort location [ləʊ'keɪʃn]
einschalten (Computer usw.) turn on [ˌtɜːn_'ɒn]
einschüchtern bully ['bʊli]
einst (früher einmal) once [wʌns]
einsteigen (in den Zug/Bus) get on (the train/bus) [ˌget_'ɒn]
eintreffen (ankommen) arrive [ə'raɪv]
eintreten (in) enter ['entə]
Eintrittskarte ticket ['tɪkɪt]
Einzelheit detail ['diːteɪl]
einziehen (in Wohnung) move in [ˌmuːv_'ɪn]
einzig: der einzige Gast the only guest ['əʊnli]
Eis ice [aɪs]; (Speiseeis) ice cream [ˌaɪs 'kriːm]
Eisenbahn railway ['reɪlweɪ]
Elefant elephant ['elɪfənt]
elektrisch electric [ɪ'lektrɪk]
Elektro- electric [ɪ'lektrɪk]
elektronisch electronic [ɪˌlek'trɒnɪk]
Eltern parents ['peərənts]
E-Mail (an) e-mail (to) ['iːmeɪl]
End- (letzte/r/s) final ['faɪnl]
Ende 1. end [end]; (einer Geschichte, eines Films usw.) ending ['endɪŋ]
am Ende (von) at the end (of) • **zu Ende machen** finish ['fɪnɪʃ] • **zu Ende sein** be over ['əʊvə]
2. oberes Ende (Spitze) top [tɒp]
am oberen Ende at the top
3. unteres Ende bottom ['bɒtəm]
am unteren Ende at the bottom ['bɒtəm]
enden finish ['fɪnɪʃ]
endlich at last [ət 'lɑːst]
Endstand (beim Sport) final score [ˌfaɪnl 'skɔː]
▶ S.159 A football match
eng tight [taɪt]
Engel angel ['eɪndʒl]
Englisch; englisch English ['ɪŋglɪʃ]
Enkel/in grandchild ['græntʃaɪld], pl grandchildren ['græntʃɪldrən]
Entdecker/in (Forscher/in) explorer [ɪk'splɔːrə]
entkommen escape [ɪ'skeɪp]
entlang der Straße / die Straße entlang along the street [ə'lɒŋ]
entscheiden: Das kannst/musst du (selbst) entscheiden. That's up to you.
entschuldigen: sich entschuldigen say sorry ['sɒri]
Entschuldigung 1. (Tut mir leid.) I'm sorry. ['sɒri] • **Entschuldigung, dass ich zu spät bin/komme.** Sorry, I'm late.
2. Entschuldigung, ... / Entschuldi-

gen Sie, ... (Darf ich mal stören?) Excuse me, ... [ɪk'skjuːz miː]
entspannen; sich entspannen relax [rɪ'læks]
entsperren unlock [ˌʌn'lɒk]
entwerfen design [dɪ'zaɪn]
er 1. (männliche Person) he [hiː] 2. (Ding, Tier) it [ɪt]
Erbse pea [piː]
Erdbeere strawberry ['strɔːbəri]
Erdboden ground [graʊnd]
Erdkunde geography [dʒi'ɒgrəfi]
erfahren: etwas über etwas erfahren learn sth. about sth. [lɜːn]
erforschen explore [ɪk'splɔː]
ergänzen add (to) [æd]
Ergebnis result [rɪ'zʌlt]
erinnern: sich erinnern (an) remember [rɪ'membə]
erkältet sein have a cold [kəʊld]
Erkältung cold [kəʊld] • **eine Erkältung haben** have a cold
erklären: jm. etwas erklären explain sth. to sb. [ɪk'spleɪn]
Erklärung explanation [ˌeksplə'neɪʃn]
erkunden explore [ɪk'splɔː]
erlauben: jm. erlauben, etwas zu tun let sb. do sth. [let]
erläutern: jm. etwas erläutern explain sth. to sb. [ɪk'spleɪn]
erraten guess [ges]
erschießen shoot [ʃuːt]
erstaunlich amazing [ə'meɪzɪŋ]
erste(r, s) first [fɜːst] • **als Erstes** first • **der erste Tag** the first day **der/die Erste sein** be first
erwachsen werden grow up [ˌgrəʊ_'ʌp]
Erwachsene(r) adult ['ædʌlt]
erwarten expect [ɪk'spekt] • **ich kann es kaum erwarten, ... zu sehen** I can't wait to see ... [weɪt]
erwischen (fangen) catch [kætʃ]
erzählen (von) tell (about) [tel]
Erzählung story ['stɔːri]
erzielen: einen Treffer erzielen (ein Tor schießen) score (a goal) [skɔː], [gəʊl]
es it [ɪt] • **es gibt** (es ist vorhanden) there's; (es sind vorhanden) there are
Essen food [fuːd]; (Mahlzeit) meal [miːl]
essen eat [iːt] • **Abendbrot essen** have dinner • **Toast zum Frühstück essen** have toast for breakfast
Esszimmer dining room ['daɪnɪŋ ruːm]
Etagenbett bunk (bed) [bʌŋk]
etwas something ['sʌmθɪŋ]; (irgendetwas) anything ['eniθɪŋ]; (ein bisschen) a bit [bɪt] • **etwas Käse/Saft** some cheese/juice [səm, sʌm]

euch you [juː] • **euch (selbst)** yourselves [jə'selvz, jɔː'selvz]
▶ S.163 Reflexive pronouns
euer, eure ... your ... [jɔː]
eurer, eure, eures yours [jɔːz]
Euro euro ['jʊərəʊ]

F

Fabrik factory ['fæktri]
fähig sein, etwas zu tun be able to do sth. ['eɪbl]
Fähre ferry ['feri]
fahren go [gəʊ]; (ein Auto / mit dem Auto) drive [draɪv] • **in Urlaub fahren** go on holiday • **mit dem Auto/Zug/Rad/... fahren** go by car/train/bike/... • **Inliner/Skateboard fahren** skate [skeɪt] • **Rad fahren** cycle ['saɪkl]; ride a bike [ˌraɪd_ə 'baɪk]
Fahrer/in driver ['draɪvə]
Fahrkarte ticket ['tɪkɪt] • **einfache Fahrkarte** (nur Hinfahrt) single (ticket) ['sɪŋgl]
Fahrplan timetable ['taɪmteɪbl]
Fahrrad bike [baɪk]
Fahrstuhl lift [lɪft] (BE); elevator ['elɪveɪtə] (AE)
Fahrt journey ['dʒɜːni] • **(Auto-)Fahrt** drive [draɪv] • **(Rad-)Fahrt** (bike) ride [raɪd]
fair fair [feə]
Fakt (Tatsache) fact [fækt]
Fall (Kriminalfall) case [keɪs]
fallen fall [fɔːl]
fallen lassen drop [drɒp]
falls if [ɪf]
falsch wrong [rɒŋ] • **in die falsche Richtung** the wrong way
Familie family ['fæməli]
Fan fan [fæn]; (Unterstützer/in) supporter [sə'pɔːtə]
fangen catch [kætʃ]
fantastisch fantastic [fæn'tæstɪk]
Farbe colour ['kʌlə] • **Welche Farbe hat ...?** What colour is ...?
färben (bunt an-, ausmalen) colour ['kʌlə]
Farm farm [fɑːm]
Fassung: jd. aus der Fassung bringen upset sb. [ʌp'set]
Fastfood fast food [ˌfɑːst 'fuːd]
Februar February ['februəri]
Federball badminton ['bædmɪntən]
Federmäppchen pencil case ['pensl keɪs]
fehlen be missing ['mɪsɪŋ]
Fehler mistake [mɪ'steɪk]
Feind/in enemy ['enəmi]

Feld 1. field [fiːld] • **auf dem Feld** in the field
2. *(bei Brettspielen)* **Geh ein Feld vor.** Move on one space. [speɪs] **Geh ein Feld zurück.** Move back one space.
Fels, Felsen rock
Fenster window [ˈwɪndəʊ]
Ferien holidays [ˈhɒlɪdeɪz] *(BE);* vacation [vəˈkeɪʃn, AE: veɪˈkeɪʃn] *(AE)*
Ferienwohnung holiday flat [ˈhɒlədeɪ flæt]
Fernsehen television [ˈtelɪvɪʒn]; TV [tiːˈviː] • **im Fernsehen** on TV
fernsehen watch TV [ˌwɒtʃ tiːˈviː]
fertig *(bereit)* ready [ˈredi] • **sich fertig machen (für)** *(sich vorbereiten)* get ready (for) • **Dinge fertig machen (für)** *(vorbereiten)* get things ready (for)
Fest, Festival festival [ˈfestɪvl]
Festspiele festival [ˈfestɪvl]
Feuer fire [ˈfaɪə]
Feuerwehrfrau firewoman [ˈfaɪəˌwʊmən]
Feuerwehrmann fireman [ˈfaɪəmən]
Fieber haben have a temperature [ˈtemprətʃə]
Fiedel fiddle [ˈfɪdl] *(infml)* • **Fiedel spielen** play the fiddle
Film film [fɪlm]; movie [ˈmuːvi]
Filmemacher film-maker [ˈfɪlmmeɪkə]
Filmstar film star [ˈfɪlm stɑː]
Filzstift felt tip [ˈfelt tɪp]
Finale final [ˈfaɪnl]
finden *(entdecken)* find [faɪnd]
Finder finder [ˈfaɪndə]
Finger finger [ˈfɪŋgə]
Fisch fish, *pl* fish [fɪʃ]
fischen fish [fɪʃ]
fit sein be fit [fɪt]
Flasche bottle [ˈbɒtl] • **eine Flasche Milch** a bottle of milk
Fleisch meat [miːt]
Fleischer butcher [ˈbʊtʃə] • **beim Fleischer** at the butcher's
▶ S.154 at the butcher's / to the doctor's ...
fliegen fly [flaɪ]
fliehen (vor jm. / aus etwas) escape (from sb./sth.) [ɪˈskeɪp]
Flug flight [flaɪt] • **ein 14-stündiger Flug, ein 14-Stunden-Flug** a 14-hour flight
Flughafen airport [ˈeəpɔːt]
Flugsteig gate [geɪt]
Flugzeug plane [pleɪn] • **im Flugzeug** on the plane
Flur hall [hɔːl]
Fluss river [ˈrɪvə]
Flusspferd hippo [ˈhɪpəʊ]
flüstern whisper [ˈwɪspə]
folgen follow [ˈfɒləʊ]

Folk folk (music) [ˈfəʊk ˌmjuːzɪk]
Football American football [əˌmerɪkən ˈfʊtbɔːl]
Forscher/in explorer [ɪkˈsplɔːrə]
fort away [əˈweɪ]
Foto photo [ˈfəʊtəʊ] • **auf dem Foto** in the photo • **Fotos machen** take photos
Fotoapparat camera [ˈkæmərə]
Fotograf/in photographer [fəˈtɒgrəfə]
fotografieren take photos [teɪk ˈfəʊtəʊz]
Frage question [ˈkwestʃn] • **Fragen stellen** ask questions • **Kommt nicht in Frage!** No way!
fragen ask [ɑːsk] • **nach etwas fragen** ask about sth. • **jn. nach dem Weg fragen** ask sb. the way • **sich fragen** wonder [ˈwʌndə]
Französisch French [frentʃ]
Frau woman [ˈwʊmən], *pl* women [ˈwɪmɪn] • **Frau Brown** Mrs Brown [ˈmɪsɪz]; Ms Brown [mɪz, məz] • **Frau White** *(unverheiratet)* Miss White [mɪs]
frei free [friː] • **freie Zeit** free time
Freitag Friday [ˈfraɪdeɪ, ˈfraɪdi] **freitagabends, am Freitagabend** on Friday evening • **freitagnachts, Freitagnacht** on Friday night
Freizeit free time [ˌfriː ˈtaɪm]
Freizeitzentrum, -park leisure centre [ˈleʒə sentə]
Fremdenverkehrsamt tourist information [ˈtʊərɪst ˌɪnfəˈmeɪʃn]
Freund/in friend [frend]; *(Kumpel)* mate [meɪt] *(infml)*
freundlich friendly [ˈfrendli]
frieren be cold [kəʊld]
froh happy [ˈhæpi]; glad [glæd]
Frosch frog [frɒg]
Frucht, Früchte fruit [fruːt]
früh early [ˈɜːli]
früher *(einst, früher einmal)* once [wʌns]
Frühling spring [sprɪŋ]
Frühstück breakfast [ˈbrekfəst] **zum Frühstück** for breakfast
frühstücken have breakfast
Frühstückspension Bed and Breakfast (B&B) [ˌbed ən ˈbrekfəst]
Fuchs fox [fɒks]
fühlen; sich fühlen feel [fiːl]
Führer/in leader [ˈliːdə]
Füller pen [pen]
funktionieren work [wɜːk]
für for [fə, fɔː] • **Was für ein Auto ...?** What kind of car ...?
furchtbar terrible [ˈterəbl]; awful [ˈɔːfl]
fürchterlich aussehen be a mess [mes]
Fuß foot [fʊt], *pl* feet [fiːt]

Fußball football [ˈfʊtbɔːl] • **Fußball spielen** play football
Fußballplatz pitch [pɪtʃ]
Fußballschuhe, -stiefel football boots [ˈfʊtbɔːl buːts]
Fußboden floor [flɔː]
Futter food [fuːd]
füttern feed [fiːd]

G

Gabel fork [fɔːk]
gähnen yawn [jɔːn]
ganz: auf der ganzen Welt all over the world • **aus der ganzen Welt** from all over the world • **den ganzen Tag (lang)** all day • **die ganze Zeit** all the time • **Das ist ganz falsch.** This is all wrong.
Garage garage [ˈgærɑːʒ]
Garten garden [ˈgɑːdn]
Gasse lane [leɪn]
Gast guest [gest]; *(Besucher/in)* visitor [ˈvɪzɪtə]
Gebäude building [ˈbɪldɪŋ]
geben give [gɪv] • **es gibt** *(es ist vorhanden)* there's; *(es sind vorhanden)* there are • **jm. die Schuld geben (an)** blame sb. (for) [bleɪm]
geboren sein/werden be born [bɔːn]
gebraucht *(aus zweiter Hand)* second-hand [ˌsekənd ˈhænd]
gebrochen *(Arm, Bein)* broken [ˈbrəʊkən]
Geburtstag birthday [ˈbɜːθdeɪ] **Herzlichen Glückwunsch zum Geburtstag.** Happy birthday. **Ich habe im Mai / am 13. Juni Geburtstag.** My birthday is in May / on 13th June. • **Wann hast du Geburtstag?** When's your birthday?
Gedicht poem [ˈpəʊɪm]
Gefahr danger [ˈdeɪndʒə]
gefährlich dangerous [ˈdeɪndʒərəs]; *(nicht sicher)* unsafe [ʌnˈseɪf]
gegen against [əˈgenst] • **gegen sechs** *(um sechs Uhr herum)* around six
▶ S.155 around
gegenseitig: sich gegenseitig each other [iːtʃ ˈʌðə]
▶ S.164 each other – themselves
Gegenteil opposite [ˈɒpəzɪt]
Gegenwart present [ˈpreznt]
gehen 1. go [gəʊ]; *(zu Fuß gehen)* walk [wɔːk]; *(weggehen)* leave [liːv] **Auf geht's!** Let's go. • **einkaufen gehen** go shopping; shop [ʃɒp] **Geh ein Feld vor.** Move on one space. [speɪs] • **Geh ein Feld zurück.** Move back one space. • **in**

die Sauna gehen have a sauna • **ins Bett gehen** go to bed • **ins Kino gehen** go to the cinema • **nach Hause gehen** go home • **reiten/schwimmen gehen** go riding/swimming • **spazieren gehen** go for a walk [wɔːk]
2. Es geht mir/ihm gut. I'm/He's fine. [faɪn]
3. Es geht um Mr Green. This is about Mr Green.
4. Das geht dich nichts an! Mind your own business. [ˌmaɪnd jərˌəʊn ˈbɪznəs]
gehören zu (passen zu) go with
Geige violin [ˌvaɪəˈlɪn]; fiddle (infml) [ˈfɪdl] • **Geige spielen** play the violin
Geist (Gespenst) ghost [ɡəʊst]
gekränkt (wegen) upset (about) [ˌʌpˈset]
Gelächter laughter [ˈlɑːftə]
gelangen (hinkommen) get [ɡet]
gelb yellow [ˈjeləʊ]
Geld money [ˈmʌni] • **Geld ausgeben (für)** spend money (on) [spend]
Geldbörse purse [pɜːs]
Gemeindehalle, -saal community hall [kəˈmjuːnəti]
Gemüse: (ein) **Gemüse** vegetable [ˈvedʒtəbl]
genau exactly [ɪɡˈzæktli] • **genau in dem Moment** just then • **genau wie du** just like you
genial brilliant [ˈbrɪliənt]
genießen enjoy [ɪnˈdʒɔɪ]
genug enough [ɪˈnʌf]
geöffnet open [ˈəʊpən]
Geografie geography [dʒiˈɒɡrəfi]
gepflegt neat [niːt]
gerade at the moment; (eben, soeben) just [dʒʌst] • **gerade dann** (genau in dem Moment) just then • **jetzt gerade** (in diesem Moment) right now [raɪt ˈnaʊ]
geradeaus weiter straight on [streɪtˌˈɒn]
Geräusch noise [nɔɪz]
gerecht fair [feə]
Gericht (Speise) dish [dɪʃ]
gern: Ich hätte gern ... / Ich möchte gern ... I'd like ... (= I would like ...) • **Ich schwimme/tanze/... gern.** I like swimming/dancing/... • **Ich würde gern über ... reden** I'd like to talk about ... • **Gern geschehen.** You're welcome. [ˈwelkəm]
gernhaben like [laɪk]
Geruch smell
gesamt: aus dem gesamten Vereinigten Königreich from all over the United Kingdom

Geschäft shop [ʃɒp]
geschehen (mit) happen (to) [ˈhæpən]
Geschenk present [ˈpreznt]
Geschichte 1. story [ˈstɔːri] **2.** (vergangene Zeiten) history [ˈhɪstri]
geschieden divorced [dɪˈvɔːst]
Geschirrspülmaschine dishwasher [ˈdɪʃwɒʃə]
Geschlecht sex [seks]
geschlossen closed [kləʊzd]
Gesicht face [feɪs]
Gespenst (Geist) ghost [ɡəʊst]
Gespräch (Dialog) dialogue [ˈdaɪəlɒɡ]
gestalten design [dɪˈzaɪn]
gestern yesterday [ˈjestədeɪ, ˈjestədi] • **gestern Morgen/Nachmittag/Abend** yesterday morning/afternoon/evening • **die Hausaufgaben von gestern** yesterday's homework
gesund healthy [ˈhelθi]; well [wel]
Getränk drink [drɪŋk]
Gewinn prize [praɪz]
gewinnen win [wɪn]
Gewinner/in winner [ˈwɪnə]
Gewitter storm [stɔːm]
gewöhnlich usually [ˈjuːʒuəli]
Giraffe giraffe [dʒəˈrɑːf]
Gitarre guitar [ɡɪˈtɑː] • **Gitarre spielen** play the guitar
Glas glass [ɡlɑːs] • **ein Glas Wasser** a glass of water
glauben think [θɪŋk] • **Glaubst du das wirklich?** Do you really think so?
gleich sein/aussehen be/look the same [seɪm]
Glocke bell [bel]
Glück: Viel Glück (bei/mit ...)! Good luck (with ...)! [ɡʊd ˈlʌk] • **zum Glück** (glücklicherweise) luckily [ˈlʌkɪli]
glücklich happy [ˈhæpi]
glücklicherweise luckily [ˈlʌkɪli]
Gokart go-kart [ˈɡəʊkɑːt]
Grad degree [dɪˈɡriː]
Grafiker/in artist [ˈɑːtɪst]
Grammatik grammar [ˈɡræmə]
grau grey [ɡreɪ]
grauenhaft horrible [ˈhɒrəbl]
groß big [bɪɡ]; large [lɑːdʒ]; (riesig) huge [hjuːdʒ]
▶ S.156 big – large – huge
großartig great [ɡreɪt]
Größe (Schuhgröße usw.) size [saɪz]
Großeltern grandparents [ˈɡrænpeərənts]
Großmutter grandmother [ˈɡrænmʌðə]
Großstadt city [ˈsɪti]

Großvater grandfather [ˈɡrænfɑːðə]
grün green [ɡriːn]
Grund reason [ˈriːzn] • **aus vielen Gründen** for lots of reasons
Gruppe group [ɡruːp]; (Musikgruppe) band [bænd]
gruselig scary [ˈskeəri]
Gruß: Liebe Grüße, ... (Briefschluss) Love ... [lʌv]
Grüß Dilip von mir. Say hi to Dilip for me.
gucken look [lʊk]
gut good [ɡʊd]; (okay) OK [əʊˈkeɪ]; (in Ordnung) all right [ɔːl ˈraɪt]; (gesundheitlich gut, wohlauf) well [wel]; fine [faɪn] • **Es geht mir/ihm gut.** I'm/He's fine. • **gute Arbeit leisten** do a good job • **Guten Morgen.** Good morning. • **Guten Tag.** Hello.; (nachmittags) Good afternoon. • **gut abschneiden (in)** do well (in) • **gut (ver)laufen** (gutgehen, klappen) go well • **Das hast du gut gemacht.** You did well.
gutgehen (gut (ver)laufen, klappen) go well

H

Haar, Haare hair (no pl) [heə]
haben have got [ˈhæv ɡɒt]; have [həv, hæv] • **Ich habe keinen Stuhl.** I haven't got a chair. • **Ich habe am 13. Juni/im Mai Geburtstag.** My birthday is on 13th June/in May. **Wann hast du Geburtstag?** When's your birthday? • **haben wollen** want [wɒnt] • **Was haben wir als Hausaufgabe auf?** What's for homework?
Hafen harbour [ˈhɑːbə]
Hähnchen chicken [ˈtʃɪkɪn]
halb: eine halbe Stunde half an hour [ˌhɑːfˌənˈaʊə] • **halb zwölf** half past 11 [hɑːf]
Halbfinale semi-final [ˌsemiˈfaɪnl]
Halbzeit half • **die erste Halbzeit** the first half • **Halbzeit(pause)** half-time [ˌhɑːfˈtaɪm]
Hälfte half [hɑːf], pl halves [hɑːvs]
Hallo! Hi! [haɪ]; Hello. [həˈləʊ]; Hey! [heɪ]
Hals throat [θrəʊt]
Halsschmerzen haben have a sore throat [sɔː ˈθrəʊt]
halten 1. hold [həʊld] **2.** (aufbewahren) keep [kiːp] • **etwas warm/kühl/offen/... halten** keep sth. warm/cool/open/... **3.** (behalten) keep • **Kontakt halten** keep in touch [ˌkiːpˌɪn ˈtʌtʃ]

4. **Halt den Mund!** Shut up. [ˌʃʌt_ˈʌp]

5. **Was hältst du von …?** What do you think about/of …?

Hamburger hamburger [ˈhæmbɜːgə]

Hamster hamster [ˈhæmstə]

Hand hand [hænd] • **aus zweiter Hand** (gebraucht) second-hand

Handball handball [ˈhændbɔːl]

Handy mobile (phone) [ˈməʊbaɪl]

hänseln: jn. mit Schimpfwörtern hänseln call sb. names

Happyend happy ending [ˌhæpi_ˈendɪŋ]

hart hard [hɑːd] • **hart arbeiten** work hard

hassen hate [heɪt]

häufig often [ˈɒfn]

Hauptstadt capital [ˈkæpɪtl]

Haus house [haʊs] • **im Haus der Shaws / bei den Shaws zu Hause** at the Shaws' house • **nach Hause gehen** go home [həʊm] • **nach Hause kommen** come home; get home • **zu Hause** at home

Hausarrest haben be grounded [ˈgraʊndɪd]

Hausaufgabe(n) homework (no pl) [ˈhəʊmwɜːk] • **die Hausaufgabe(n) machen** do homework • **Was haben wir als Hausaufgabe auf?** What's for homework?

Hausmeister/in caretaker [ˈkeəteɪkə]

Haustier pet [pet]

Haustür front door [ˌfrʌnt 'dɔː]

Heim home [həʊm]

heiß hot [hɒt]

heißen: 1. Ich heiße … My name is … • **Wie heißt du?** What's your name?

2. **Sie heißen dich in … willkommen** They welcome you to … [ˈwelkəm]

helfen help [help]

Helikopter helicopter [ˈhelɪkɒptə]

hell (leuchtend) bright [braɪt]

Helm helmet [ˈhelmɪt]

Hemd shirt [ʃɜːt]

herauf up [ʌp]

heraus out [aʊt] • **aus … heraus** out of … [ˈaʊt_əv]

herausfinden find out [ˌfaɪnd_ˈaʊt] **etwas über etwas herausfinden** learn sth. about sth. [lɜːn]

herausnehmen take out [ˌteɪk_ˈaʊt]

Herberge hostel [ˈhɒstl]

herbringen bring [brɪŋ]

Herbst autumn [ˈɔːtəm]

Herd cooker [ˈkʊkə]

hereinkommen come in [ˌkʌm_ˈɪn]

Herr Brown Mr Brown [ˈmɪstə]

herstellen produce [prəˈdjuːs]

herum: anders herum the other way round [raʊnd] • **um … herum** round, around [əˈraʊnd] • **um sechs Uhr herum** (gegen sechs) • around six

▶ S.155 around

herum-: etwas herumgeben pass sth. round [ˌpɑːs ˈraʊnd] • **herumgehen** walk around [əˈraʊnd] **herumrennen** run around **herumspringen** jump around

▶ S.155 around

herunter down [daʊn]

herunterfallen (von) fall off [ˌfɔːl_ˈɒf]

Herz heart [hɑːt]

Herzlichen Glückwunsch zum Geburtstag. Happy birthday. [ˌhæpi 'bɜːθdeɪ]

heute today [təˈdeɪ] • **heute Morgen/Nachmittag/Abend** this morning/afternoon/evening **heute Nacht** tonight [təˈnaɪt] **das Programm von heute** today's programme

heutig: das heutige Programm today's programme

hier here [hɪə] • **Hier bitte.** (Bitte sehr.) Here you are. • **hier drinnen** in here [ˌɪn 'hɪə] • **hier entlang** this way [ˈðɪs weɪ] • **Hier spricht Isabel. / Hier ist Isabel.** (am Telefon) This is Isabel. • **Hier steht: … / Es heißt hier: …** (im Text) It says here: …

hierher here [hɪə]

Hilfe help [help]

Himmel sky [skaɪ]

hinauf up [ʌp] • **den Hügel hinauf** up the hill • **auf … hinauf** onto [ˈɒntə, ˈɒntʊ]

hinaufklettern (auf) climb [klaɪm]

hinaus out [aʊt] • **aus … hinaus** out of … [ˈaʊt_əv]

hinein: in … hinein into … [ˈɪntə, ˈɪntʊ]

hinfallen fall [fɔːl]; fall down

hinkommen (gelangen) get [get]

hinsetzen: sich hinsetzen sit down

hinstellen: sich hinstellen stand [stænd]

hinter behind [bɪˈhaɪnd]

Hintergrund background [ˈbækgraʊnd]

Hintertür back door

hinüber zu/nach … over to … [ˈəʊvə]

hinunter down [daʊn]

hinzufügen (zu) add (to) [æd]

Hirsch deer, pl deer [dɪə]

Hobby hobby [ˈhɒbi], pl hobbies

hoch high [haɪ]

hochheben: etwas hochheben pick sth. up [ˌpɪk_ˈʌp]

hochsehen (von) look up (from) [ˌlʊk_ˈʌp]

Hockey hockey [ˈhɒki]

Hockeyplatz, -feld hockey pitch [ˈhɒki pɪtʃ]

Hockeyschuhe hockey shoes [ˈhɒki ʃuːz]

Hof yard [jɑːd] • **auf dem Hof** in the yard

hoffen hope [həʊp]

Hoffnung hope [həʊp]

holen (besorgen) get [get]

hören hear [hɪə] • **Na hör mal!** Come on. [ˌkʌm_ˈɒn]

Hose trousers (pl) [ˈtraʊzəz]

Hotel hotel [həʊˈtel]

Hotline hotline [ˈhɒtlaɪn]

hübsch pretty [ˈprɪti]

Hubschrauber helicopter [ˈhelɪkɒptə]

Hügel hill [hɪl]

hügelig hilly [ˈhɪli]

Huhn chicken [ˈtʃɪkɪn]

Hülle cover [ˈkʌvə]

Hund dog [dɒg]

hundert hundred [ˈhʌndrəd]

Hunger haben be hungry [ˈhʌngri]

hungrig sein be hungry [ˈhʌngri]

Hurra! Hooray! [hʊˈreɪ]

Hut hat [hæt]

Hütte cabin [ˈkæbɪn]

I

ich I [aɪ] • **Ich auch.** Me too. [ˌmiː 'tuː] • **Das bin ich.** That's me. **Warum ich?** Why me?

Idee idea [aɪˈdɪə] • **Ideen sammeln** brainstorm [ˈbreɪnstɔːm]

Igel hedgehog [ˈhedʒhɒg]

igitt yuck [jʌk]

ihm him; (bei Dingen, Tieren) it

ihn him; (bei Dingen, Tieren) it

ihnen them [ðəm, ðem]

Ihnen (höfliche Anrede) you [juː]

ihr (Plural von „du") you [juː] • **ihr zwei** you two [juː 'tuː]

ihr: Hilf ihr. Help her. [hə, hɜː]

ihr(e) (besitzanzeigend) (zu „she") her [hə, hɜː]; (zu „they") their [ðeə]

Ihr(e) (höfliche Anrede) your [jɔː]

ihrer, ihre, ihrs (zu „she") hers [hɜːz]; (zu „they") theirs [ðeəz]

Ihrer, Ihre, Ihrs (höfliche Anrede) yours [jɔːz]

im: im Fernsehen on TV • **im Flugzeug** on the plane • **im Haus der Shaws** at the Shaws' house • **im Mai** in May • **im Radio** on the radio • **im Zug** on the train

Imbiss snack [snæk]

Imbissstube café [ˈkæfeɪ]

immer always [ˈɔːlweɪz] • **immer noch** still [stɪl]

in in • **in ... (hinein)** into ... ['ɪntə, 'ɪntʊ] • **in den Zug/Bus einsteigen** get on the train/bus • **in der Stadt umher** around the town • **in der ...straße** in ... Street • **in der Hamiltonstraße 7** at 7 Hamilton Street • **in der Nacht** at night **in der Nähe von** near • **in der Pause** *(zwischen Schulstunden)* at break • **in der Schule** at school **in die falsche Richtung** the wrong way • **in die Sauna gehen** have a sauna • **in Eile sein** be in a hurry **ins Bett gehen** go to bed • **ins Kino gehen** go to the cinema • **in Urlaub fahren** go on holiday • **in Verbindung bleiben** keep in touch [ˌkiːp_ɪn 'tʌtʃ] • **in welche Richtung?** which way? • **in Wirklichkeit** *(eigentlich)* actually ['æktʃuəli]
Information(en) (über) information (about/on) *(no pl)* [ˌɪnfə'meɪʃn]
Ingenieur/in engineer [ˌendʒɪ'nɪə]
Inliner skates [skeɪts] • **Inliner fahren** skate
innen (drin) inside [ˌɪn'saɪd]
Innenstadt city centre [ˌsɪti 'sentə]
Insel island ['aɪlənd]
installieren install [ɪn'stɔːl]
Instrument instrument ['ɪnstrəmənt]
interessant interesting ['ɪntrəstɪŋ]
Interesse interest ['ɪntrəst]
interessieren: sich interessieren (für) be interested (in) ['ɪntrəstɪd]
interessiert sein (an) be interested (in) ['ɪntrəstɪd]
international international [ˌɪntə'næʃnəl]
Internet internet ['ɪntənet] • **im Internet surfen** surf the internet [sɜːf]
Interview interview ['ɪntəvjuː]
interviewen interview ['ɪntəvjuː]
irgendetwas anything ['eniθɪŋ]
irgendjemand anybody ['enibɒdi]
irgendwelche any ['eni]
irgendwo(hin) somewhere ['sʌmweə]; anywhere ['eniweə]
irren: sich irren be wrong [rɒŋ]

J

ja yes [jes]
Jacke, Jackett jacket ['dʒækɪt]
Jagd hunt [hʌnt]
jagen hunt [hʌnt]
Jahr year [jɪə]
Jahrgangsstufe year [jɪə]
Jahrhundert century ['sentʃəri]
...jährig: ein(e) Sechzehnjährige(r) a sixteen-year-old • **ein sechzehn-**

jähriges Mädchen a sixteen-year-old girl
Januar January ['dʒænjuəri]
Jazz jazz [dʒæz]
je? *(jemals?)* ever? ['evə]
Jeans jeans *(pl)* [dʒiːnz]
jede(r, s) ... *(Begleiter)* **1.** every ... ['evri]
 2. *(jeder einzelne)* each ... [iːtʃ]
jeder *(alle)* everybody ['evribɒdi]
jemals? ever? ['evə]
jemand somebody ['sʌmbədi]; *(irgendjemand)* anybody ['enibɒdi]
jene(r, s) *(Singular)* that [ðət, ðæt]; *(Plural)* those [ðəʊz]
jetzt now [naʊ] • **jetzt gerade, jetzt sofort** right now
Job job [dʒɒb]
jubeln cheer [tʃɪə]
Judo judo ['dʒuːdəʊ] • **Judo machen** do judo
Jugend youth [juːθ]
Jugendclub youth club ['juːθ ˌklʌb]
Jugend- junior ['dʒuːniə]; *(Teenager-)* teen [tiːn]
Jugendherberge youth hostel ['juːθ ˌhɒstl]
Jugendliche(r) kid [kɪd]; teenager ['tiːneɪdʒə]
Juli July [dʒu'laɪ]
jung young [jʌŋ]
Junge boy [bɔɪ]
Juni June [dʒuːn]
Junioren- junior ['dʒuːniə]

K

Käfig cage [keɪdʒ]
Kai *(Kaimauer)* quay [kiː]
Kaimauer quay [kiː]
Kalender calendar ['kælɪndə]
kalt cold [kəʊld]
Kamel camel ['kæml]
Kamera camera ['kæmərə]
kämpfen (für, um) fight (for) [faɪt]
Kanal canal [kə'næl]
Känguru kangaroo [ˌkæŋgə'ruː]
Kaninchen rabbit ['ræbɪt]
Kantine canteen [kæn'tiːn]
Kanu canoe [kə'nuː] • **Kanu fahren** canoe [kə'nuː]
Kapitän/in captain ['kæptɪn]
Kappe cap [kæp]
kaputt broken ['brəʊkən]
Karotte carrot ['kærət]
Karriere career [kə'rɪə]
Karte *(Post-, Spielkarte)* card [kɑːd]
Kartoffel potato [pə'teɪtəʊ], *pl* -toes
Kartoffelbrei mashed potatoes [ˌmæʃt pə'teɪtəʊz]
Kartoffelchips crisps *(pl)* [krɪsps]

Kartoffelpüree mashed potatoes [ˌmæʃt pə'teɪtəʊz]
Käse cheese [tʃiːz]
Kästchen, Kasten box [bɒks]
Kathedrale cathedral [kə'θiːdrəl]
Katze cat [kæt]
kaufen buy [baɪ]
Kaufhaus department store [dɪ'pɑːtmənt stɔː]
Kehle throat [θrəʊt]
kein(e) no; not a; not (...) any • **Ich habe keinen Stuhl.** I haven't got a chair. • **keine Musik mehr** no more music
Keks biscuit ['bɪskɪt]
Kellner waiter ['weɪtə]
Kellnerin waitress ['weɪtrəs]
kennen know [nəʊ]
kennenlernen meet [miːt] • **Nett, dich/euch/Sie kennenzulernen.** Nice to meet you.
kennzeichnen mark up [ˌmɑːk_'ʌp]
Keyboard *(elektronisches Tasten- instrument)* keyboard ['kiːbɔːd]
Kilogramm, Kilo (kg) kilogram (kg) ['kiːləgræm], kilo ['kiːləʊ] • **ein 150 Kilo- gramm schwerer Bär** a 150-kilo- gram bear
Kilometer (km) kilometre (km) ['kɪləmiːtə] • **eine Zehn-Kilometer- Wanderung** a ten-kilometre walk
Kind child [tʃaɪld], *pl* children ['tʃɪldrən]; kid [kɪd] • **ein Kind be- kommen** have a child
Kino cinema ['sɪnəmə] • **ins Kino gehen** go to the cinema
Kirche church [tʃɜːtʃ]
Kirsche cherry ['tʃeri]
Kiste box [bɒks]
Kiwi kiwi ['kiːwiː]
Klang sound [saʊnd]
klar clear [klɪə]
Klasse class [klɑːs]; form [fɔːm]
Klassenkamerad/in classmate ['klɑːsmeɪt]
Klassenlehrer/in class teacher; form teacher
Klassenzimmer classroom ['klɑːsruːm]
klassisch classical ['klæsɪkl]
klatschen: Beifall klatschen cheer [tʃɪə]
Klavier piano [pi'ænəʊ] • **Klavier spielen** play the piano
kleben: (auf-, ein)kleben glue [gluː]
Klebestift glue stick ['gluː stɪk]
Klebstoff glue [gluː]
Kleid dress [dres]
Kleider *(Kleidungsstücke)* clothes *(pl)* [kləʊðz, kləʊz]
Kleiderschrank wardrobe ['wɔːdrəʊb]

Kleiderordnung dress code ['dres kəʊd]

Kleidung(sstücke) clothes (pl) [kləʊðz, kləʊz]

klein little ['lɪtl]; small [smɔːl]

Kleinstadt town [taʊn]

klettern climb [klaɪm] • **Klettere auf einen Baum.** Climb a tree.

Klingel bell [bel]

klingeln ring [rɪŋ] • **Es klingelte.** The bell rang.

Klingelton ringtone ['rɪŋtəʊn]

klingen sound [saʊnd]

Klinik clinic ['klɪnɪk]

Klon clone [kləʊn]

Klub club [klʌb]

klug clever ['klevə]

knapp: Das war knapp. That was close. [kləʊs]

Kneipe pub [pʌb]

Knie knee [niː]

Knieschützer pad [pæd]

Knopf button ['bʌtn]

Koch cook [kʊk]

kochen cook [kʊk]

Köchin cook [kʊk]

Koffer suitcase ['suːtkeɪs]

Koje (Etagenbett) bunk (bed) [bʌŋk]

kolorieren colour ['kʌlə]

komisch funny ['fʌni]

Komma: 10,4 (zehn Komma vier) 10.4 (ten point four)
▶ S.151 Numbers

kommen come [kʌm]; (hinkommen) get [get] • **Ich komme aus ...** I'm from ... • **Wo kommst du her?** Where are you from? • **nach Hause kommen** come home; get home • **zu spät kommen** be late **Kommt nicht in Frage!** No way! **Ach komm!** Come on. [ˌkʌm_'ɒn] **Na los, komm.** Come on.

König king [kɪŋ]

Königin queen [kwiːn]

Königreich: das Vereinigte Königreich (Großbritannien und Nordirland) the United Kingdom (UK) [juˌnaɪtɪd 'kɪŋdəm, juː'keɪ]

können can [kən, kæn]; be able to ['eɪbl] • **ich kann nicht ...** I can't ... [kɑːnt] • **Kann ich Ihnen helfen? / Was kann ich für Sie tun?** (im Laden) Can I help you?
▶ S.162 „können" und „dürfen"

könnte(n): ich/er könnte ... I/he could ... [kəd, kʊd]

konnte(n): ich/er konnte ... I/he could ... [kəd, kʊd]

Kontakt halten keep in touch [ˌkiːp_ɪn 'tʌtʃ]

kontrollieren (überprüfen) check [tʃek]

Konzert concert ['kɒnsət] • **ein Konzert geben** (einen Auftritt haben) do a gig (infml)

Kopf head [hed]

Kopfschmerzen headache ['hedeɪk]

Kopie copy ['kɒpi]

kopieren copy ['kɒpi]

Korb basket ['bɑːskɪt] • **ein Korb Äpfel** a basket of apples

Körper body ['bɒdi]

korrigieren correct [kə'rekt]

kosten (Essen probieren) try [traɪ]

kosten: Er/Sie/Es kostet 1 Pfund. It's £1. • **Sie kosten 35 Pence.** They are 35 p. • **Wie viel kostet/kosten ...?** How much is/are ...?

kostenlos free [friː]

köstlich delicious [dɪ'lɪʃəs]

Kram stuff [stʌf]

krank ill [ɪl]

kränken: jd. kränken (aus der Fassung bringen) upset sb. [ʌp'set]

Krankenhaus hospital ['hɒspɪtl]

Krankenwagen ambulance ['æmbjələns]

kriegen get [get]

Krokodil crocodile ['krɒkədaɪl]

Krug jug [dʒʌg] • **ein Krug Orangensaft** a jug of orange juice

Küche kitchen ['kɪtʃɪn]

Kuchen cake [keɪk]

Kugelschreiber pen [pen]

Kuh cow [kaʊ]

kühl cool [kuːl]

Kühlschrank fridge [frɪdʒ]

Kummer worry ['wʌri]

kümmern 1. sich um etwas/jn. kümmern look after sth./sb. [ˌlʊk_'ɑːftə] **2. Kümmere dich um deine eigenen Angelegenheiten!** Mind your own business. [ˌmaɪnd jər_ˌəʊn 'bɪznəs]

Kumpel mate [meɪt]

Kunde, Kundin customer ['kʌstəmə]

Kunst art [ɑːt]

Künstler/in artist ['ɑːtɪst]

künstlich artificial [ˌɑːtɪ'fɪʃl]

Kurs (Lehrgang) course [kɔːs]

kurz short [ʃɔːt] • **kurze Hose** shorts (pl) [ʃɔːts]

Küste coast [kəʊst] • **an der Küste** on the coast

L

lächeln smile [smaɪl]

Lächeln smile [smaɪl]

lachen laugh [lɑːf]

Laden (Geschäft) shop [ʃɒp]

Lage: in der Lage sein, etwas zu tun be able to do sth. [eɪbl]

Lamm(fleisch) lamb [læm]

Lampe lamp [læmp]

Land (auch als Gegensatz zur Stadt) country ['kʌntri]; (Grund und Boden) land [lænd] • **auf dem Land** (im Gegensatz zur Stadt) in the country; (nicht auf dem Wasser) on land

landen land [lænd]

Landkarte map [mæp]

lang long [lɒŋ] • **drei Tage lang** for three days

langsam slow [sləʊ]

langweilig boring ['bɔːrɪŋ]

Lärm noise [nɔɪz]

lärmend noisy ['nɔɪzi]

Lasagne lasagne [lə'zænjə]

lassen let [let] • **Lass uns ... / Lasst uns ...** Let's ... • **Lass das!** Stop that!

Lastkraftwagen lorry ['lɒri]

Lauf run [rʌn]

laufen run [rʌn]

Läufer/in runner ['rʌnə]

Laufschuhe running shoes

laut loud [laʊd]; (lärmend) noisy ['nɔɪzi]

Laut sound [saʊnd]

läuten ring [rɪŋ]

leben live [lɪv]

Leben life [laɪf], pl lives [laɪvz]

Lebensmittel food [fuːd]

Leber liver ['lɪvə]

lecker delicious [dɪ'lɪʃəs]

ledig single ['sɪŋgl]

leer empty ['empti]

legen (hin-, ablegen) put [pʊt]

lehren teach [tiːtʃ]

Lehrer/in teacher-['tiːtʃə]

Lehrgang (Kurs, Seminar) workshop ['wɜːkʃɒp]; course [kɔːs]

leicht (nicht schwierig) easy ['iːzi]

Leichtathletik athletics [æθ'letɪks]

leider I'm afraid [ə'freɪd]

leidtun: Tut mir leid. I'm sorry. ['sɒri]

leise quiet ['kwaɪət]

Leiter/in (Anführer/in) leader ['liːdə]

Lektion (im Schulbuch) unit ['juːnɪt]

lernen learn [lɜːn]

Lern- und Arbeitstechniken study skills ['stʌdi skɪlz]

lesen read [riːd]

Leser/in reader ['riːdə]

letzte(r, s) last [lɑːst]; final ['faɪnl]

leuchtend bright [braɪt]

Leute people ['piːpl]; guys [gaɪz] (AE, infml)

Licht light [laɪt]

Lichtblitz flash [flæʃ]

Liebe love [lʌv]

Liebe Grüße, ... (Briefschluss) Love ... [lʌv]

lieben love [lʌv]

Lieber Jay, ... Dear Jay ... [dɪə]

lieber: etwas lieber mögen like sth. better

Liebling dear [dɪə]; sweetheart ['swiːthɑːt]

Lieblings-: meine Lieblingsfarbe my favourite colour ['feɪvərɪt]

liebsten: etwas am liebsten mögen like sth. best

Lied song [sɒŋ]

liegen: Das liegt bei dir. *(Das kannst/ musst du (selbst) entscheiden.)* That's up to you.

lila purple ['pɜːpl]

Limonade lemonade [ˌleməˈneɪd]

Lineal ruler ['ruːlə]

Linie: (U-Bahn-)Linie line [laɪn]

linke(r, s) left [left] • **links, auf der linken Seite** on the left • **(nach) links abbiegen** turn left • **nach links schauen** look left

Liste list [lɪst]

Livemusik live music [laɪv]

Löffel spoon [spuːn]

Lokal *(Kneipe)* pub [pʌb]

Löwe lion ['laɪən]

M

machen do [duː]; make [meɪk] • **die Hausaufgabe(n) machen** do homework • **einen Ausflug machen** go on a trip • **einen Spaziergang machen** go for a walk • **eine Übung machen** do an exercise • **ein Picknick machen** have a picnic • **Fotos machen** take photos • **jm. Vorwürfe machen (wegen)** blame sb. (for) • **Judo machen** do judo **sich Notizen machen** take notes **sich Sorgen machen (um, wegen)** worry (about) ['wʌri] • **(Zauber-) Kunststücke machen** do tricks **Reiten macht Spaß.** Riding is fun.

Mädchen girl [gɜːl]

Magazin *(Zeitschrift)* magazine [ˌmægəˈziːn]

Magen stomach ['stʌmək]

Magenschmerzen stomach ache ['stʌmək_eɪk]

Magst du ...? Do you like ...? [laɪk] *(siehe auch unter „mögen")*

Mahlzeit meal [miːl]

Mai May [meɪ]

mailen: jm. etwas mailen mail sb. sth. [meɪl]

Make-up make-up ['meɪkʌp]

Mal(e); -mal time(s) [taɪm(z)]

malen paint [peɪnt]

Maler/in painter ['peɪntə]

Mama mum [mʌm] *(BE)*; mom [mɒm, AE: mɑːm] *(AE)*

manchmal sometimes ['sʌmtaɪmz]

Mann man [mæn], *pl* men [men]

männlich male [meɪl]

Mannschaft team [tiːm]

Mappe *(des Sprachenportfolios)* dossier ['dɒsieɪ]

markieren mark up [ˌmɑːk_'ʌp]

Markt market ['mɑːkɪt]

Marmelade *(Orangenmarmelade)* marmalade ['mɑːməleɪd]

März March [mɑːtʃ]

Maschine machine [məˈʃiːn]

Mathematik maths [mæθs]

Matrose sailor ['seɪlə]

Mauer wall [wɔːl]

Maulwurf mole [məʊl]

Maus mouse [maʊs], *pl* mice [maɪs]

Medaille medal ['medl]

Mediation *(Sprachmittlung)* mediation [ˌmiːdiˈeɪʃn]

Medien media *(pl)* ['miːdiə]

Meer sea [siː]

Meerschweinchen guinea pig ['gɪni pɪg]

mehr more [mɔː] • **mehr als** more than • **mehr als ich** more than me • **nicht mehr** not ... any more **viel mehr** lots more • **keine Musik mehr** no more music

Meile *(= ca. 1,6 km)* mile [maɪl]

meilenweit for miles [maɪlz]

mein(e) ... my ... [maɪ] • **meine neuen** my new ones [wʌnz]

meinen think [θɪŋk]; *(sagen wollen)* mean [miːn] • **Meinst du wirklich?** Do you really think so?

meiner, meine, meins mine [maɪn]

meist: (der/die/das) meiste ...; am meisten most [məʊst] • **die meisten Leute** most people

meistens usually ['juːʒuəli]

Meister/in *(Champion)* champion ['tʃæmpiən]

Meisterschaft championship ['tʃæmpiənʃɪp]

Menschen people ['piːpl]

merken: sich etwas merken remember sth. [rɪˈmembə]

Messer knife [naɪf], *pl* knives [naɪvz]

Meter metre ['miːtə]

Metzger butcher ['bʊtʃə] • **beim Metzger** at the butcher's
▶ S.154 at the butcher's / to the doctor's

mich me [miː] • **mich (selbst)** myself [maɪˈself]
▶ S.163 Reflexive pronouns

Mikrofon microphone ['maɪkrəfəʊn]

Milch milk [mɪlk]

mild mild [maɪld]

Million million ['mɪljən]

Mindmap mind map ['maɪnd mæp]

Minute minute ['mɪnɪt]

mir me [miː]

mischen mix [mɪks]

Mischung mix [mɪks]; mixture ['mɪkstʃə]

mit with [wɪð] • **mit dem Auto/ Zug/Rad/... fahren** go by car/ train/bike/...

mitbringen bring [brɪŋ]

mitmachen: bei etwas/jm. mitmachen join sth./sb. [dʒɔɪn]

Mitschüler/in classmate ['klɑːsmeɪt]

Mittagessen lunch [lʌntʃ] • **zum Mittagessen** for lunch

Mittagspause lunch break ['lʌntʃ breɪk]

Mitte centre ['sentə]; middle (of) ['mɪdl]

Mitteilung *(Notiz)* note [nəʊt]

Mittel- *(Zentral-)* central ['sentrəl]

mittel(groß) medium ['miːdiəm]

Mittelteil middle ['mɪdl]

Mittwoch Wednesday ['wenzdeɪ, 'wenzdi] *(siehe auch unter „Freitag")*

Mix mix [mɪks]

mixen mix [mɪks]

Mobiltelefon mobile phone [ˌməʊbaɪl 'fəʊn]; mobile ['məʊbaɪl]

möchte: Ich möchte gern ... (haben) I'd like ... (= I would like ...) • **Ich möchte über ... reden** I'd like to talk about ... • **Möchtest du etwas (Saft) / ein paar (Kekse)?** Would you like some (juice/biscuits)?

Mode fashion ['fæʃn]

Modell(-auto, -schiff; *Fotomodell)* model ['mɒdl]

Moderator/in presenter [prɪˈzentə]

modern modern ['mɒdən]

modisch *(schick, im Trend)* trendy ['trendi]

mögen like [laɪk]; *(sehr mögen)* love [lʌv] • **etwas lieber mögen** like sth. better • **etwas am liebsten/wenigsten mögen** like sth. best/least

möglich possible ['pɒsəbl]

Möhre carrot ['kærət]

Moment moment ['məʊmənt] **genau in dem Moment** just then • **Moment mal!** Wait a minute. ['mɪnɪt]

Monat month [mʌnθ]

Mond moon [muːn]

Monitor monitor ['mɒnɪtə]

Monster monster ['mɒnstə]

Montag Monday ['mʌndeɪ, 'mʌndi] *(siehe auch unter „Freitag")*

morgen tomorrow [təˈmɒrəʊ] • **das Wetter von morgen** tomorrow's weather

Morgen morning ['mɔːnɪŋ] • **am Morgen, morgens** in the morning

Guten Morgen. Good morning.
Montagmorgen Monday morning
MP3-Spieler MP3 player
[ˌempiːˈθriː ˌpleɪə]
müde tired ['taɪəd]
Müll rubbish ['rʌbɪʃ]
Mülltonne bin [bɪn]; dustbin ['dʌstbɪn]
Multiple-Choice multiple choice
[ˌmʌltɪpl 'tʃɔɪs]
Mund mouth [maʊθ] • **Halt den
Mund!** Shut up. [ˌʃʌt_'ʌp]
murren grumble ['grʌmbl]
Museum museum [mjuˈziːəm]
Musical musical ['mjuːzɪkl]
Musik music ['mjuːzɪk]
müssen have to; must [mʌst]
nicht müssen needn't ['niːdnt]
Mutter mother ['mʌðə]
Mutti mum [mʌm] *(BE)*; mom [mɒm,
AE: maːm] *(AE)*
Mütze cap [kæp]

N

Na ja … / Na gut … Oh well …
[əʊ 'wel]
Na und? So? [səʊ]
nach 1. *(örtlich)* to [tə, tu] • **nach
draußen** outside • **nach drinnen**
inside • **nach Hause gehen** go
home • **nach Hause kommen**
come home; get home • **nach
oben** up; *(im Haus)* upstairs
[ˌʌp'steəz] • **nach unten** down; *(im
Haus)* downstairs [ˌdaʊn'steəz]
2. *(zeitlich)* after ['ɑːftə] • **Viertel
nach 11** quarter past 11 [pɑːst]
3. **nach etwas fragen** ask about
sth. [əˈbaʊt]
Nachbar/in neighbour ['neɪbə]
nachdem after ['ɑːftə]
nachdenken über think about
Nachmittag afternoon [ˌɑːftə'nuːn]
am Nachmittag, nachmittags in
the afternoon
Nachricht message ['mesɪdʒ]
Nachrichten *(im Fernsehen, Radio;
Neuigkeiten)* news *(no pl)* [njuːz]
Das sind gute Nachrichten. That's
good news.
**nachrufen: jm. Schimpfwörter nach-
rufen** call sb. names
nachschlagen: etwas nachschlagen
look sth. up [ˌlʊk_'ʌp]
nächste(r, s): am nächsten Tag the
next day [nekst] • **der Nächste sein**
be next • **Was haben wir als
Nächstes?** What have we got
next?

Nacht night [naɪt] • **heute Nacht**
tonight [təˈnaɪt] • **in der Nacht,
nachts** at night
nahe (bei) near [nɪə]
Nähe: in der Nähe von near [nɪə]
Name name [neɪm]
Nase nose [nəʊz] • **die Nase voll
haben (von etwas)** be fed up (with
sth.) [ˌfed_'ʌp]
Nashorn rhino ['raɪnəʊ]
nass wet [wet]
national national ['næʃnəl]
natürlich of course [əv 'kɔːs]
Naturwissenschaft science ['saɪəns]
Nebel fog [fɒg]
neben next to ['nekst tə]
neblig foggy ['fɒgi]
nehmen take [teɪk] • **Wir nehmen
es.** *(beim Einkaufen)* We'll take it.
neidisch (auf) jealous (of) ['dʒeləs]
nein no [nəʊ]
nennen *(rufen, bezeichnen)* call
[kɔːl]; *(benennen)* name [neɪm]
nervös nervous ['nɜːvəs]
nett nice [naɪs]
neu new [njuː]
neueste(r, s) latest ['leɪtɪst]
Neuigkeiten news [njuːz]
nicht not [nɒt] • **nicht mehr** not (…)
any more • **Du brauchst eine
Schultasche, nicht wahr?** You need
a school bag, right? [raɪt] • **Ich
weiß es nicht.** I don't know. [ˌdəʊnt
'nəʊ] • **noch nicht** not (…) yet [jet]
nichts nothing ['nʌθɪŋ]; not (…) anything ['eniθɪŋ] • **Nichts zu danken.**
You're welcome. ['welkəm]
nicken (mit) nod [nɒd]
nie, niemals never ['nevə]
niemand nobody ['nəʊbədi]; not (…)
anybody ['enibɒdi]
Niere kidney ['kɪdni]
nirgendwo(hin) not (…) anywhere
['eniweə]
noch: noch ein(e) … another …
[əˈnʌðə] • **noch 45 Pence** another
45 p • **noch einmal** again [əˈgen] •
noch nicht not (…) yet [jet] •
(immer) noch still [stɪl]
Norden north [nɔːθ] • **nach Norden**
north
nördlich north [nɔːθ]
Nordosten north-east [ˌnɔːθ'iːst]
nach Nordosten north-east
nordöstlich north-east [ˌnɔːθ'iːst]
Nordwesten north-west [ˌnɔːθ'west]
nach Nordwesten north-west
nordwestlich north-west [ˌnɔːθ'west]
nörgeln grumble ['grʌmbl]
normalerweise usually ['juːʒuəli]
Notiz note [nəʊt] • **sich Notizen
machen** take notes

November November [nəʊ'vembə]
null o [əʊ]; zero ['zɪərəʊ];
(beim Sport) nil [nɪl]
▶ S.159 A football match
Nummer number ['nʌmbə]
nun now [naʊ] • **Nun, …** Well, …
[wel]
nur only ['əʊnli]; just [dʒʌst] • **nur
zum Spaß** just for fun

O

ob if [ɪf]
oben *(an der Spitze)* at the top (of)
[tɒp]; *(im Haus)* upstairs [ˌʌp'steəz]
nach oben up; *(im Haus)* upstairs
Oberbegriff group word ['gruːp wɜːd]
oberhalb von over ['əʊvə]
Oberteil top [tɒp]
Obst fruit [fruːt]
Obstkuchen pie [paɪ]
Obstsalat fruit salad ['fruːt ˌsæləd]
oder or [ɔː] • **Das ist nicht dein
Ernst, oder?** You're joking, aren't
you?
offen open ['əʊpən]
öffnen open ['əʊpən]
oft often ['ɒfn]
ohne without [wɪˈðaʊt]
Ohr ear [ɪə]
Ohrenschmerzen earache ['ɪəreɪk]
Ohrring earring ['ɪərɪŋ]
Oje! Oh dear! [əʊ 'dɪə]
okay OK [əʊ'keɪ]
Oktober October [ɒk'təʊbə]
Öl oil [ɔɪl]
Ölbohrinsel oil rig ['ɔɪl rɪg]
Oma grandma ['grænmaː]; granny
['græni]
Onkel uncle ['ʌŋkl]
online, Online- online [ˌɒn'laɪn]
Opa grandpa ['grænpaː]
Operation (an) operation (on)
[ˌɒpəˈreɪʃn]
Opfer victim ['vɪktɪm]
Orange orange ['ɒrɪndʒ]
orange(farben) orange ['ɒrɪndʒ]
Orangenmarmelade marmalade
['maːməleɪd]
Orangensaft orange juice ['ɒrɪndʒ
dʒuːs]
ordentlich tidy ['taɪdi]
Ordnung: in Ordnung all right
[ɔːl 'raɪt]; fine [faɪn]
organisieren organize ['ɔːgənaɪz]
Ort place [pleɪs]; *(Veranstaltungs-,
Wohnort)* location [ləʊ'keɪʃn]
Orts-, örtlich local ['ləʊkl]
Osten east [iːst] • **nach Osten** east
östlich east [iːst]

Outfit *(Kleidung; Ausrüstung)* outfit ['aʊtfɪt]

P

paar: ein paar some [səm, sʌm]; *(einige wenige)* a few [fju:]
Paar: ein Paar a pair (of) [peə]
Päckchen packet ['pækɪt] • **ein Päckchen Pfefferminzbonbons** a packet of mints
packen pack [pæk]
Packung packet ['pækɪt] • **eine Packung Pfefferminzbonbons** a packet of mints
Paddel paddle ['pædl]
paddeln paddle ['pædl]; canoe [kə'nu:]
Paket parcel ['pɑ:sl]
Palast palace ['pæləs]
pantomimisch darstellen mime [maɪm]
Papa dad [dæd]
Papagei parrot ['pærət]
Papier paper ['peɪpə]
Paralympische Spiele *(Olympische Spiele für Sportler/innen mit körperlicher Behinderung)* Paralympics [,pærə'lɪmpɪks]
Park park [pɑ:k]
Parkplatz *(für viele Autos)* car park ['kɑ: pɑ:k]
Parlament parliament ['pɑ:ləmənt]
Partner/in partner ['pɑ:tnə]
Party party ['pɑ:ti]
passen fit [fɪt] • **passen zu** go with
passieren (mit) happen (to) ['hæpən]
Pause break [breɪk] • **in der Pause** *(zwischen Schulstunden)* at break
Pence pence (p) [pens]
Person person ['pɜ:sn]
persönliche(r, s) personal ['pɜ:sənl]
Pfad path [pɑ:θ]
Pfefferminzbonbons mints [mɪnts]
pfeifen whistle ['wɪsl]
Pferd horse [hɔ:s]
Pfund *(britische Währung)* pound (£) [paʊnd] • **Es kostet 1 Pfund.** It's £1.
Piano piano [pi'ænəʊ]
Picknick picnic ['pɪknɪk] • **ein Picknick machen** have a picnic
piepsen bleep [bli:p]
Piepton bleep [bli:p]
Piercing piercing ['pɪəsɪŋ]
Pilz mushroom ['mʌʃrʊm, -ru:m]
pink(farben) pink [pɪŋk]
Pirat/in pirate ['paɪrət]
Pizza pizza ['pi:tsə]
Plan plan [plæn]
planen plan [plæn]
Planet planet ['plænɪt]

Platz *(Ort, Stelle)* place [pleɪs]; *(in der Stadt)* square [skweə]; *(runder Platz in der Stadt)* circus ['sɜ:kəs]; *(Einsatzort)* location [ləʊ'keɪʃn]
Plätzchen biscuit ['bɪskɪt]
plaudern chat [tʃæt]
plötzlich suddenly ['sʌdnli]
Pokal cup [kʌp]
Polizei police *(pl)* [pə'li:s]
Polizeiwache, Polizeirevier police station [pə'li:s steɪʃn]
Polizist/in policeman [pə'li:smən]/ policewoman [pə'li:swʊmən]
Poltergeist poltergeist ['pəʊltəgaɪst]
Pommes frites chips *(pl)* [tʃɪps]
Popcorn popcorn ['pɒpkɔ:n]
Pop(musik) pop (music) [pɒp]
populär (bei) popular ['pɒpjələ]
Porträt *(Steckbrief)* profile ['prəʊfaɪl]
Postamt post office ['pəʊst ˌɒfɪs]
Poster poster ['pəʊstə]
Postkarte postcard ['pəʊstkɑ:d]
Präsentation presentation [,prezn'teɪʃn]
Preis *(Kaufpreis)* price [praɪs]; *(Gewinn)* prize [praɪz]
pro per [pɜ:, pə] • **einmal pro Woche** once a week / once per week
Probe *(am Theater)* rehearsal [rɪ'hɜ:sl]
proben *(am Theater)* rehearse [rɪ'hɜ:s]
probieren try [traɪ]
Problem problem ['prɒbləm]
produzieren produce [prə'dju:s]
Programm programme ['prəʊgræm]
Projekt (über, zu) project (on, about) ['prɒdʒekt] • **ein Projekt machen, durchführen** do a project
Prospekt brochure ['brəʊʃə]
Prozent per cent (%) [pə'sent]
prüfen *(überprüfen)* check [tʃek]
Prüfung test [test]
PS *(Nachschrift unter Briefen)* PS [,pi:_'es] (postscript ['pəʊstskrɪpt])
Publikum audience ['ɔ:dɪəns]
Pullover pullover ['pʊləʊvə]
Punkt *(bei Test, Quiz)* point [pɔɪnt]
Punktestand *(Spielstand)* score [skɔ:]
▶ S.159 A football match
Pute/Puter turkey ['tɜ:ki]
putzen clean [kli:n] • **Ich putze mir die Zähne.** I clean my teeth.
Putzfrau, -mann cleaner ['kli:nə]

Q

Querflöte flute [flu:t]
Quiz quiz [kwɪz], *pl* quizzes ['kwɪzɪz]

R

Rad **1.** wheel ['wi:l] **2.** *(Fahrrad)* bike [baɪk]
Rad fahren cycle ['saɪkl]; ride a bike [,raɪd_ə 'baɪk]
Radfahrt bike ride ['baɪk raɪd]
Radiergummi rubber ['rʌbə]
Radio radio ['reɪdiəʊ] • **im Radio** on the radio
Radweg cycle path ['saɪkl pɑ:θ]
Rap rap [ræp]
Rat advice *(no pl)* [əd'vaɪs]
raten *(erraten, schätzen)* guess [ges]
Ratespiel quiz [kwɪz], *pl* quizzes ['kwɪzɪz]
Ratschläge advice *(no pl)* [əd'vaɪs]
Rauch smoke [sməʊk]
rauchen smoke [sməʊk] • **Rauchen verboten.** No smoking.
Raum room [ru:m, rʊm]
realistisch realistic [,ri:ə'lɪstɪk]
Rechnung bill [bɪl]
Recht haben be right [raɪt]
rechte(r, s) right [raɪt] • **rechts, auf der rechten Seite** on the right **(nach) rechts abbiegen** turn right **nach rechts schauen** look right
Rechtschreibung spelling ['spelɪŋ]
rechtzeitig in time [ɪn 'taɪm]
recycelt recycled [,ri:'saɪkld]
Recycling recycling [,ri:'saɪklɪŋ]
Redakteur/in editor ['edɪtə]
reden (mit, über) talk (to, about) [tɔ:k]; speak (to, about) [spi:k] **Wovon redest du?** What are you talking about?
Refrain chorus ['kɔ:rəs]
Regal(brett) shelf [ʃelf], *pl* shelves [ʃelvz]
Regel *(Vorschrift)* rule [ru:l]
Regen rain [reɪn]
Reggae reggae [re'geɪ]
regnen rain [reɪn]
regnerisch rainy ['reɪni]
Reh deer, *pl* deer [dɪə]
reich rich [rɪtʃ]
reichen *(weitergeben)* pass [pɑ:s]
Reihe **1. Du bist an der Reihe.** It's your turn. [tɜ:n] **2.** *(Sendereihe, Serie)* series, *pl* series ['sɪəri:z]
Reise trip [trɪp]; *(Fahrt)* journey ['dʒɜ:ni] • **eine Reise unterbrechen** break a journey
reisen travel ['trævl]
reiten ride [raɪd] • **reiten gehen** go riding
Religion *(Religionsunterricht)* RE [,ɑ:r_'i:], Religious Education [rɪ,lɪdʒəs_edʒu'keɪʃn]
rennen run [rʌn]

Reportage (über) report (on) [rɪˈpɔːt]
repräsentieren represent [ˌreprɪˈzent]
Rest rest [rest]
Restaurant restaurant [ˈrestrɒnt]; *(Imbissstube, Café)* café [ˈkæfeɪ]
Resultat result [rɪˈzʌlt]
retten save [seɪv]
Rettungshubschrauber rescue helicopter [ˈreskjuː ˌhelɪkɒptə]
richtig right [raɪt]
Richtung way [weɪ] • **in diese Richtung** this way • **in die falsche Richtung** the wrong way • **in welche Richtung?** which way?
riechen smell [smel]
Riesenrad big wheel [ˌbɪg ˈwiːl]
riesig huge [hjuːdʒ]
▶ S.156 big – large – huge
Rindfleisch beef [biːf]
Ring ring [rɪŋ]
Rock skirt [skɜːt]
Rolle role [rəʊl]
Rollenspiel role play [ˈrəʊl pleɪ]
Rollstuhl wheelchair [ˈwiːltʃeə]
römisch; Römer, Römerin Roman [ˈrəʊmən]
rosa pink [pɪŋk]
rot red [red]
Rückfahrkarte return ticket [rɪˈtɜːn ˌtɪkɪt]
Rucksack rucksack [ˈrʌksæk]
rufen call [kɔːl]; shout [ʃaʊt] • **die Polizei rufen** call the police
ruhig quiet [ˈkwaɪət]
rumhängen (mit Freunden/Freundinnen) *(abhängen)* hang out (with friends) [ˌhæŋ ˈaʊt]
rund round [raʊnd]
Rundgang (durch das Haus) tour (of the house) [tʊə]
runterladen *(downloaden)* download [ˌdaʊnˈləʊd]

S

Sache thing [θɪŋ]
Saft juice [dʒuːs]
sagen say [seɪ] • **Sagt mir eure Namen.** Tell me your names. [tel]
Salat 1. *(Kopfsalat)* lettuce [ˈletɪs]
2. *(Gericht, Beilage)* salad [ˈsæləd]
sammeln collect [kəˈlekt] • **Ideen sammeln** brainstorm [ˈbreɪnstɔːm]
Sammler/in collector [kəˈlektə]
Samstag Saturday [ˈsætədeɪ, ˈsætədi] *(siehe auch unter „Freitag")*
Sandwich sandwich [ˈsænwɪtʃ, ˈ-wɪdʒ]
Sänger/in singer [ˈsɪŋə]
Sanitäter/in paramedic [ˌpærəˈmedɪk]
Sattel saddle [ˈsædl]
Satz sentence [ˈsentəns]

sauber clean [kliːn] • **sauber machen** clean
sauer sein (auf) be cross (with) [krɒs]
Sauna sauna [ˈsɔːnə] • **in die Sauna gehen** have a sauna
Saxophon saxophone [ˈsæksəfəʊn]
Schachtel packet [ˈpækɪt]; box [bɒks]
Schaf sheep, *pl* sheep [ʃiːp]
Schal scarf [skɑːf], *pl* scarves [skɑːvz]
Schale bowl [bəʊl] • **eine Schale Cornflakes** a bowl of cornflakes
scharf *(würzig)* spicy [ˈspaɪsi]
Schatz dear [dɪə]; sweetheart [ˈswiːthɑːt]
schätzen *(raten, erraten)* guess [ges]
schauen look [lʊk] • **nach links/ rechts schauen** look left/right
Schaufenster shop window [ˌʃɒp ˈwɪndəʊ]
Schauspiel drama [ˈdrɑːmə]
Schauspieler/in actor [ˈæktə]
scheinen *(Sonne)* shine [ʃaɪn]
scherzen joke [dʒəʊk]
scheu shy [ʃaɪ]
scheußlich horrible [ˈhɒrəbl]
schick *(modisch, im Trend)* trendy [ˈtrendi]
schicken (an) *(Post, E-Mail)* send (to) [send]; mail (to) [meɪl] • **jm. eine SMS schicken** text sb. [tekst]
schieben push [pʊʃ]
schießen shoot [ʃuːt]; *(ein Tor schießen)* score (a goal) [skɔː], [gəʊl]
Schiff boat [bəʊt]; ship [ʃɪp]
Schild sign [saɪn]
Schildkröte tortoise [ˈtɔːtəs]
Schimpfwort: jn. mit Schimpf-wörtern hänseln, jm. Schimpf-wörter nachrufen call sb. names
Schinkenspeck bacon [ˈbeɪkən]
Schlaf sleep [sliːp]
Schlafanzug pyjamas *(pl)* [pəˈdʒɑːməz]
schlafen sleep [sliːp]; *(nicht wach sein)* be asleep [əˈsliːp]
Schlafparty sleepover [ˈsliːpəʊvə]
Schlafzimmer bedroom [ˈbedruːm]
schlagen hit [hɪt]; *(besiegen)* beat [biːt]
Schlagzeug drums *(pl)* [drʌmz] • **Schlagzeug spielen** play the drums
Schlange snake [sneɪk]
schlau clever [ˈklevə]; smart [smɑːt]
schlecht bad [bæd] • **schlechter** worse [wɜːs] • **am schlechtesten; der/die/das schlechteste** (the) worst [wɜːst] • **schlecht abschnei-den (in)** do badly (in) • **schlechtes Timing** bad timing
Schleuse lock [lɒk]
schließen *(zumachen)* close [kləʊz]

schließlich at last [ət ˈlɑːst]; *(zum Schluss)* in the end
schlimm bad [bæd] • **schlimmer** worse [wɜːs] • **am schlimmsten; der/die/das schlimmste** (the) worst [wɜːst]
Schlitten sledge [sledʒ]
Schlittschuhbahn ice rink [ˈaɪs rɪŋk]
Schloss castle [ˈkɑːsl]; *(Palast)* palace [ˈpæləs]
Schluss 1. end [end] • **zum Schluss** in the end
2. *(einer Geschichte, eines Films usw.)* ending [ˈendɪŋ]
Schlüssel key [kiː]
Schlüsselring key ring [ˈkiː rɪŋ]
Schlüsselwort key word [ˈkiː wɜːd]
Schmuck jewellery [ˈdʒuːəlri]
schmutzig dirty [ˈdɜːti]
Schnee snow [snəʊ]
Schneeschuh snowshoe [ˈsnəʊʃuː]
Schneeschuhwandern snowshoeing [ˈsnəʊʃuːɪŋ]
schneiden cut [kʌt]
schnell quick [kwɪk]; fast [fɑːst]
schockiert shocked [ʃɒkt]
Schokolade chocolate [ˈtʃɒklət]
schon already [ɔːlˈredi] • **schon?** yet? [jet] • **schon mal?** ever? [ˈevə]
schön beautiful [ˈbjuːtɪfl]; *(nett)* nice [naɪs]; *(gut, in Ordnung)* fine [faɪn]
schön ordentlich neat and tidy
Schönheit beauty [ˈbjuːti]
Schrank cupboard [ˈkʌbəd]; *(Kleider-schrank)* wardrobe [ˈwɔːdrəʊb]
schrecklich terrible [ˈterəbl]; awful [ˈɔːfl]
schreiben (an) write (to) [raɪt]
Schreiber/in writer [ˈraɪtə]
Schreibtisch desk [desk]
Schreibung *(Rechtschreibung, Schreibweise)* spelling [ˈspelɪŋ]
schreien shout [ʃaʊt]
Schriftsteller/in writer [ˈraɪtə]
Schritt step [step]
schüchtern shy [ʃaɪ]
Schuh shoe [ʃuː]
Schuld: Das ist nicht meine Schuld. It's not my fault. [fɔːlt] • **jm. die Schuld geben (an)** blame sb. (for) [bleɪm]
Schule school [skuːl] • **in der Schule** at school
Schüler/in student [ˈstjuːdənt]
Schulfach (school) subject [ˈsʌbdʒɪkt]
Schulheft exercise book [ˈeksəsaɪz bʊk]
Schulleiter/in head teacher [ˌhed ˈtiːtʃə]
Schulmensa canteen [kænˈtiːn]
Schultasche school bag [ˈskuːl bæg]
Schulter shoulder [ˈʃəʊldə]

Schulterpolster *(beim American Football)* pad [pæd]
Schüssel bowl [baʊl]
Schützer *(Knieschützer usw. für In-lineskater)* pad [pæd]
schwach weak [wiːk]
schwarz black [blæk] • **schwarzes Brett** notice board [ˈnaʊtɪs bɔːd]
Schwein pig [pɪg]
Schweinefleisch pork [pɔːk]
schwer 1. *(Gewicht)* heavy [ˈhevi] • **ein 150 Kilogramm schwerer Bär** a 150-kilogram bear
2. *(schwierig)* difficult [ˈdɪfɪkəlt]; hard [hɑːd]
3. *(anstrengend)* hard [hɑːd]
Schwester sister [ˈsɪstə]
schwierig difficult [ˈdɪfɪkəlt]; hard [hɑːd]
Schwierigkeiten trouble [ˈtrʌbl] • **in Schwierigkeiten sein** be in trouble
Schwimmbad, -becken swimming pool [ˈswɪmɪŋ puːl]
schwimmen swim [swɪm]
schwimmen gehen go swimming
Schwimmer/in swimmer [ˈswɪmə]
See 1. *(Binnensee)* lake [leɪk]
2. *(die See, das Meer)* sea [siː]
Seemann sailor [ˈseɪlə]
sehen see [siː] • **Siehst du?** See?
Sehenswürdigkeiten sights *(pl)* [saɪts]
sehr very [ˈveri] • **Danke sehr!** Thanks very much! • **Er mag sie sehr.** He likes her a lot. [ə ˈlɒt] **etwas sehr mögen / sehr lieben** like/love sth. very much
Seife soap [saʊp]
sein *(Verb)* be [biː]
sein(e) *(besitzanzeigend) (zu „he")* his; *(zu „it")* its
seiner, seine, seins his [hɪz]
Seite 1. side [saɪd] • **auf der linken Seite** on the left • **auf der rechten Seite** on the right
2. *(Buch-, Heftseite)* page [peɪdʒ]
Auf welcher Seite sind wir? What page are we on?
selbstverständlich of course [əv ˈkɔːs]
senden (an) *(Post, E-Mail)* send (to) [send]; mail (to) [meɪl]
Sendereihe series, *pl* series [ˈsɪəriːz]
September September [sepˈtembə]
Serie *(Sendereihe)* series, *pl* series [ˈsɪəriːz]
Sessel armchair [ˈɑːmtʃeə]
Setup setup [ˈsetʌp]
setzen: sich setzen sit [sɪt] • **Setz dich / Setzt euch zu mir.** Sit with me.
Shorts shorts *(pl)* [ʃɔːts]
Show show [ʃaʊ]

sich (selbst) 1. *(zu „she")* herself [həˈself, hɜːˈself]
2. *(zu „he")* himself [hɪmˈself]
3. *(zu „it")* itself [ɪtˈself]
4. *(zu „they")* themselves [ðəmˈselvz]
5. **sich (gegenseitig)** *(einander)* each other [iːtʃ_ˈʌðə]; one another [wʌn_əˈnʌðə]
▶ S.163 Reflexive pronouns
▶ S.164 each other – themselves
sicher 1. *(in Sicherheit)* safe (from) [seɪf] • **nicht sicher** unsafe [ʌnˈseɪf]
2. **sicher sein** *(nicht zweifeln)* be sure [ʃʊə, ʃɔː]
Sicherheit: in Sicherheit (vor) safe (from) [seɪf]
sie 1. *(weibliche Person)* she [ʃiː] **Frag sie.** Ask her. [hə, hɜː]
2. *(Ding, Tier)* it [ɪt]
3. *(Plural)* they [ðeɪ] • **Frag sie.** Ask them. [ðəm, ðem]
Sie *(höfliche Anrede)* you [juː]
Sieg win [wɪn]
Sieger/in winner [ˈwɪnə]
Silbe syllable [ˈsɪləbl]
singen sing [sɪŋ]
Single single [ˈsɪŋgl]
sitzen sit [sɪt]
Skateboard skateboard [ˈskeɪtbɔːd]
Skateboard fahren skate [skeɪt]
skaten skate [skeɪt]
Sketch sketch [sketʃ]
Ski ski [skiː] • **Ski fahren/laufen** ski [skiː]
Sklave, Sklavin slave [sleɪv]
SMS text message [tekst ˌmesɪdʒ]
jm . eine SMS schicken text sb. [tekst]
Snack snack [snæk]
so 1. so weit/gut/schlecht/… that far/good/bad/… • **so süß** so sweet [saʊ]
2. so alt/groß wie as old/big as
Socke sock [sɒk]
soeben just [dʒʌst]
Sofa sofa [ˈsaʊfə]
Software software [ˈsɒftweə]
sogar even [ˈiːvn]
Sohn son [sʌn]
Sommer summer [ˈsʌmə]
Song song [sɒŋ]
Sonnabend Saturday [ˈsætədeɪ, ˈsætədi] *(siehe auch unter „Freitag")*
Sonne sun [sʌn]
Sonnenbrille: (eine) Sonnenbrille sunglasses *(pl)* [ˈsʌnglɑːsɪz]
sonnig sunny [ˈsʌni]
Sonntag Sunday [ˈsʌndeɪ, ˈsʌndi] *(siehe auch unter „Freitag")*
Sorge worry [ˈwʌri] • **sich Sorgen machen (wegen, um)** worry

(about) • **Mach dir keine Sorgen.** Don't worry.
sorgfältig careful [ˈkeəfl]
Sorte sort [sɔːt]
Soundfile sound file [ˈsaʊnd faɪl]
sowieso anyway [ˈeniweɪ]
Spaghetti spaghetti [spəˈgeti]
spannend exciting [ɪkˈsaɪtɪŋ]
sparen save [seɪv]
Spaß fun [fʌn] • **Spaß haben** have fun • **nur zum Spaß** just for fun **Reiten macht Spaß.** Riding is fun. **Viel Spaß!** Have fun! / Enjoy yourself.
spät late [leɪt] • **Wie spät ist es?** What's the time? • **zu spät sein/kommen** be late
später later [ˈleɪtə]
spätestens: bis spätestens 10 (Uhr) by ten (o'clock)
▶ S.163 German „bis"
spazieren gehen go for a walk [wɔːk]
Spaziergang walk [wɔːk] • **einen Spaziergang machen** go for a walk
Specht woodpecker [ˈwʊdpekə]
Speise dish [dɪʃ]
Speisekarte menu [ˈmenjuː]
sperren lock [lɒk]
Spiegel mirror [ˈmɪrə]
Spiel game [geɪm]; *(Wettkampf)* match [mætʃ]
spielen play [pleɪ]; *(Szene, Dialog)* act [ækt] • **Fußball spielen** play football • **Gitarre/Klavier spielen** play the guitar/the piano
Spieler/in player [ˈpleɪə]
Spielstand *(Punktestand)* score [skɔː]
▶ S.159 A football match
Spion/in spy [spaɪ]
Spitze *(oberes Ende)* top [tɒp] • **an der Spitze (von)** at the top (of)
Sport; Sportart sport [spɔːt] • **Sport treiben** do sport
sportlich sporty [ˈspɔːti]
Sportunterricht PE [ˌpiːˈiː], Physical Education [ˌfɪzɪkəl_edʒuˈkeɪʃn]
Sportzentrum sports centre [ˈspɔːts ˌsentə]
Sprache language [ˈlæŋgwɪdʒ]
Sprachmittlung *(Mediation)* mediation [ˌmiːdiˈeɪʃn]
sprechen (mit) speak (to) [spiːk] **Hier spricht Isabel.** *(am Telefon)* This is Isabel.
springen jump [dʒʌmp]
Spülbecken, Spüle sink [sɪŋk]
Staat state [steɪt] • **die Vereinigten Staaten (von Amerika)** the United States (US) [juːˌnaɪtɪd ˈsteɪts], [ˌjuːˈes]
Stadion stadium [ˈsteɪdiəm]
Stadt *(Großstadt)* city [ˈsɪti]; *(Kleinstadt)* town [taʊn]

Stadtplan map [mæp]
Stadtzentrum city centre [ˌsɪti 'sentə]
Stahl steel [stiːl]
Stall *(für Kaninchen)* hutch [hʌtʃ]
Stammbaum family tree ['fæməli triː]
Standort location [ləʊ'keɪʃn]
Star *(Film-, Popstar)* star [stɑː]
stark strong [strɒŋ]
starten start [stɑːt]
Statue statue ['stætʃuː]
Steak steak [steɪk]
Steckbrief *(Beschreibung)* profile ['prəʊfaɪl]
Stecker plug [plʌg]
Steeldrum steel drum [ˌstiːl 'drʌm]
stehen stand [stænd] • **Hier steht: …** *(im Text)* It says here: … • **Wie steht es?** *(beim Sport)* What's the score?
▶ S.159 A football match
stehlen steal [stiːl]
Steigerung comparison [kəm'pærɪsn]
Stein stone [stəʊn]
stellen *(hin-, abstellen)* put [pʊt]
Fragen stellen ask questions
sich (hin)stellen stand [stænd]
sterben (an) die (of) [daɪ]
Stereoanlage stereo ['steriəʊ]
Stern star [stɑː]
Stichwort *(Schlüsselwort)* key word ['kiː wɜːd]
Stiefel boot [buːt]
still quiet ['kwaɪət]
stimmen: Das stimmt. That's right. [raɪt] • **Du brauchst ein Lineal, stimmt's?** You need a ruler, right?
stolz (auf jn./etwas) proud (of sb./ sth.) [praʊd]
stoßen push [pʊʃ]
Strand beach [biːtʃ] • **am Strand** on the beach
Straße road [rəʊd]; street [striːt]
Straßenbahn tram [træm]
Streich trick [trɪk]
Streik strike [straɪk] • **in den Streik treten** go on strike • **sich im Streik befinden** be on strike
streiken 1. *(sich im Streik befinden)* be on strike [straɪk]
2. *(in den Streik treten)* go on strike [straɪk]
streiten; sich streiten argue ['ɑːgjuː]
streng strict [strɪkt]
strukturieren structure ['strʌktʃə]
Strumpf sock [sɒk]
Stück piece [piːs] • **ein Stück Papier** a piece of paper
Student/in student ['stjuːdənt]
Stuhl chair [tʃeə]
stumm: „stummer" Buchstabe *(nicht gesprochener Buchstabe)* silent letter [ˌsaɪlənt 'letə]
Stunde hour ['aʊə]; *(Schulstunde)* lesson ['lesn] • **eine halbe Stunde**

half an hour [ˌhɑːf_ən_'aʊə] • **ein 14-Stunden-Flug** a 14-hour flight
ein Supermarkt, der 24 Stunden geöffnet ist a 24-hour supermarket
Stundenplan timetable ['taɪmteɪbl]
…stündig: ein 14-stündiger Flug a 14-hour flight
Sturm storm [stɔːm]
stürmisch stormy ['stɔːmi]
stürzen *(hinfallen)* fall [fɔːl]
suchen look for ['lʊk fɔː]
Süden south [saʊθ] • **nach Süden**
südlich south [saʊθ]
Südosten south-east [ˌsaʊθ'iːst]
nach Südosten south-east
südöstlich south-east [ˌsaʊθ'iːst]
Südwesten south-west [ˌsaʊθ'west]
nach Südwesten south-west
südwestlich south-west [ˌsaʊθ'west]
Supermarkt supermarket ['suːpəmɑːkɪt]
Suppe soup [suːp]
Surfbrett surfboard ['sɜːfbɔːd]
surfen surf [sɜːf] • **im Internet surfen** surf the internet [sɜːf]
süß sweet [swiːt]
Süßigkeiten sweets *(pl)* [swiːts]
Sweatshirt sweatshirt ['swetʃɜːt]
Szene scene [siːn]

T

Tabak tobacco [tə'bækəʊ]
Tafel *(Wandtafel)* board [bɔːd] • **an der/die Tafel** on the board
Tag day [deɪ] • **drei Tage (lang)** for three days • **eines Tages** one day **Guten Tag.** Hello.; *(nachmittags)* Good afternoon. [gʊd_ˌɑːftə'nuːn]
Tagebuch diary ['daɪəri]
Tagesfahrkarte all-day ticket; *(der Londoner Verkehrsbetriebe)* Travelcard ['trævlkɑːd]
Tal valley ['væli]
Tante aunt [ɑːnt]; auntie ['ɑːnti]
Tanz dance [dɑːns]
tanzen dance [dɑːns]
Tanzen dancing ['dɑːnsɪŋ]
Tänzer/in dancer ['dɑːnsə]
Tanzstunden, Tanzunterricht dancing lessons ['dɑːnsɪŋ ˌlesnz]
Tasche *(Tragetasche, Beutel)* bag [bæg]; *(Hosentasche, Jackentasche)* pocket ['pɒkɪt]
Taschengeld pocket money ['pɒkɪt mʌni]
Tasse cup [kʌp] • **eine Tasse Tee** a cup of tea
Tätigkeit activity [æk'tɪvəti]
Tatsache fact [fækt]

tausend thousand ['θaʊznd]
Taxi taxi ['tæksi]
Team team [tiːm]
Teddy teddy ['tedi]
Tee tea [tiː]
Teelöffel teaspoon ['tiːspuːn]
Teenager teenager ['tiːneɪdʒə]
Teenager- *(Jugend-)* teen [tiːn]
Teil part [pɑːt]; *(Abschnitt)* section ['sekʃn]
teilen: sich etwas teilen (mit jm.) share sth. (with sb.) [ʃeə]
Telefon (tele)phone ['telɪfəʊn] • **am Telefon** on the phone
telefonieren phone [fəʊn]
Telefonnummer (tele)phone number ['telɪfəʊn ˌnʌmbə]
Teller plate [pleɪt] • **ein Teller Pommes frites** a plate of chips
Temperatur temperature ['temprətʃə]
Tennis tennis ['tenɪs]
Termin appointment [ə'pɔɪntmənt]
Terminkalender diary ['daɪəri]
Test test [test]
teuer expensive [ɪk'spensɪv]
Text text [tekst]
Theater theatre ['θɪətə]
Theaterstück play [pleɪ]
Thema, Themenbereich topic ['tɒpɪk]
Thermometer thermometer [θə'mɒmɪtə]
Tier animal ['ænɪml]; *(Haustier)* pet [pet]
Tierhandlung pet shop ['pet ʃɒp]
Tiger tiger ['taɪgə]
Tipp tip [tɪp]
Tisch table ['teɪbl]
Tischtennis table tennis ['teɪbl tenɪs]
Tischtennisschläger table tennis bat [bæt]
Titel title ['taɪtl]
Toast(brot) toast [təʊst]
Tochter daughter ['dɔːtə]
Toilette toilet ['tɔɪlət]
toll fantastic [fæn'tæstɪk]; great [greɪt]; brilliant ['brɪliənt]
Tomate tomato [tə'mɑːtəʊ], *pl* tomatoes
Tondatei sound file ['saʊnd faɪl]
Top *(Oberteil)* top [tɒp]
Tor gate [geɪt]; *(im Sport)* goal [gəʊl] • **ein Tor schießen** score (a goal) [skɔː]
Torfrau, Torwart goalkeeper ['gəʊlkiːpə]
Tornado tornado [tɔː'neɪdəʊ]
Torte cake [keɪk]
tot dead [ded]
töten kill [kɪl]
Tour (durch das Haus) tour (of the house) [tʊə]
Tourist/in tourist ['tʊərɪst]
tragen *(Kleidung)* wear [weə]

Trainer/in coach [kəʊtʃ]
trainieren practise ['præktɪs]; train [treɪn]
Trainingsstunde, -einheit training session ['seʃn]
Transport *(Beförderung)* transport ['trænspɔːt]
Traum dream [driːm]
Traumhaus dream house
traurig sad [sæd]
treffen; sich treffen meet [miːt]
Treffer: einen Treffer erzielen score (a goal) [skɔː], [gəʊl]
Treppe(nstufen) stairs *(pl)* [steəz]
Trick *(Zauberkunststück)* trick [trɪk]
Trimester term [tɜːm]
trinken drink [drɪŋk] • **Milch zum Frühstück trinken** have milk for breakfast
Trommel drum [drʌm]
Trompete trumpet ['trʌmpɪt]
trotzdem anyway ['eniweɪ]
Truthahn turkey ['tɜːki]
Tschüs. Bye. [baɪ]; See you. ['siː juː]
T-Shirt T-shirt ['tiːʃɜːt]
tun do [duː] • **Tue, was ich tue.** Do what I do. • **tun müssen** have to do • **tun wollen** want to do [wɒnt] **Tut mir leid.** I'm sorry. ['sɒri]
Tunnel tunnel ['tʌnl]
Tür door [dɔː]
Türklingel doorbell ['dɔːbel]
Turm tower ['taʊə]
Turnen *(Sportunterricht)* PE [ˌpiːˈiː], Physical Education [ˌfɪzɪkəl_edʒuˈkeɪʃn]
Turnschuhe trainers *(pl)* ['treɪnəz]
Tut mir leid. I'm sorry. ['sɒri]
Tüte bag [bæg]
Typ type [taɪp] *(infml)*
Tyrann *(Schultyrann)* bully ['bʊli]
tyrannisieren bully ['bʊli]

U

U-Bahn: die U-Bahn the underground ['ʌndəgraʊnd] *(BE)*; the subway ['sʌbweɪ] *(AE)*; *(in London)* the Tube *(no pl)* [tjuːb]
U-Bahnlinie line [laɪn]
üben practise ['præktɪs]
über 1. about [əˈbaʊt] • **über dich selbst** about yourself **2.** *(räumlich)* over ['əʊvə]; *(quer über)* across [əˈkrɒs]; *(oberhalb von)* above [əˈbʌv]
überarbeiten revise [rɪˈvaɪz]
übereinstimmen: mit jm./etwas übereinstimmen agree with sb./ sth. [əˈgriː]

überfliegen: einen Text überfliegen *(um den Inhalt grob zu erfassen)* skim a text [skɪm]
überleben survive [səˈvaɪv]
übernachten *(über Nacht bleiben)* stay [steɪ]
überprüfen check [tʃek]
überqueren cross [krɒs]
Überraschung surprise [səˈpraɪz]
Überschrift title ['taɪtl]
übersetzen (aus … ins) translate (from … into) [trænsˈleɪt]
Übersetzung translation [trænsˈleɪʃn]
übrigens by the way [ˌbaɪ ðə ˈweɪ]
Übung *(im Schulbuch)* exercise ['eksəsaɪz] • **eine Übung machen** do an exercise
Übungsheft exercise book ['eksəsaɪz bʊk]
Uhr 1. *(Armbanduhr)* watch [wɒtʃ]; *(Wand-, Stand-, Turmuhr)* clock [klɒk]
2. elf Uhr eleven o'clock • **7 Uhr morgens/vormittags** 7 am [ˌeɪˈem] **7 Uhr nachmittags/abends** 7 pm [ˌpiːˈem] • **um 8 Uhr 45** at 8.45
Uhrzeit time [taɪm]
um 1. *(örtlich)* **um … (herum)** round [raʊnd]; around [əˈraʊnd] • **um den See (herum)** around the lake **ganz um die Burg herum** all around the castle
▶ S.155 around
2. *(zeitlich)* **um 8.45** at 8.45 • **um sechs herum** *(gegen sechs)* around six
▶ S.155 around
3. Es geht um Mr Green. This is about Mr Green.
4. um zu to
umdrehen: sich umdrehen turn [tɜːn]
Umfrage (über) survey (on) ['sɜːveɪ]
umher: in … umher round [raʊnd]; around [əˈraʊnd] • **in der Stadt umher** around the town
▶ S.155 around
umher-: umhergehen; umherspazieren walk around • **umherrennen** run around • **umherspringen** jump around
▶ S.155 around
umschreiben *(anders ausdrücken)* paraphrase ['pærəfreɪz]
umsehen: sich umsehen look round [ˌlʊk ˈraʊnd]
umsteigen change [tʃeɪndʒ]
umziehen (nach, in) *(die Wohnung wechseln)* move (to) [muːv]
uncool uncool [ˌʌnˈkuːl] *(infml)*
und and [ənd, ænd] • **Und? / Na und?** So? [səʊ]

unfair unfair [ˌʌnˈfeə]
Unfall accident ['æksɪdənt]
unfreundlich unfriendly [ʌnˈfrendli]
ungefähr about [əˈbaʊt]
Ungeheuer monster ['mɒnstə]
ungerecht unfair [ˌʌnˈfeə]
ungesund unhealthy [ʌnˈhelθi]
unglaublich amazing [əˈmeɪzɪŋ]
unglücklich unhappy [ʌnˈhæpi]
unheimlich scary ['skeəri]
unhöflich rude [ruːd]
Uniform uniform ['juːnɪfɔːm]
unmöglich impossible [ɪmˈpɒsɪbl]
unordentlich untidy [ʌnˈtaɪdi] • **sehr unordentlich sein** *(Zimmer)* be a mess [mes]
Unordnung: alles in Unordnung bringen make a mess [ˌmeɪk_ə ˈmes]
Unrecht haben be wrong [rɒŋ]
uns us [əs, ʌs] • **uns (selbst)** ourselves [aʊəˈselvz]
▶ S.163 Reflexive pronouns
unser(e) … our … ['aʊə] • **unser eigenes Schwimmbad** our own pool [əʊn]
unserer, unsere, unseres ours ['aʊəz]
unten *(im Haus)* downstairs [ˌdaʊnˈsteəz] • **am unteren Ende (von)** at the bottom (of) ['bɒtəm] **dort unten** down there • **nach unten** down [daʊn]; *(im Haus)* downstairs
unter under ['ʌndə]
unterbrechen: eine Reise unterbrechen break a journey [ˌbreɪk_ə ˈdʒɜːni]
unterhalten: sich unterhalten (mit, über) talk (to, about) [tɔːk]
Unterricht lessons *(pl)* ['lesnz]
unterrichten teach [tiːtʃ]
unterschiedlich different ['dɪfrənt]
Untersuchung (über) *(Umfrage)* survey (on) ['sɜːveɪ]
Unterwäsche underwear ['ʌndəweə]
unverschämt rude [ruːd]
Urlaub holiday ['hɒlədeɪ] *(BE)*; vacation [vəˈkeɪʃn, AE: veɪˈkeɪʃn] *(AE)* • **in Urlaub fahren** go on holiday • **in Urlaub sein** be on holiday • **ein zweiwöchiger Urlaub** a two-week holiday

V

Vater father ['fɑːðə]
Vati dad [dæd]
Verabredung appointment [əˈpɔɪntmənt]
verabschieden: sich verabschieden say goodbye [ˌseɪ gʊdˈbaɪ]
verängstigt scared [skeəd]

Veranstaltungsort location [ləʊˈkeɪʃn]

verbinden *(einander zuordnen)* link [lɪŋk]

Verbindung *(Verknüfung)* link [lɪŋk] • **in Verbindung bleiben** keep in touch [ˌkiːp_ɪn ˈtʌtʃ]

verboten: Rauchen verboten. No smoking.

verbringen: Zeit verbringen (mit) spend time (on) [spend]

Verein club [klʌb]

vereinigt: das Vereinigte Königreich *(Großbritannien und Nordirland)* the United Kingdom (UK) [juˌnaɪtɪd ˈkɪŋdəm], [ˌjuːˈkeɪ] • **die Vereinigten Staaten (von Amerika)** the United States (US) [juˌnaɪtɪd ˈsteɪts], [juː_ˈes]

verfolgen follow [ˈfɒləʊ]

vergessen forget [fəˈget]

Vergleich comparison [kəmˈpærɪsn]

verheiratet (mit) married (to) [ˈmærɪd]

verkaufen sell [sel]

Verkäufer/in *(im Geschäft)* shop assistant [ˈʃɒp_əˌsɪstənt]

Verkehr traffic [ˈtræfɪk]

Verkehrsmittel transport *(no pl)* [ˈtrænspɔːt]

verkehrsreich *(Straße)* busy [ˈbɪzi]

verkehrt *(falsch)* wrong [rɒŋ]

verknüpfen *(einander zuordnen)* link [lɪŋk]

Verknüpfung link [lɪŋk]

verlassen leave [liːv]

verletzen hurt [hɜːt]

verletzt hurt [hɜːt]

verlieren lose [luːz]

vermissen miss [mɪs]

Vermittlung *(Sprachmittlung, Mediation)* mediation [ˌmiːdiˈeɪʃn]

veröffentlichen publish [ˈpʌblɪʃ]

verrückt mad [mæd] • **verrückt nach/auf etwas sein** be mad about sth.

Versammlung *(morgendliche Schulversammlung, oft mit Andacht)* Assembly [əˈsembli]

verschieden *(anders)* different [ˈdɪfrənt]

verschwinden disappear [ˌdɪsəˈpɪə]

versprechen promise [ˈprɒmɪs]

verstecken; sich verstecken hide [haɪd]

verstehen understand [ˌʌndəˈstænd]

versuchen try [traɪ] • **versuchen zu tun** try and do / try to do

vertreten *(repräsentieren)* represent [ˌreprɪˈzent]

verwenden use [juːz]

verwirrt puzzled [ˈpʌzld]

Video video [ˈvɪdiəʊ]

viel a lot (of) [lɒt]; lots (of) [lɒts]; much [mʌtʃ] • **viele** a lot (of) [lɒt]; lots (of) [lɒts]; many [ˈmeni] • **Viel Glück (bei/mit ...)!** Good luck (with ...)! • **viel mehr** lots more **Viel Spaß!** Have fun! / Enjoy yourself. • **wie viel?** how much? **wie viele?** how many? • **Vielen Dank!** Thanks a lot!

vielleicht maybe [ˈmeɪbi]

Viertel: Viertel nach 11 quarter past 11 [ˈkwɔːtə] • **Viertel vor 12** quarter to 12

violett purple [ˈpɜːpl]

Violine violin [ˌvaɪəˈlɪn]

Vogel bird [bɜːd]

Vogelkäfig birdcage [ˈbɜːdkeɪdʒ]

Vokabelverzeichnis vocabulary [vəˈkæbjələri]

voll full [fʊl] • **die Nase voll haben (von etwas)** be fed up (with sth.) [ˌfed_ˈʌp]

Volleyball volleyball [ˈvɒlibɔːl]

von of [əv, ɒv]; from [frəm, frɒm] **ein Aufsatz von ...** an essay by ... [baɪ] • **von Montag bis Freitag** from Mondays to Fridays ▶ S.163 German „bis"

vor 1. *(räumlich)* in front of [ɪn ˈfrʌnt_əv] 2. *(zeitlich)* **vor dem Abendessen** before dinner [bɪˈfɔː] • **vor einer Minute** a minute ago [əˈgəʊ] **Viertel vor 12** quarter to 12

vorankommen: Wie komme ich voran? *(Wie sind meine Fortschritte?)* How am I doing?

vorbei (an) *(vorüber)* past [pɑːst]

vorbei sein be over [ˈəʊvə]

vorbereiten prepare [prɪˈpeə] • **sich vorbereiten (auf)** prepare (for); get ready (for) [ˈredi] • **Dinge vorbereiten** get things ready

Vordergrund foreground [ˈfɔːgraʊnd]

Vormittag morning [ˈmɔːnɪŋ]

Vorschrift *(Regel)* rule [ruːl]

vorsichtig careful [ˈkeəfl]

vorspielen *(pantomimisch darstellen)* mime [maɪm]

Vorstellung *(Präsentation)* presentation [ˌpreznˈteɪʃn]; *(Show)* show [ʃəʊ]

vorüber (an) *(vorbei)* past [pɑːst]

Vorwürfe: jm. Vorwürfe machen machen (wegen) blame sb. (for) [bleɪm]

W

wählen *(auswählen, aussuchen)* choose [tʃuːz]

wahr true [truː]

während as [əz, æz]; while [waɪl]

wahrscheinlich probably [ˈprɒbəbli]

Wald forest [ˈfɒrɪst]

walisisch; Walisisch Welsh [welʃ]

Wand wall [wɔːl]

wann when [wen]

warm warm [wɔːm]

warten (auf) wait (for) [weɪt] **Warte mal!** Wait a minute. [ˈmɪnɪt] **Wart's ab!** Wait and see!

warum why [waɪ] • **Warum ich?** Why me?

was what [wɒt] • **Was für ein Auto ...?** What kind of car ...? **Was haben wir als Hausaufgabe auf?** What's for homework? **Was haben wir als Nächstes?** What have we got next? • **Was ist los? / Was ist denn?** What's the matter? [ˈmætə] • **Was ist mit ...?** What about ...? • **Was kostet/kosten ...?** How much is/are ...? **Was war das Beste an ...?** What was the best thing about ...?

waschen wash [wɒʃ] • **Ich wasche mir das Gesicht.** I wash my face.

Waschmaschine washing machine [ˈwɒʃɪŋ məˌʃiːn]

Wasser water [ˈwɔːtə]

Webcam webcam [ˈwebkæm]

Website website [ˈwebsaɪt]

Wechselgeld change [tʃeɪndʒ]

weg away [əˈweɪ]

Weg way [weɪ]; *(Pfad)* path [pɑːθ]; *(Gasse)* lane [leɪn] • **auf dem Weg (zu/nach)** on the way (to) • **jm. den Weg beschreiben** tell sb. the way • **jn. nach dem Weg fragen** ask sb. the way • **etwas auf den Weg bringen** get sth. off the ground

weggehen leave [liːv]

wehtun hurt [hɜːt]

weiblich female [ˈfiːmeɪl]

Weide field [fiːld]

Weihnachten Christmas [ˈkrɪsməs]

weil because [bɪˈkɒz]

Weise *(Art und Weise)* way [weɪ]

weiß white [waɪt]

weit 1. *(entfernt)* far [fɑː] 2. *(geschnitten)* baggy [ˈbægi]

weiter: geradeaus weiter straight on [streɪt_ˈɒn]

weitere(r, s): weitere 45 Pence another 45 p [əˈnʌðə]

weiter-: weitergeben pass [pɑːs] **weitermachen** go on **weiterreden** go on

welche(r, s) which [wɪtʃ] • **Auf welcher Seite sind wir?** What page are we on? [wɒt] • **Welche Farbe hat …?** What colour is …?

wellenreiten gehen go surfing ['sɜːfɪŋ]

Wellensittich budgie ['bʌdʒi]

Welt world [wɜːld] • **auf der ganzen Welt** all over the world • **aus der ganzen Welt** from all over the world

wem? who? [huː] • **Wem gehören diese?** Whose are these? [huːz]

wen? who? [huː]

wenden: sich an jn. wenden turn to sb. [tɜːn]

wenig: am wenigsten least [liːst] **etwas am wenigsten mögen** like sth. least

wenigstens at least [ət 'liːst]

wenn 1. *(zeitlich)* when [wen] **2.** *(falls)* if [ɪf]

wer? who? [huː] • **Wer ist dran / an der Reihe?** Whose turn is it? [huːz]

werden become [bɪ'kʌm] • **wütend/ heiß/… werden** get angry/hot/… **du wirst frieren; ihr werdet frieren** you'll be cold (= you will be cold) [wɪl] • **du wirst nicht frieren; ihr werdet nicht frieren** you won't be cold (= you will not be cold) [wəʊnt]

werfen throw [θrəʊ]

wessen? whose? [huːz]

West- western ['westən]

Westen west [west] • **nach Westen** west

westlich *(westlich von)* west [west]; *(Gebiet)* western ['westən]

Wettbewerb *(Wettkampf)* competition [ˌkɒmpə'tɪʃn]

wetten bet [bet]

Wetter weather ['weðə]

Wettkampf match [mætʃ]; competition [ˌkɒmpə'tɪʃn]

Whisky whisky ['wɪski]

wichtig important [ɪm'pɔːtnt]

wie 1. *(Fragewort)* how [haʊ] • **Wie bitte?** Sorry? ['sɒri] • **Wie geht es dir/Ihnen/euch?** How are you? [ˌhaʊ_'ɑː jʊ] • **Wie heißt du?** What's your name? • **Wie komme ich voran?** *(Wie sind meine Fortschritte?)* How am I doing? • **Wie spät ist es?** What's the time? **Wie steht es jetzt?** *(beim Sport)* What's the score? • **wie viel?** how much? • **wie viele?** how many? • **Wie war …?** How was …? • **Wie war das Wetter?** What was the weather like? • **Wie wär's mit …?** What about …? **2. so alt/groß wie** as old/big as **3. wie ein Filmstar** like a film star [laɪk]

wieder again [ə'gen]

wiederholen *(Lernstoff)* revise [rɪ'vaɪz]

Wiederholung *(des Lernstoffs)* revision [rɪ'vɪʒn]

Wiedersehen: Auf Wiedersehen. Goodbye. [ˌgʊd'baɪ]

wiederverwendet/-verwertet recycled [ˌriː'saɪkld]

Wiederverwertung recycling [ˌriː'saɪklɪŋ]

wild wild [waɪld]

willkommen: Willkommen (in Bristol). Welcome (to Bristol). ['welkəm] • **Sie heißen dich in … willkommen** They welcome you to …

Wind wind [wɪnd]

windig windy ['wɪndi]

Windjacke anorak ['ænəræk]

Windsurfen windsurfing ['wɪndsɜːfɪŋ]

winken wave [weɪv]

Winter winter ['wɪntə]

wir we [wiː]

Wirbelsturm tornado [tɔː'neɪdəʊ]

wirklich 1. *(tatsächlich)* really ['rɪəli] • **Meinst du wirklich? / Glaubst du das wirklich?** Do you really think so? **2.** *(echt)* real [rɪəl]

wirklichkeitsnah realistic [ˌrɪə'lɪstɪk]

wissen know [nəʊ] • **wissen wollen** wonder ['wʌndə] • **Ich weiß es nicht.** I don't know. • **von etwas wissen; über etwas Bescheid wissen** know about sth. • **…, wissen Sie. / …, weißt du.** …, you know. **Weißt du was, Sophie?** You know what, Sophie? • **Woher weißt du …?** How do you know …?

Witz joke [dʒəʊk] • **Witze machen** joke

witzig funny ['fʌni]

wo where [weə] • **Wo kommst du her?** Where are you from?

Woche week [wiːk]

Wochenende weekend [ˌwiːk'end] **am Wochenende** at the weekend

Wochentage days of the week

…wöchig: ein zweiwöchiger Urlaub a two-week holiday

Wofür? What for? [ˌwɒt 'fɔː]

Woher weißt du …? How do you know …? [nəʊ]

wohin where [weə]; *(in welche Richtung)* which way

wohlauf *(gesund)* well [wel]

Wohltätigkeitsbasar jumble sale ['dʒʌmbl seɪl]

wohnen live [lɪv]

Wohnheim hostel ['hɒstl]

Wohnort location [ləʊ'keɪʃn]

Wohnung flat [flæt]

Wohnungstür front door [ˌfrʌnt 'dɔː]

Wohnwagen caravan ['kærəvæn]

Wohnzimmer living room ['lɪvɪŋ ruːm]

Wolf wolf, *pl* wolves [wʊlf, wʊlvz]

Wolke cloud [klaʊd]

wollen *(haben wollen)* want [wɒnt] **tun wollen** want to do

Workshop workshop ['wɜːkʃɒp]

Wort word [wɜːd]

Wortbildung word building ['wɜːd ˌbɪldɪŋ]

Wörterbuch dictionary ['dɪkʃənri]

Wörterverzeichnis vocabulary [və'kæbjələri]; *(alphabetisches)* dictionary ['dɪkʃənri]

Wovon redest du? What are you talking about?

würden: ich würde … / du würdest … I would … / you would … [wəd, wʊd]

Würfel dice, *pl* dice [daɪs]

Wurst, Würstchen sausage ['sɒsɪdʒ]

würzig *(scharf gewürzt)* spicy ['spaɪsi]

wütend (über etwas/auf jn.) angry (about sth./with sb.) ['æŋgri]

Y

Yoga yoga ['jəʊgə]

Z

Zahl number ['nʌmbə]

zählen count [kaʊnt]

Zahn tooth [tuːθ], *pl* teeth [tiːθ] • **Ich putze mir die Zähne.** I clean my teeth.

Zahnschmerzen toothache ['tuːθeɪk]

zanken; sich zanken argue ['ɑːgjuː]

Zauberkunststück trick [trɪk] • **Zauberkunststücke machen** do tricks

Zebra zebra ['zebrə]

Zeh toe [təʊ]

Zeichen *(Schild)* sign [saɪn]

zeichnen draw [drɔː]

Zeichnung drawing ['drɔːɪŋ]

zeigen show [ʃəʊ] • **auf etwas zeigen** point at/to sth. [pɔɪnt]

Zeile line [laɪn]

Zeit time [taɪm] • **Zeit verbringen (mit)** spend time (on) [spend]

Zeitschrift magazine [ˌmægə'ziːn]

Zeitung newspaper ['njuːspeɪpə]; paper ['peɪpə]

Zeitungsartikel article ['ɑːtɪkl]

zelten camp [kæmp]

Zentimeter centimetre (cm) ['sentɪmiːtə]

Zentral- *(Mittel-)* central ['sentrəl]

Zentrum centre ['sentə]

zerbrochen broken ['brəʊkən]

Zeug *(Kram)* stuff [stʌf]

ziehen pull [pʊl]

ziemlich gut pretty good ['prɪti]; quite good [kwaɪt]

Ziffer number ['nʌmbə]

Zimmer room [ruːm, rʊm]

zu 1. *(örtlich)* to [tə, tu] • **zu Jenny** to Jenny's • **zu Hause** at home **zum Arzt** to the doctor's • **Setz dich zu mir.** Sit with me. • **auf jn./etwas zu** towards sb./sth. [təˈwɔːdz]

2. zum Beispiel for example [ˌfər_ɪgˈzɑːmpl] • **zum Frühstück/Mittagessen/Abendbrot** for breakfast/lunch/dinner [fə, fɔː]

zum Schluss in the end

3. zu viel too much [tuː] • **zu spät sein/kommen** be late

4. versuchen zu tun try and do / try to do

5. *(geschlossen)* closed [kləʊzd]

zubereiten *(kochen)* cook [kʊk]

Zucker sugar ['ʃʊgə]

zuerst first [fɜːst]

Zug train [treɪn] • **im Zug** on the train

Zuhause home [həʊm]

zuhören listen (to) ['lɪsn]

Zuhörer/in listener ['lɪsnə] • **Zuhörer/innen** *(Publikum)* audience ['ɔːdɪəns]

zum *siehe „zu"*

zumachen close [kləʊz]

zumindest at least [ət 'liːst]

zurück (nach) back (to) [bæk]

zurücklassen leave [liːv]

zusammen together [təˈgeðə]

zusammenpassen, -gehören go together

zusätzlich extra ['ekstrə]

Zuschauer/innen *(Publikum)* audience ['ɔːdɪəns]

zusehen watch [wɒtʃ]

zustimmen: jm./etwas zustimmen agree with sb./sth. [əˈgriː]

zuwenden: sich jm. zuwenden turn to sb. [tɜːn]

zweimal twice [twaɪs]

zweite(r, s) second ['sekənd]

Zwiebel onion ['ʌnjən]

Zwillinge twins *(pl)* [twɪnz]

Zwillingsbruder twin brother ['twɪn ˌbrʌðə]

zwischen between [bɪˈtwiːn]

Quellenverzeichnis

Illustrationen

Roland Beier, Berlin (S. 17 oben; S. 18; S. 20; S. 23 oben; S. 24–25; S. 29; S. 37; S. 40 unten; S. 43; S. 47; S. 50; S. 55; S. 62–65; S. 67 oben; S. 77 (u. 108); S. 80; S. 83; S. 86; S. 98; S. 101; S. 122–123 (u.110); S. 128–139 oben; S. 140–165); **Carlos Borrell**, Berlin (vordere u. hintere Umschlaginnenseite; S. 6 (u. 52); S. 17 unten; S. 30; S. 43 (u. 99); S. 74); **Julie Colthorpe**, New York (S. 22; S. 139 unten); **Graham-Cameron Illustrations**, UK: **Fliss Cary** (S. 23 unten (u. 103); S. 26–28; S. 34; S. 40 oben; S. 42 (u. 105); S. 44–46; S. 56; S. 67 unten; S. 71–72; S. 78–79; S. 82; S. 95 (u. 109); S. 106); **John Rabou** (S. 48; S. 51); **Stella Ludin/Aksinia Raphael**, Berlin (S. 60 (u. 99); **Linda Rogers Associates**, London: **Gary Rees** (S. 112 (u. 110)); **Korinna Wilkes**, Berlin (S. 115)

Bildquellen

action press, Hamburg (S. 36 oben re.: Rex Features Ltd., S. 53 trainers (M).: ALTERPHOTOS; S. 61 Bild 5: Everett Collection, Inc.; S. 97 unten: 2Vista; S. 112 oben re.: Photographers International; S. 135: ALL ACTION DIGITAL; **akg-images**, Berlin (S. 75 oben li.: Johann Brandste); **Alamy**, Abingdon (Inhaltsverz. bear (u. 121), S. 6 (u. 52) unten re.: Paul Doyle, oben Mitte: The Photolibrary Wales, unten Mitte: Photofusion Picture Library/Vehbi Koca; S. 12 Bild 1: Peter Barritt, Bild 2: Ernst Wrba, Bild 3: TNT MAGAZINE; S. 13 Bild 4: Keith Erskine; S. 15 Bild B: Kevin Allen, Bild C: Richard Cooke; S. 16 road sign: Alice de Maria, oben li.: Alex Segre; S. 18 Mitte: PCL/picturescolourlibrary; S. 19 oben li. (u. 136): The Print Collector; Mitte: Alex Beaton; S. 20: Brand X Pictures/Burke/Triolo Productions; S. 21 oben li.: imagestopshop, oben Mitte: Stan Kujawa, oben re.: Trevor Smith, unten (u. 102): Jeremy Hoare; S. 22 oben li.: Martin Fowler, oben re.: Justin Kase; S. 30 Bild 2: orkneypics; S. 31 Bild 4: Malcolm Fife, Bild 7: Doug Houghton, lamb and sheep: Suzy Bennett, sheep: orkneypics; S. 36 oben li.: Steve Allen Travel Photography; S. 37 shortbread: Ingram Publishing (Superstock Limited);

S. 57 football (u. 117): artpartner-images.com; S. 58 oben li.: Mike Booth, Mitte li. u. Mitte: Colin Edwards, Mitte re.: Jim West, unten re.: JUPITERIMAGES/BananaStock; S. 59 oben li.: David Hancock, oben re.: Bradley Ireland, football: Mark J. Barrett; S. 61 Bild 2: Eric Nathan, Bild 3: Hayley Madden, Bild 7: UKraft; S. 68 Bild A/camping (M): Chris Cheadle, Bild B: image100; Bild C/background (M): Robert Estall photo agency; girl (M): JUPITERIMAGES/Comstock Images, Bild E: Steve Skjold; S. 70 Mitte li.: Geoff du Feu; unten li.: david sanger photography/davidsanger.com, unten re.: RubberBall; S. 74 unten li.: Winston Fraser, unten re.: Keith Douglas; S. 75 oben re.: North Wind Picture Archives; S. 76 bear: Alaska Stock LLC: C&C Bear Imagery, stop sign: Robert McGouey, unten: ACE STOCK LTD; S. 79 Bild C: Elvele Images/Fritz Poelking; S. 80 oben li.: Content Mine International; S. 81 li.: Arco Images; re.: Helene Rogers, S. 88 medal: Radius Images, model: Adrian Sherratt, rock climbing: shockpix.com; S. 89 oben: Bubbles Photolibrary, Mitte: Digital Vision, unten: John Powell Photographer; S. 90 oben li.: JUPITERIMAGES/ABLESTOCK, unten Mitte: Digital Vision; S. 100 unten: George S de Blonsky; S. 121 oben (u. 110): Wolfgang Kaehler, unten li.: ImageState/Rosemary Calvert, unten re.: david tipling; S. 124 unten: Hugh Threlfall; S. 126 video game character (M): JUPITERIMAGES/Brand X/Colin Anderson, unten: Andrew Woodley; **Peter Arnold**, New York: Steven Kazlowski (S. 79 Bild A); **David Askew** (S. 31 Bild 3); **ATW Photography**, Hitchin (S. 115 unten (u. 110)); **Avenue Images**, Hamburg (S. 15 Bild A: Index Stock/David Ball); **Bildmaschine**, Berlin (S. 91 Bild 3: Peter Engelke); John **Birdsall Social Issues Photolibrary**, Nottingham (Inhaltsverz. kids: S. 7–11; S. 15 (u. 132) Bild D foreground (M); S. 16 Mitte; S. 32 oben; S. 35; S. 52 portrait: S. 54; S. 56–57 oben; S. 61 Bild 1; S. 70 oben li.: S. 73 Mitte); **Blickwinkel**, Witten (S. 30 bird: H.J. Igelmund); **The Anthony Blake Photo Library** (S. 37 pancakes: ABPL/Sian Irvine); **Britain on View**, London (S. 15 (u. 132) Bild D background (M): Nigel Hicks; S. 18

First names (Vornamen)

Alexander [ˌælɪgˈzɑːndə]
Alice [ˈælɪs]
Alisha [əˈlɪʃə]
Alison [ˈælɪsn]
Alistair [ˈælɪstə]
Andy [ˈændi]
Arthur [ˈɑːθə]
Asif [æˈsiːf]
Avril [ˈævrɪl]
Charlie [ˈtʃɑːli]
Christopher [ˈkrɪstəfə]
Conan [ˈkəʊnən]
Dermot [ˈdɜːmət]
Diana [daɪˈænə]
Dora [ˈdɔːrə]
Dylan [ˈdɪlən]
Elizabeth [ɪˈlɪzəbəθ]
Elvis [ˈelvɪs]
Emily [ˈeməli]
Emma [ˈemə]
Faith [feɪθ]
Fiona [fiˈəʊnə]
Fred [fred]
Giles [dʒaɪlz]
Grace [greɪs]
Graham [ˈgreɪəm]
Hagrid [ˈhægrɪd]
Hannah [ˈhænə]
Hassan [həˈsɑːn]
Helen [ˈhelən]
Jake [dʒeɪk]
Jaz [dʒæz]
Jenny [ˈdʒeni]
Jessica [ˈdʒesɪkə]
Jill [dʒɪl]
Joe [dʒəʊ]
Johnny [ˈdʒɒni]
Jordan [ˈdʒɔːdn]
Julie [ˈdʒuːli]
Kahasi [kəˈhɑːʃi]
Karen [ˈkærən]
Kate [keɪt]
Katrina [kəˈtriːnə]
Kaz [kæz]
Keira [ˈkɪərə]
Kylie [ˈkaɪli]
Lara [ˈlɑːrə]
Latisha [ləˈtɪʃə]
Laura [ˈlɔːrə]
Lisa [ˈliːsə], [ˈliːzə]
Liz [lɪz]
Lucy [ˈluːsi]
Madonna [məˈdɒnə]
Marc [mɑːk]
Michael [ˈmaɪkəl]
Mika [ˈmiːkə]
Minnie [ˈmɪni]
Nate [neɪt]
Nathan [ˈneɪθən]
Nick [nɪk]
Patrick [ˈpætrɪk]

Paul [pɔːl]
Robbie [ˈrɒbi]
Robert [ˈrɒbət]
Rocky [ˈrɒki]
Sandy [ˈsændi]
Sarah [ˈseərə]
Shakira [ʃəˈkɪərə]
Shaz [ʃæz]
Sheena [ˈʃiːnə]
Tommy [ˈtɒmi]
Vanessa [vəˈnesə]
Walter [ˈwɔːltə]
Wayne [weɪn]
Will [ˈwɪl]

Family names (Familiennamen)

Balboa [bælˈbəʊə]
Bale [beɪl]
Beckham [ˈbekəm]
Browne [braʊn]
Burns [bɜːnz]
Byrd [bɜːd]
Cartwright [ˈkɑːtraɪt]
Coltrane [kɒlˈtreɪn]
Cookson [ˈkʊksn]
Cooper [ˈkuːpə]
Costelloe [kɒˈsteləʊ]
Crutwell [ˈkrʌtwel]
Depp [dep]
Devlin [ˈdevlɪn]
Doyle [dɔɪl]
Fagan [ˈfeɪgən]
Holmes [həʊmz]
Hooley [ˈhuːli]
Jones [dʒəʊnz]
Kelly [ˈkeli]
Knightley [ˈnaɪtli]
Knowles [nəʊlz]
Kumar [ˈkuːmə]
Lavigne [læˈviːn]
Macintosh [ˈmækɪntɒʃ]
McCartney [məˈkɑːtni]
McDonald [məkˈdɒnld]
McFadden [məkˈfædn]
McNamara [ˌmæknəˈmɑːrə]
Minogue [mɪˈnəʊg]
Owen [ˈəʊɪn]
Parker [ˈpɑːkə]
Parsons [ˈpɑːsnz]
Perry [ˈperi]
Potter [ˈpɒtə]
Presley [ˈprezli]
Raleigh [ˈrɔːli]
Rooney [ˈruːni]
Rowling [ˈrəʊlɪŋ]
Sparrow [ˈspærəʊ]
Stephens [ˈstiːvnz]
Tilley [ˈtɪli]
Tunstall [ˈtʌnstəl]
Williams [ˈwɪljəmz]

Place names (Ortsnamen)

Aberdeen [ˌæbəˈdiːn]
Albert Street [ˈælbət striːt]
Aldgate East [ˌɔːldgeɪt ˈiːst]
Barcelona [ˌbɑːsɪˈləʊnə]
Ben Nevis [ˌben ˈnevɪs]
Bond Street [ˈbɒnd striːt]
Brick Lane [ˌbrɪk ˈleɪn]
Camden Lock [ˌkæmdən ˈlɒk]
Chapleau [ˈʃæpləʊ]
Cologne [kəˈləʊn] *Köln*
Cornwall [ˈkɔːnwɔːl]
Ealing [ˈiːlɪŋ]
Earls Court [ˌɜːlz ˈkɔːt]
Edinburgh [ˈedɪnbərə]
Elm Street [ˈelm striːt]
Flotta [ˈflɒtə]
Glasgow [ˈglæzgəʊ, ˈglɑːzgəʊ]
Haymarket [ˈheɪˌmɑːkɪt]
Houton [ˈhuːtn]
Hoy [hɔɪ]
Hyde Park [ˌhaɪd ˈpɑːk]
Kentucky [kenˈtʌki]
Kirkwall [ˈkɜːkwɔːl]
Leicester Square [ˌlestə ˈskweə]
Liverpool [ˈlɪvəpuːl]
Loch Ness [ˌlɒx ˈnes]
London [ˈlʌndən]
Los Angeles [ˌlɒs ˈændʒəliːz]
Lyness [ˈlaɪnes]
Manchester [ˈmæntʃestə]
Missinaibi Lake [ˌmɪsɪˈneɪbi ˈleɪk]
Montreal [ˌmɒntriˈɔːl]
Nunavut [ˈnuːnəvuːt]
Old Trafford [ˌəʊld ˈtræfəd]
Ontario [ɒnˈteəriəʊ]
The Orkney Islands [ˈɔːkniˌaɪləndz]
Ottawa [ˈɒtəwə]
Pall Mall [ˌpæl ˈmæl]
Paris [ˈpærɪs]
Piccadilly Circus [ˌpɪkədɪli ˈsɜːkəs]
Portobello Road [ˌpɔːtəʊbeləʊ ˈrəʊd]
The Quays [kiːz]
Quebec [kwɪˈbek]
Queensway [ˈkwiːnzweɪ]
Redcliffe [ˈredklɪf]
Richmond [ˈrɪtʃmənd]
The River Thames [ˌrɪvə ˈtemz]
Rochdale [ˈrɒtʃdeɪl]
San Francisco [ˌsæn frənˈsɪskəʊ]
Stoke-on-Trent [ˌstəʊk ɒn ˈtrent]
Stromness [ˈstrɒmnes]
Toronto [təˈrɒntəʊ]

Trafalgar Square [trəˌfælgə ˈskweə]
The Trocadero [ˌtrɒkəˈdɪərəʊ]
Vancouver [vænˈkuːvə]
Victoria Station [vɪkˌtɔːriə ˈsteɪʃn]
Waterloo [ˌwɔːtəˈluː]
Wawa [ˈwɑːwɑː]
Westminster [ˈwestmɪnstə]
Wimbledon [ˈwɪmbldən]

Other names (Andere Namen)

The Bloody Tower [ˌblʌdi ˈtaʊə]
The Central Line [ˈsentrəl ˌlaɪn]
The Circle Line [ˈsɜːkl ˌlaɪn]
The District Line [ˈdɪstrɪkt ˌlaɪn]
The Docklands Light Railway (DLR) [ˌdɒkləndz ˌlaɪt ˈreɪlweɪ]
Franz Ferdinand [ˌfræns ˈfɜːdɪnænd]
Global Deejays [ˌgləʊbl ˈdiːdʒeɪz]
The Hammersmith Line [ˈhæməsmɪθ ˌlaɪn]
The Highland Games [ˌhaɪlənd ˈgeɪmz]
The Jubilee Line [ˈdʒuːbɪliː ˌlaɪn]
The London Dungeon [ˌlʌndən ˈdʌndʒən]
The Lovin' Spoonful [ˌlʌvɪn ˈspuːnfʊl]
Manchester United [ˌmæntʃestə juˈnaɪtəd]
The Maple Leafs [ˌmeɪpl ˈliːfs]
The Metropolitan Line [ˌmetrəˈpɒlɪtən ˌlaɪn]

Country/Continent	Adjective	Person	People
Africa ['æfrɪkə] *Afrika*	African ['æfrɪkən]	an African	the Africans
America [ə'merɪkə] *Amerika*	American [ə'merɪkən]	an American	the Americans
Asia ['eɪʃə, 'eɪʒə] *Asien*	Asian ['eɪʃn, 'eɪʒn]	an Asian	the Asians
Australia [ɒ'streɪliə] *Australien*	Australian [ɒ'streɪliən]	an Australian	the Australians
Austria ['ɒstriə] *Österreich*	Austrian ['ɒstriən]	an Austrian	the Austrians
Bangladesh [ˌbæŋglə'deʃ] *Bangladesch*	Bangladeshi [ˌbæŋglə'deʃi]	a Bangladeshi	the Bangladeshis
Belgium ['beldʒəm] *Belgien*	Belgian ['beldʒən]	a Belgian	the Belgians
Canada ['kænədə] *Kanada*	Canadian [kə'neɪdiən]	a Canadian	the Canadians
the Caribbean [ˌkærə'biːən] *die Karibik*	Caribbean [ˌkærə'biːən]	a Caribbean	the Caribbeans
China ['tʃaɪnə] *China*	Chinese [ˌtʃaɪ'niːz]	a Chinese	the Chinese
Colombia [kə'lɒmbiə] *Kolumbien*	Colombian [kə'lɒmbiən]	a Colombian	the Colombians
Croatia [krəʊ'eɪʃə] *Kroatien*	Croatian [krəʊ'eɪʃn]	a Croatian	the Croatians
the Czech Republic [ˌtʃek rɪ'pʌblɪk] *Tschechien, die Tschechische Republik*	Czech [tʃek]	a Czech	the Czechs
Denmark ['denmɑːk] *Dänemark*	Danish ['deɪnɪʃ]	a Dane [deɪn]	the Danes
England ['ɪŋglənd] *England*	English ['ɪŋglɪʃ]	an Englishman/-woman	the English
Europe ['jʊərəp] *Europa*	European [ˌjʊərə'piːən]	a European	the Europeans
Finland ['fɪnlənd] *Finnland*	Finnish ['fɪnɪʃ]	a Finn [fɪn]	the Finns
France [frɑːns] *Frankreich*	French [frentʃ]	a Frenchman/-woman	the French
Georgia ['dʒɔːdʒə] *Georgien*	Georgian ['dʒɔːdʒən]	a Georgian	the Georgians
Germany ['dʒɜːməni] *Deutschland*	German ['dʒɜːmən]	a German	the Germans
(Great) Britain ['brɪtn] *Großbritannien*	British ['brɪtɪʃ]	a Briton ['brɪtn]	the British
Greece [griːs] *Griechenland*	Greek [griːk]	a Greek	the Greeks
Holland ['hɒlənd] *Holland, die Niederlande*	Dutch [dʌtʃ]	a Dutchman/-woman	the Dutch
Hungary ['hʌŋgəri] *Ungarn*	Hungarian [hʌŋ'geəriən]	a Hungarian	the Hungarians
India ['ɪndiə] *Indien*	Indian ['ɪndiən]	an Indian	the Indians
Iran [ɪ'rɑːn, ɪ'ræn] *Iran*	Iranian [ɪ'reɪniən]	a Iranian	the Iranians
Ireland ['aɪələnd] *Irland*	Irish ['aɪrɪʃ]	an Irishman/-woman	the Irish
Italy ['ɪtəli] *Italien*	Italian [ɪ'tæliən]	an Italian	the Italians
Japan [dʒə'pæn] *Japan*	Japanese [ˌdʒæpə'niːz]	a Japanese	the Japanese
Lebanon ['lebənən] *Libanon*	Lebanese [ˌlebə'niːz]	a Lebanese	the Lebanese
the Netherlands ['neðələndz] *die Niederlande, Holland*	Dutch [dʌtʃ]	a Dutchman/-woman	the Dutch
New Zealand [ˌnjuː 'ziːlənd] *Neuseeland*	New Zealand [ˌnjuː 'ziːlənd]	a New Zealander	the New Zealanders
Norway ['nɔːweɪ] *Norwegen*	Norwegian [nɔː'wiːdʒən]	a Norwegian	the Norwegians
Pakistan [ˌpækɪ'stæn, ˌpɑːkɪ'stɑːn] *Pakistan*	Pakistani [ˌpækɪ'stæni, ˌpɑːkɪ'stɑːni]	a Pakistani	the Pakistanis
Poland ['pəʊlənd] *Polen*	Polish ['pəʊlɪʃ]	a Pole [pəʊl]	the Poles
Portugal ['pɔːtʃʊgl] *Portugal*	Portuguese [ˌpɔːtʃʊ'giːz]	a Portuguese	the Portuguese
Russia ['rʌʃə] *Russland*	Russian ['rʌʃn]	a Russian	the Russians
Scotland ['skɒtlənd] *Schottland*	Scottish ['skɒtɪʃ]	a Scotsman/-woman, a Scot [skɒt]	the Scots, the Scottish
Slovakia [sləʊ'vɑːkiə, sləʊ'vækiə] *die Slowakei*	Slovak ['sləʊvæk]	a Slovak	the Slovaks
Slovenia [sləʊ'viːniə] *Slowenien*	Slovenian [sləʊ'viːniən], Slovene ['sləʊviːn]	a Slovene, a Slovenian	the Slovenes, the Slovenians
South Africa [ˌsaʊθ 'æfrɪkə] *Südafrika*	South African [ˌsaʊθ 'æfrɪkn]	South African	the South Africans
Spain [speɪn] *Spanien*	Spanish ['spænɪʃ]	a Spaniard ['spænɪəd]	the Spaniards
Sweden ['swiːdn] *Schweden*	Swedish ['swiːdɪʃ]	a Swede [swiːd]	the Swedes
Switzerland ['swɪtsələnd] *die Schweiz*	Swiss [swɪs]	a Swiss	the Swiss
Turkey ['tɜːki] *die Türkei*	Turkish ['tɜːkɪʃ]	a Turk [tɜːk]	the Turks
the United Kingdom (the UK) [juˌnaɪtɪd 'kɪŋdəm, juːˈkeɪ] *das Vereinigte Königreich (Großbritannien und Nordirland)*	British ['brɪtɪʃ]	a Briton ['brɪtn]	the British
the United States of America [juˌnaɪtɪd ˌsteɪts_əv_ə'merɪkə] *die Vereinigten Staaten von Amerika* **(the USA)** [ˌjuː_es_'eɪ]	American [ə'merɪkən]	an American	the Americans
Wales [weɪlz] *Wales*	Welsh [welʃ]	a Welshman/-woman	the Welsh

Infinitive	Simple past form	Past participle	
(to) **be**	**was/were**	**been**	sein
(to) **beat**	**beat**	**beaten**	schlagen; besiegen
(to) **become**	**became**	**become**	werden
(to) **bet**	**bet**	**bet**	wetten
(to) **break** a journey	**broke**	**broken**	eine Reise unterbrechen
(to) **bring**	**brought**	**brought**	(mit-, her)bringen
(to) **build**	**built**	**built**	bauen
(to) **buy**	**bought**	**bought**	kaufen
(to) **catch**	**caught**	**caught**	fangen; erwischen
(to) **choose** [uː]	**chose** [əʊ]	**chosen** [əʊ]	(aus)wählen; (sich) aussuchen
(to) **come**	**came**	**come**	kommen
(to) **cut**	**cut**	**cut**	schneiden
(to) **do**	**did**	**done** [ʌ]	tun, machen
(to) **draw**	**drew**	**drawn**	zeichnen
(to) **drink**	**drank**	**drunk**	trinken
(to) **drive** [aɪ]	**drove**	**driven** [ɪ]	*(ein Auto)* fahren
(to) **eat**	**ate** [et, eɪt]	**eaten**	essen
(to) **fall**	**fell**	**fallen**	(hin)fallen, stürzen
(to) **feed**	**fed**	**fed**	füttern
(to) **feel**	**felt**	**felt**	(sich) fühlen; sich anfühlen
(to) **fight**	**fought**	**fought**	kämpfen
(to) **find**	**found**	**found**	finden
(to) **fly**	**flew**	**flown**	fliegen
(to) **forget**	**forgot**	**forgotten**	vergessen
(to) **get**	**got**	**got**	bekommen; holen; werden; (hin)kommen
(to) **give**	**gave**	**given**	geben
(to) **go**	**went**	**gone** [ɒ]	gehen, fahren
(to) **grow**	**grew**	**grown**	wachsen; anbauen, anpflanzen
(to) **hang out** *(infml)*	**hung out**	**hung out**	rumhängen, abhängen
(to) **have (have got)**	**had**	**had**	haben, besitzen
(to) **hear** [ɪə]	**heard** [ɜː]	**heard** [ɜː]	hören
(to) **hide** [aɪ]	**hid** [ɪ]	**hidden** [ɪ]	(sich) verstecken
(to) **hit**	**hit**	**hit**	schlagen
(to) **hold**	**held**	**held**	halten
(to) **hurt**	**hurt**	**hurt**	wehtun; verletzen
(to) **keep**	**kept**	**kept**	(be)halten
(to) **know** [nəʊ]	**knew** [njuː]	**known** [nəʊn]	wissen; kennen
(to) **lay** the table	**laid**	**laid**	den Tisch decken
(to) **leave**	**left**	**left**	(weg)gehen; abfahren; verlassen; zurücklassen

Infinitive	Simple past form	Past participle	
(to) **let**	**let**	**let**	lassen
(to) **lose** [uː]	**lost** [ɒ]	**lost** [ɒ]	verlieren
(to) **make**	**made**	**made**	machen; bauen; bilden
(to) **mean** [iː]	**meant** [e]	**meant** [e]	bedeuten; meinen
(to) **meet**	**met**	**met**	(sich) treffen
(to) **pay**	**paid**	**paid**	bezahlen
(to) **put**	**put**	**put**	legen, stellen, *(wohin)* tun
(to) **read** [iː]	**read** [e]	**read** [e]	lesen
(to) **ride** [aɪ]	**rode**	**ridden** [ɪ]	reiten; *(Rad)* fahren
(to) **ring**	**rang**	**rung**	klingeln, läuten
(to) **run**	**ran**	**run**	rennen, laufen
(to) **say** [eɪ]	**said** [e]	**said** [e]	sagen
(to) **see**	**saw**	**seen**	sehen; besuchen, aufsuchen
(to) **sell**	**sold**	**sold**	verkaufen
(to) **send**	**sent**	**sent**	schicken, senden
(to) **shine**	**shone** [ɒ]	**shone** [ɒ]	scheinen *(Sonne)*
(to) **shoot** [uː]	**shot** [ɒ]	**shot** [ɒ]	schießen, erschießen
(to) **show**	**showed**	**shown**	zeigen
(to) **shut up**	**shut**	**shut**	den Mund halten
(to) **sing**	**sang**	**sung**	singen
(to) **sit**	**sat**	**sat**	sitzen; sich setzen
(to) **sleep**	**slept**	**slept**	schlafen
(to) **speak**	**spoke**	**spoken**	sprechen
(to) **spend**	**spent**	**spent**	*(Zeit)* verbringen; *(Geld)* ausgeben
(to) **stand**	**stood**	**stood**	stehen; sich (hin)stellen
(to) **steal**	**stole**	**stolen**	stehlen
(to) **swim**	**swam**	**swum**	schwimmen
(to) **take**	**took**	**taken**	nehmen; (weg-, hin)bringen; dauern, *(Zeit)* brauchen
(to) **teach**	**taught**	**taught**	unterrichten, lehren
(to) **tell**	**told**	**told**	erzählen, berichten
(to) **think**	**thought**	**thought**	denken, glauben, meinen
(to) **throw**	**threw**	**thrown**	werfen
(to) **understand**	**understood**	**understood**	verstehen
(to) **upset**	**upset**	**upset**	ärgern, kränken, aus der Fassung bringen
(to) **wear** [eə]	**wore** [ɔː]	**worn** [ɔː]	tragen *(Kleidung)*
(to) **win**	**won** [ʌ]	**won** [ʌ]	gewinnen
(to) **write**	**wrote**	**written**	schreiben

Key to the self-assessment tests

Unit 1 ▶ How am I doing? (p. 29)

1 B Thames
2 A the Tube
3 A a big wheel
4 B Piccadilly Circus
5 B Buckingham Palace
6 B tickets
7 C get

8 C a sandwich
9 C views
10 A Hello from London!
11 C Tomorrow
12 C Dear Dora
13 B went
14 A didn't

15 C Have
16 C Yes, he has.
17 C How much is a single ticket for an adult?
18 B Can I help you?

Unit 2 ▶ How am I doing? (p. 47)

1 A islands / Orkney Islands
2 C Edinburgh
3 A dance
4 C rock
5 C in a car park
6 B mountain
7 B text message

8 D great
9 D Person
10 B funktionieren
11 C sends
12 A If my brother goes to the party, I will stay at home.

13 A If I was you, I'd tell my teacher.
14 B This is Emily speaking.
15 A Can I leave a message?

Unit 3 ▶ How am I doing? (p. 67)

1 A the steel drum
2 B Old Trafford
3 C Enjoy.
4 B Trinidad
5 A kiwi

6 B It's somebody who trains a team.
7 D bat
8 D pet
9 B fridge
10 B

11 A B C D
12 A who
13 that I want to visit.
14 B That was delicious.
15 C

Unit 4 ▶ How am I doing? (p. 83)

1 A Ottawa
2 B Toronto
3 A bigger
4 B smaller
5 C French
6 C football
7 B a sleepover
8 C You're grounded.

9 A You're so old-fashioned.
10 D You're mad.
11 C B A
    a beginning, a middle and an end
12 A so
13 B after

14 D I am not allowed to go to the disco …
15 B …, you'll have to do more jobs at home.
16 C himself
17 C What are you doing at the weekend?

Key to the self-assessment tests _____

Unit 1–5 ▸ *How am I doing? (p. 98)*

1 Wales   1 point
2 London, Thames   2 points
3 Tube   1 point
4 Scotland   1 point
5 Manchester   1 point
6 word field: transport
   airport, bike, boat, bus, bus stop, car,
   driver, harbour, helicopter, line, lorry,
   plane, road, river, sea, ship, station, street,
   taxi, tram, Travelcard, Tube, map,
   underground, ...;
   1 point for word field,
   1 point for more words
7 word field: electronic media
   phone calls, text messages, e-mails, instant
   messages, video, DVD, logo, ringtone,
   computer, games, mix music, chat,
   internet, ...;
   1 point for the word field,
   1 point for more words
8 word field: the town
   castle, cathedral, church, department store,
   hotel, lake, market, palace, park, post
   office, pub, river, school, station, street,
   supermarket, tower, town centre, ...;
   1 point for the word field,
   1 point for more words
9 word field: sport
   basketball, football, handball, rugby,
   tennis, hockey, judo, competition, coach,
   goalkeeper, pitch, half-time, swimming
   pool, badminton racket, table tennis bat,
   skis, skates and pads, saddle, swimsuit,
   swimming trunks, running shoes, ...;
   1 point for the word field,
   1 point for more words

10 word field: music
   guitar, steel drum, violin, piano, recorder,
   flute, trumpet, classical music, folk music,
   rap, jazz, concert, dance, workshop,
   album, single, club, CD player, choir,
   chorus, MP3 player, songs, concert hall, ...;
   1 point for the word field,
   1 point for more words
11 word field: the country
   canal, castle, rock, cow, coast, farmhouse,
   farmer, field, hill, lake, valley, village,
   sheep, ...;
   1 point for the word field,
   1 point for more words
12 **A** first
13 who, what, when, where, why
   1 point for all of the 5 Ws
14 message   1 point
15 one-day ticket/Travelcard   1 point
16 full   1 point
17 **C** will be   1 point
18 **B** that   1 point
19 **B** My sister and I aren't allowed to ride
   our bikes in the street because my mum is
   afraid we'll hurt ourselves.   1 point
20 skimming   1 point
21 paraphrasing   1 point
22 brainstorming   1 point

Classroom English

Was *du* im Klassenzimmer sagen kannst | **What *you* can say in the classroom**

Du brauchst Hilfe
Können Sie mir bitte helfen?
Auf welcher Seite sind wir, bitte?
Was heißt ... auf Englisch/Deutsch?
Wie spricht man das erste Wort in Zeile 2 aus?
Können Sie bitte ... buchstabieren?
Können Sie es bitte an die Tafel schreiben?
Kann ich es auf Deutsch sagen?
Können Sie/Kannst du bitte lauter sprechen?
Können Sie/Kannst du das bitte noch mal sagen?

You need help
Can you help me, please?
What page are we on, please?
What's ... in English/German?
How do you say the first word in line 2?
Can you spell ..., please?
Can you write it on the board, please?
Can I say it in German?
Can you speak louder, please?
Can you say that again, please?

Über Texte und Themen sprechen
Ich finde die Geschichte ...
schön/interessant/langweilig/schrecklich/....
Es war lustig/gruselig/langweilig/..., als ...
Ich fand es gut/nicht gut, als ...
Ich finde, Tom hat recht/nicht recht, weil ...
Ich bin mir nicht sicher. Vielleicht ...
Was meinst du?
Ich stimme ... zu/nicht zu, weil ...

Talking about texts and topics
I think the story is ...
nice/interesting/boring/terrible/...
It was funny/scary/boring/... when ...
I liked it/didn't like it when ...
I think Tom is right/wrong because ...
I'm not sure. Maybe ...
What do you think?
I agree/disagree (with ...) because ...

Hausaufgaben und Übungen
Tut mir leid, ich habe mein Schulheft nicht dabei, Herr ...
Ich habe meine Hausaufgaben vergessen, Frau ...
Ich kann Nummer 3 nicht lösen.
Entschuldigung, ich bin noch nicht fertig.
Ich habe ... Ist das auch richtig?
Tut mir leid, das weiß ich nicht.
Was haben wir (als Hausaufgabe) auf?

Homework and exercises
Sorry, I haven't got my exercise book, Mr ...
I've forgotten my homework, Mrs/Ms/Miss ...
I can't do number 3.
Sorry, I haven't finished yet.
I've got ... Is that right too?
Sorry, I don't know.
What's for homework?

Bei der Partnerarbeit
Kann ich mit Julian arbeiten?
Wer ist dran? - Du bist dran.
Ich finde, wir sollten/könnten ...
Was machen wir zuerst?

Work with a partner
Can I work with Julian?
Whose turn is it? - It's your turn.
I think we should/could ...
What are we going to do first?

What your teacher says
Open your books at page 24, please.
Look at the picture/line 8/... on page 24.
Copy/Complete the chart/network/...
Correct the mistakes.
Take notes.
Do exercise 3 for homework, please.
Have you finished?
Switch off your mobile phones.
Walk around the class and ask other students.
Discuss ... with ...
Give a presentation about ...
Report to the class.

Was dein/e Lehrer/in sagt
Schlagt bitte Seite 24 auf.
Seht euch das Bild/Zeile 8/... auf Seite 24 an.
Übertragt/Vervollständigt die Tabelle/das Wörternetz/...
Verbessert die Fehler.
Macht euch Notizen.
Macht bitte Übung 3 als Hausaufgabe.
Seid ihr fertig? / Bist du fertig?
Schaltet eure Handys aus.
Geht durch die Klasse und fragt andere Schüler/innen.
Diskutiere/Diskutiert ... mit ...
Halte/Haltet einen Vortrag über ...
Berichte/Berichtet der Klasse.